HARLEY QUINN

VOL. 1: NO GOOD DEED

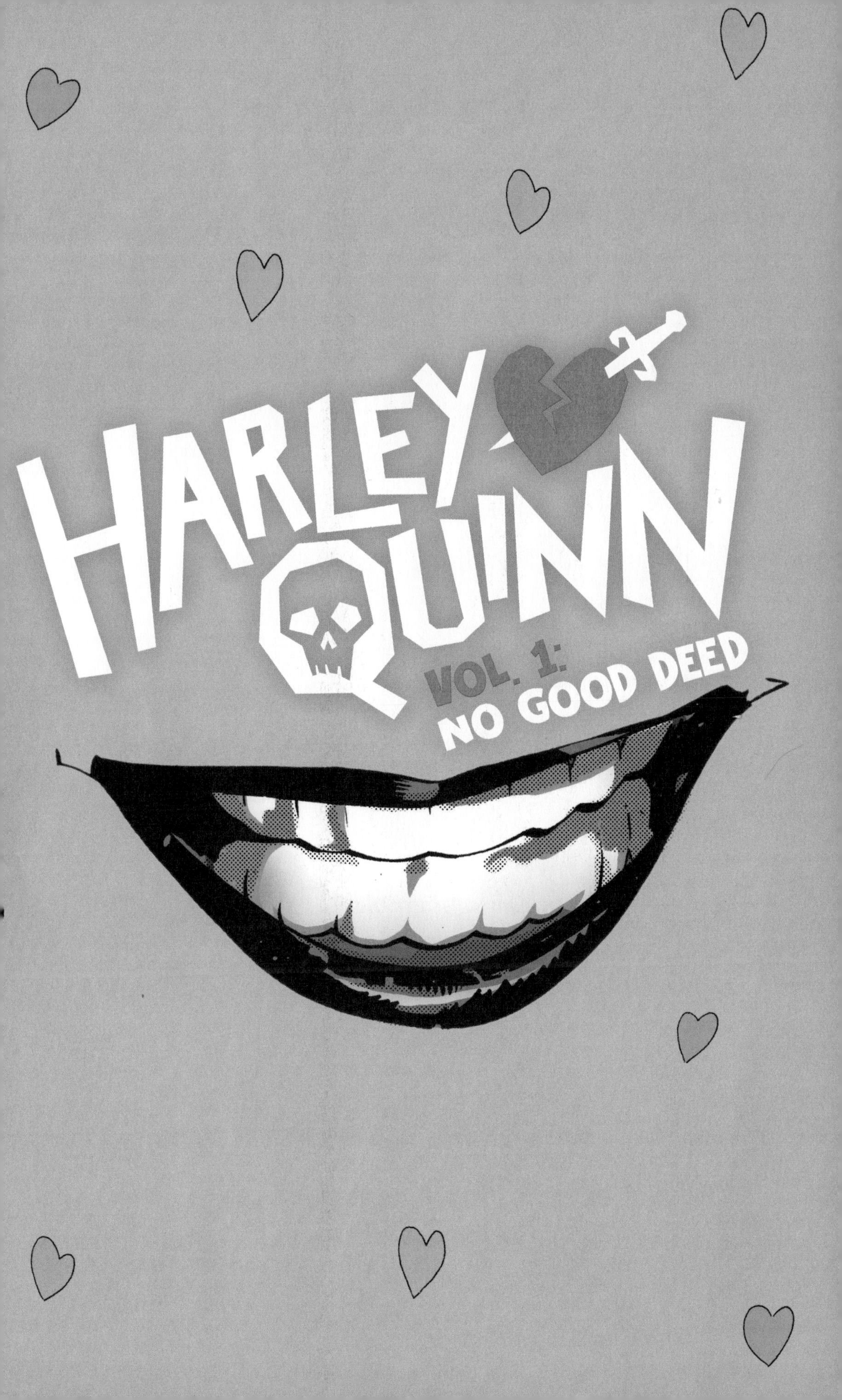

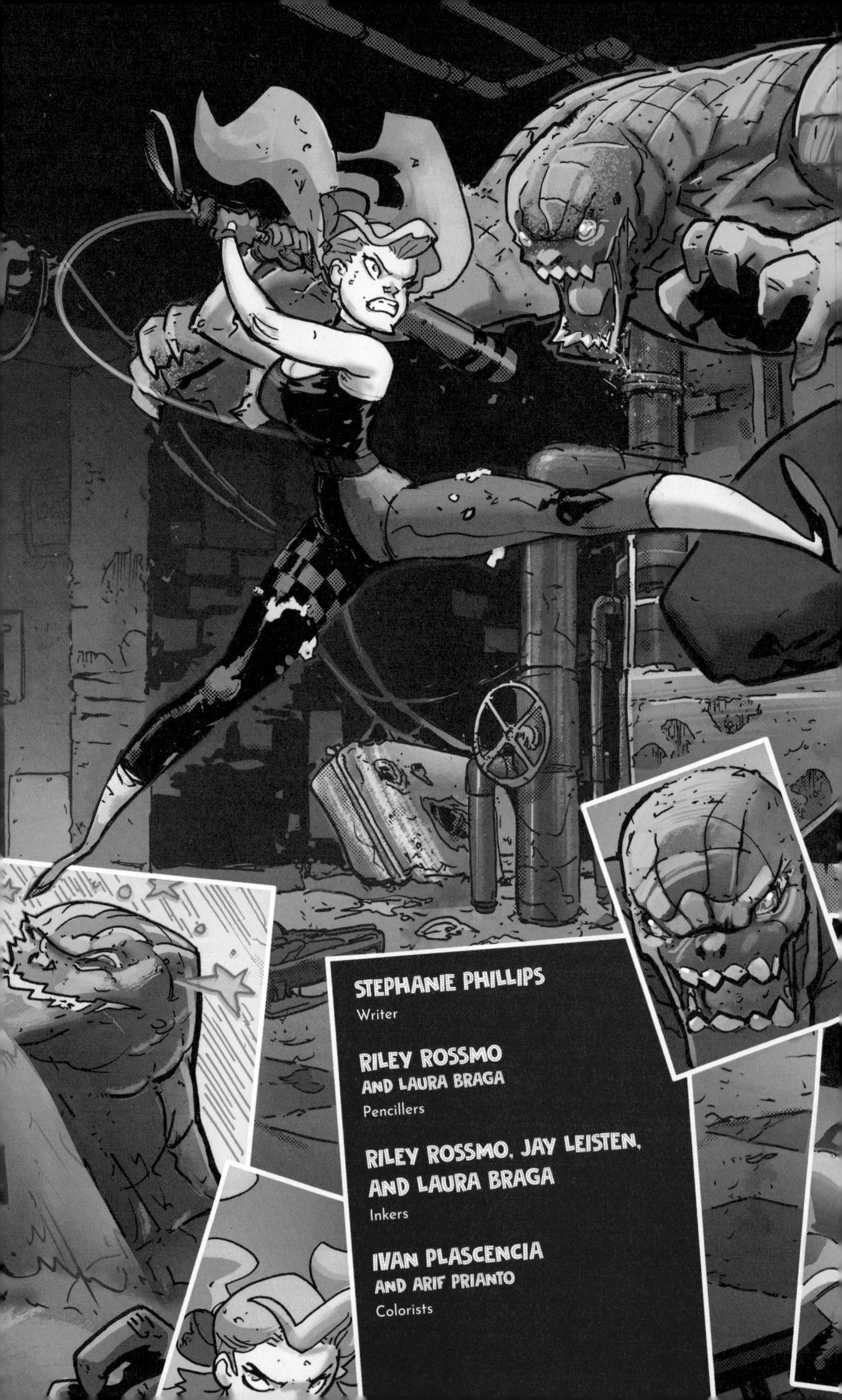

STEPHANIE PHILLIPS
Writer

RILEY ROSSMO AND LAURA BRAGA
Pencillers

RILEY ROSSMO, JAY LEISTEN, AND LAURA BRAGA
Inkers

IVAN PLASCENCIA AND ARIF PRIANTO
Colorists

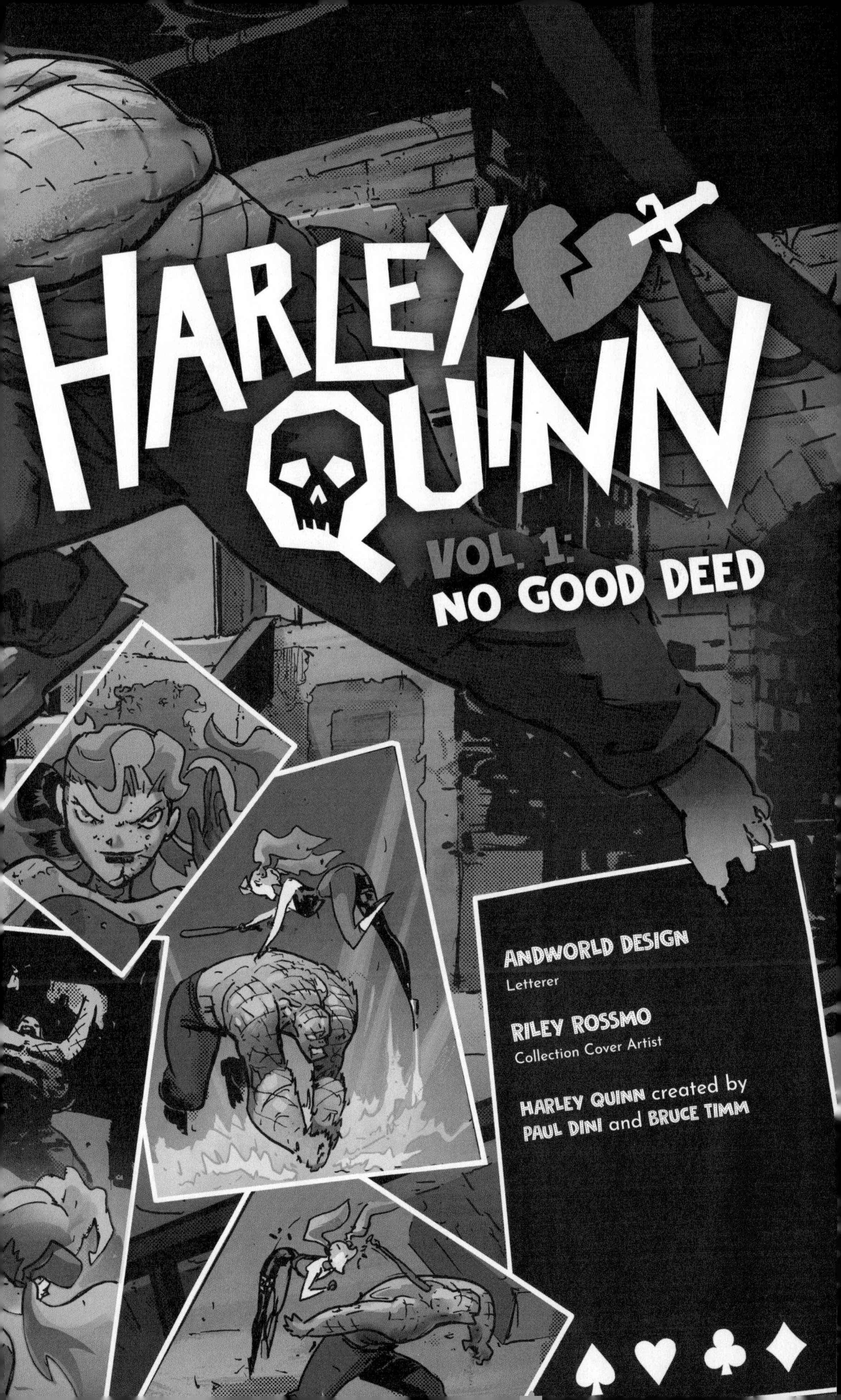

HARLEY QUINN

VOL. 1: NO GOOD DEED

ANDWORLD DESIGN
Letterer

RILEY ROSSMO
Collection Cover Artist

HARLEY QUINN created by
PAUL DINI and **BRUCE TIMM**

BEN ABERNATHY
Editor - Original Series & Collected Edition

DAVE WIELGOSZ
Editor - Original Series

STEVE COOK
Design Director - Books

MEGEN BELLERSEN
Publication Design

SUZANNAH ROWNTREE
Publication Production

MARIE JAVINS
Editor-in-Chief, DC Comics

DANIEL CHERRY III
Senior VP - General Manager

JIM LEE
Publisher & Chief Creative Officer

JOEN CHOE
VP - Global Brand & Creative Services

DON FALLETTI
VP - Manufacturing Operations
& Workflow Management

LAWRENCE GANEM
VP - Talent Services

ALISON GILL
Senior VP - Manufacturing & Operations

NICK J. NAPOLITANO
VP - Manufacturing Administration & Design

NANCY SPEARS
VP - Revenue

HARLEY QUINN VOL. 1: NO GOOD DEED

DC Comics
2900 West Alameda Ave.
Burbank, CA 91505
Printed by Transcontinental Interglobe,
Beauceville, QC, Canada.
10/29/21. First Printing.
ISBN: 978-1-77951-346-5

Library of Congress
Cataloging-in-Publication
Data is available.

PEFC Certified

This product is
from sustainably
managed forests and
controlled sources

PEFC/01-31-106   www.pefc.org

Batman: Urban Legends #1
Cover Art by Hicham Habchi

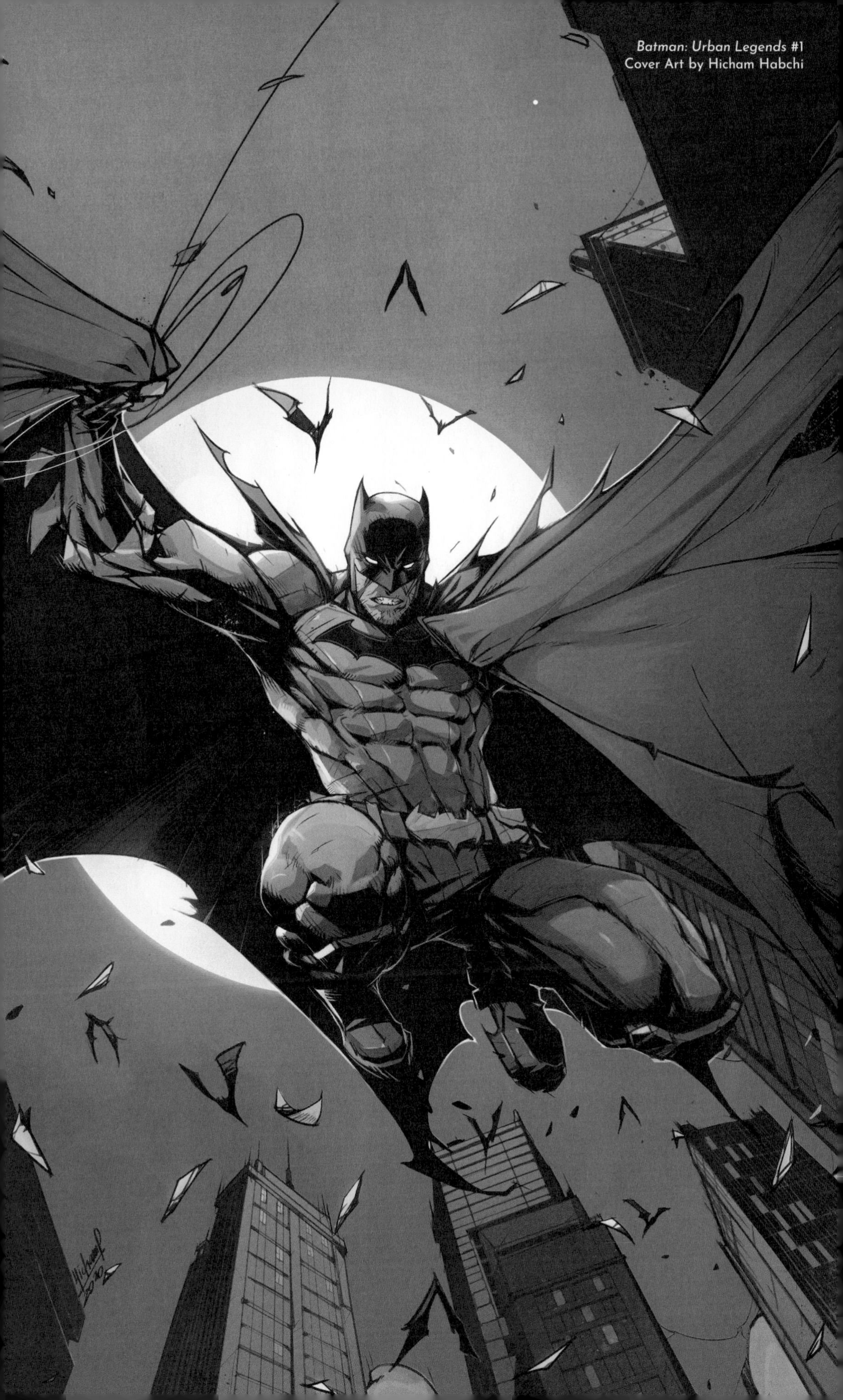

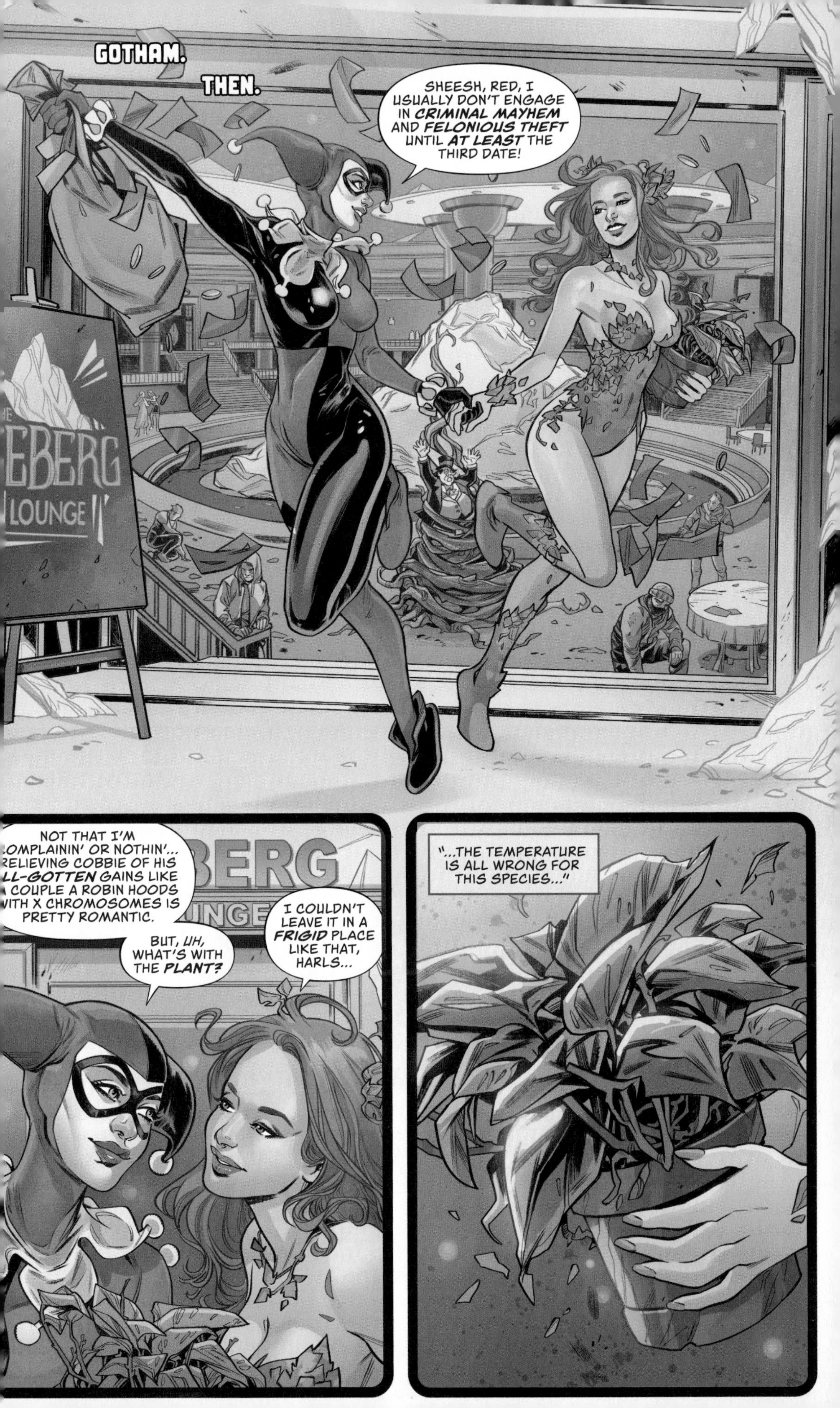
GOTHAM.
THEN.
SHEESH, RED, I USUALLY DON'T ENGAGE IN **CRIMINAL MAYHEM** AND **FELONIOUS THEFT** UNTIL **AT LEAST** THE THIRD DATE!
EBERG LOUNGE
NOT THAT I'M COMPLAININ' OR NOTHIN'... RELIEVING COBBIE OF HIS ILL-GOTTEN GAINS LIKE A COUPLE A ROBIN HOODS WITH X CHROMOSOMES IS PRETTY ROMANTIC.
BUT, *UH,* WHAT'S WITH THE **PLANT?**
I COULDN'T LEAVE IT IN A **FRIGID** PLACE LIKE THAT, HARLS...
"...THE TEMPERATURE IS ALL WRONG FOR THIS SPECIES..."

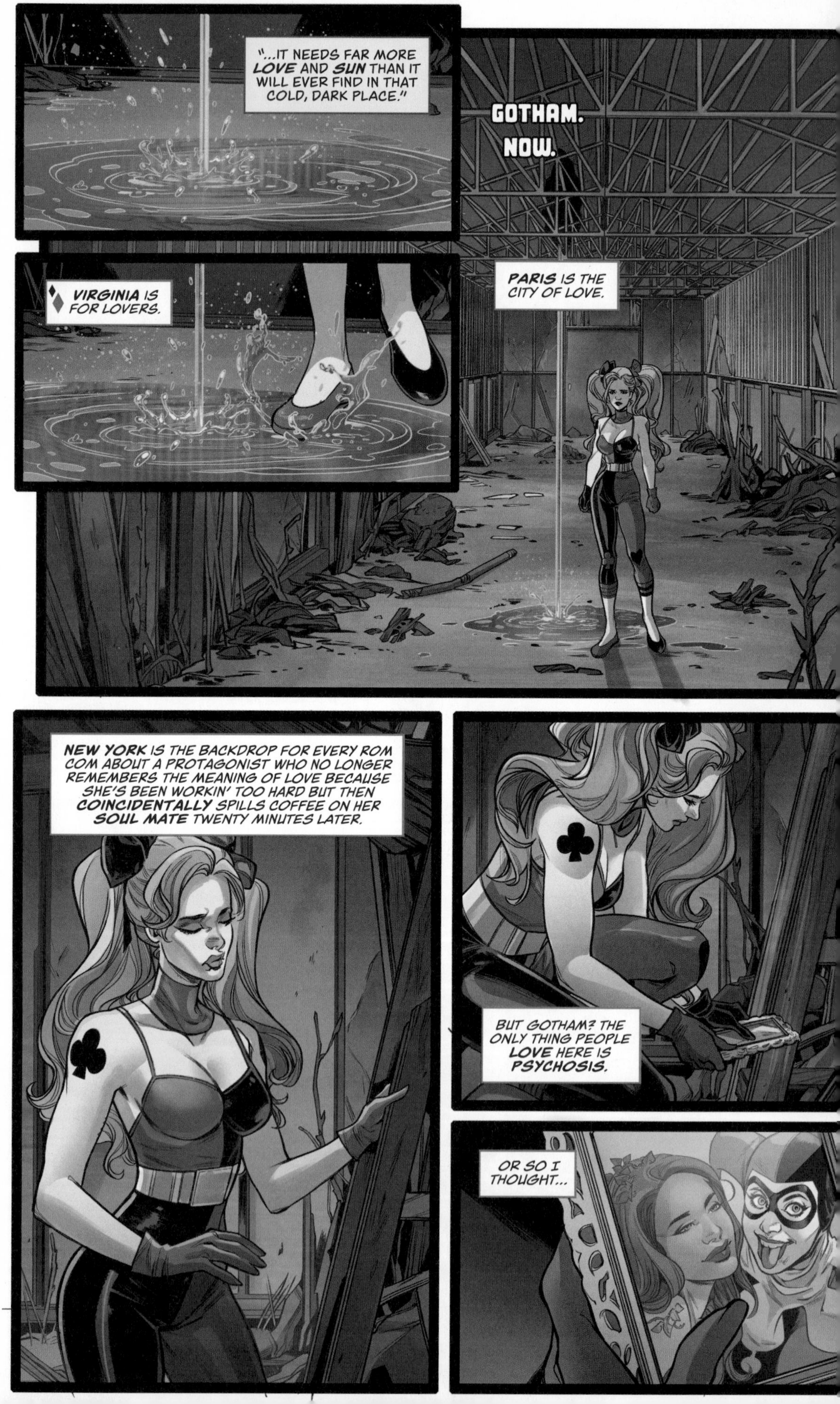

"...IT NEEDS FAR MORE LOVE AND SUN THAN IT WILL EVER FIND IN THAT COLD, DARK PLACE."
GOTHAM.
NOW.
VIRGINIA IS FOR LOVERS.
PARIS IS THE CITY OF LOVE.
NEW YORK IS THE BACKDROP FOR EVERY ROM COM ABOUT A PROTAGONIST WHO NO LONGER REMEMBERS THE MEANING OF LOVE BECAUSE SHE'S BEEN WORKIN' TOO HARD BUT THEN COINCIDENTALLY SPILLS COFFEE ON HER SOUL MATE TWENTY MINUTES LATER.
BUT GOTHAM? THE ONLY THING PEOPLE LOVE HERE IS PSYCHOSIS.
OR SO I THOUGHT...

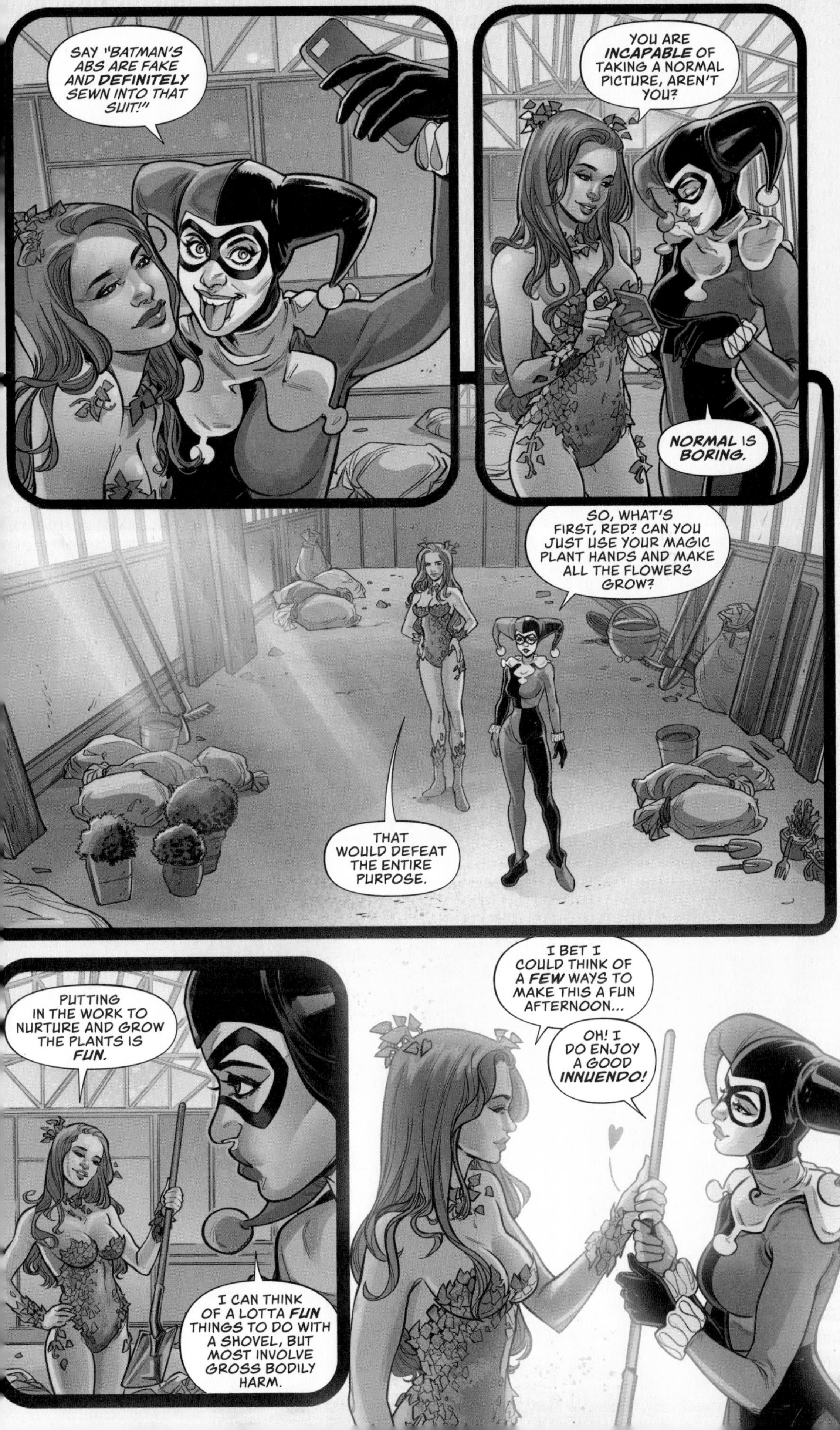

SAY "BATMAN'S ABS ARE FAKE AND DEFINITELY SEWN INTO THAT SUIT!"
YOU ARE INCAPABLE OF TAKING A NORMAL PICTURE, AREN'T YOU?
NORMAL IS BORING.
SO, WHAT'S FIRST, RED? CAN YOU JUST USE YOUR MAGIC PLANT HANDS AND MAKE ALL THE FLOWERS GROW?
THAT WOULD DEFEAT THE ENTIRE PURPOSE.
PUTTING IN THE WORK TO NURTURE AND GROW THE PLANTS IS FUN.
I CAN THINK OF A LOTTA FUN THINGS TO DO WITH A SHOVEL, BUT MOST INVOLVE GROSS BODILY HARM.
I BET I COULD THINK OF A FEW WAYS TO MAKE THIS A FUN AFTERNOON...
OH! I DO ENJOY A GOOD INNUENDO!

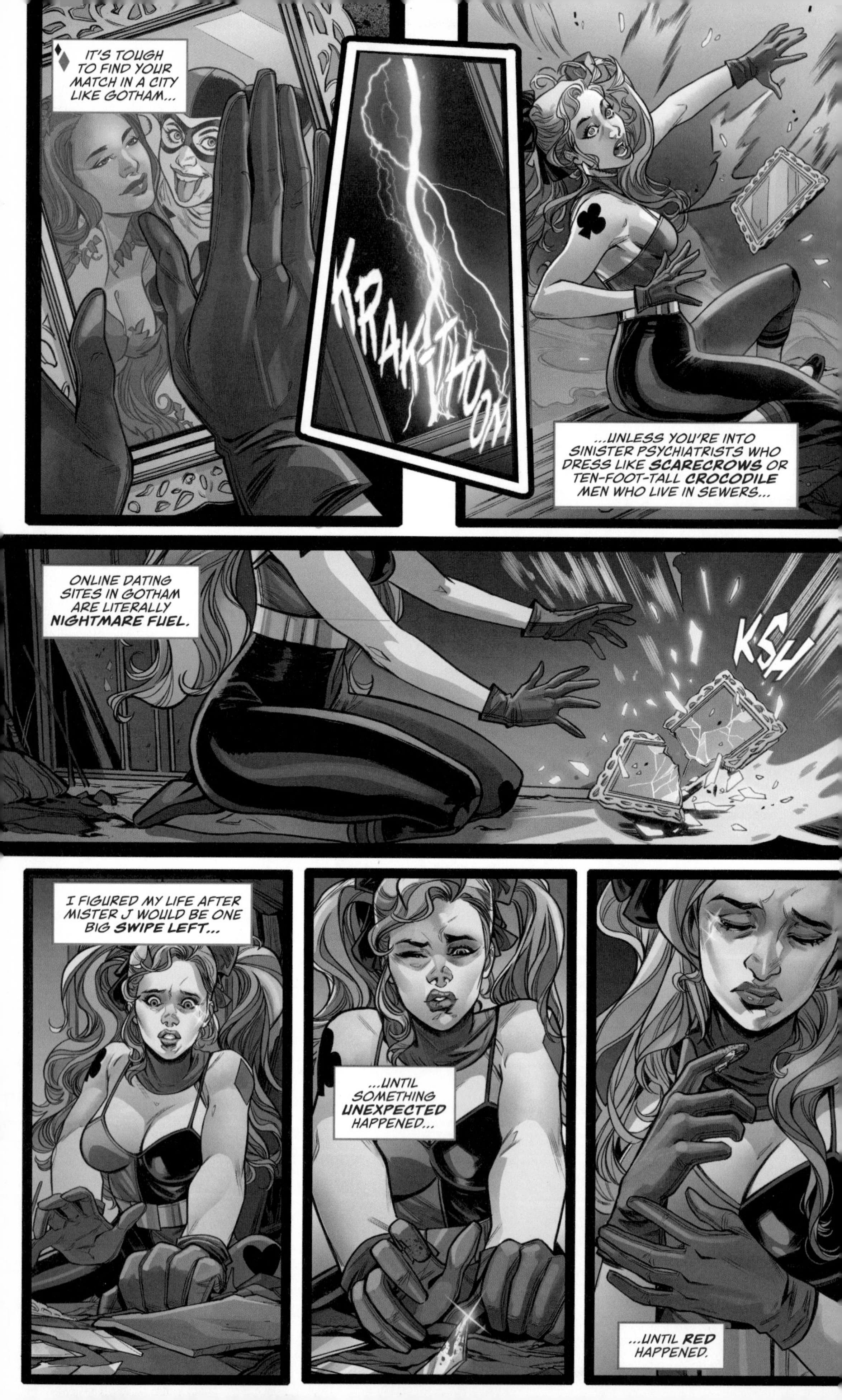
IT'S TOUGH TO FIND YOUR MATCH IN A CITY LIKE GOTHAM...
KRAK-THOOM
...UNLESS YOU'RE INTO SINISTER PSYCHIATRISTS WHO DRESS LIKE SCARECROWS OR TEN-FOOT-TALL CROCODILE MEN WHO LIVE IN SEWERS...
ONLINE DATING SITES IN GOTHAM ARE LITERALLY NIGHTMARE FUEL.
KSH
I FIGURED MY LIFE AFTER MISTER J WOULD BE ONE BIG SWIPE LEFT...
...UNTIL SOMETHING UNEXPECTED HAPPENED...
...UNTIL RED HAPPENED.

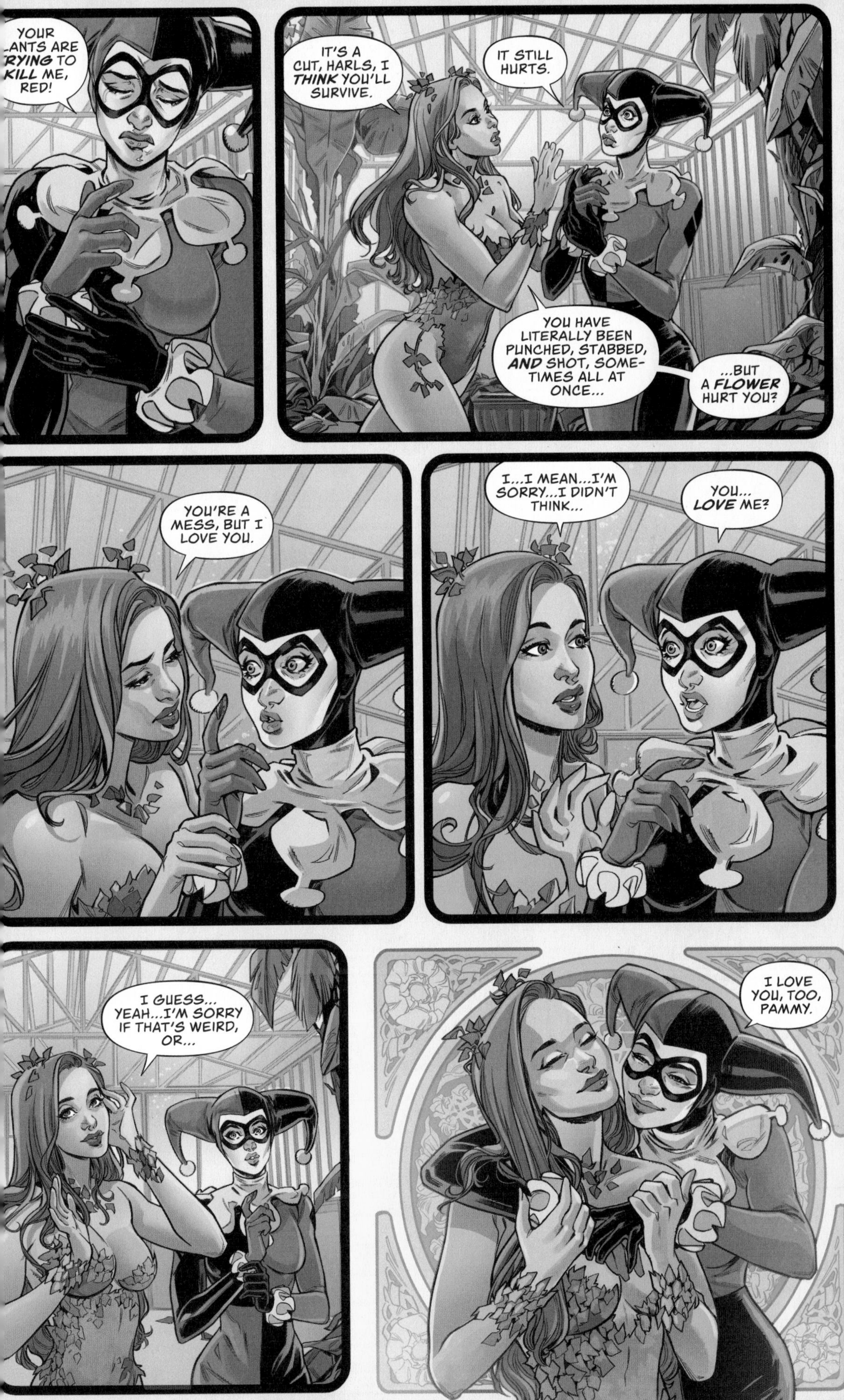
YOUR PLANTS ARE TRYING TO KILL ME, RED!
IT'S A CUT, HARLS, I THINK YOU'LL SURVIVE.
IT STILL HURTS.
YOU HAVE LITERALLY BEEN PUNCHED, STABBED, AND SHOT, SOMETIMES ALL AT ONCE...
...BUT A FLOWER HURT YOU?
YOU'RE A MESS, BUT I LOVE YOU.
I...I MEAN...I'M SORRY...I DIDN'T THINK...
YOU... LOVE ME?
I GUESS... YEAH...I'M SORRY IF THAT'S WEIRD, OR...
I LOVE YOU, TOO, PAMMY.

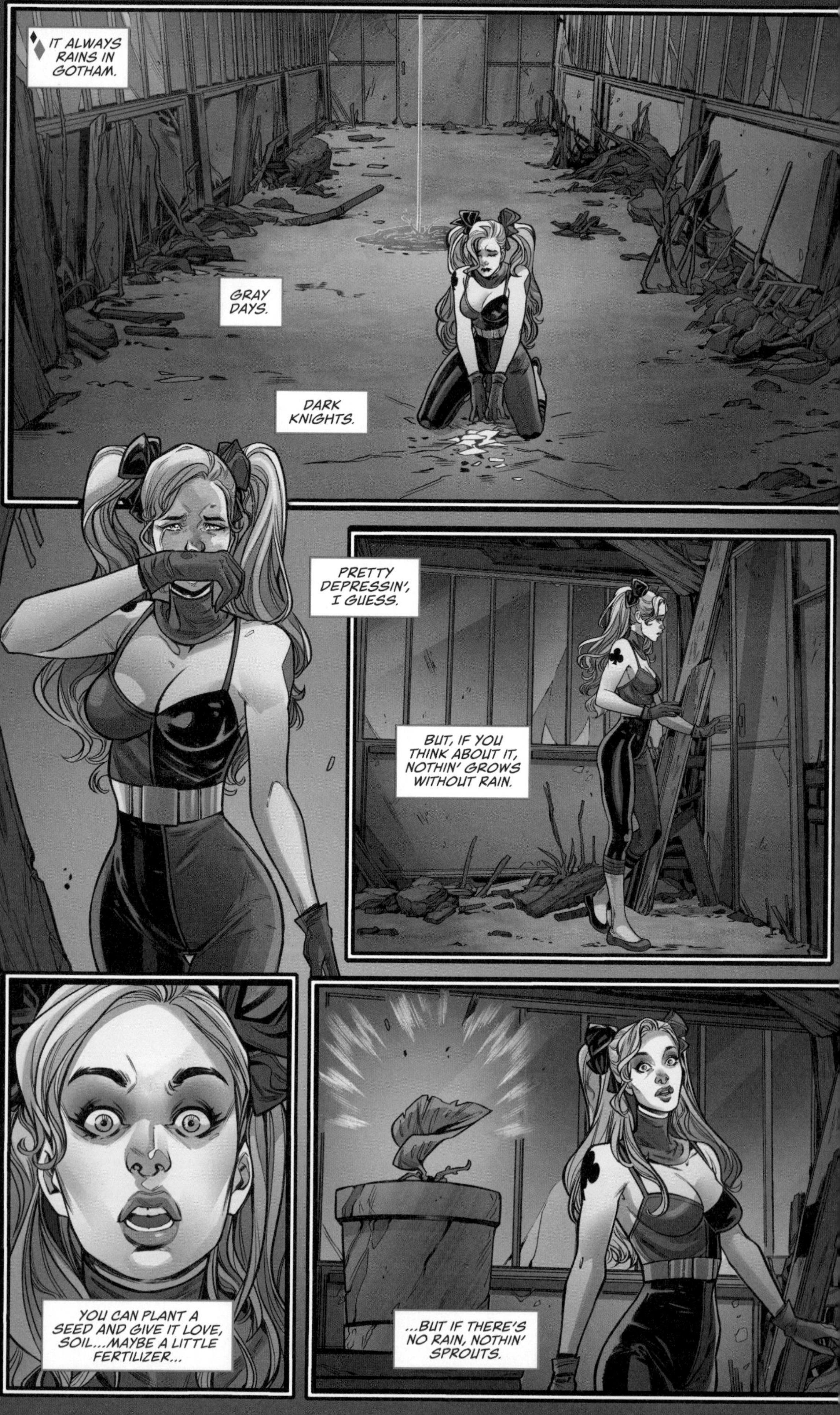
IT ALWAYS RAINS IN GOTHAM.
GRAY DAYS.
DARK KNIGHTS.
PRETTY DEPRESSIN', I GUESS.
BUT, IF YOU THINK ABOUT IT, NOTHIN' GROWS WITHOUT RAIN.
YOU CAN PLANT A SEED AND GIVE IT LOVE, SOIL...MAYBE A LITTLE FERTILIZER...
...BUT IF THERE'S NO RAIN, NOTHIN' SPROUTS.

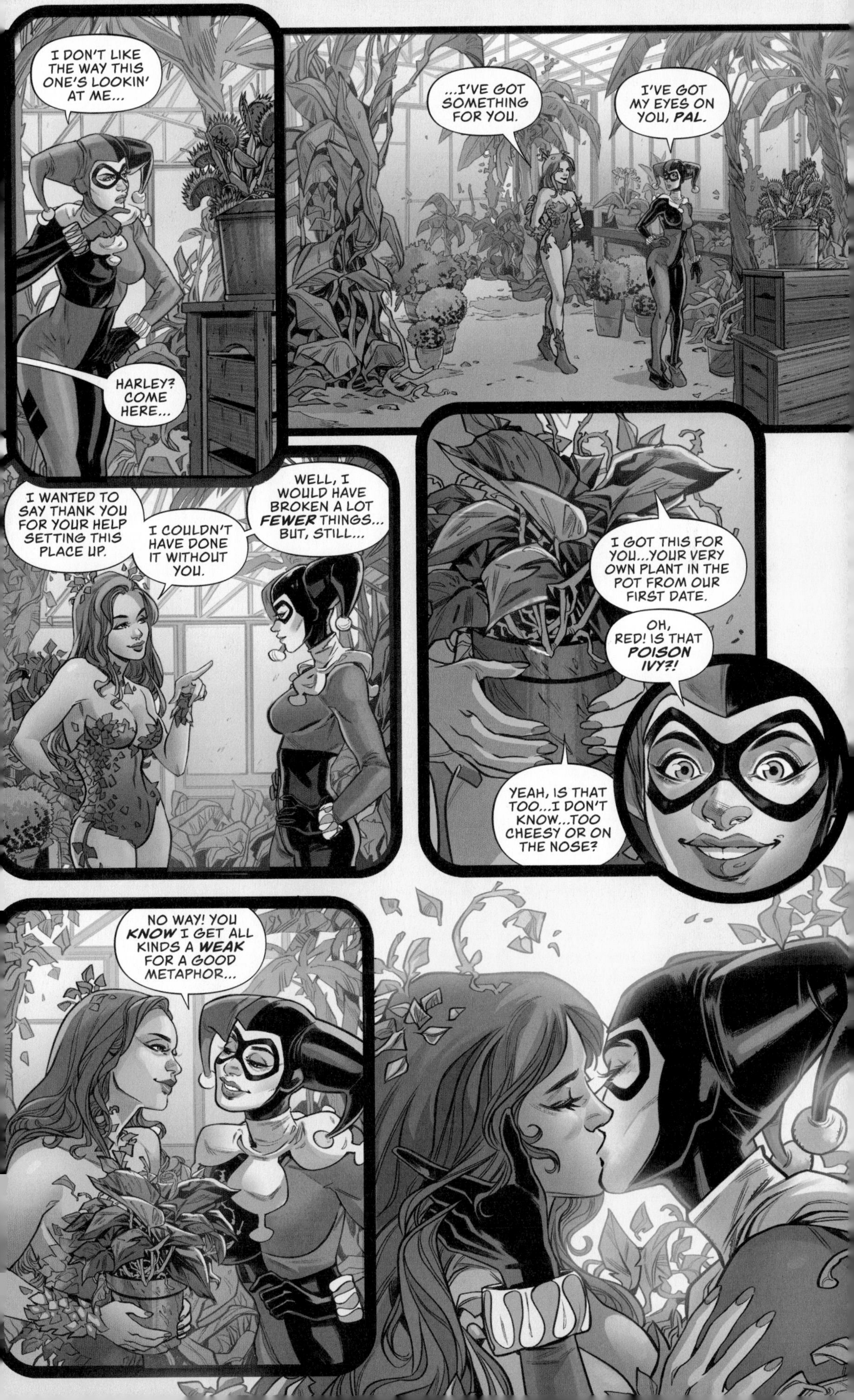
I DON'T LIKE THE WAY THIS ONE'S LOOKIN' AT ME...
HARLEY? COME HERE...
...I'VE GOT SOMETHING FOR YOU.
I'VE GOT MY EYES ON YOU, *PAL.*
I WANTED TO SAY THANK YOU FOR YOUR HELP SETTING THIS PLACE UP.
I COULDN'T HAVE DONE IT WITHOUT YOU.
WELL, I WOULD HAVE BROKEN A LOT *FEWER* THINGS... BUT, STILL...
I GOT THIS FOR YOU...YOUR VERY OWN PLANT IN THE POT FROM OUR FIRST DATE.
OH, RED! IS THAT *POISON IVY?!*
YEAH, IS THAT TOO...I DON'T KNOW...TOO CHEESY OR ON THE NOSE?
NO WAY! YOU *KNOW* I GET ALL KINDS A *WEAK* FOR A GOOD METAPHOR...

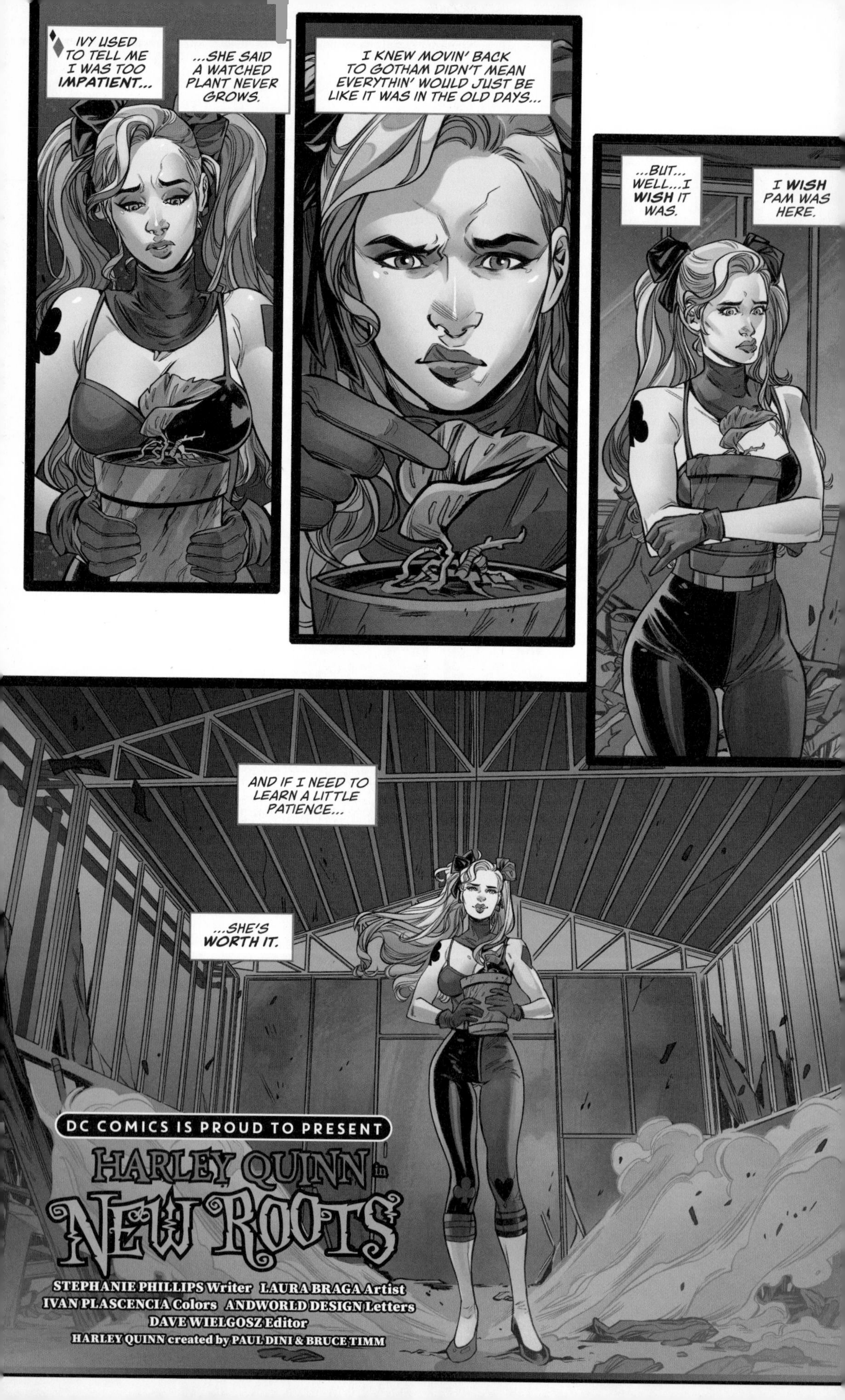
IVY USED TO TELL ME I WAS TOO IMPATIENT...
...SHE SAID A WATCHED PLANT NEVER GROWS.
I KNEW MOVIN' BACK TO GOTHAM DIDN'T MEAN EVERYTHIN' WOULD JUST BE LIKE IT WAS IN THE OLD DAYS...
...BUT... WELL...I WISH IT WAS.
I WISH PAM WAS HERE.
AND IF I NEED TO LEARN A LITTLE PATIENCE...
...SHE'S WORTH IT.
DC COMICS IS PROUD TO PRESENT
HARLEY QUINN in
NEW ROOTS
STEPHANIE PHILLIPS Writer LAURA BRAGA Artist
IVAN PLASCENCIA Colors ANDWORLD DESIGN Letters
DAVE WIELGOSZ Editor
HARLEY QUINN created by PAUL DINI & BRUCE TIMM

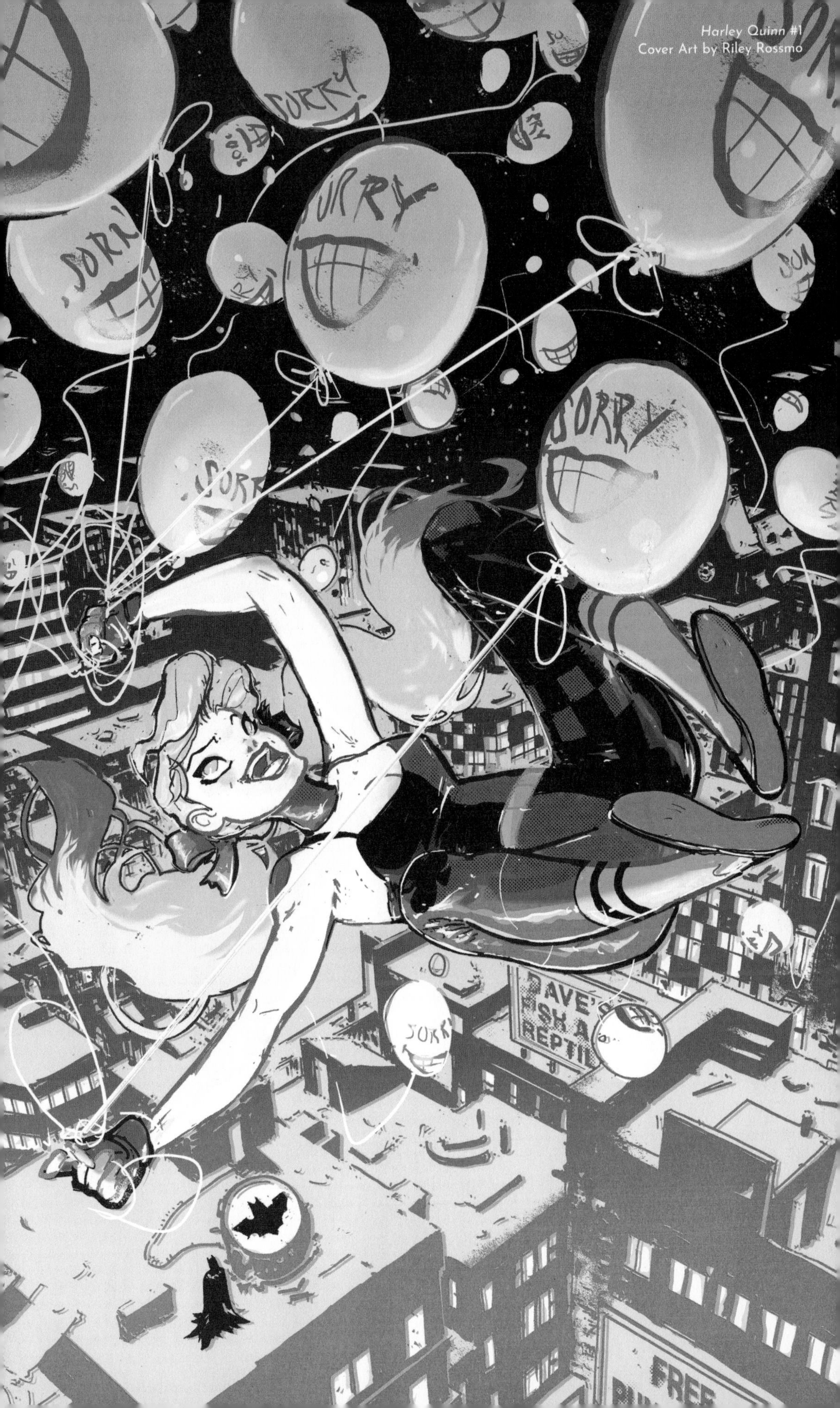
SORRY
DAVE'S
FREE

Harley Quinn #1
Cover Art by Riley Rossmo

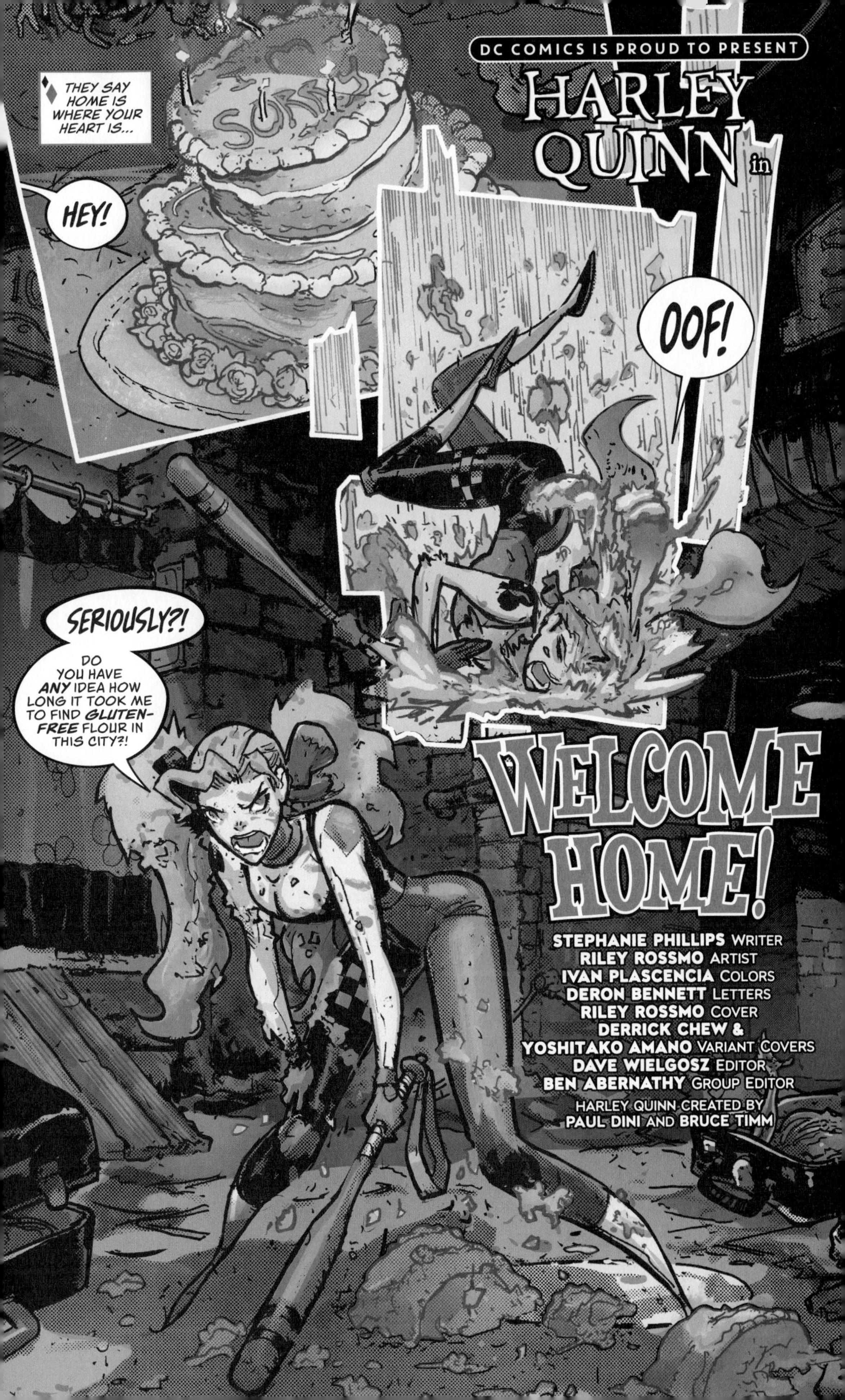
DC COMICS IS PROUD TO PRESENT
HARLEY QUINN in
THEY SAY HOME IS WHERE YOUR HEART IS...
HEY!
OOF!
SERIOUSLY?!
DO YOU HAVE ANY IDEA HOW LONG IT TOOK ME TO FIND GLUTEN-FREE FLOUR IN THIS CITY?!
WELCOME HOME!
STEPHANIE PHILLIPS WRITER
RILEY ROSSMO ARTIST
IVAN PLASCENCIA COLORS
DERON BENNETT LETTERS
RILEY ROSSMO COVER
DERRICK CHEW &
YOSHITAKO AMANO VARIANT COVERS
DAVE WIELGOSZ EDITOR
BEN ABERNATHY GROUP EDITOR
HARLEY QUINN CREATED BY
PAUL DINI AND BRUCE TIMM

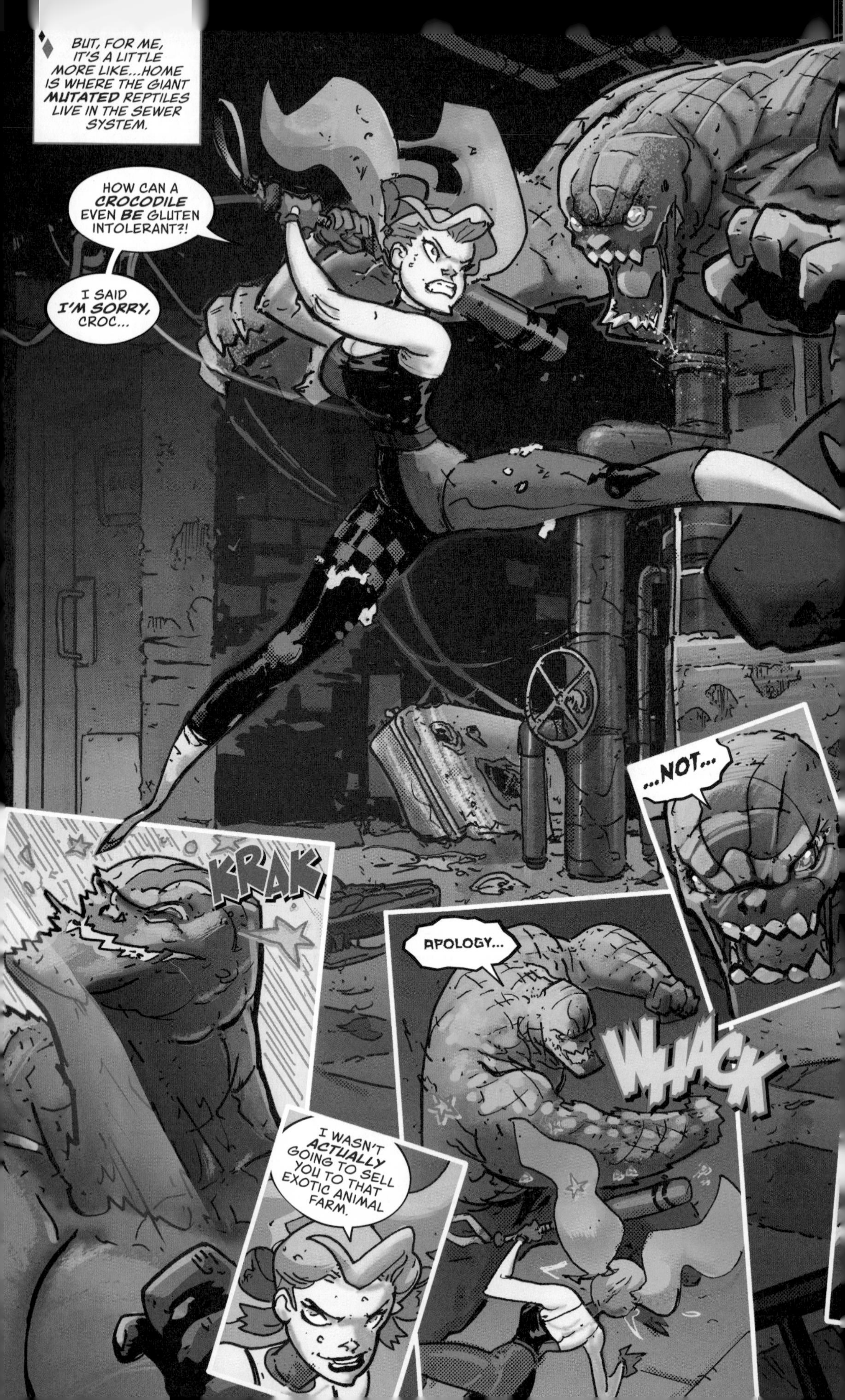

BUT, FOR ME, IT'S A LITTLE MORE LIKE...HOME IS WHERE THE GIANT MUTATED REPTILES LIVE IN THE SEWER SYSTEM.
HOW CAN A CROCODILE EVEN BE GLUTEN INTOLERANT?!
I SAID I'M SORRY, CROC...
KRAK
...NOT...
APOLOGY...
WHACK
I WASN'T ACTUALLY GOING TO SELL YOU TO THAT EXOTIC ANIMAL FARM.

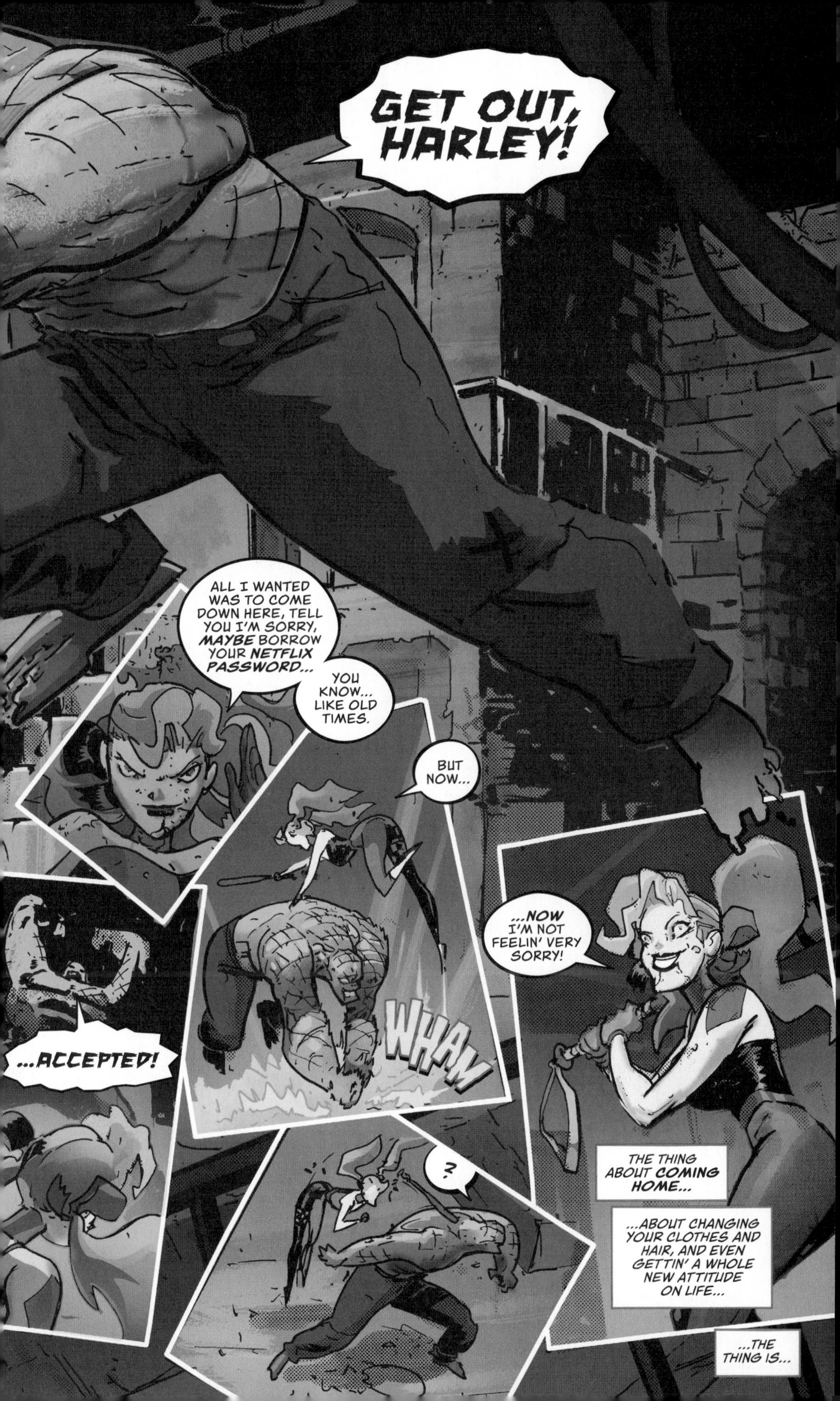
GET OUT, HARLEY!
ALL I WANTED WAS TO COME DOWN HERE, TELL YOU I'M SORRY, MAYBE BORROW YOUR NETFLIX PASSWORD...
YOU KNOW... LIKE OLD TIMES.
BUT NOW...
...NOW I'M NOT FEELIN' VERY SORRY!
WHAM
...ACCEPTED!
?
THE THING ABOUT COMING HOME...
...ABOUT CHANGING YOUR CLOTHES AND HAIR, AND EVEN GETTIN' A WHOLE NEW ATTITUDE ON LIFE...
...THE THING IS...

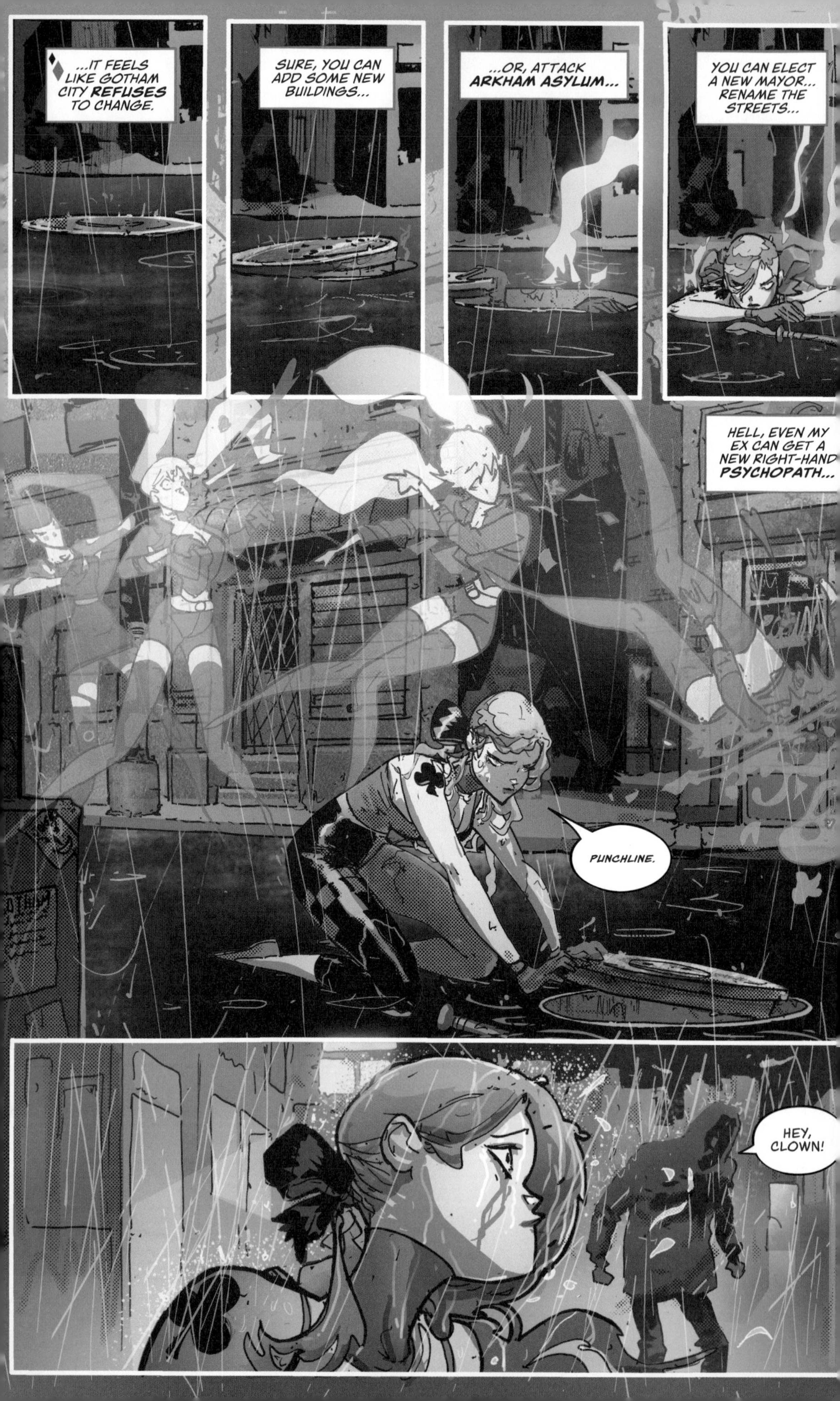
...IT FEELS LIKE GOTHAM CITY REFUSES TO CHANGE.
SURE, YOU CAN ADD SOME NEW BUILDINGS...
...OR, ATTACK ARKHAM ASYLUM...
YOU CAN ELECT A NEW MAYOR... RENAME THE STREETS...
HELL, EVEN MY EX CAN GET A NEW RIGHT-HAND PSYCHOPATH...
PUNCHLINE.
HEY, CLOWN!

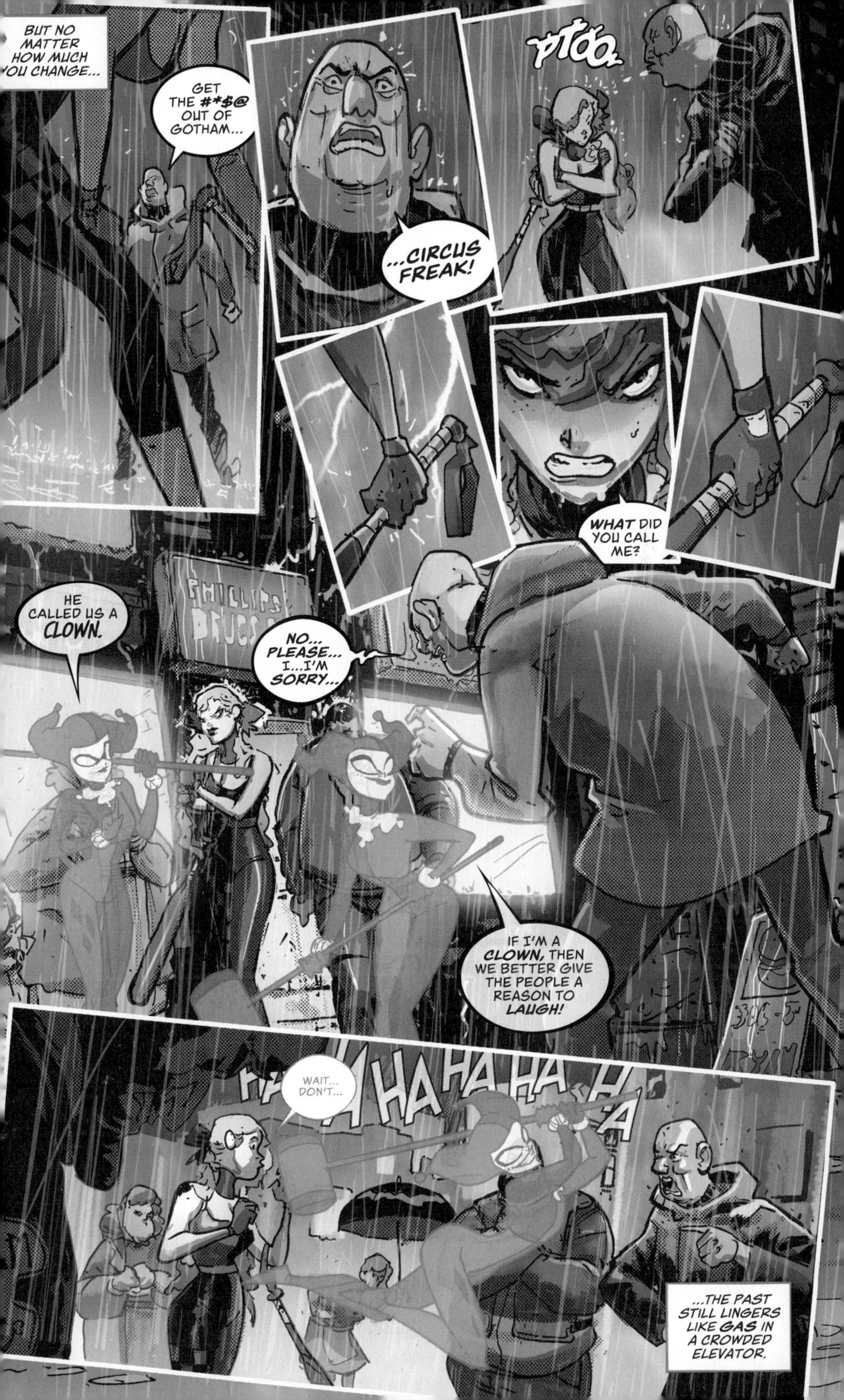
BUT NO MATTER HOW MUCH YOU CHANGE...
GET THE #*$@ OUT OF GOTHAM...
...CIRCUS FREAK!
PTOO
WHAT DID YOU CALL ME?
HE CALLED US A CLOWN.
NO... PLEASE... I...I'M SORRY...
IF I'M A CLOWN, THEN WE BETTER GIVE THE PEOPLE A REASON TO LAUGH!
HA HA HA HA HA HA HA
WAIT... DON'T...
...THE PAST STILL LINGERS LIKE GAS IN A CROWDED ELEVATOR.

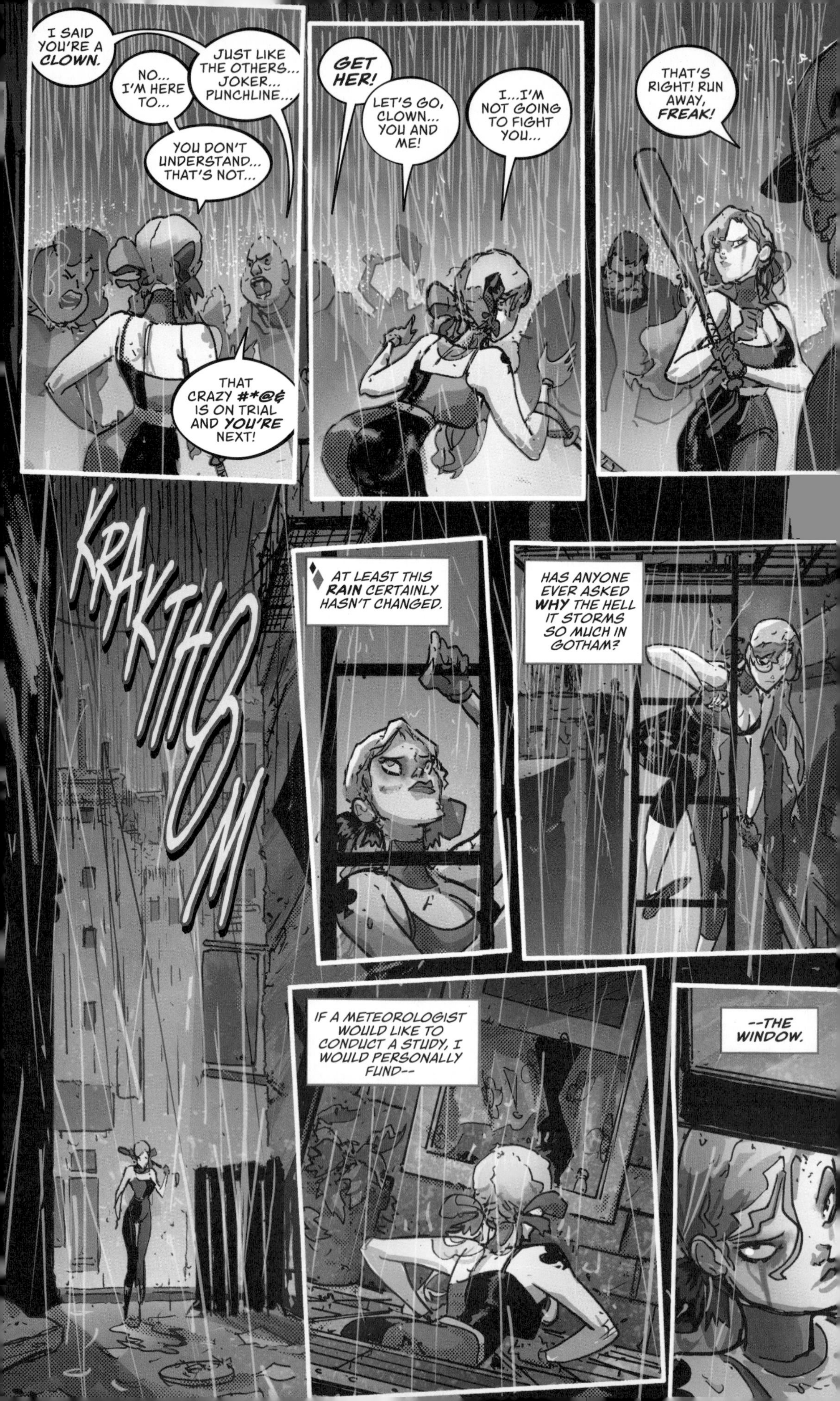

I SAID YOU'RE A CLOWN.
NO... I'M HERE TO...
JUST LIKE THE OTHERS... JOKER... PUNCHLINE...
YOU DON'T UNDERSTAND... THAT'S NOT...
THAT CRAZY #*@& IS ON TRIAL AND YOU'RE NEXT!
GET HER!
LET'S GO, CLOWN... YOU AND ME!
I...I'M NOT GOING TO FIGHT YOU...
THAT'S RIGHT! RUN AWAY, FREAK!
KRAKTHOOM
AT LEAST THIS RAIN CERTAINLY HASN'T CHANGED.
HAS ANYONE EVER ASKED WHY THE HELL IT STORMS SO MUCH IN GOTHAM?
IF A METEOROLOGIST WOULD LIKE TO CONDUCT A STUDY, I WOULD PERSONALLY FUND--
--THE WINDOW.

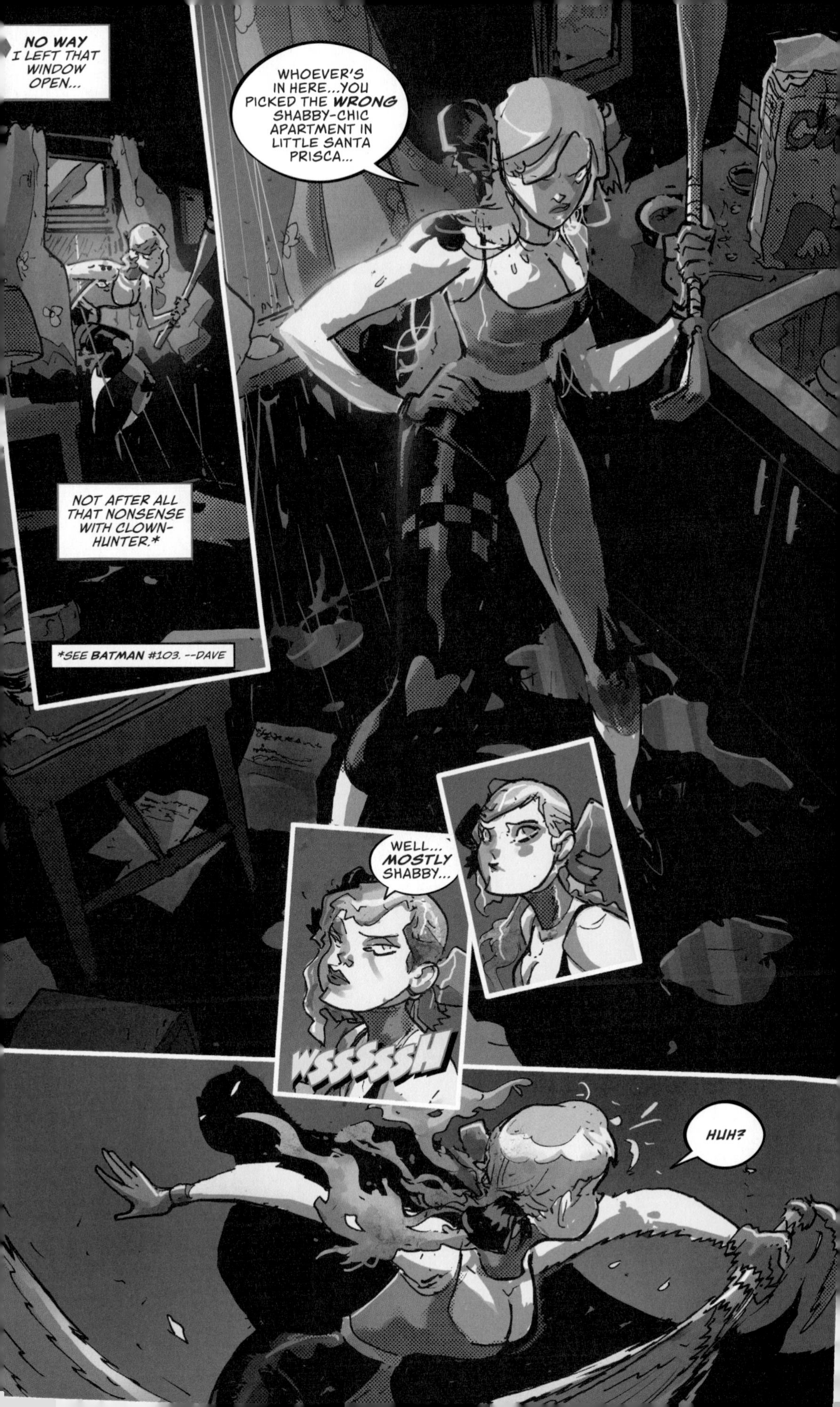
NO WAY I LEFT THAT WINDOW OPEN...
WHOEVER'S IN HERE...YOU PICKED THE WRONG SHABBY-CHIC APARTMENT IN LITTLE SANTA PRISCA...
NOT AFTER ALL THAT NONSENSE WITH CLOWN-HUNTER.*
*SEE BATMAN #103. --DAVE
WELL... MOSTLY SHABBY...
WSSSSSH
HUH?

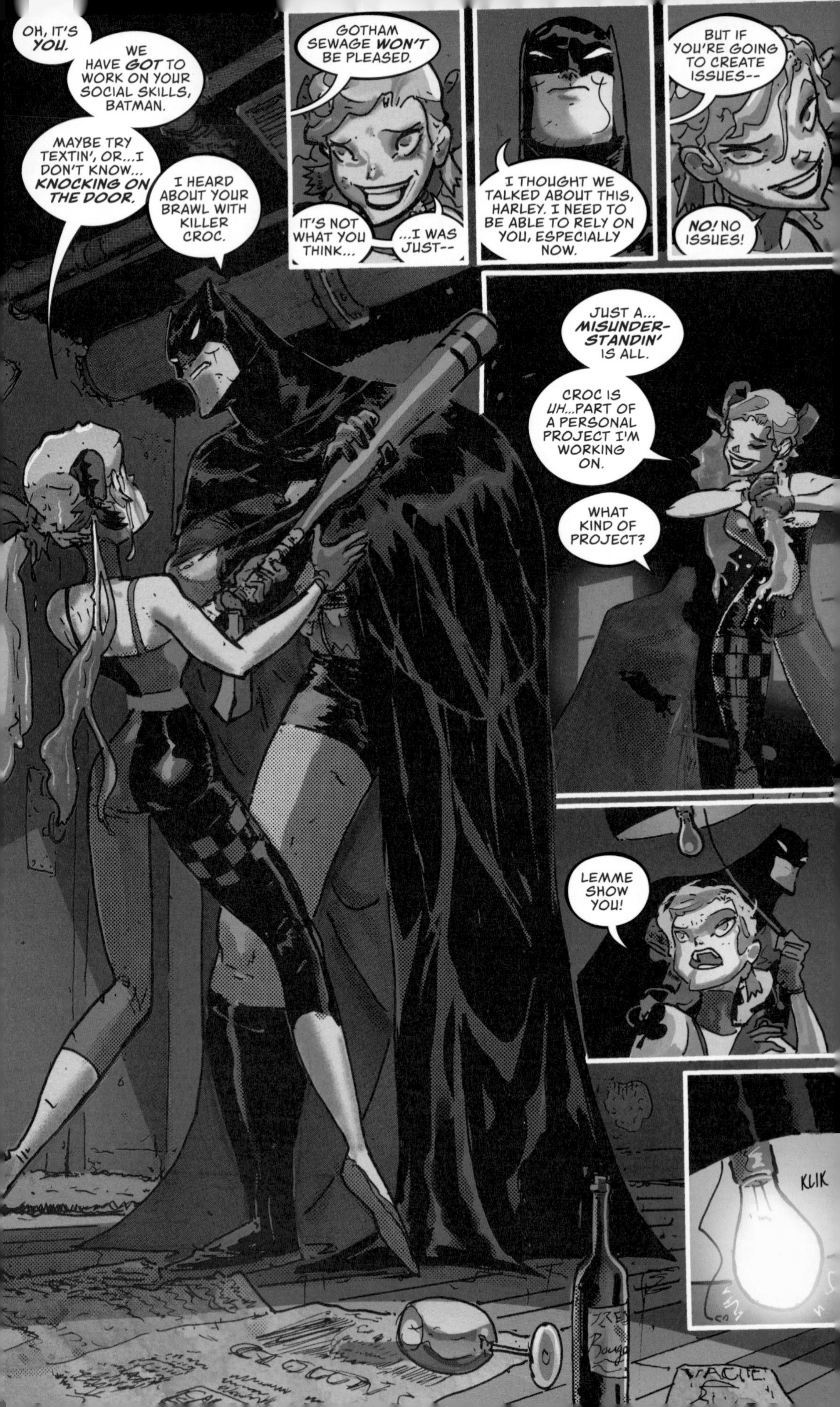
OH, IT'S *YOU.*
WE HAVE *GOT* TO WORK ON YOUR SOCIAL SKILLS, BATMAN.
MAYBE TRY TEXTIN', OR...I DON'T KNOW... ***KNOCKING ON THE DOOR.***
I HEARD ABOUT YOUR BRAWL WITH KILLER CROC.
GOTHAM SEWAGE ***WON'T*** BE PLEASED.
IT'S NOT WHAT YOU THINK...
...I WAS JUST--
I THOUGHT WE TALKED ABOUT THIS, HARLEY. I NEED TO BE ABLE TO RELY ON YOU, ESPECIALLY NOW.
BUT IF YOU'RE GOING TO CREATE ISSUES--
NO! NO ISSUES!
JUST A... ***MISUNDER-STANDIN'*** IS ALL.
CROC IS *UH*...PART OF A PERSONAL PROJECT I'M WORKING ON.
WHAT KIND OF PROJECT?
LEMME SHOW YOU!
KLIK

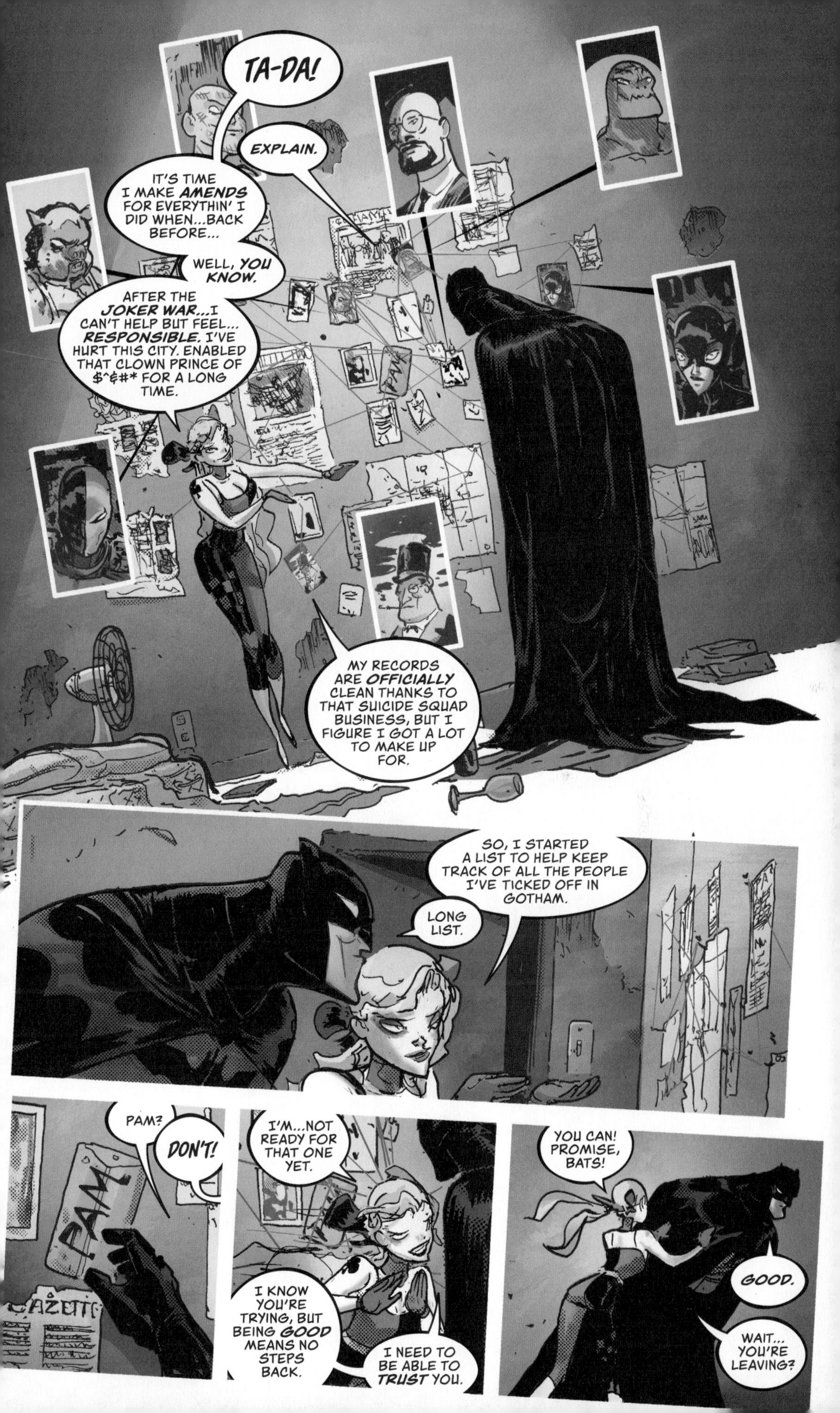
TA-DA!
EXPLAIN.
IT'S TIME I MAKE AMENDS FOR EVERYTHIN' I DID WHEN...BACK BEFORE...
WELL, YOU KNOW.
AFTER THE JOKER WAR...I CAN'T HELP BUT FEEL... RESPONSIBLE. I'VE HURT THIS CITY. ENABLED THAT CLOWN PRINCE OF $^&#* FOR A LONG TIME.
MY RECORDS ARE OFFICIALLY CLEAN THANKS TO THAT SUICIDE SQUAD BUSINESS, BUT I FIGURE I GOT A LOT TO MAKE UP FOR.
SO, I STARTED A LIST TO HELP KEEP TRACK OF ALL THE PEOPLE I'VE TICKED OFF IN GOTHAM.
LONG LIST.
PAM?
DON'T!
PAM
I'M...NOT READY FOR THAT ONE YET.
I KNOW YOU'RE TRYING, BUT BEING GOOD MEANS NO STEPS BACK.
I NEED TO BE ABLE TO TRUST YOU.
YOU CAN! PROMISE, BATS!
GOOD.
WAIT... YOU'RE LEAVING?

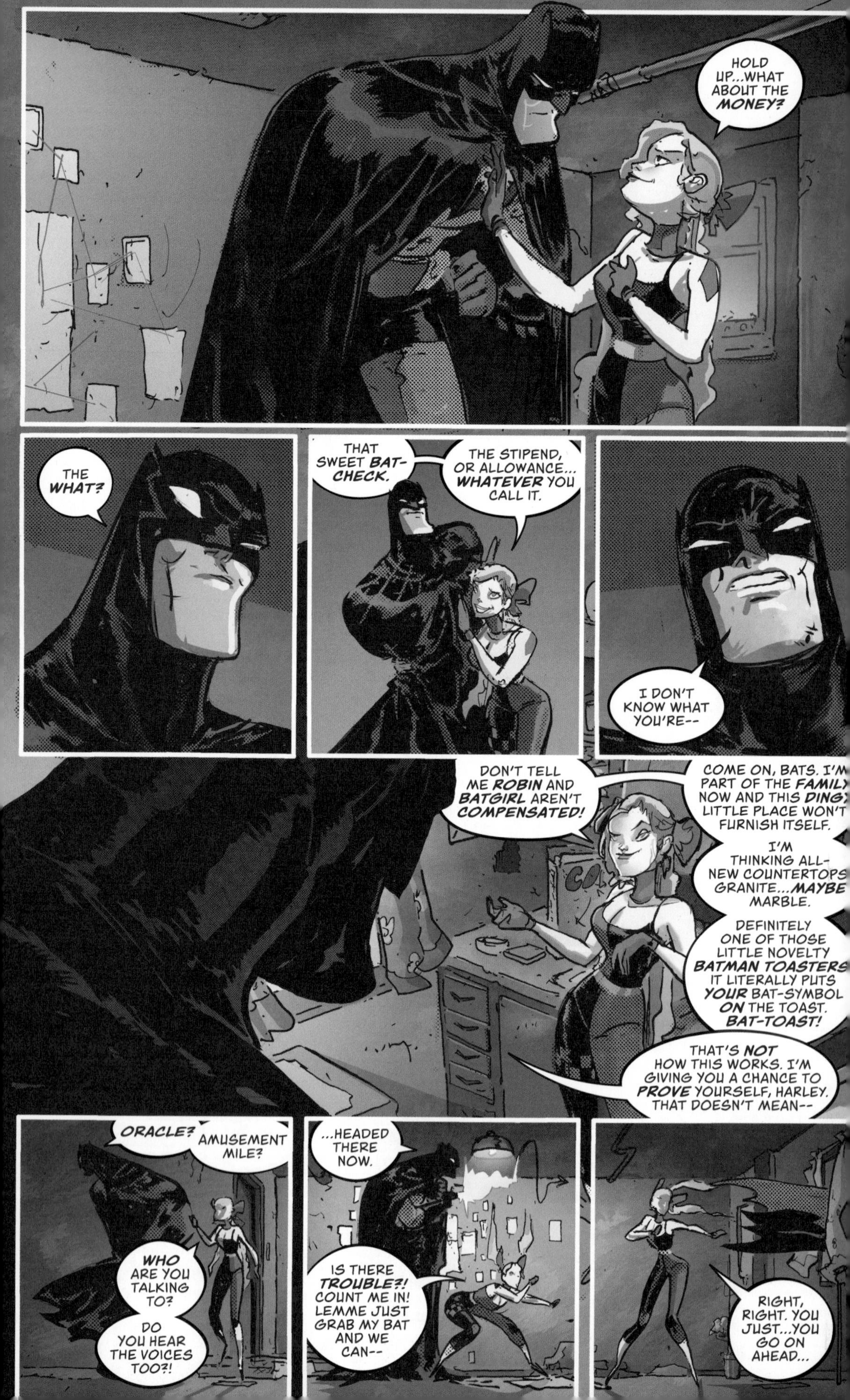

HOLD UP...WHAT ABOUT THE MONEY?
THE WHAT?
THAT SWEET BAT-CHECK.
THE STIPEND, OR ALLOWANCE... WHATEVER YOU CALL IT.
I DON'T KNOW WHAT YOU'RE--
DON'T TELL ME ROBIN AND BATGIRL AREN'T COMPENSATED!
COME ON, BATS. I'M PART OF THE FAMILY NOW AND THIS DINGY LITTLE PLACE WON'T FURNISH ITSELF.
I'M THINKING ALL-NEW COUNTERTOPS GRANITE...MAYBE MARBLE.
DEFINITELY ONE OF THOSE LITTLE NOVELTY BATMAN TOASTERS IT LITERALLY PUTS YOUR BAT-SYMBOL ON THE TOAST. BAT-TOAST!
THAT'S NOT HOW THIS WORKS. I'M GIVING YOU A CHANCE TO PROVE YOURSELF, HARLEY. THAT DOESN'T MEAN--
ORACLE?
AMUSEMENT MILE?
WHO ARE YOU TALKING TO?
DO YOU HEAR THE VOICES TOO?!
...HEADED THERE NOW.
IS THERE TROUBLE?! COUNT ME IN! LEMME JUST GRAB MY BAT AND WE CAN--
RIGHT, RIGHT. YOU JUST...YOU GO ON AHEAD...

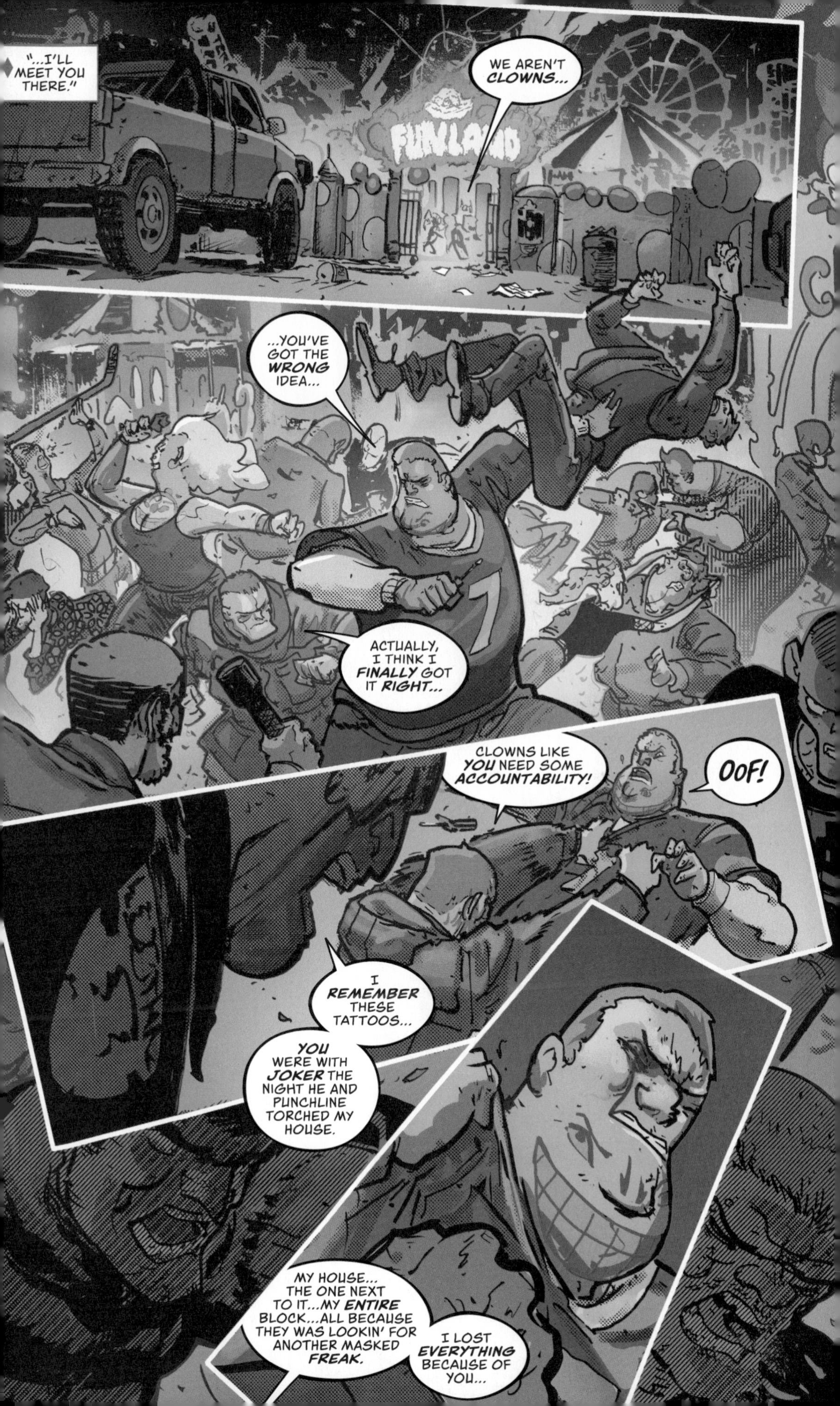
"...I'LL MEET YOU THERE."
WE AREN'T CLOWNS...
...YOU'VE GOT THE WRONG IDEA...
ACTUALLY, I THINK I FINALLY GOT IT RIGHT...
CLOWNS LIKE YOU NEED SOME ACCOUNTABILITY!
OOF!
I REMEMBER THESE TATTOOS...
YOU WERE WITH JOKER THE NIGHT HE AND PUNCHLINE TORCHED MY HOUSE.
MY HOUSE... THE ONE NEXT TO IT...MY ENTIRE BLOCK...ALL BECAUSE THEY WAS LOOKIN' FOR ANOTHER MASKED FREAK.
I LOST EVERYTHING BECAUSE OF YOU...
FUNLAND

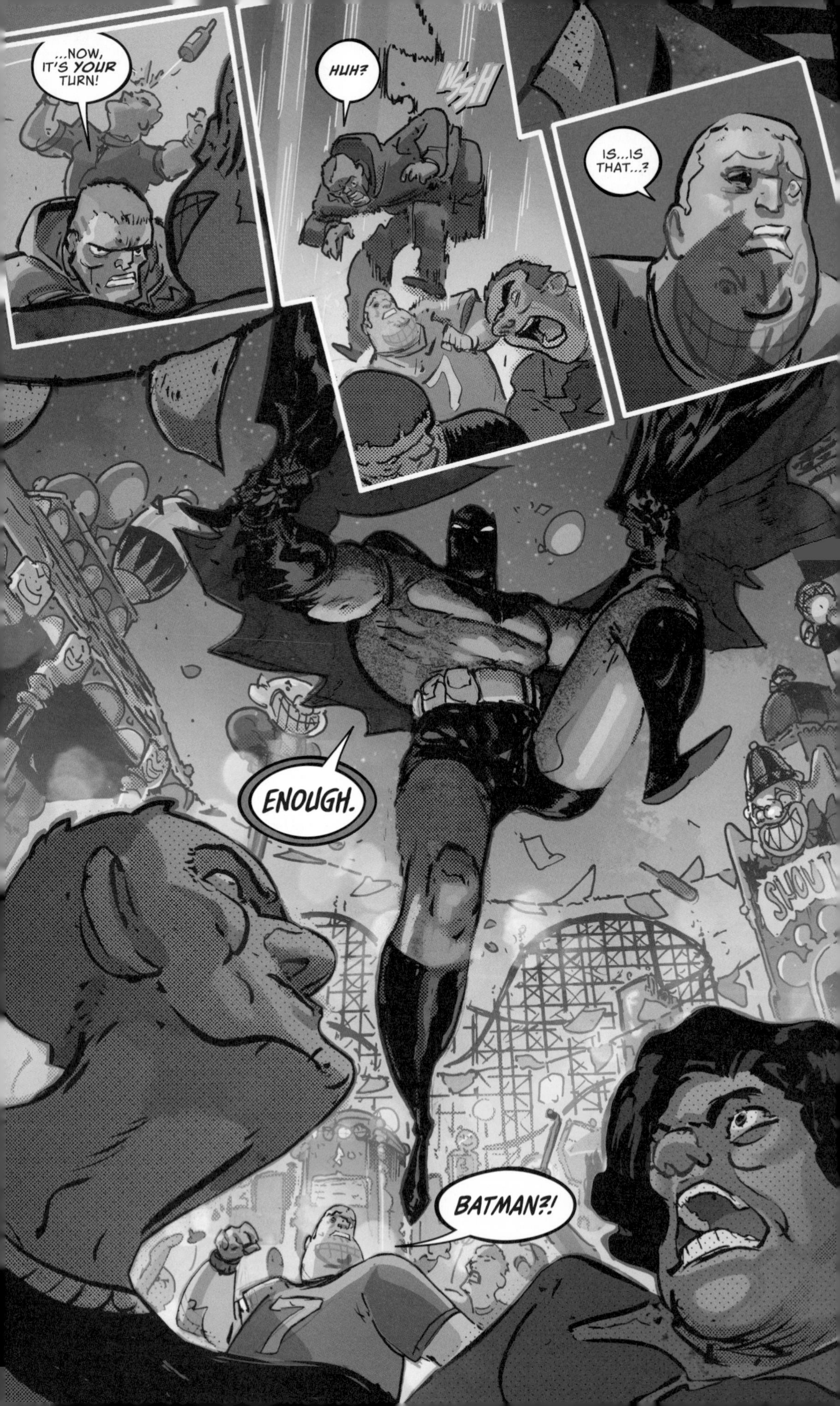

...NOW, IT'S YOUR TURN!
HUH?
WSSH
IS...IS THAT...?
ENOUGH.
BATMAN?!

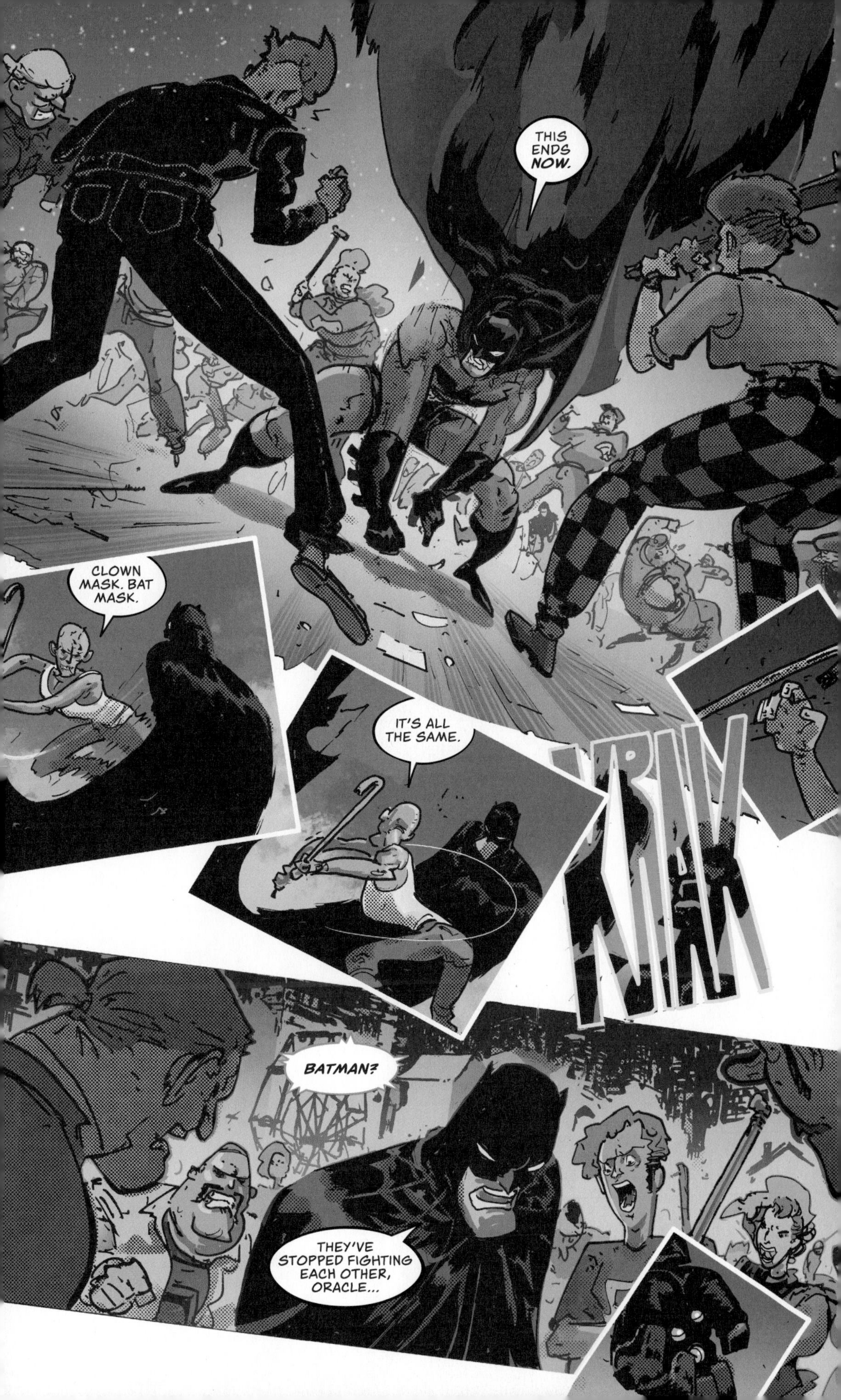
THIS ENDS NOW.
CLOWN MASK. BAT MASK.
IT'S ALL THE SAME.
KRAK
BATMAN?
THEY'VE STOPPED FIGHTING EACH OTHER, ORACLE...

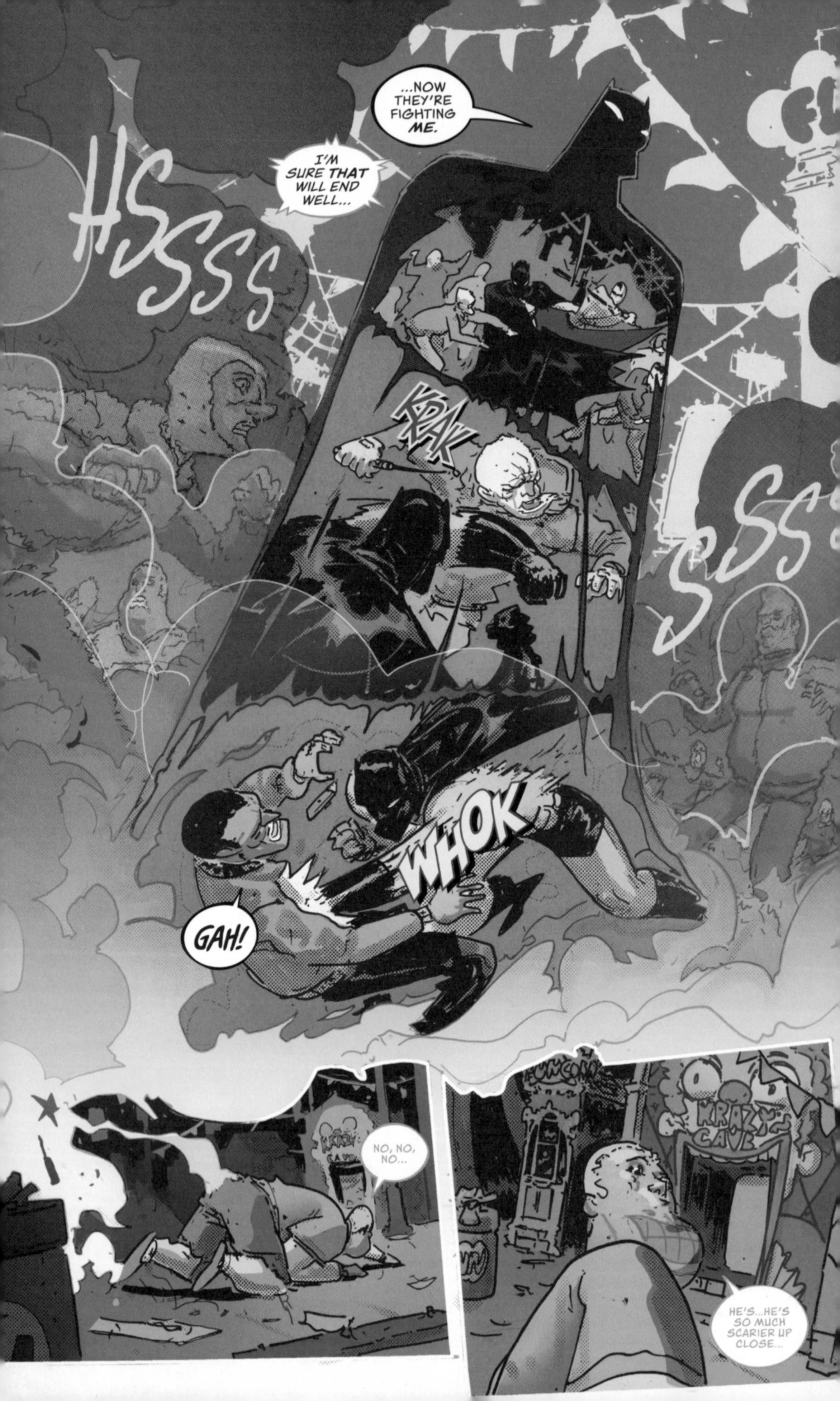

...NOW THEY'RE FIGHTING ME.
I'M SURE THAT WILL END WELL...
HSSSS
KRAK
SSSS
WHOK
GAH!
NO, NO, NO...
KRAZY CAVE
HE'S...HE'S SO MUCH SCARIER UP CLOSE...

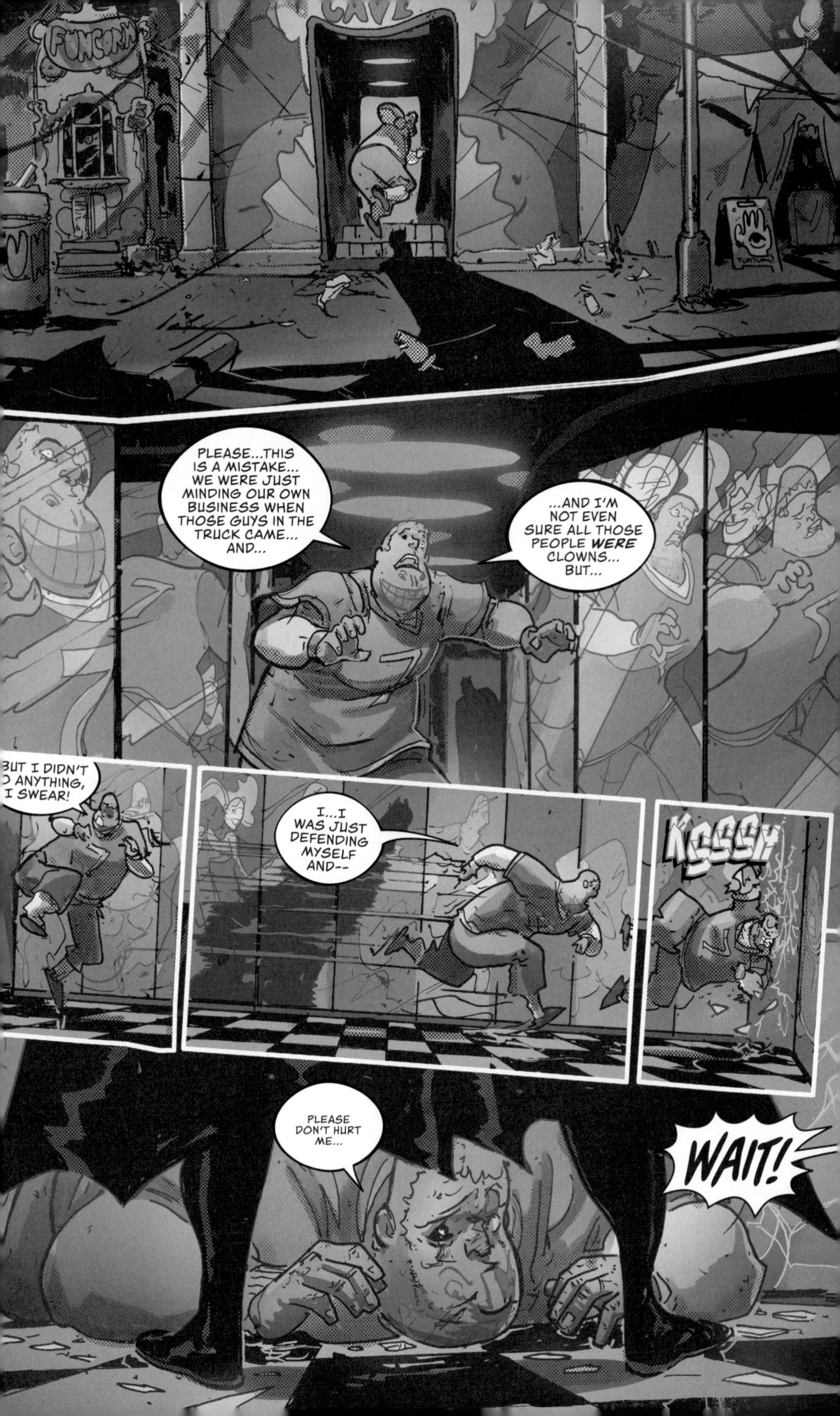
FUNCORN
CAVE
PLEASE...THIS IS A MISTAKE... WE WERE JUST MINDING OUR OWN BUSINESS WHEN THOSE GUYS IN THE TRUCK CAME... AND...
...AND I'M NOT EVEN SURE ALL THOSE PEOPLE *WERE* CLOWNS... BUT...
BUT I DIDN'T DO ANYTHING, I SWEAR!
I...I WAS JUST DEFENDING MYSELF AND--
KSSSH
PLEASE DON'T HURT ME...
WAIT!

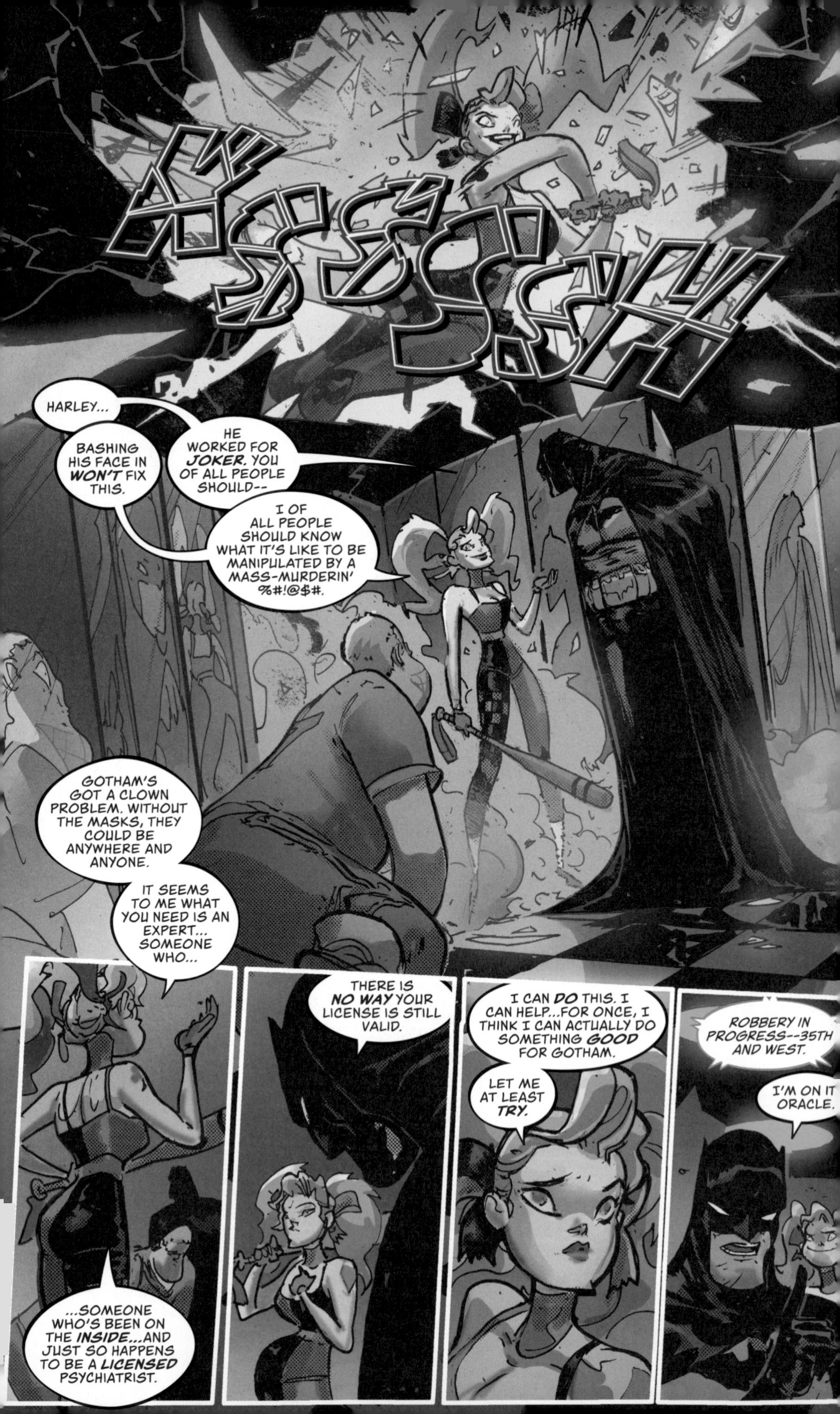

KRASSSSH!!
HARLEY...
HE WORKED FOR *JOKER*. YOU OF ALL PEOPLE SHOULD--
BASHING HIS FACE IN *WON'T* FIX THIS.
I OF ALL PEOPLE SHOULD KNOW WHAT IT'S LIKE TO BE MANIPULATED BY A MASS-MURDERIN' %#!@$#.
GOTHAM'S GOT A CLOWN PROBLEM. WITHOUT THE MASKS, THEY COULD BE ANYWHERE AND ANYONE.
IT SEEMS TO ME WHAT YOU NEED IS AN EXPERT... SOMEONE WHO...
...SOMEONE WHO'S BEEN ON THE *INSIDE*...AND JUST SO HAPPENS TO BE A *LICENSED* PSYCHIATRIST.
THERE IS *NO WAY* YOUR LICENSE IS STILL VALID.
I CAN *DO* THIS. I CAN HELP...FOR ONCE, I THINK I CAN ACTUALLY DO SOMETHING *GOOD* FOR GOTHAM.
LET ME AT LEAST *TRY*.
ROBBERY IN PROGRESS--35TH AND WEST.
I'M ON IT ORACLE.

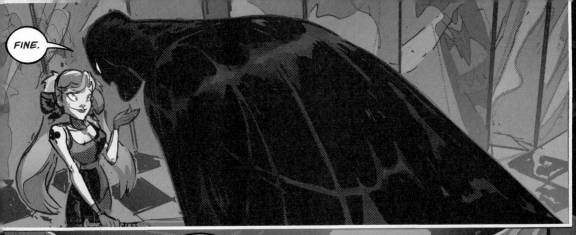

FINE.

BUT I DO NOT HAVE TIME TO CLEAN UP A MESS, HARLEY.

AYE, AYE, CAPTAIN! THERE'LL BE NO TROUBLE FROM ME!

YES! I GET TO WORK FOR BATMAN!

THAT'S... NOT REALLY THE WAY IT SOUNDED...

SHUT IT... ...WAIT... WHO ARE YOU?

KEVIN.

SHUT IT, KEVIN. YOU DON'T KNOW BATS THE WAY I DO.

WE'RE SO CLOSE THAT SOME THINGS ARE UNSPOKEN.

YOU HEARD APATHY, BUT, TO ME, HIS BODY LANGUAGE REALLY SAID...

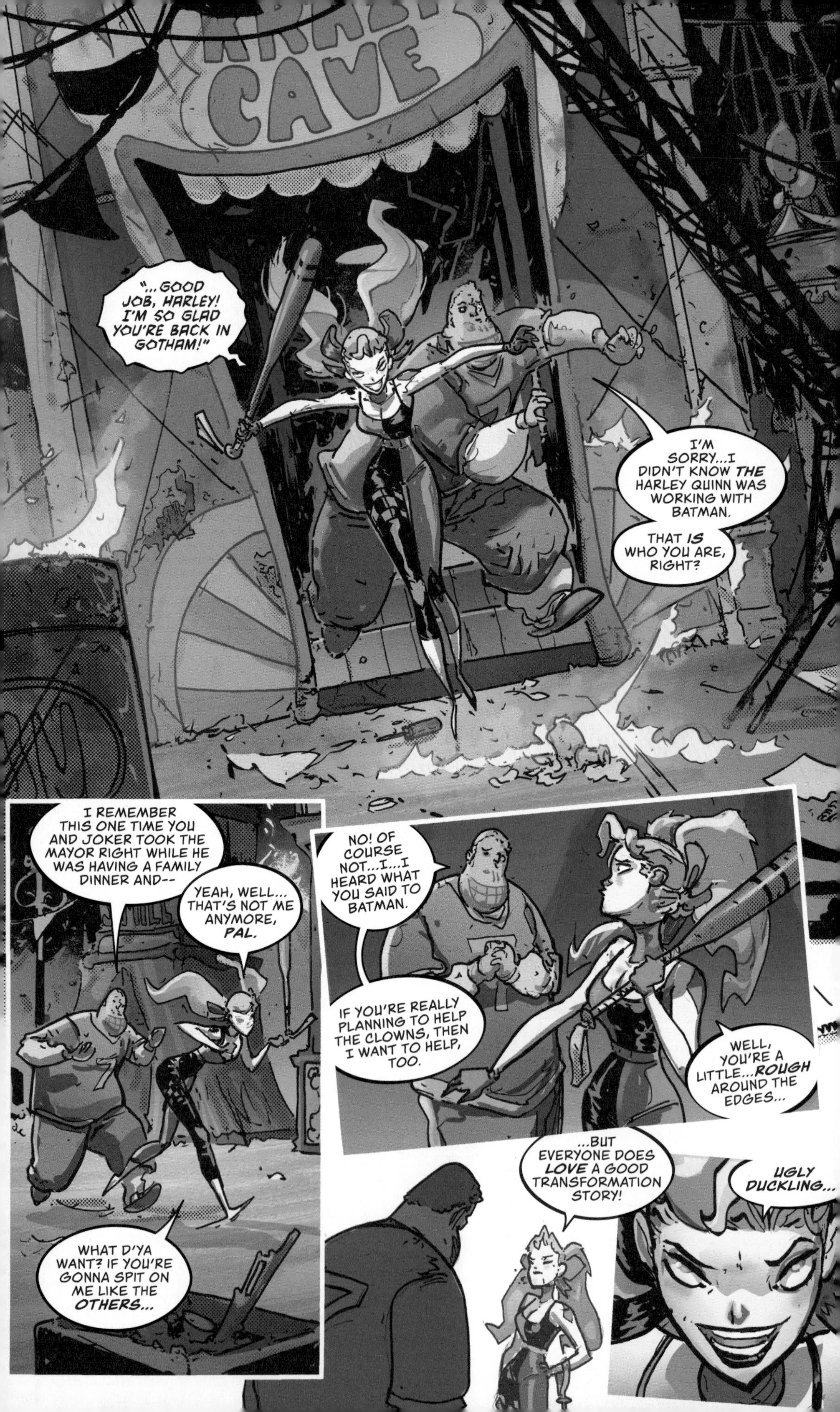
CAVE
"...GOOD JOB, HARLEY! I'M SO GLAD YOU'RE BACK IN GOTHAM!"
I'M SORRY...I DIDN'T KNOW ***THE*** HARLEY QUINN WAS WORKING WITH BATMAN.
THAT ***IS*** WHO YOU ARE, RIGHT?
I REMEMBER THIS ONE TIME YOU AND JOKER TOOK THE MAYOR RIGHT WHILE HE WAS HAVING A FAMILY DINNER AND--
YEAH, WELL... THAT'S NOT ME ANYMORE, ***PAL.***
WHAT D'YA WANT? IF YOU'RE GONNA SPIT ON ME LIKE THE ***OTHERS...***
NO! OF COURSE NOT...I...I HEARD WHAT YOU SAID TO BATMAN.
IF YOU'RE REALLY PLANNING TO HELP THE CLOWNS, THEN I WANT TO HELP, TOO.
WELL, YOU'RE A LITTLE...***ROUGH*** AROUND THE EDGES...
...BUT EVERYONE DOES ***LOVE*** A GOOD TRANSFORMATION STORY!
UGLY DUCKLING...

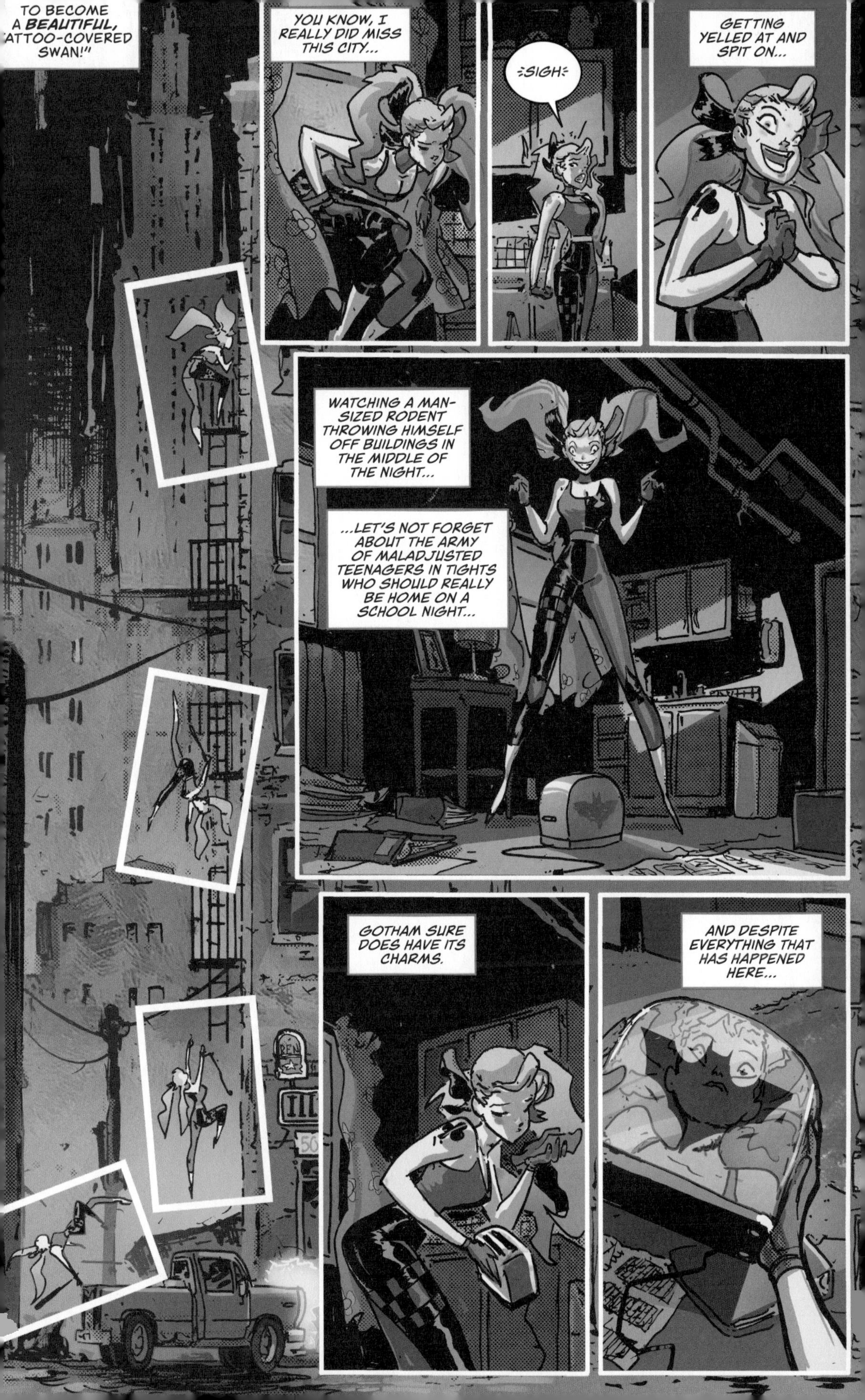
TO BECOME A **BEAUTIFUL**, TATTOO-COVERED SWAN!"
YOU KNOW, I REALLY DID MISS THIS CITY...
:SIGH:
GETTING YELLED AT AND SPIT ON...
WATCHING A MAN-SIZED RODENT THROWING HIMSELF OFF BUILDINGS IN THE MIDDLE OF THE NIGHT...
...LET'S NOT FORGET ABOUT THE ARMY OF MALADJUSTED TEENAGERS IN TIGHTS WHO SHOULD REALLY BE HOME ON A SCHOOL NIGHT...
GOTHAM SURE DOES HAVE ITS CHARMS.
AND DESPITE EVERYTHING THAT HAS HAPPENED HERE...

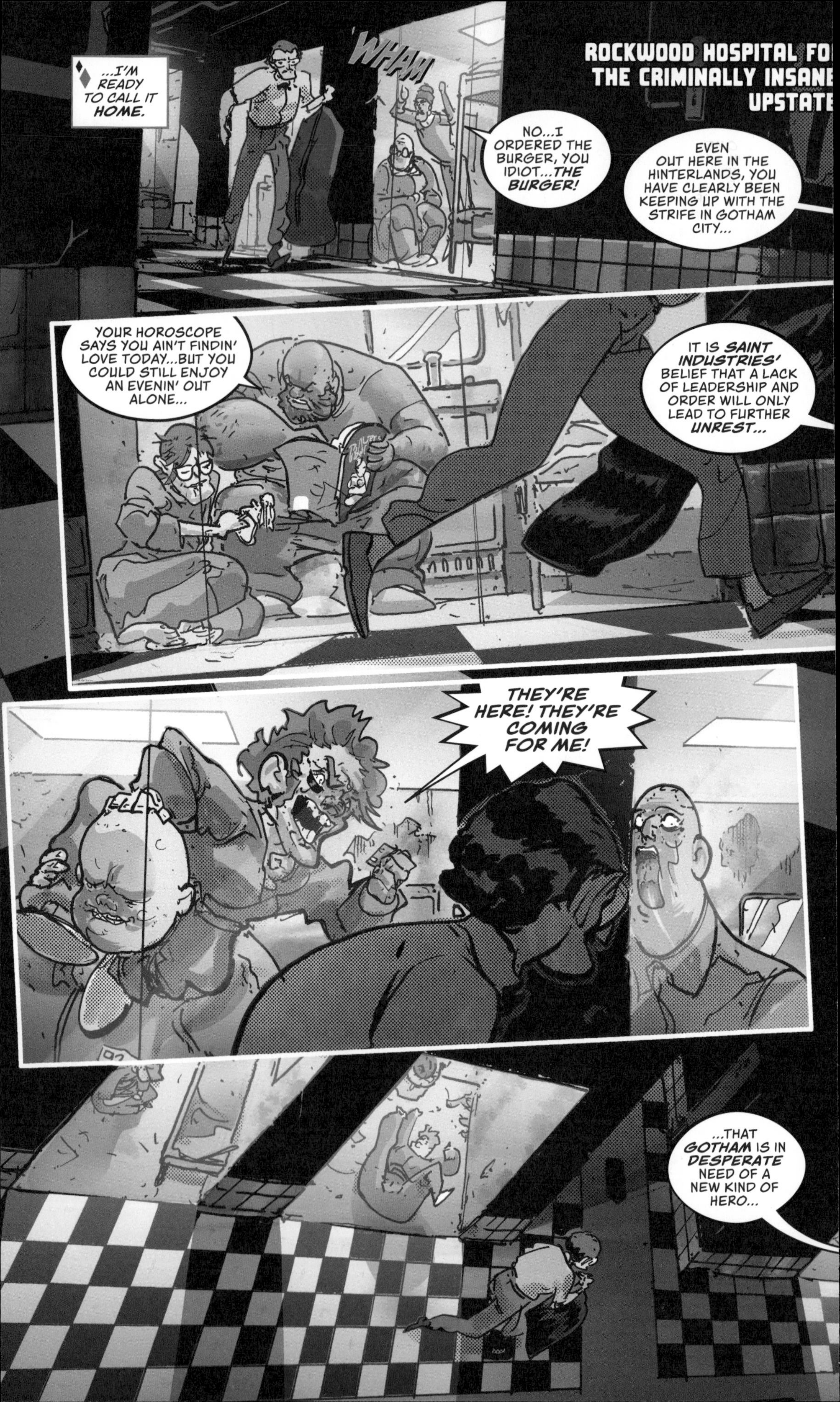

...I'M READY TO CALL IT *HOME.*
WHAM
ROCKWOOD HOSPITAL FOR THE CRIMINALLY INSANE UPSTATE
NO...I ORDERED THE BURGER, YOU IDIOT...*THE BURGER!*
EVEN OUT HERE IN THE HINTERLANDS, YOU HAVE CLEARLY BEEN KEEPING UP WITH THE STRIFE IN GOTHAM CITY...
YOUR HOROSCOPE SAYS YOU AIN'T FINDIN' LOVE TODAY...BUT YOU COULD STILL ENJOY AN EVENIN' OUT ALONE...
IT IS *SAINT INDUSTRIES'* BELIEF THAT A LACK OF LEADERSHIP AND ORDER WILL ONLY LEAD TO FURTHER *UNREST...*
THEY'RE HERE! THEY'RE COMING FOR ME!
...THAT *GOTHAM* IS IN *DESPERATE* NEED OF A NEW KIND OF HERO...

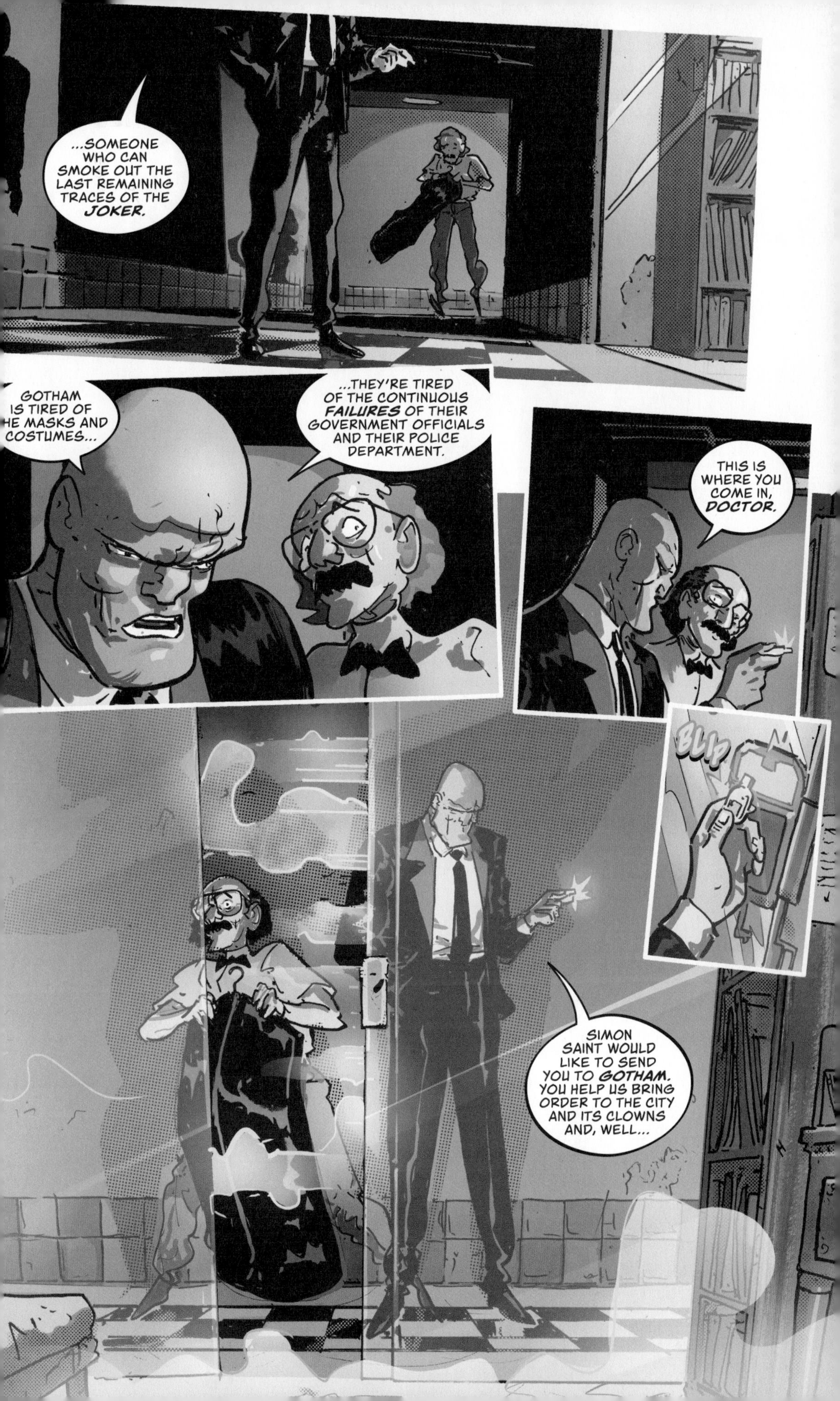
...SOMEONE WHO CAN SMOKE OUT THE LAST REMAINING TRACES OF THE JOKER.
GOTHAM IS TIRED OF HE MASKS AND COSTUMES...
...THEY'RE TIRED OF THE CONTINUOUS FAILURES OF THEIR GOVERNMENT OFFICIALS AND THEIR POLICE DEPARTMENT.
THIS IS WHERE YOU COME IN, DOCTOR.
BLIP
SIMON SAINT WOULD LIKE TO SEND YOU TO GOTHAM. YOU HELP US BRING ORDER TO THE CITY AND ITS CLOWNS AND, WELL...

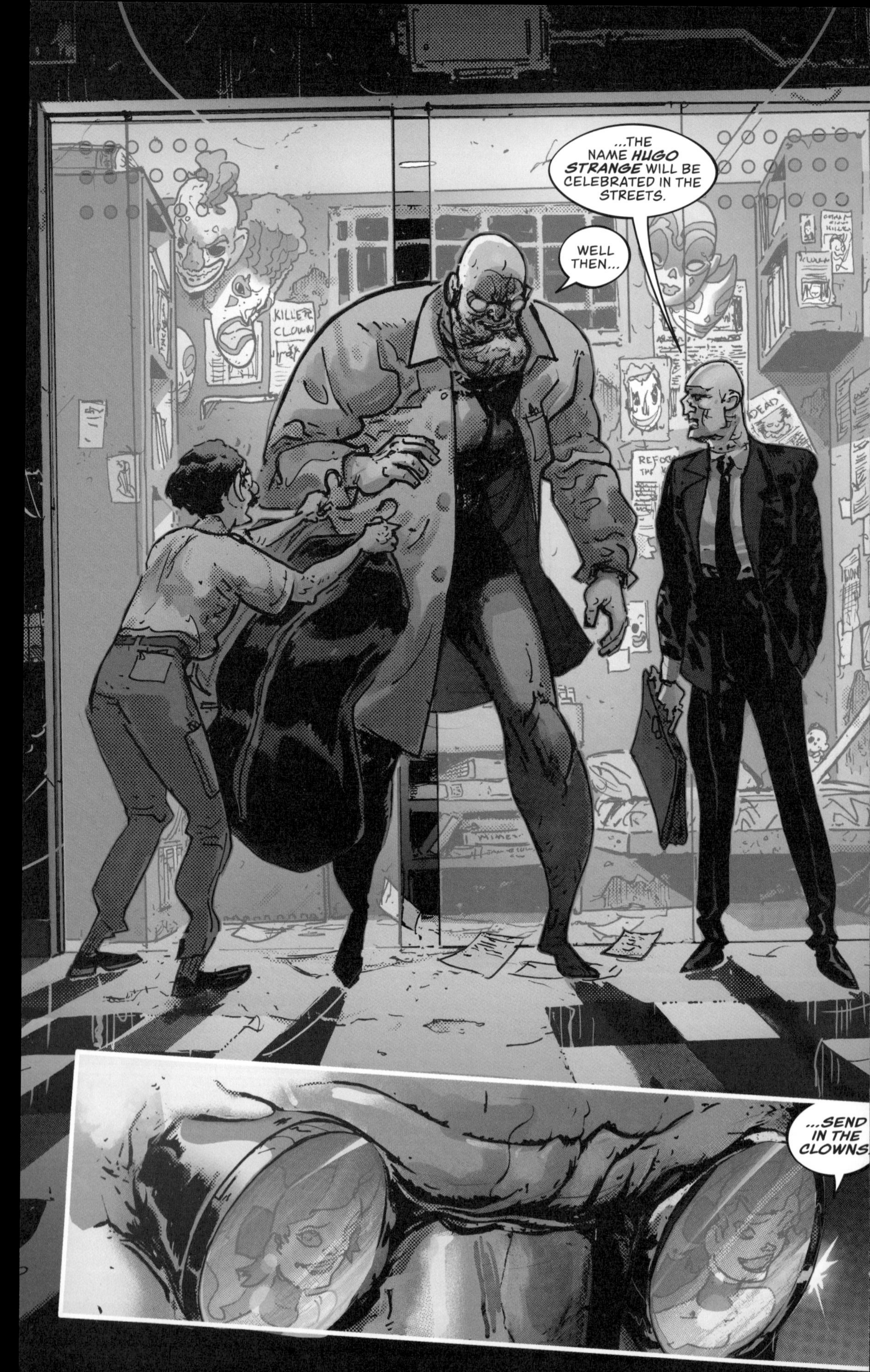
WELL THEN...
...THE NAME HUGO STRANGE WILL BE CELEBRATED IN THE STREETS.
...SEND IN THE CLOWNS

Harley Quinn #2
Cover Art by Riley Rossmo

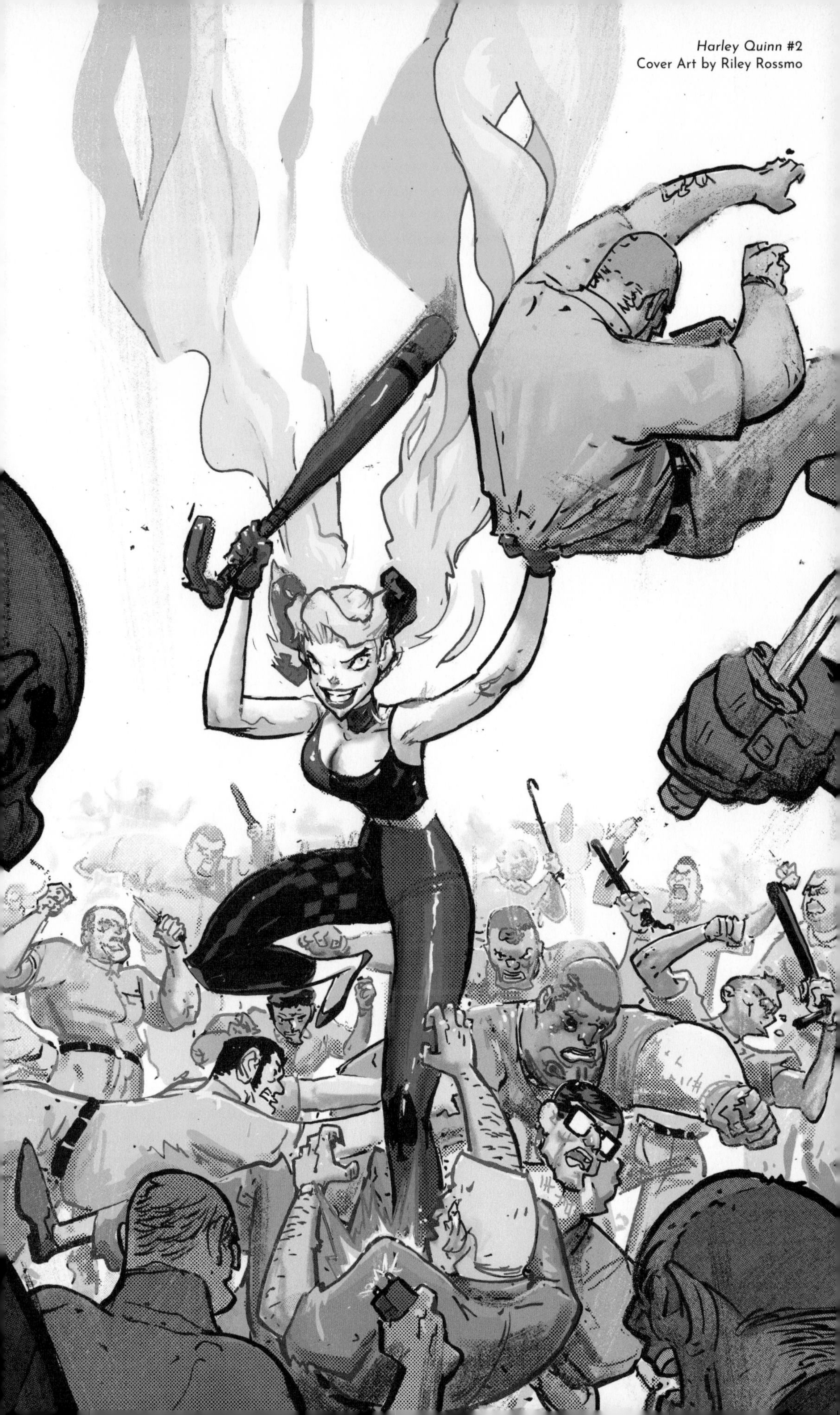

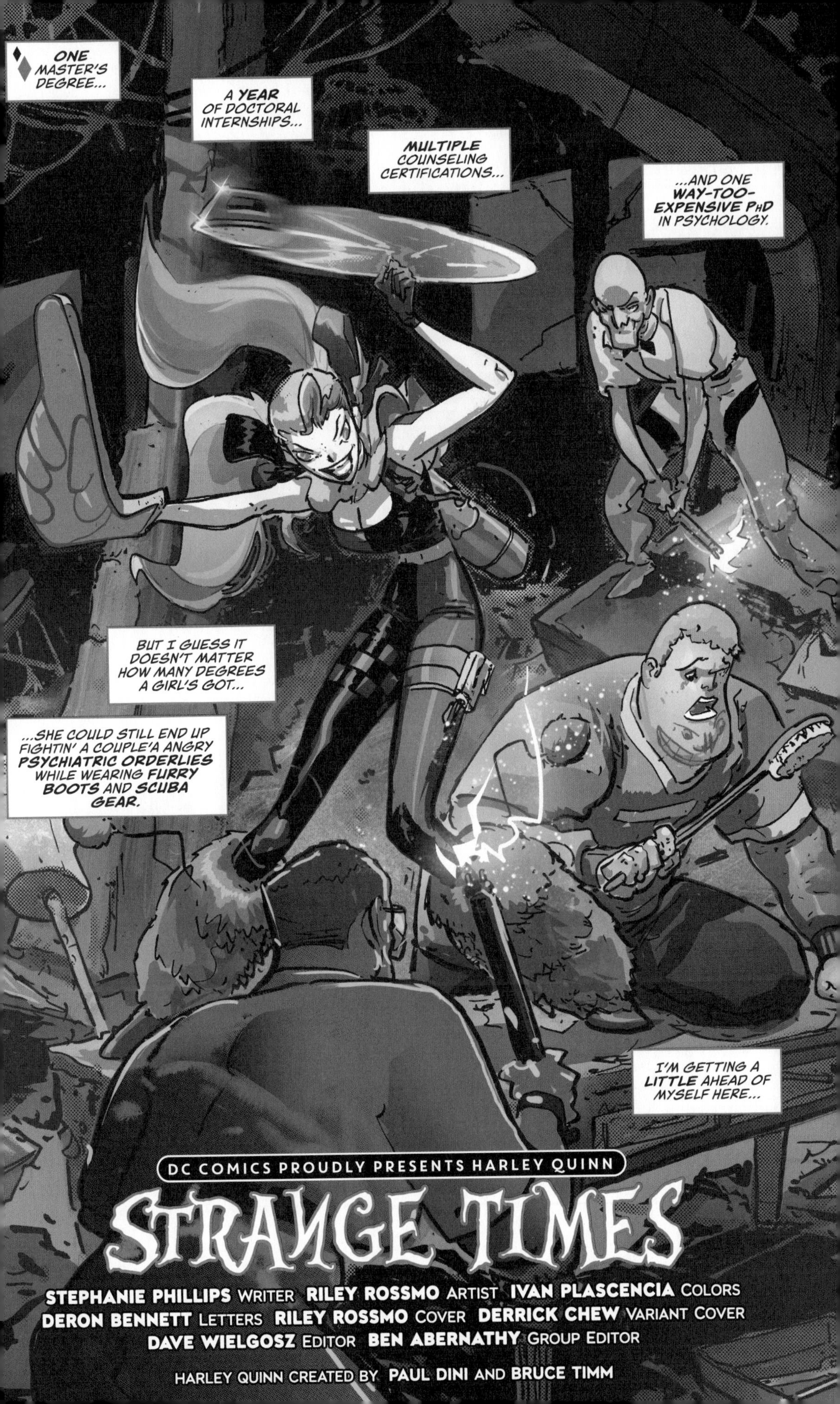
ONE MASTER'S DEGREE...
A YEAR OF DOCTORAL INTERNSHIPS...
MULTIPLE COUNSELING CERTIFICATIONS...
...AND ONE WAY-TOO-EXPENSIVE PhD IN PSYCHOLOGY.
BUT I GUESS IT DOESN'T MATTER HOW MANY DEGREES A GIRL'S GOT...
...SHE COULD STILL END UP FIGHTIN' A COUPLE'A ANGRY PSYCHIATRIC ORDERLIES WHILE WEARING FURRY BOOTS AND SCUBA GEAR.
I'M GETTING A LITTLE AHEAD OF MYSELF HERE...
DC COMICS PROUDLY PRESENTS HARLEY QUINN
STRANGE TIMES
STEPHANIE PHILLIPS WRITER RILEY ROSSMO ARTIST IVAN PLASCENCIA COLORS
DERON BENNETT LETTERS RILEY ROSSMO COVER DERRICK CHEW VARIANT COVER
DAVE WIELGOSZ EDITOR BEN ABERNATHY GROUP EDITOR
HARLEY QUINN CREATED BY PAUL DINI AND BRUCE TIMM

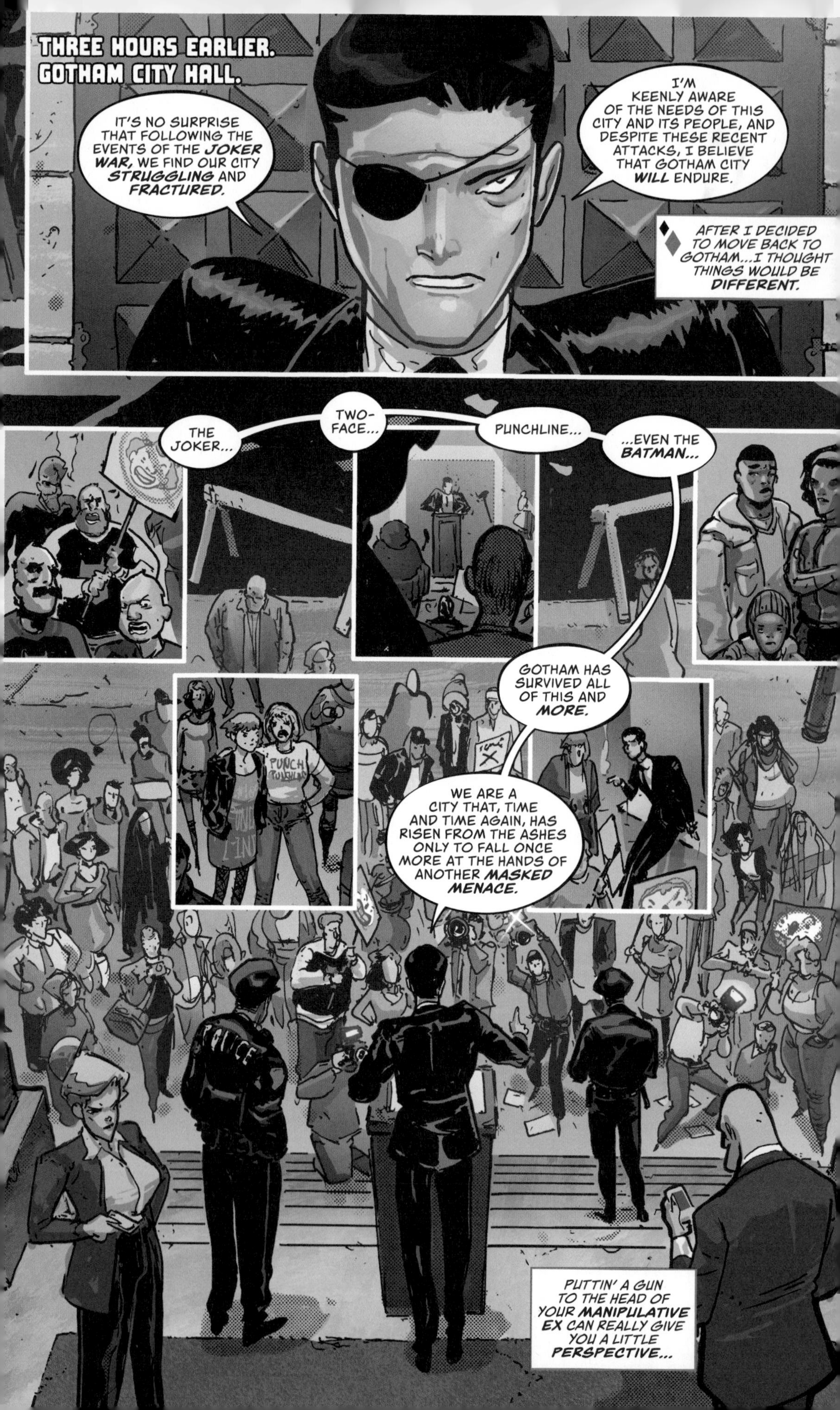

THREE HOURS EARLIER. GOTHAM CITY HALL.
IT'S NO SURPRISE THAT FOLLOWING THE EVENTS OF THE JOKER WAR, WE FIND OUR CITY STRUGGLING AND FRACTURED.
I'M KEENLY AWARE OF THE NEEDS OF THIS CITY AND ITS PEOPLE, AND DESPITE THESE RECENT ATTACKS, I BELIEVE THAT GOTHAM CITY WILL ENDURE.
AFTER I DECIDED TO MOVE BACK TO GOTHAM...I THOUGHT THINGS WOULD BE DIFFERENT.
THE JOKER...
TWO-FACE...
PUNCHLINE...
...EVEN THE BATMAN...
GOTHAM HAS SURVIVED ALL OF THIS AND MORE.
WE ARE A CITY THAT, TIME AND TIME AGAIN, HAS RISEN FROM THE ASHES ONLY TO FALL ONCE MORE AT THE HANDS OF ANOTHER MASKED MENACE.
PUNCH
POLICE
PUTTIN' A GUN TO THE HEAD OF YOUR MANIPULATIVE EX CAN REALLY GIVE YOU A LITTLE PERSPECTIVE...

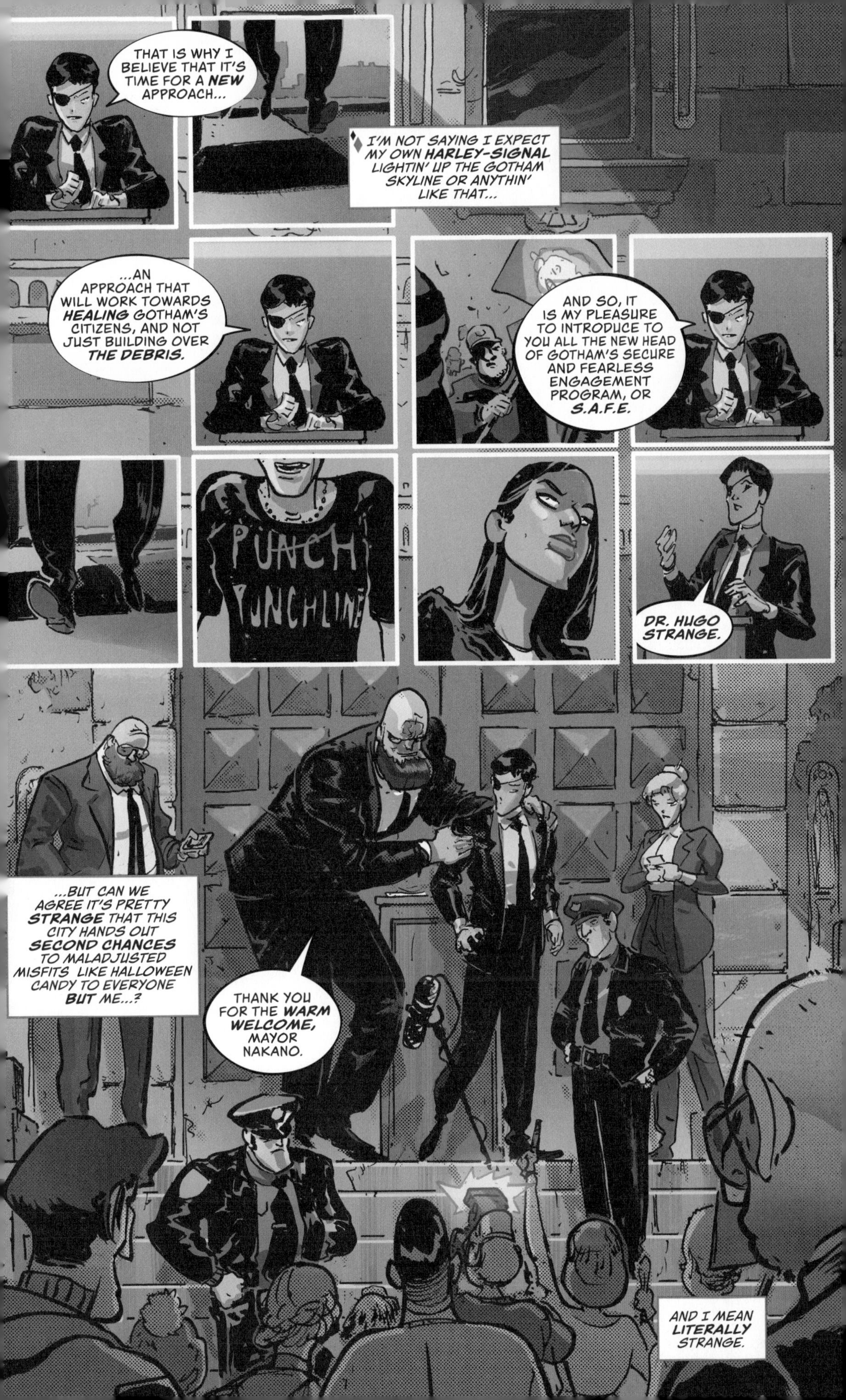

THAT IS WHY I BELIEVE THAT IT'S TIME FOR A NEW APPROACH...
I'M NOT SAYING I EXPECT MY OWN HARLEY-SIGNAL LIGHTIN' UP THE GOTHAM SKYLINE OR ANYTHIN' LIKE THAT...
...AN APPROACH THAT WILL WORK TOWARDS HEALING GOTHAM'S CITIZENS, AND NOT JUST BUILDING OVER THE DEBRIS.
AND SO, IT IS MY PLEASURE TO INTRODUCE TO YOU ALL THE NEW HEAD OF GOTHAM'S SECURE AND FEARLESS ENGAGEMENT PROGRAM, OR S.A.F.E.
PUNCH PUNCHLINE
DR. HUGO STRANGE.
...BUT CAN WE AGREE IT'S PRETTY STRANGE THAT THIS CITY HANDS OUT SECOND CHANCES TO MALADJUSTED MISFITS LIKE HALLOWEEN CANDY TO EVERYONE BUT ME...?
THANK YOU FOR THE WARM WELCOME, MAYOR NAKANO.
AND I MEAN LITERALLY STRANGE.

I AM SURE THE NAME *HUGO STRANGE* IS NOT UNFAMILIAR TO SOME OF YOU.

I HAVE NOT ALWAYS BEEN AN *ALLY* TO YOUR CITY...

BUT, MY OWN PERSONAL *REFORMATION* IS WHAT MAKES ME THE BEST...NAY...THE *ONLY* PERSON FOR THIS JOB.

I KNOW WHAT IT'S LIKE TO MAKE A *BAD DECISION* AND WHAT IT MEANS TO MAKE *AMENDS* FOR THOSE ACTIONS.

THAT IS WHY *S.A.F.E.* IS ABOUT *HEALING.* IT'S ABOUT *REFORM.* AND IT'S ABOUT *ACCOUNTABILITY.*

GOTHAM IS OVERRUN BY *CLOWNS.* THE VERY PEOPLE COMPLICIT IN THE ACTIONS OF THE *JOKER* COULD BE ANYWHERE... *DOING ANYTHING...* AND ALL *WITHOUT* CONSEQUENCE.

THE *S.A.F.E.* PROGRAM...*MY* PROGRAM...IS HERE TO CHANGE THAT.

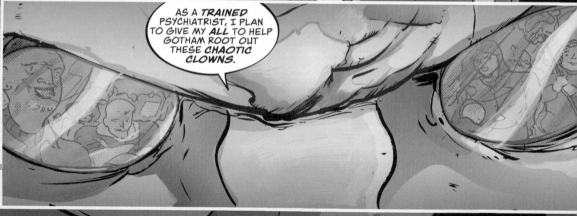

AS A *TRAINED* PSYCHIATRIST, I PLAN TO GIVE MY *ALL* TO HELP GOTHAM ROOT OUT THESE *CHAOTIC CLOWNS.*

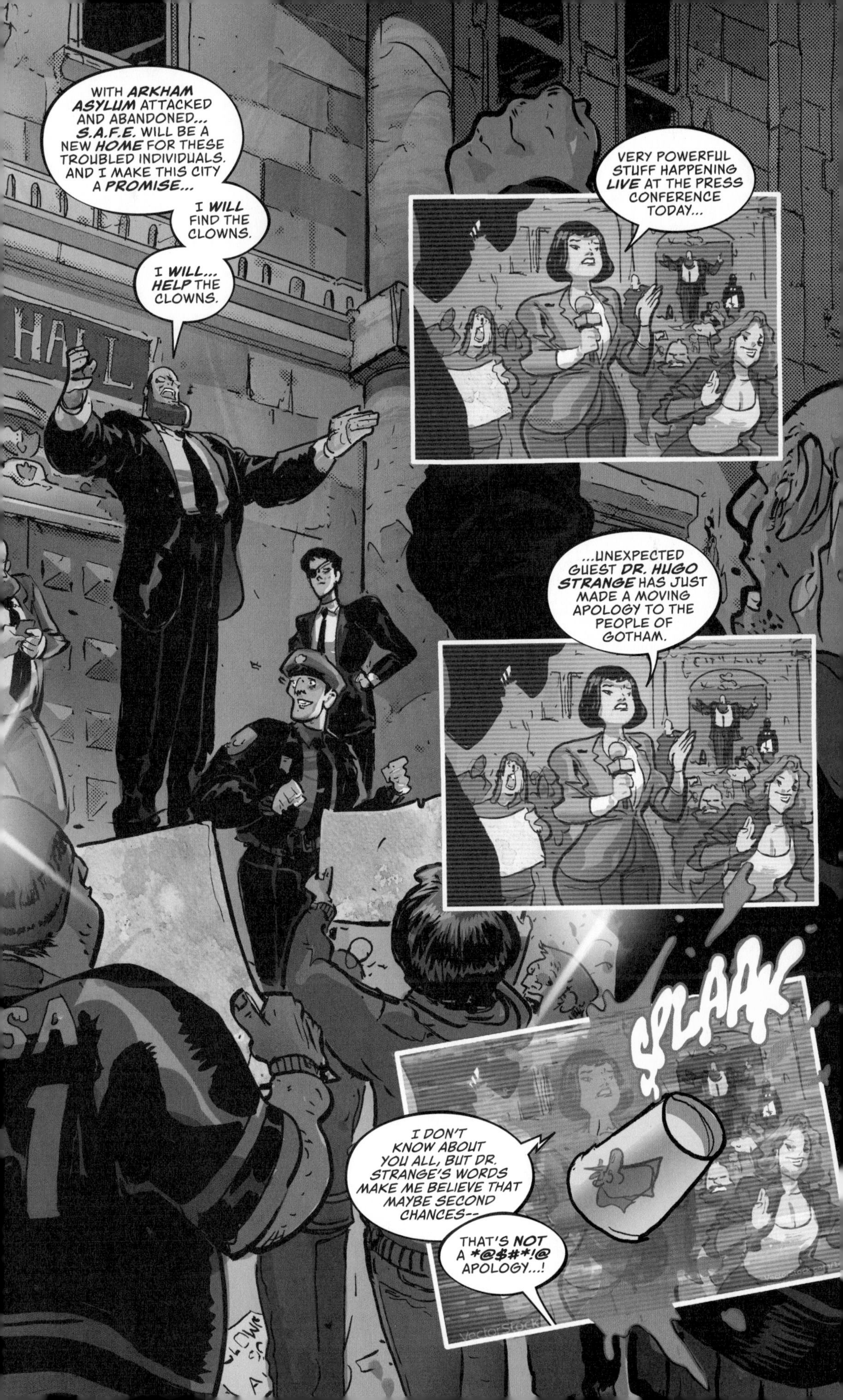
WITH ARKHAM ASYLUM ATTACKED AND ABANDONED... S.A.F.E. WILL BE A NEW HOME FOR THESE TROUBLED INDIVIDUALS. AND I MAKE THIS CITY A PROMISE...
I WILL FIND THE CLOWNS.
I WILL... HELP THE CLOWNS.
VERY POWERFUL STUFF HAPPENING LIVE AT THE PRESS CONFERENCE TODAY...
...UNEXPECTED GUEST DR. HUGO STRANGE HAS JUST MADE A MOVING APOLOGY TO THE PEOPLE OF GOTHAM.
SPLAAK
I DON'T KNOW ABOUT YOU ALL, BUT DR. STRANGE'S WORDS MAKE ME BELIEVE THAT MAYBE SECOND CHANCES--
THAT'S NOT A *@$#*!@ APOLOGY...!

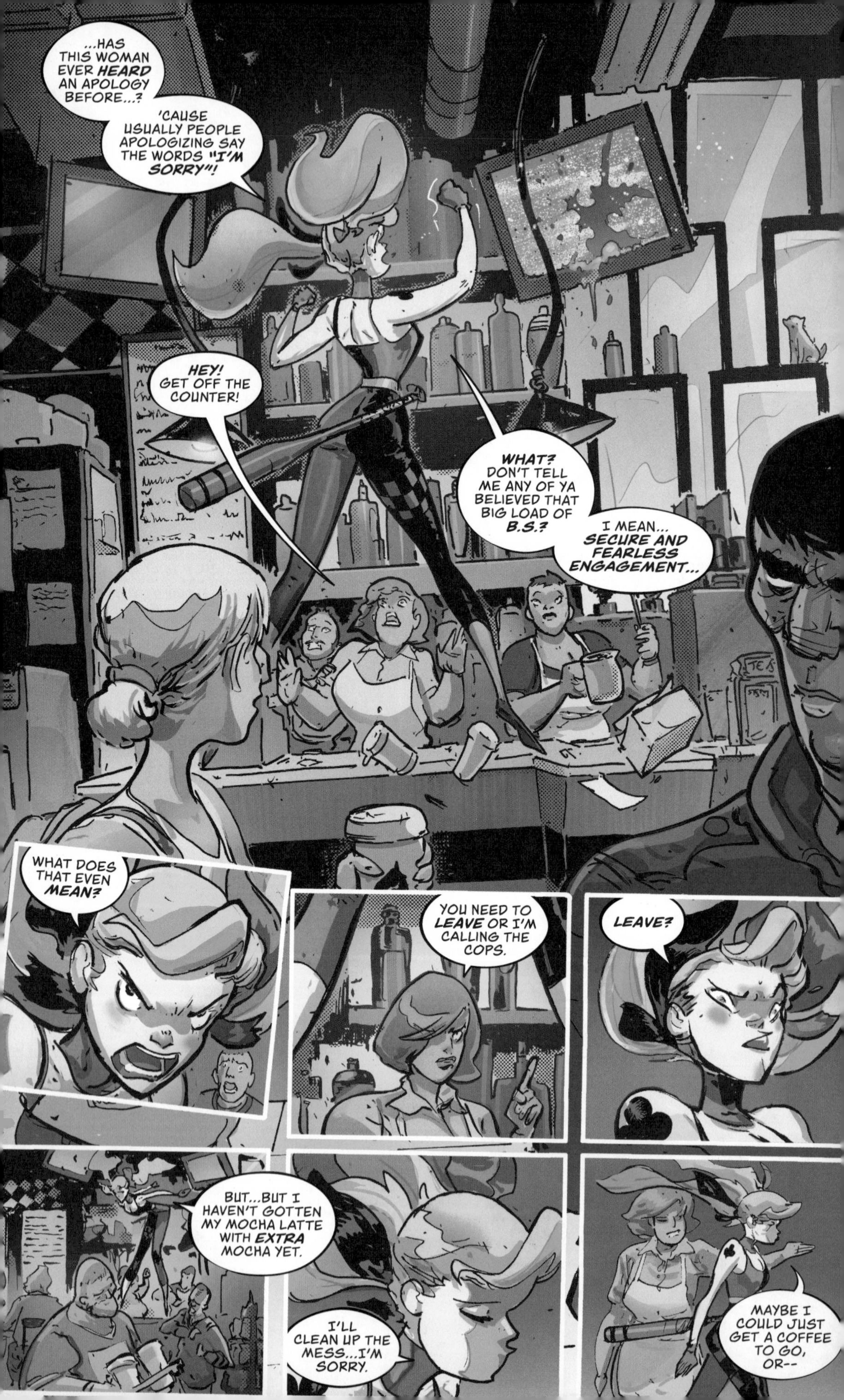
...HAS THIS WOMAN EVER HEARD AN APOLOGY BEFORE...?
'CAUSE USUALLY PEOPLE APOLOGIZING SAY THE WORDS "I'M SORRY"!
HEY! GET OFF THE COUNTER!
WHAT? DON'T TELL ME ANY OF YA BELIEVED THAT BIG LOAD OF B.S.?
I MEAN... SECURE AND FEARLESS ENGAGEMENT...
WHAT DOES THAT EVEN MEAN?
YOU NEED TO LEAVE OR I'M CALLING THE COPS.
LEAVE?
BUT...BUT I HAVEN'T GOTTEN MY MOCHA LATTE WITH EXTRA MOCHA YET.
I'LL CLEAN UP THE MESS...I'M SORRY.
MAYBE I COULD JUST GET A COFFEE TO GO, OR--

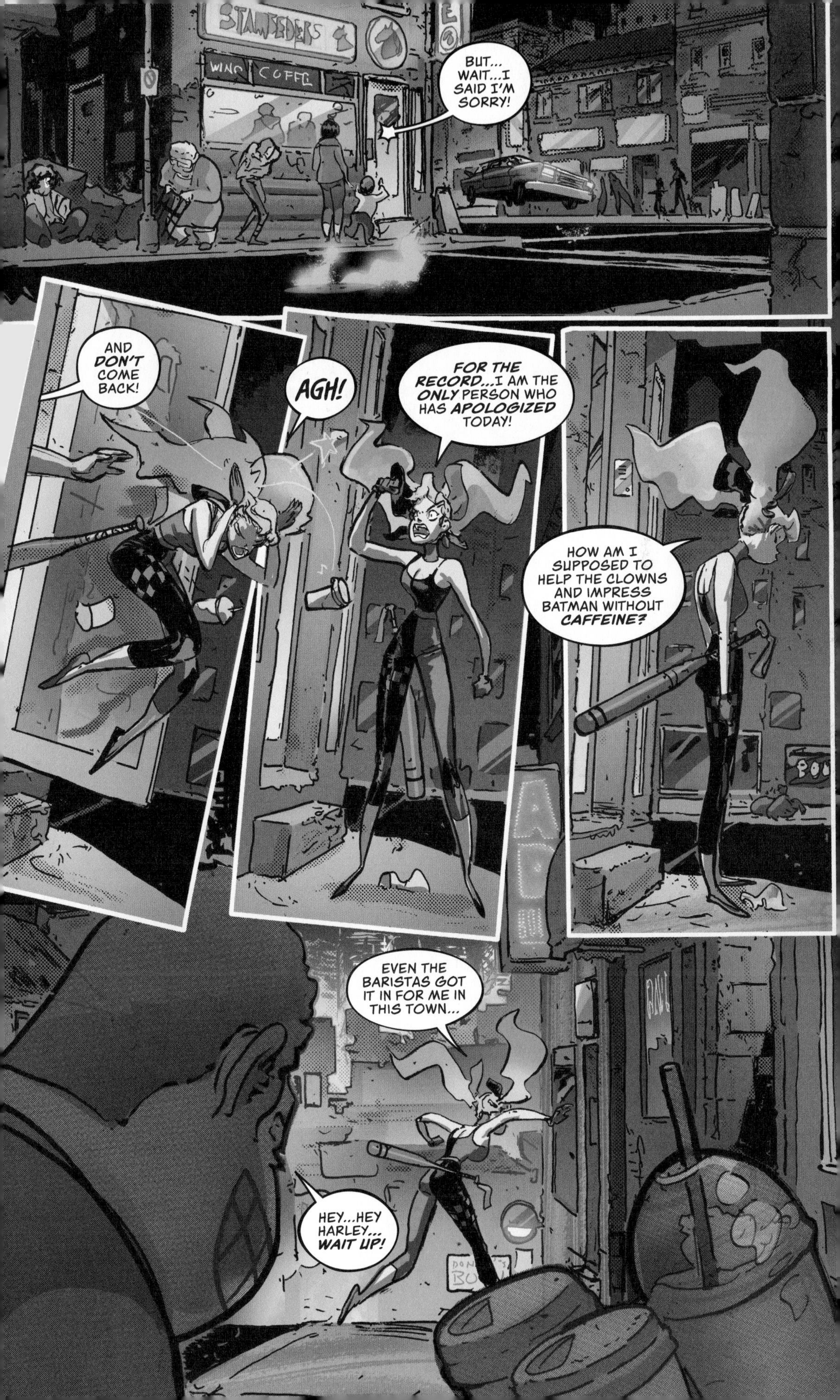
STAMPEDERS
WINC COFFE
BUT... WAIT...I SAID I'M SORRY!
AND DON'T COME BACK!
AGH!
FOR THE RECORD...I AM THE ONLY PERSON WHO HAS APOLOGIZED TODAY!
HOW AM I SUPPOSED TO HELP THE CLOWNS AND IMPRESS BATMAN WITHOUT CAFFEINE?
EVEN THE BARISTAS GOT IT IN FOR ME IN THIS TOWN...
HEY...HEY HARLEY... WAIT UP!

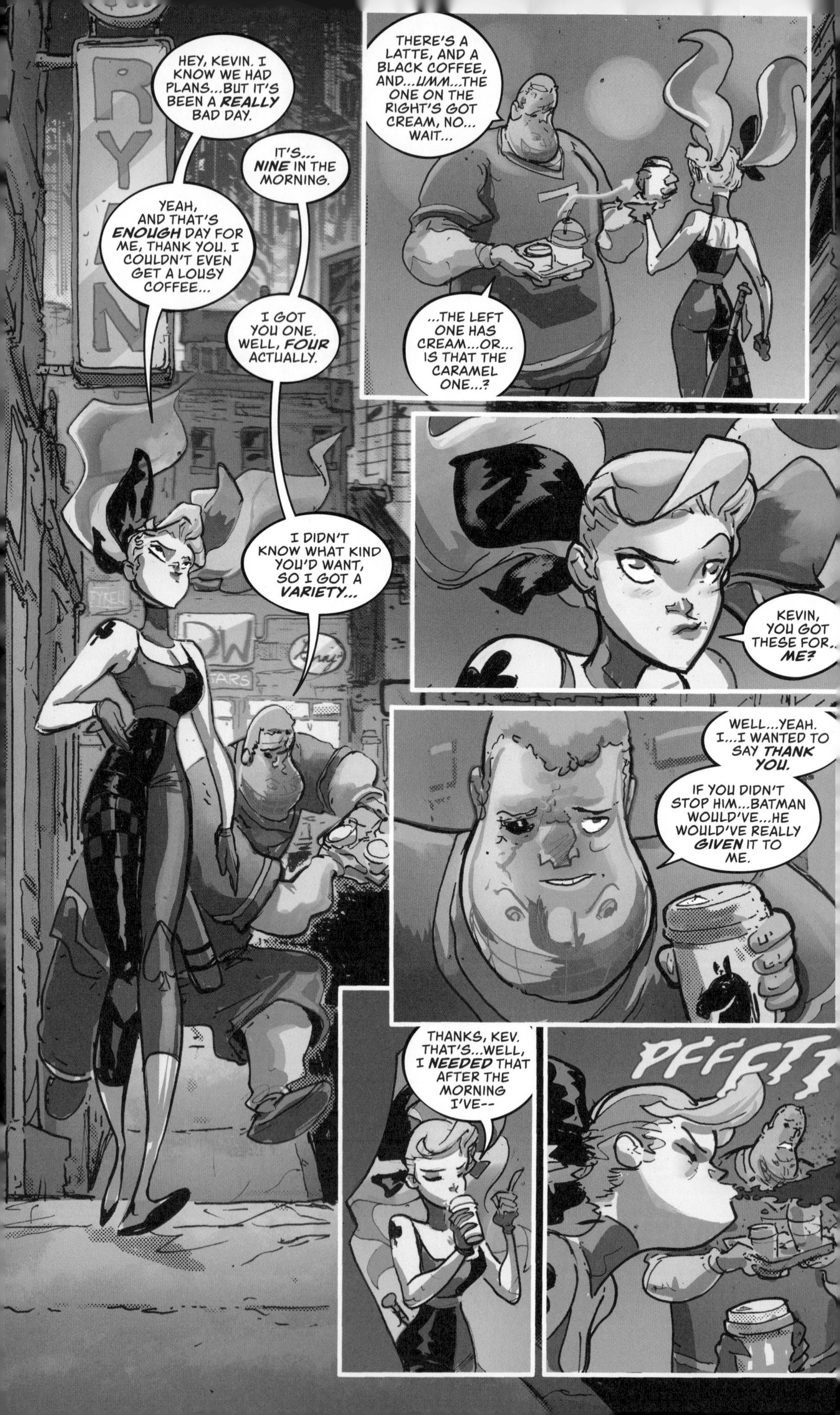
HEY, KEVIN. I KNOW WE HAD PLANS...BUT IT'S BEEN A REALLY BAD DAY.
IT'S... NINE IN THE MORNING.
YEAH, AND THAT'S ENOUGH DAY FOR ME, THANK YOU. I COULDN'T EVEN GET A LOUSY COFFEE...
I GOT YOU ONE. WELL, FOUR ACTUALLY.
I DIDN'T KNOW WHAT KIND YOU'D WANT, SO I GOT A VARIETY...
THERE'S A LATTE, AND A BLACK COFFEE, AND...UMM...THE ONE ON THE RIGHT'S GOT CREAM, NO... WAIT...
...THE LEFT ONE HAS CREAM...OR... IS THAT THE CARAMEL ONE...?
KEVIN, YOU GOT THESE FOR... ME?
WELL...YEAH. I...I WANTED TO SAY THANK YOU.
IF YOU DIDN'T STOP HIM...BATMAN WOULD'VE...HE WOULD'VE REALLY GIVEN IT TO ME.
THANKS, KEV. THAT'S...WELL, I NEEDED THAT AFTER THE MORNING I'VE--
PFFFT!

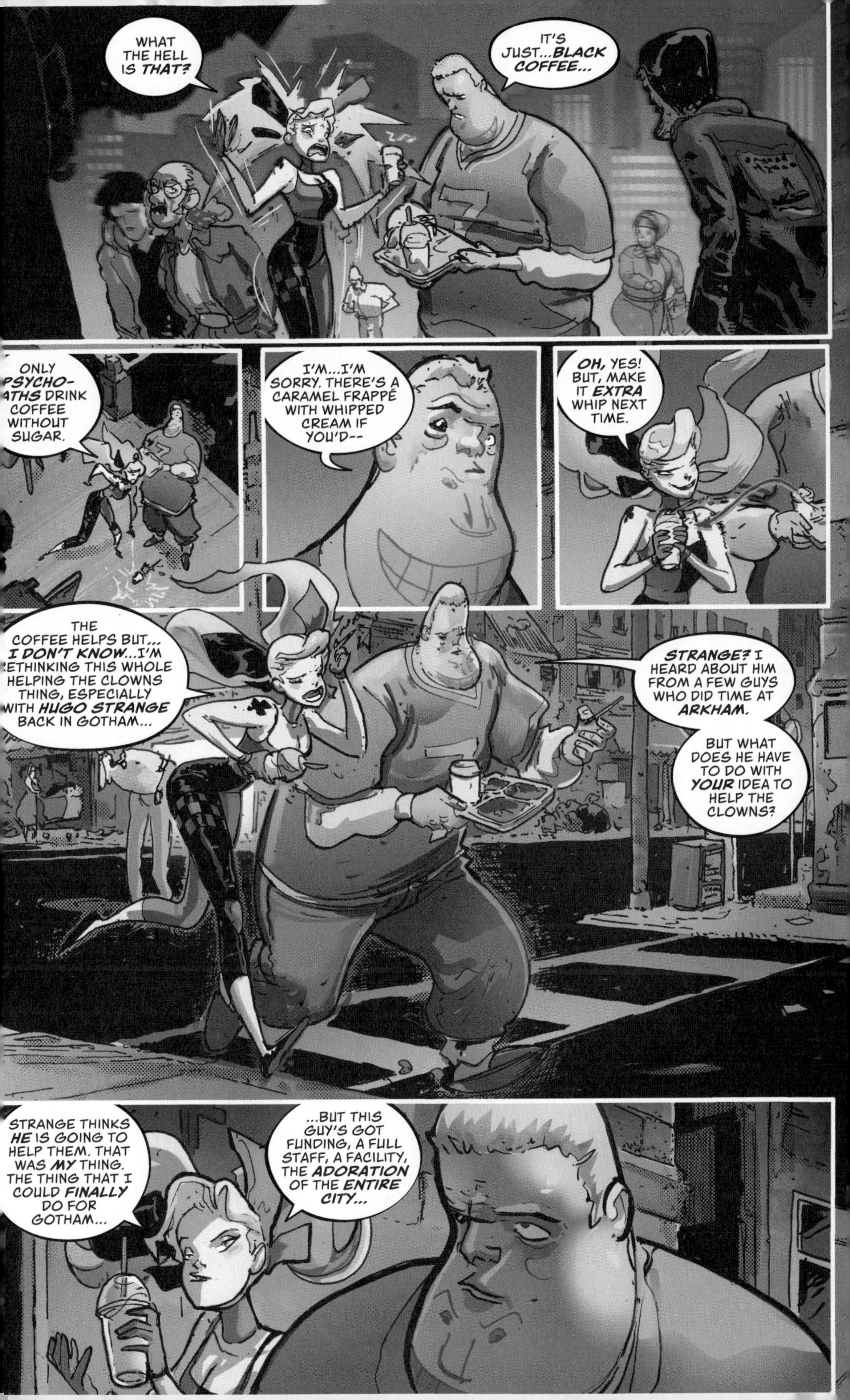
WHAT THE HELL IS THAT?
IT'S JUST...BLACK COFFEE...
ONLY PSYCHOPATHS DRINK COFFEE WITHOUT SUGAR.
I'M...I'M SORRY. THERE'S A CARAMEL FRAPPÉ WITH WHIPPED CREAM IF YOU'D--
OH, YES! BUT, MAKE IT EXTRA WHIP NEXT TIME.
THE COFFEE HELPS BUT... I DON'T KNOW...I'M RETHINKING THIS WHOLE HELPING THE CLOWNS THING, ESPECIALLY WITH HUGO STRANGE BACK IN GOTHAM...
STRANGE? I HEARD ABOUT HIM FROM A FEW GUYS WHO DID TIME AT ARKHAM.
BUT WHAT DOES HE HAVE TO DO WITH YOUR IDEA TO HELP THE CLOWNS?
STRANGE THINKS HE IS GOING TO HELP THEM. THAT WAS MY THING. THE THING THAT I COULD FINALLY DO FOR GOTHAM...
...BUT THIS GUY'S GOT FUNDING, A FULL STAFF, A FACILITY, THE ADORATION OF THE ENTIRE CITY...

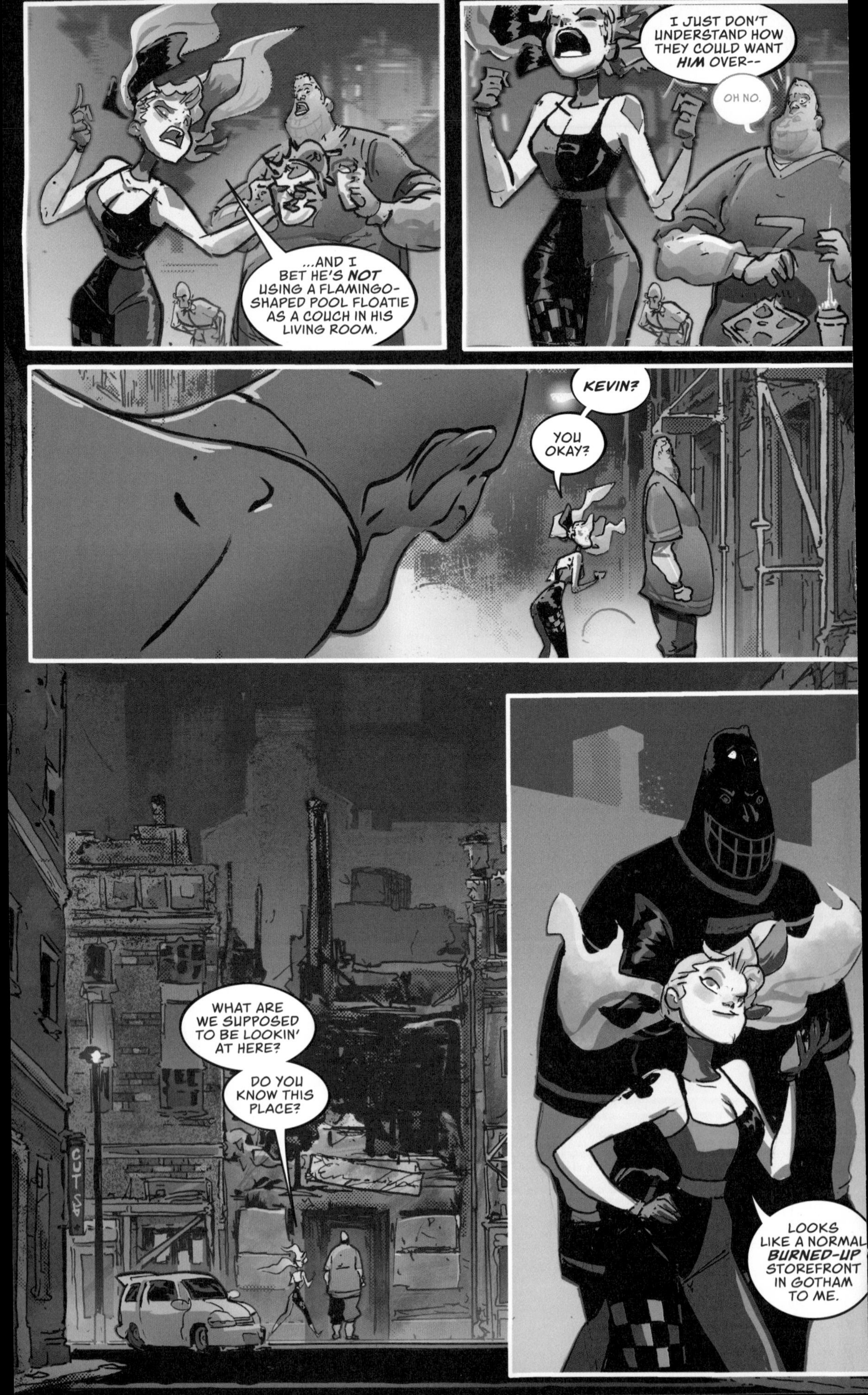
...AND I BET HE'S NOT USING A FLAMINGO-SHAPED POOL FLOATIE AS A COUCH IN HIS LIVING ROOM.
I JUST DON'T UNDERSTAND HOW THEY COULD WANT HIM OVER--
OH NO.
KEVIN?
YOU OKAY?
WHAT ARE WE SUPPOSED TO BE LOOKIN' AT HERE?
DO YOU KNOW THIS PLACE?
CUTS
LOOKS LIKE A NORMAL BURNED-UP STOREFRONT IN GOTHAM TO ME.

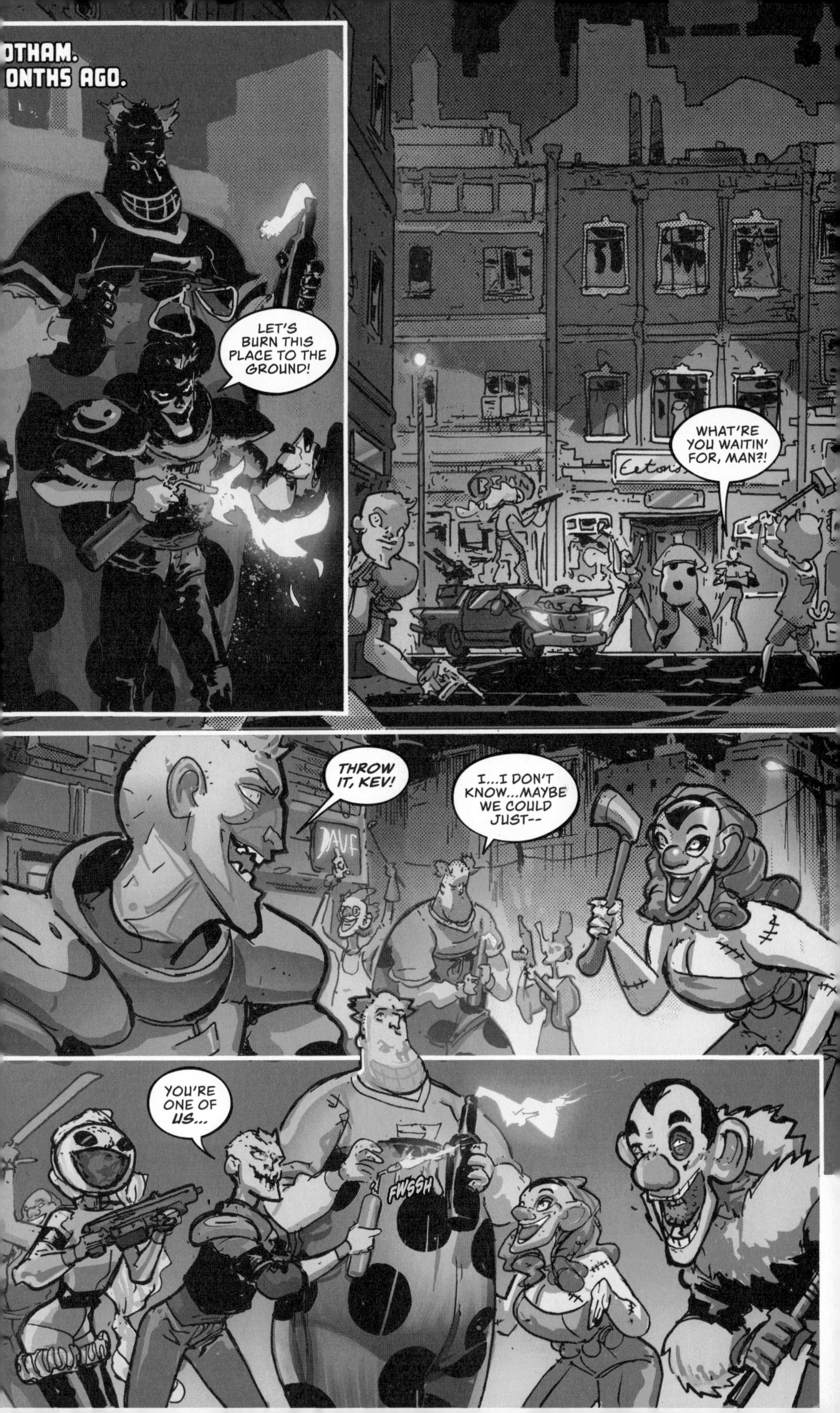

OTHAM.
ONTHS AGO.
LET'S BURN THIS PLACE TO THE GROUND!
WHAT'RE YOU WAITIN' FOR, MAN?!
Eeton's
THROW IT, KEV!
I...I DON'T KNOW...MAYBE WE COULD JUST--
YOU'RE ONE OF US...
FWSSH

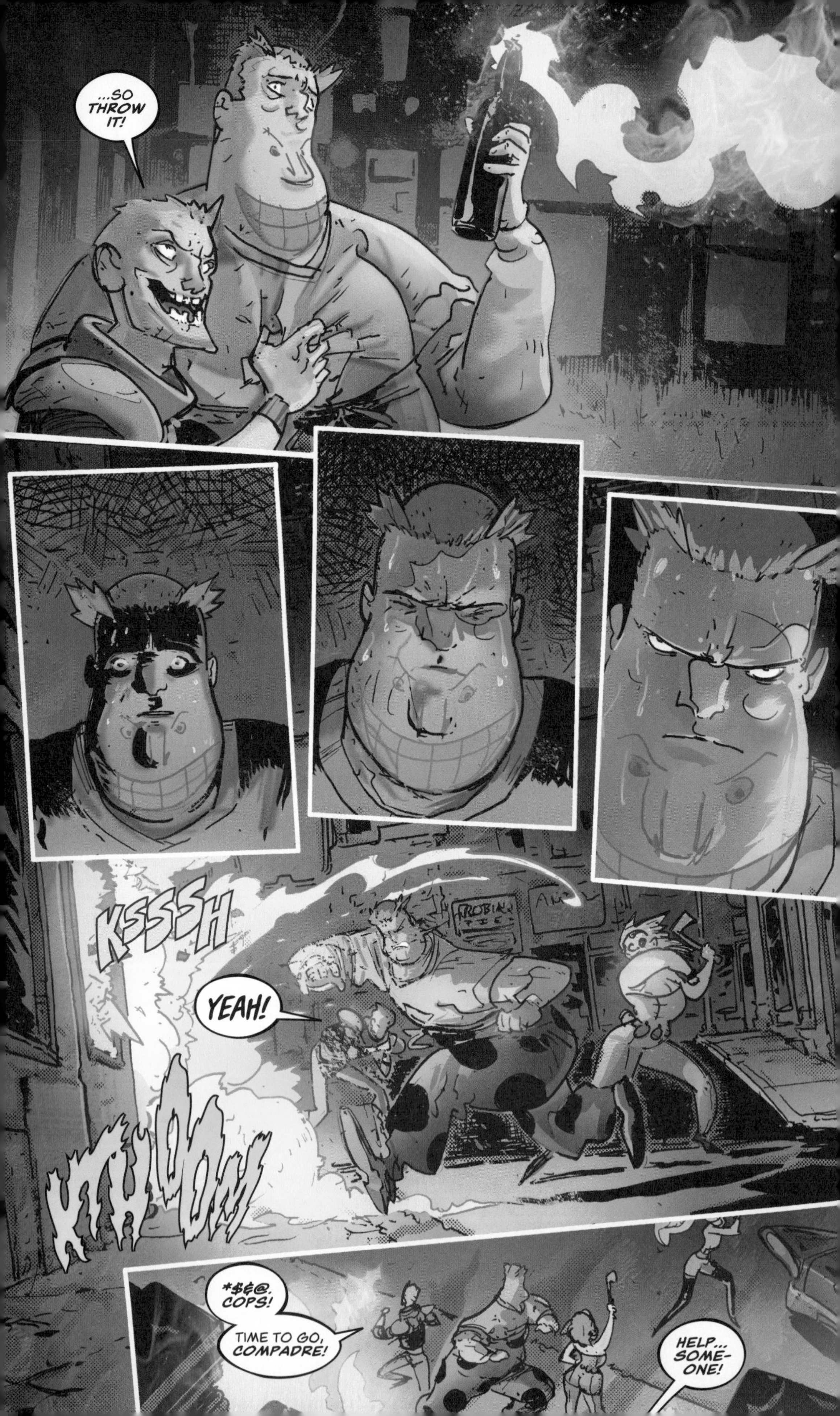
...SO THROW IT!
KSSSH
YEAH!
KTHOOM
*$£@. COPS!
TIME TO GO, COMPADRE!
HELP... SOME-ONE!

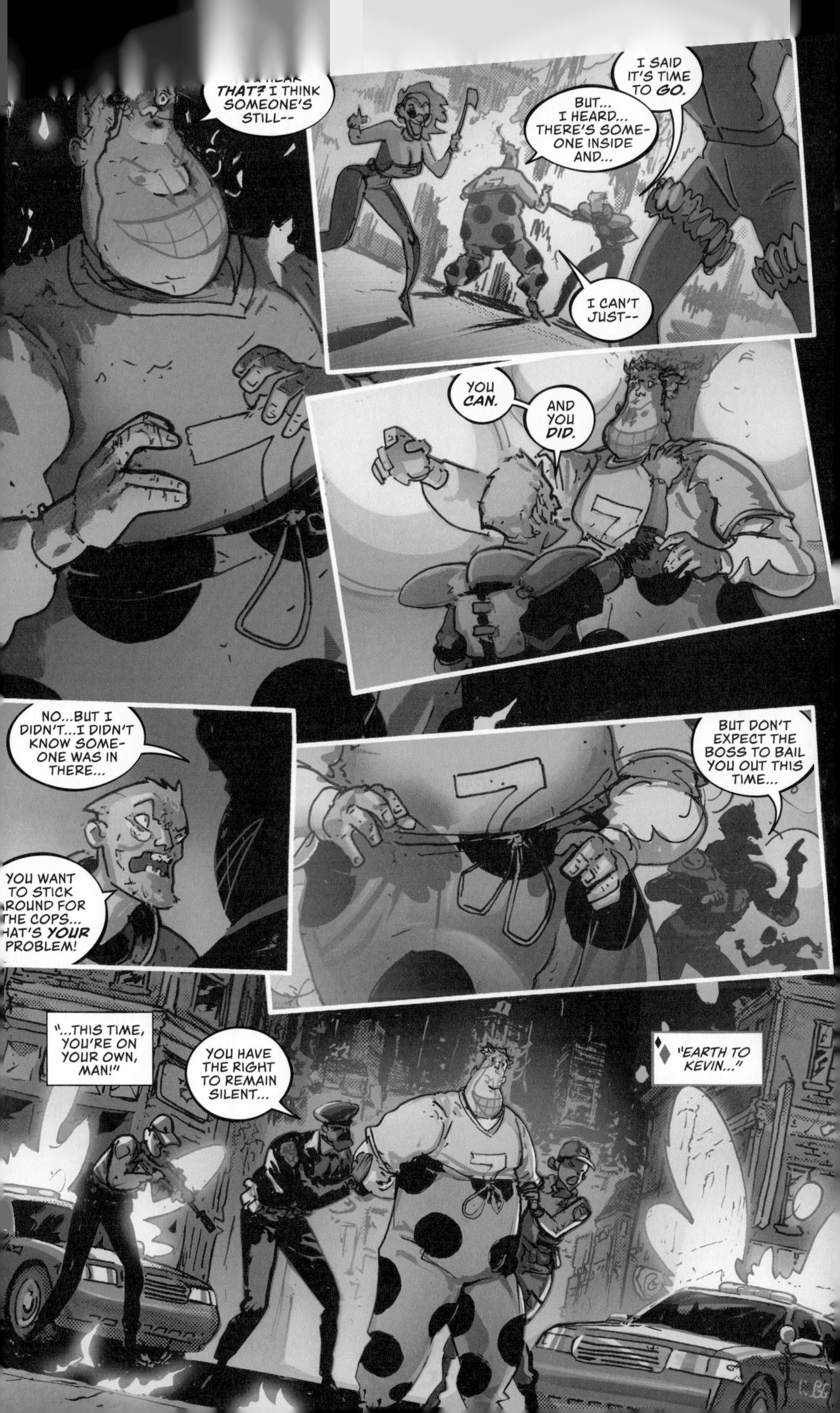

THAT? I THINK SOMEONE'S STILL--
BUT... I HEARD... THERE'S SOME-ONE INSIDE AND...
I SAID IT'S TIME TO GO.
I CAN'T JUST--
YOU CAN.
AND YOU DID.
NO...BUT I DIDN'T...I DIDN'T KNOW SOME-ONE WAS IN THERE...
YOU WANT TO STICK ROUND FOR THE COPS... HAT'S YOUR PROBLEM!
BUT DON'T EXPECT THE BOSS TO BAIL YOU OUT THIS TIME...
"...THIS TIME, YOU'RE ON YOUR OWN, MAN!"
YOU HAVE THE RIGHT TO REMAIN SILENT...
"EARTH TO KEVIN..."

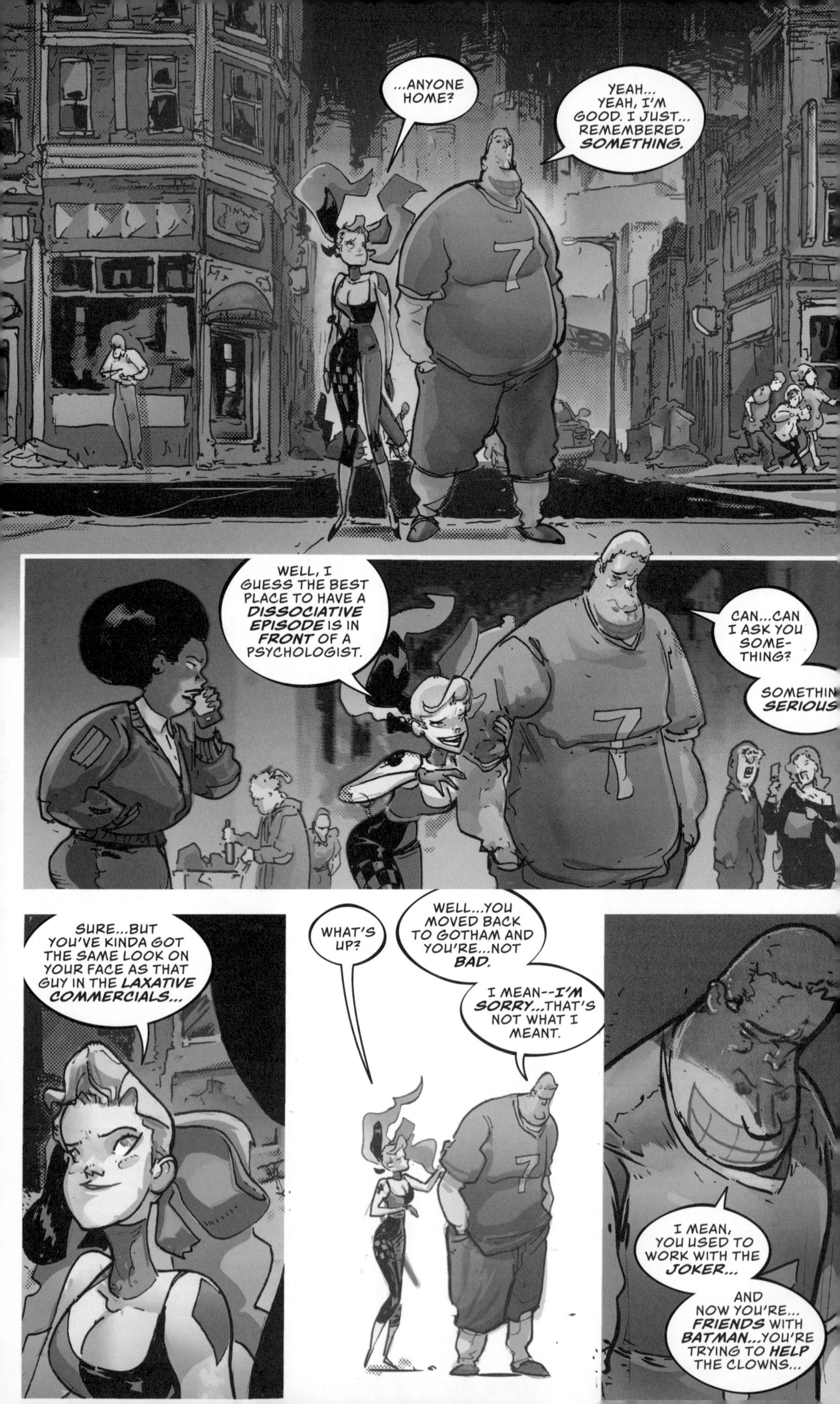
...ANYONE HOME?
YEAH... YEAH, I'M GOOD. I JUST... REMEMBERED SOMETHING.
WELL, I GUESS THE BEST PLACE TO HAVE A DISSOCIATIVE EPISODE IS IN FRONT OF A PSYCHOLOGIST.
CAN...CAN I ASK YOU SOME-THING?
SOMETHIN SERIOUS
SURE...BUT YOU'VE KINDA GOT THE SAME LOOK ON YOUR FACE AS THAT GUY IN THE LAXATIVE COMMERCIALS...
WHAT'S UP?
WELL...YOU MOVED BACK TO GOTHAM AND YOU'RE...NOT BAD.
I MEAN--I'M SORRY...THAT'S NOT WHAT I MEANT.
I MEAN, YOU USED TO WORK WITH THE JOKER...
AND NOW YOU'RE... FRIENDS WITH BATMAN...YOU'RE TRYING TO HELP THE CLOWNS...

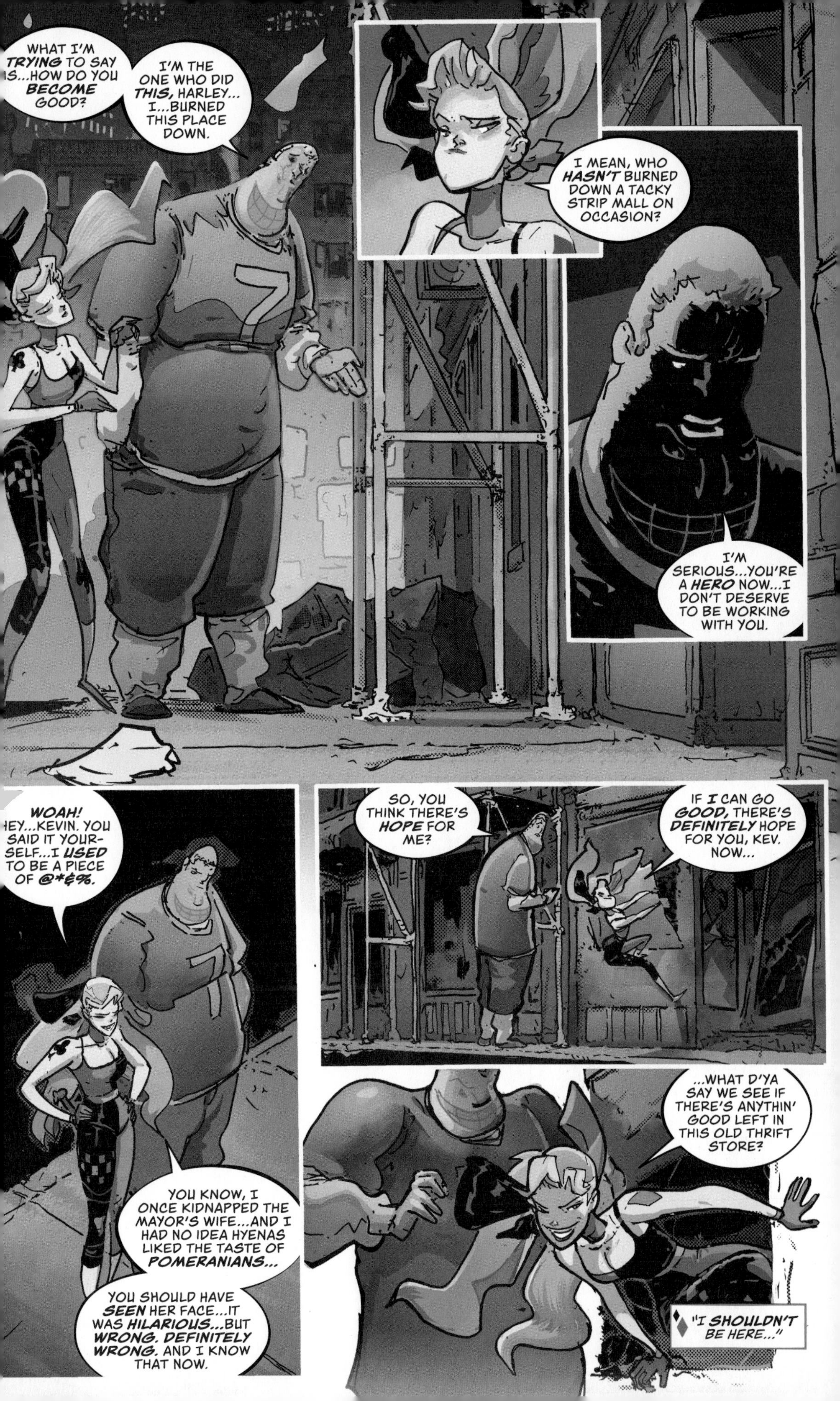
WHAT I'M TRYING TO SAY IS...HOW DO YOU BECOME GOOD?
I'M THE ONE WHO DID THIS, HARLEY... I...BURNED THIS PLACE DOWN.
I MEAN, WHO HASN'T BURNED DOWN A TACKY STRIP MALL ON OCCASION?
I'M SERIOUS...YOU'RE A HERO NOW...I DON'T DESERVE TO BE WORKING WITH YOU.
WOAH! HEY...KEVIN. YOU SAID IT YOURSELF...I USED TO BE A PIECE OF @*&%.
YOU KNOW, I ONCE KIDNAPPED THE MAYOR'S WIFE...AND I HAD NO IDEA HYENAS LIKED THE TASTE OF POMERANIANS...
YOU SHOULD HAVE SEEN HER FACE...IT WAS HILARIOUS...BUT WRONG. DEFINITELY WRONG. AND I KNOW THAT NOW.
SO, YOU THINK THERE'S HOPE FOR ME?
IF I CAN GO GOOD, THERE'S DEFINITELY HOPE FOR YOU, KEV. NOW...
...WHAT D'YA SAY WE SEE IF THERE'S ANYTHIN' GOOD LEFT IN THIS OLD THRIFT STORE?
"I SHOULDN'T BE HERE..."

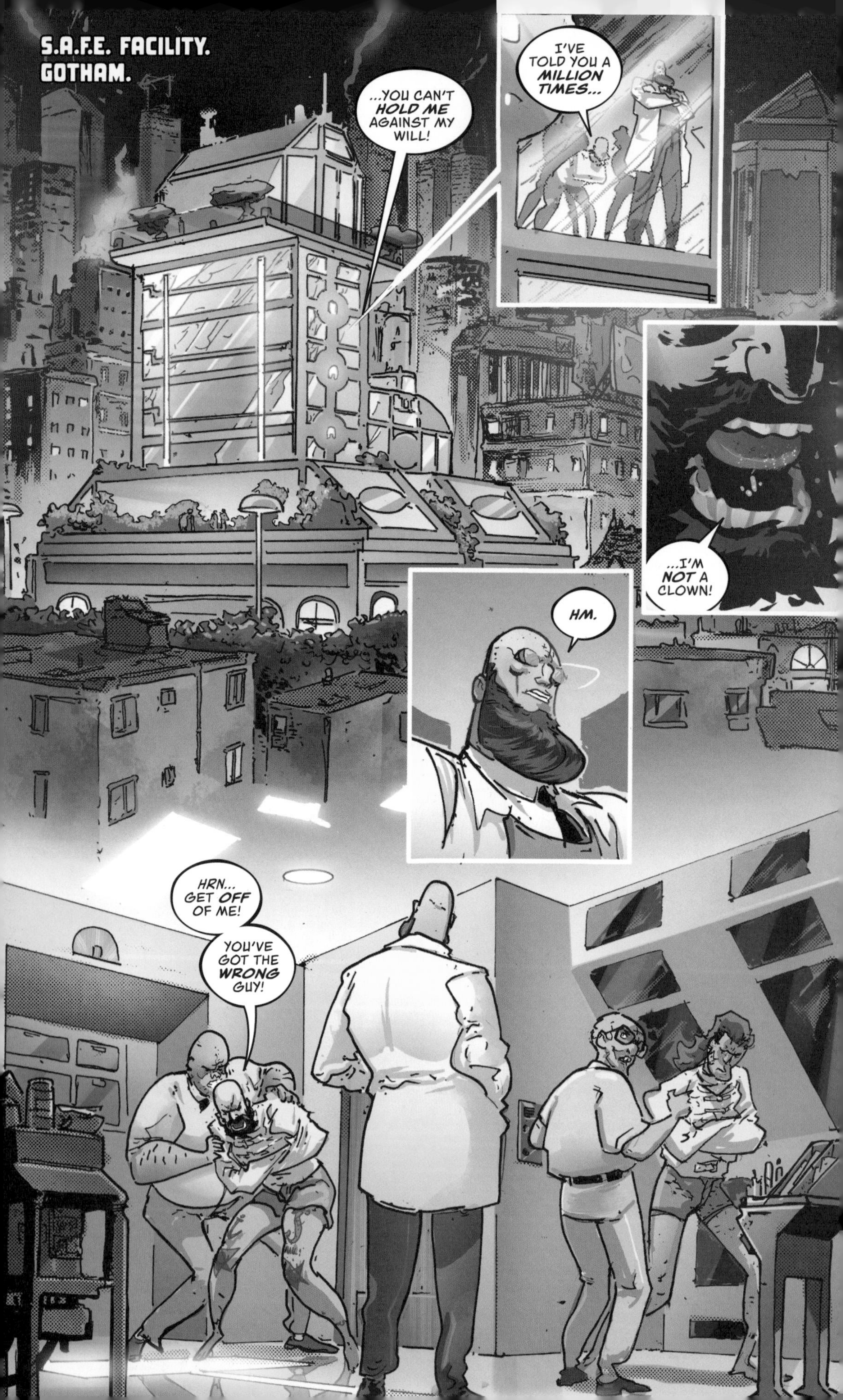

S.A.F.E. FACILITY. GOTHAM.
...YOU CAN'T HOLD ME AGAINST MY WILL!
I'VE TOLD YOU A MILLION TIMES...
...I'M NOT A CLOWN!
HM.
HRN... GET OFF OF ME!
YOU'VE GOT THE WRONG GUY!

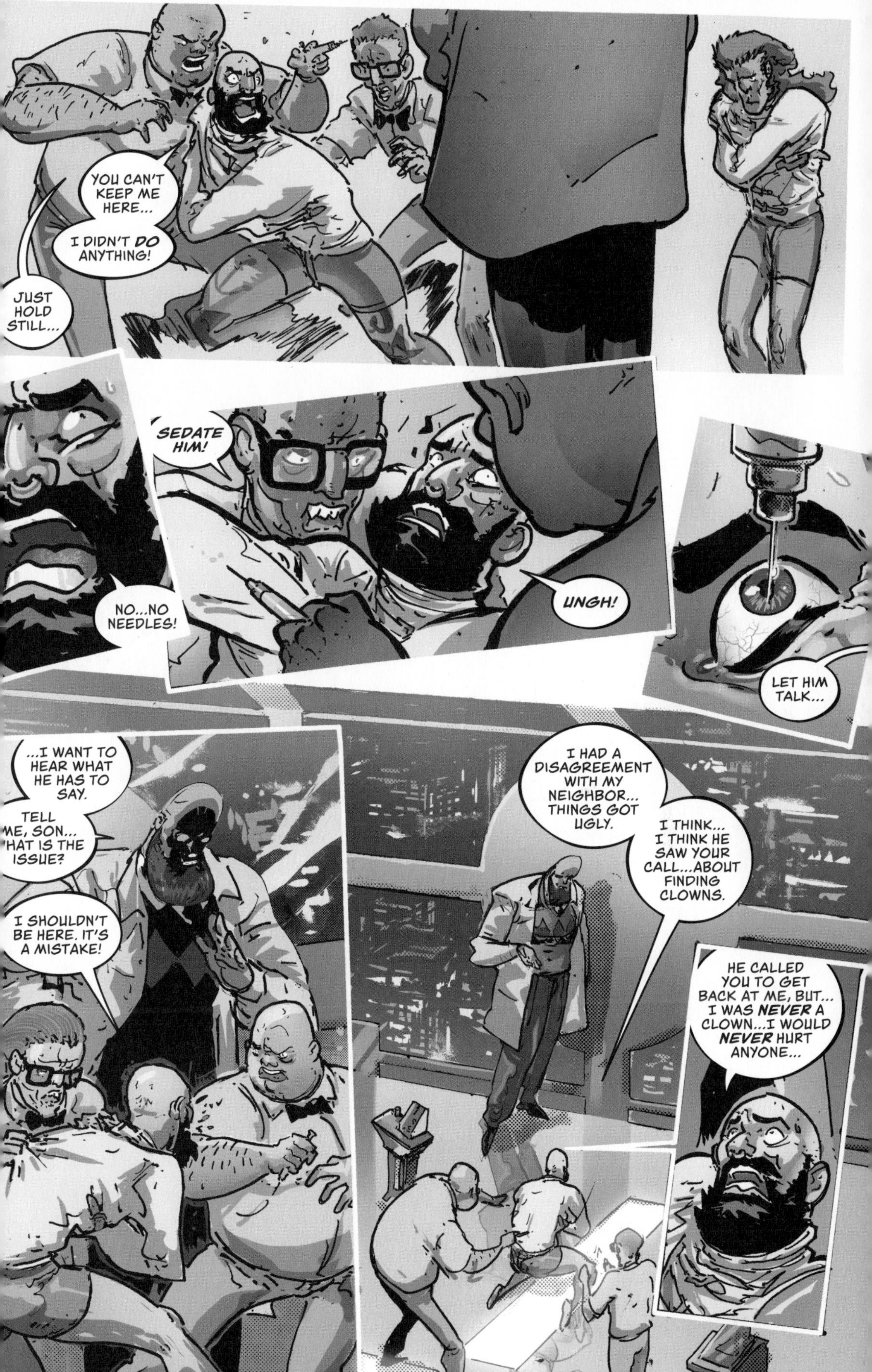
YOU CAN'T KEEP ME HERE...
I DIDN'T DO ANYTHING!
JUST HOLD STILL...
NO...NO NEEDLES!
SEDATE HIM!
UNGH!
LET HIM TALK...
...I WANT TO HEAR WHAT HE HAS TO SAY.
TELL ME, SON... WHAT IS THE ISSUE?
I SHOULDN'T BE HERE. IT'S A MISTAKE!
I HAD A DISAGREEMENT WITH MY NEIGHBOR... THINGS GOT UGLY.
I THINK... I THINK HE SAW YOUR CALL...ABOUT FINDING CLOWNS.
HE CALLED YOU TO GET BACK AT ME, BUT... I WAS NEVER A CLOWN...I WOULD NEVER HURT ANYONE...

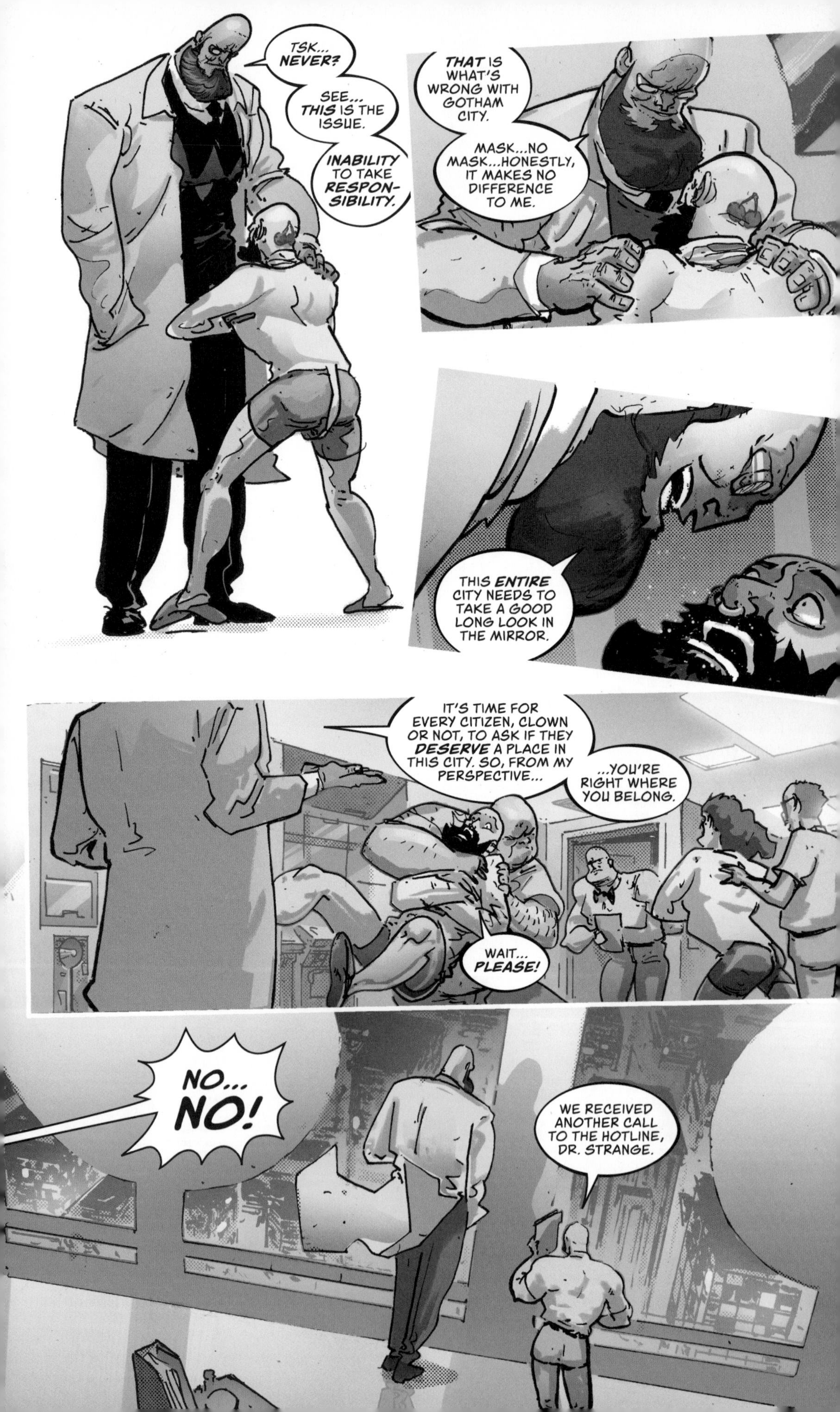
TSK... NEVER?
SEE... THIS IS THE ISSUE.
INABILITY TO TAKE RESPON-SIBILITY.
THAT IS WHAT'S WRONG WITH GOTHAM CITY.
MASK...NO MASK...HONESTLY, IT MAKES NO DIFFERENCE TO ME.
THIS ENTIRE CITY NEEDS TO TAKE A GOOD LONG LOOK IN THE MIRROR.
IT'S TIME FOR EVERY CITIZEN, CLOWN OR NOT, TO ASK IF THEY DESERVE A PLACE IN THIS CITY. SO, FROM MY PERSPECTIVE...
...YOU'RE RIGHT WHERE YOU BELONG.
WAIT... PLEASE!
NO... NO!
WE RECEIVED ANOTHER CALL TO THE HOTLINE, DR. STRANGE.

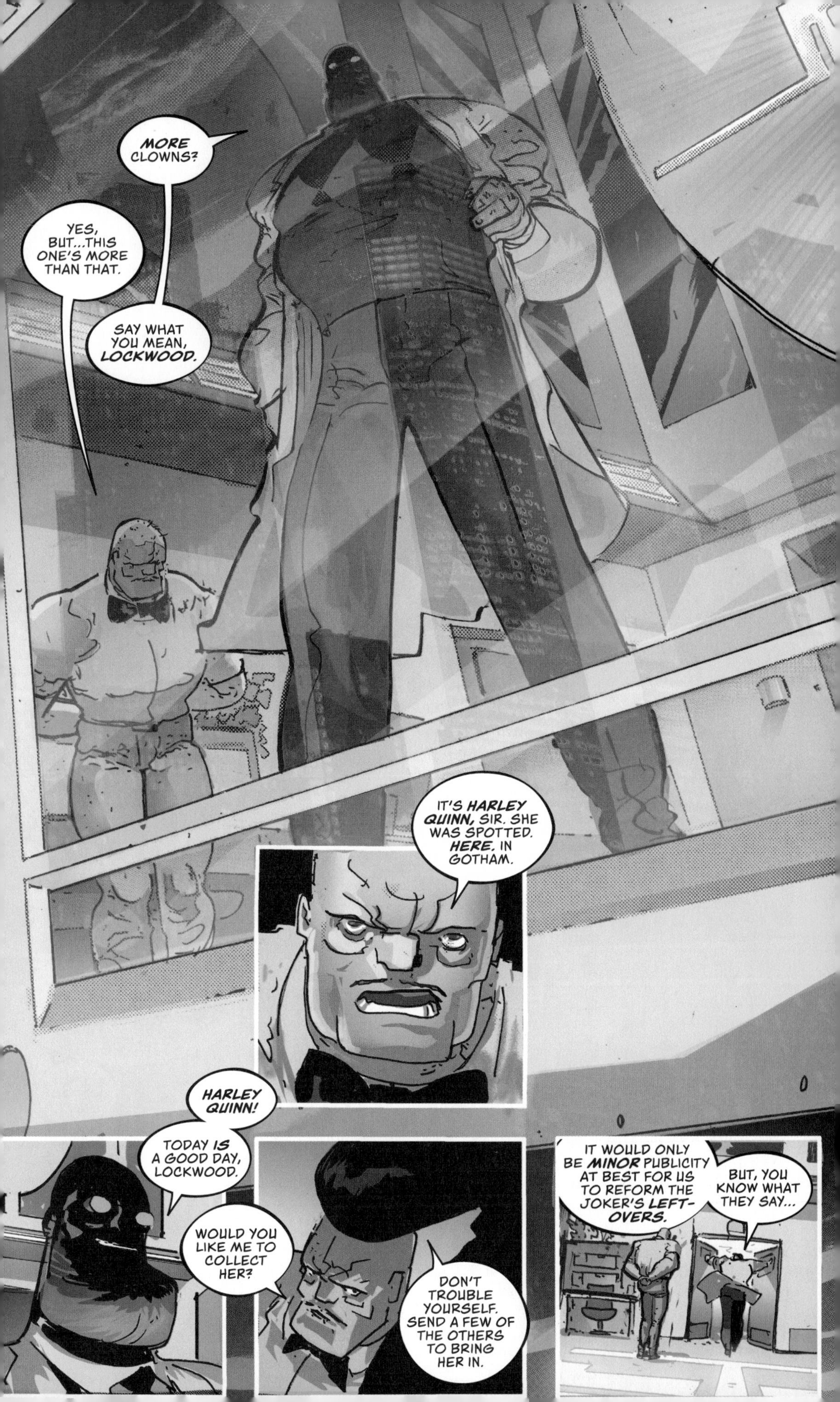

MORE CLOWNS?
YES, BUT...THIS ONE'S MORE THAN THAT.
SAY WHAT YOU MEAN, LOCKWOOD.
IT'S HARLEY QUINN, SIR. SHE WAS SPOTTED. HERE. IN GOTHAM.
HARLEY QUINN!
TODAY IS A GOOD DAY, LOCKWOOD.
WOULD YOU LIKE ME TO COLLECT HER?
DON'T TROUBLE YOURSELF. SEND A FEW OF THE OTHERS TO BRING HER IN.
IT WOULD ONLY BE MINOR PUBLICITY AT BEST FOR US TO REFORM THE JOKER'S LEFT-OVERS.
BUT, YOU KNOW WHAT THEY SAY...

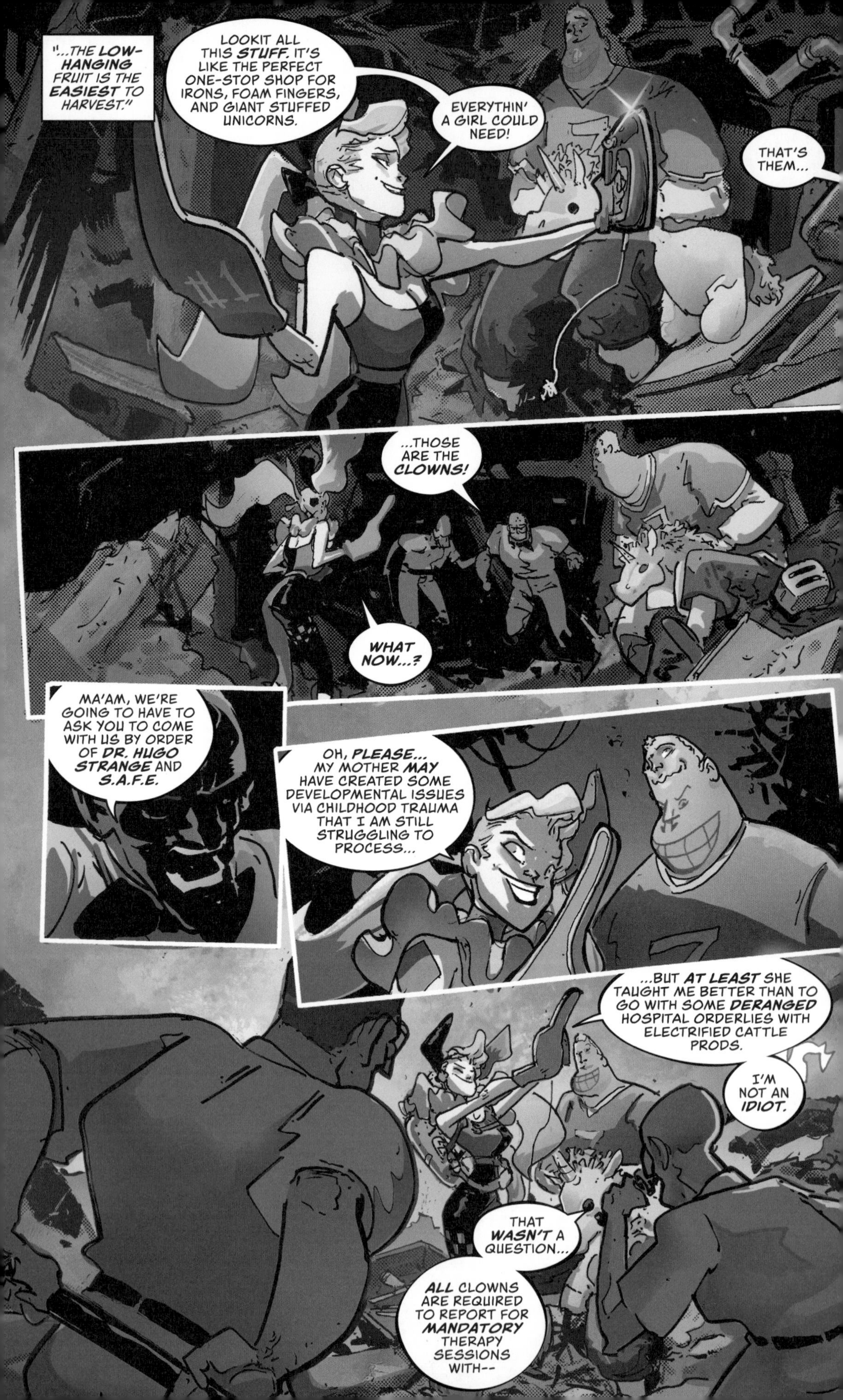
"...THE LOW-HANGING FRUIT IS THE EASIEST TO HARVEST."
LOOKIT ALL THIS STUFF. IT'S LIKE THE PERFECT ONE-STOP SHOP FOR IRONS, FOAM FINGERS, AND GIANT STUFFED UNICORNS.
EVERYTHIN' A GIRL COULD NEED!
THAT'S THEM...
...THOSE ARE THE CLOWNS!
WHAT NOW...?
MA'AM, WE'RE GOING TO HAVE TO ASK YOU TO COME WITH US BY ORDER OF DR. HUGO STRANGE AND S.A.F.E.
OH, PLEASE... MY MOTHER MAY HAVE CREATED SOME DEVELOPMENTAL ISSUES VIA CHILDHOOD TRAUMA THAT I AM STILL STRUGGLING TO PROCESS...
...BUT AT LEAST SHE TAUGHT ME BETTER THAN TO GO WITH SOME DERANGED HOSPITAL ORDERLIES WITH ELECTRIFIED CATTLE PRODS.
I'M NOT AN IDIOT.
THAT WASN'T A QUESTION...
ALL CLOWNS ARE REQUIRED TO REPORT FOR MANDATORY THERAPY SESSIONS WITH--

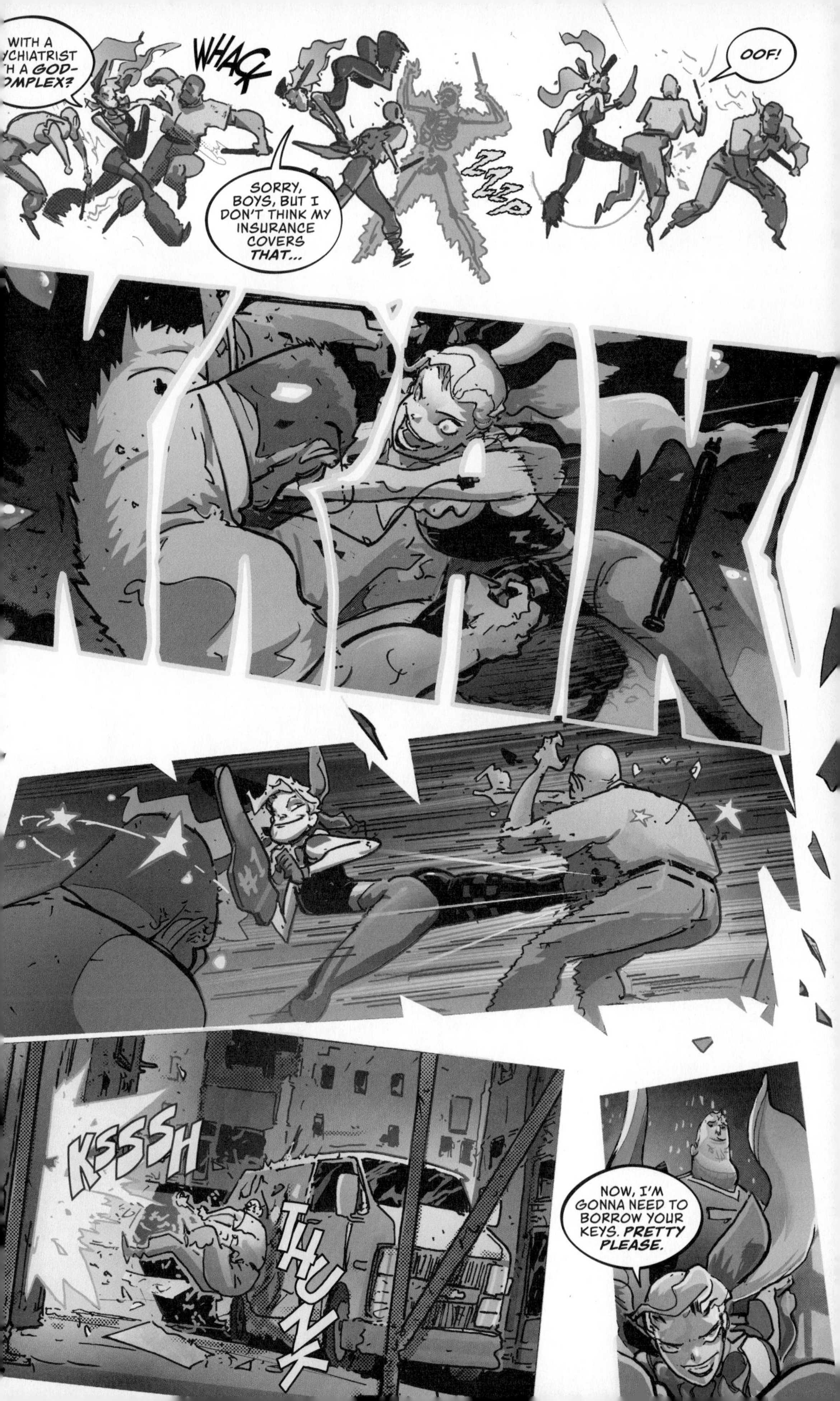

WITH A
YCHIATRIST
H A GOD-
OMPLEX?
WHACK
SORRY, BOYS, BUT I DON'T THINK MY INSURANCE COVERS THAT...
ZZZP
OOF!
KSSSH
THUNK
NOW, I'M GONNA NEED TO BORROW YOUR KEYS. PRETTY PLEASE.

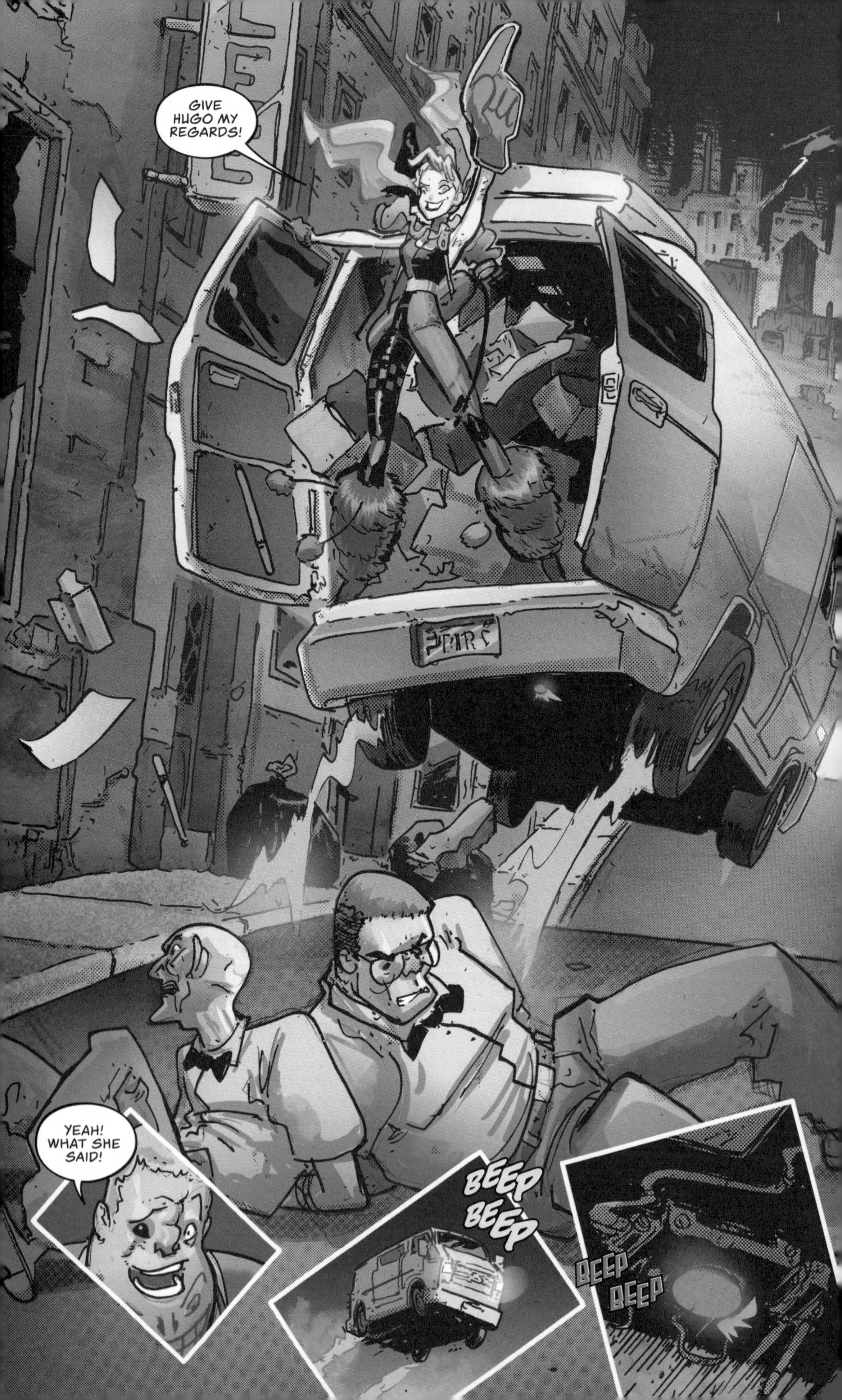
GIVE HUGO MY REGARDS!
YEAH! WHAT SHE SAID!
BEEP BEEP
BEEP BEEP

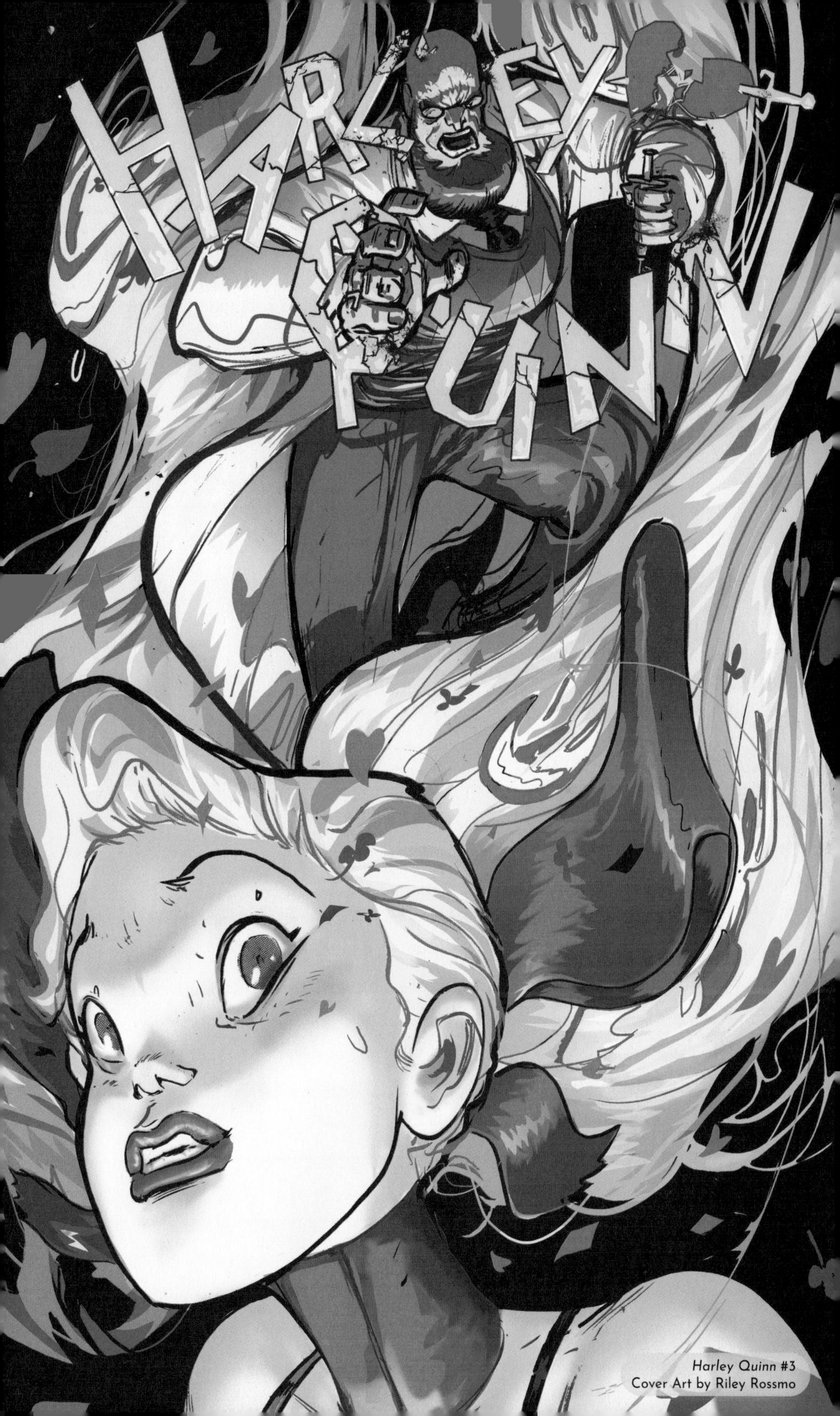
HARLEY QUINN

Harley Quinn #3
Cover Art by Riley Rossmo

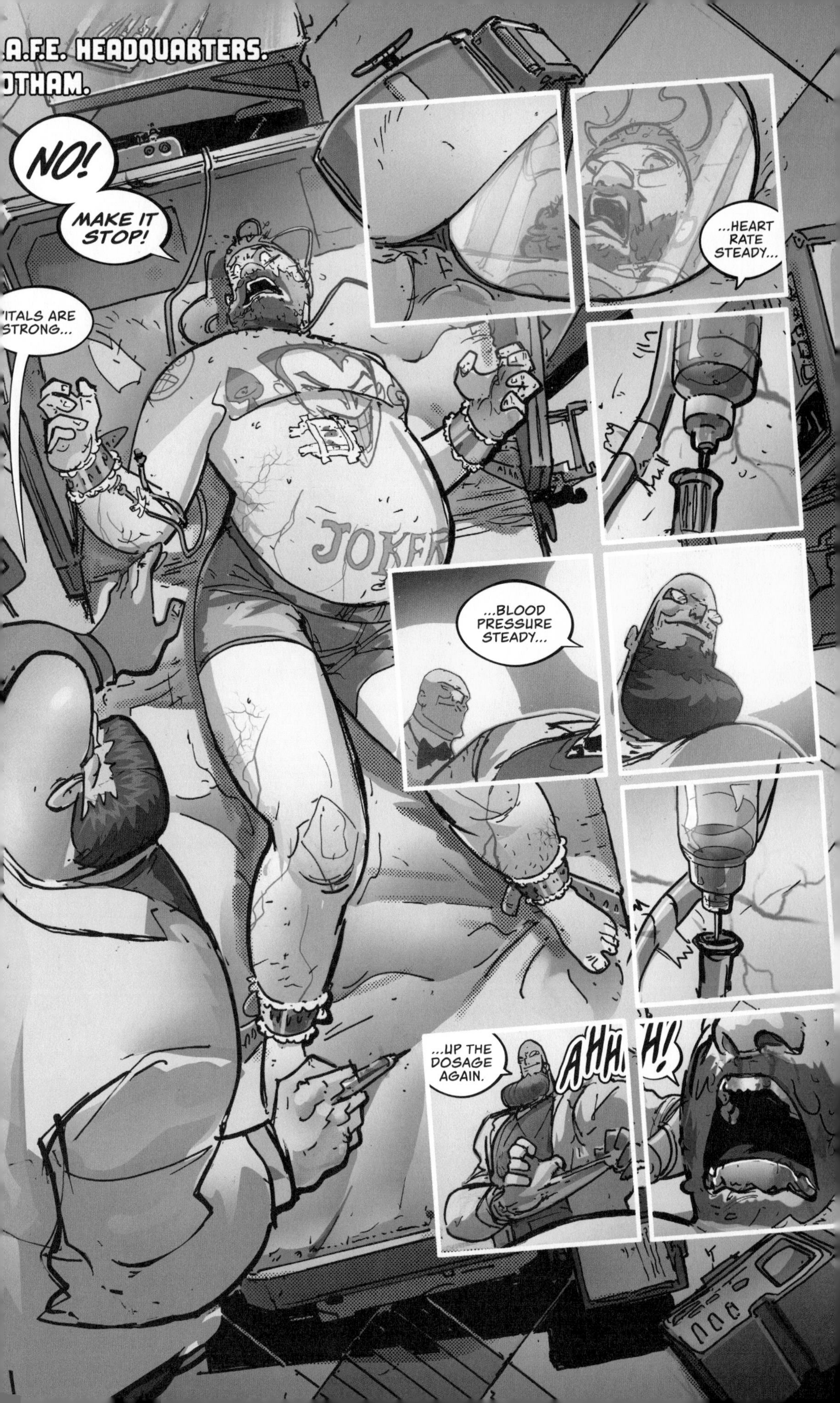

.A.F.E. HEADQUARTERS.
OTHAM.
NO!
MAKE IT STOP!
ITALS ARE STRONG...
...HEART RATE STEADY...
JOKER
...BLOOD PRESSURE STEADY...
...UP THE DOSAGE AGAIN.
AHHHH!

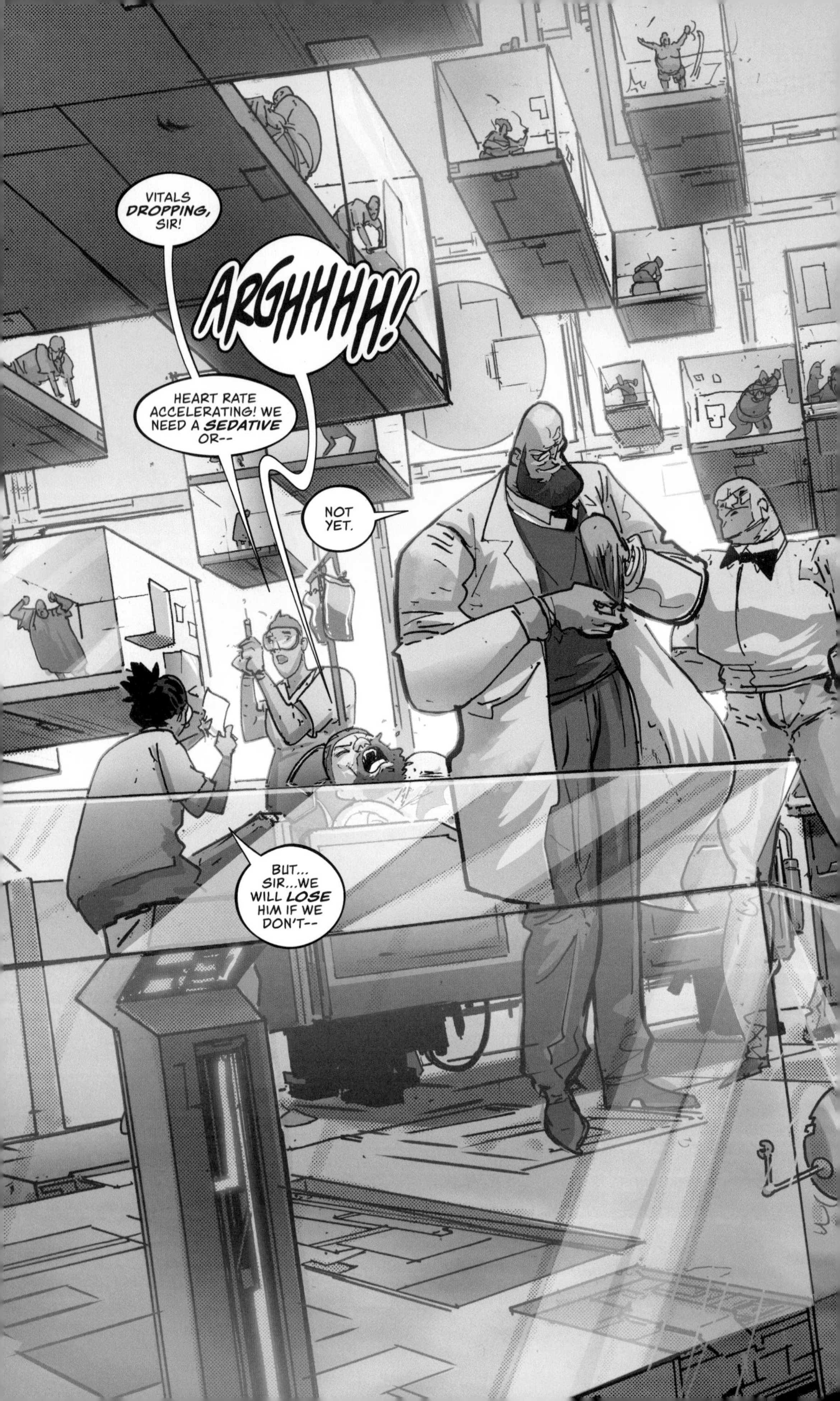
VITALS DROPPING, SIR!
ARGHHHH!
HEART RATE ACCELERATING! WE NEED A SEDATIVE OR--
NOT YET.
BUT... SIR...WE WILL LOSE HIM IF WE DON'T--

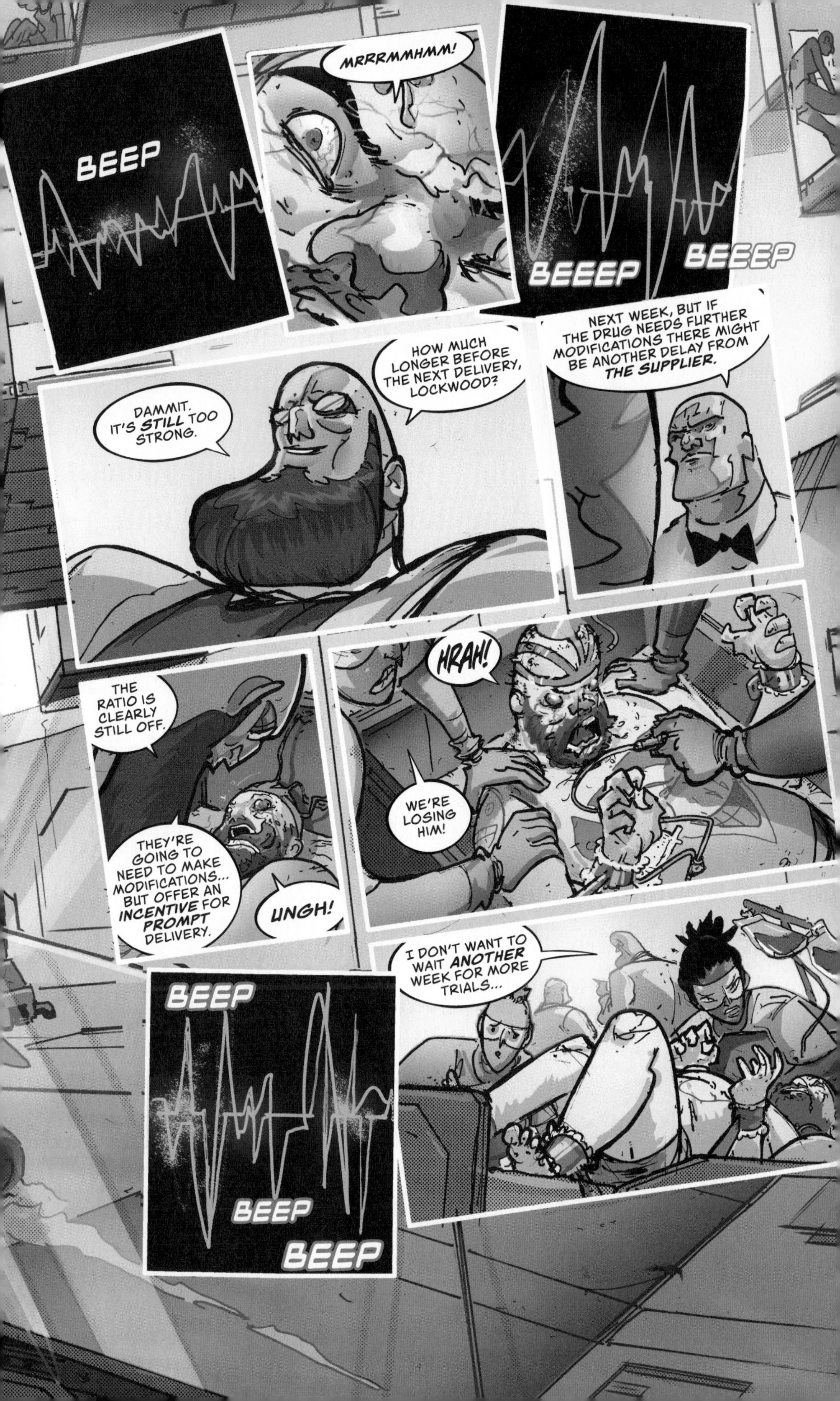
BEEP
MRRRMMHMM!
BEEEP
BEEEP
HOW MUCH LONGER BEFORE THE NEXT DELIVERY, LOCKWOOD?
NEXT WEEK, BUT IF THE DRUG NEEDS FURTHER MODIFICATIONS THERE MIGHT BE ANOTHER DELAY FROM THE SUPPLIER.
DAMMIT. IT'S STILL TOO STRONG.
THE RATIO IS CLEARLY STILL OFF.
THEY'RE GOING TO NEED TO MAKE MODIFICATIONS... BUT OFFER AN INCENTIVE FOR PROMPT DELIVERY.
UNGH!
HRAH!
WE'RE LOSING HIM!
BEEP
BEEP
BEEP
I DON'T WANT TO WAIT ANOTHER WEEK FOR MORE TRIALS...

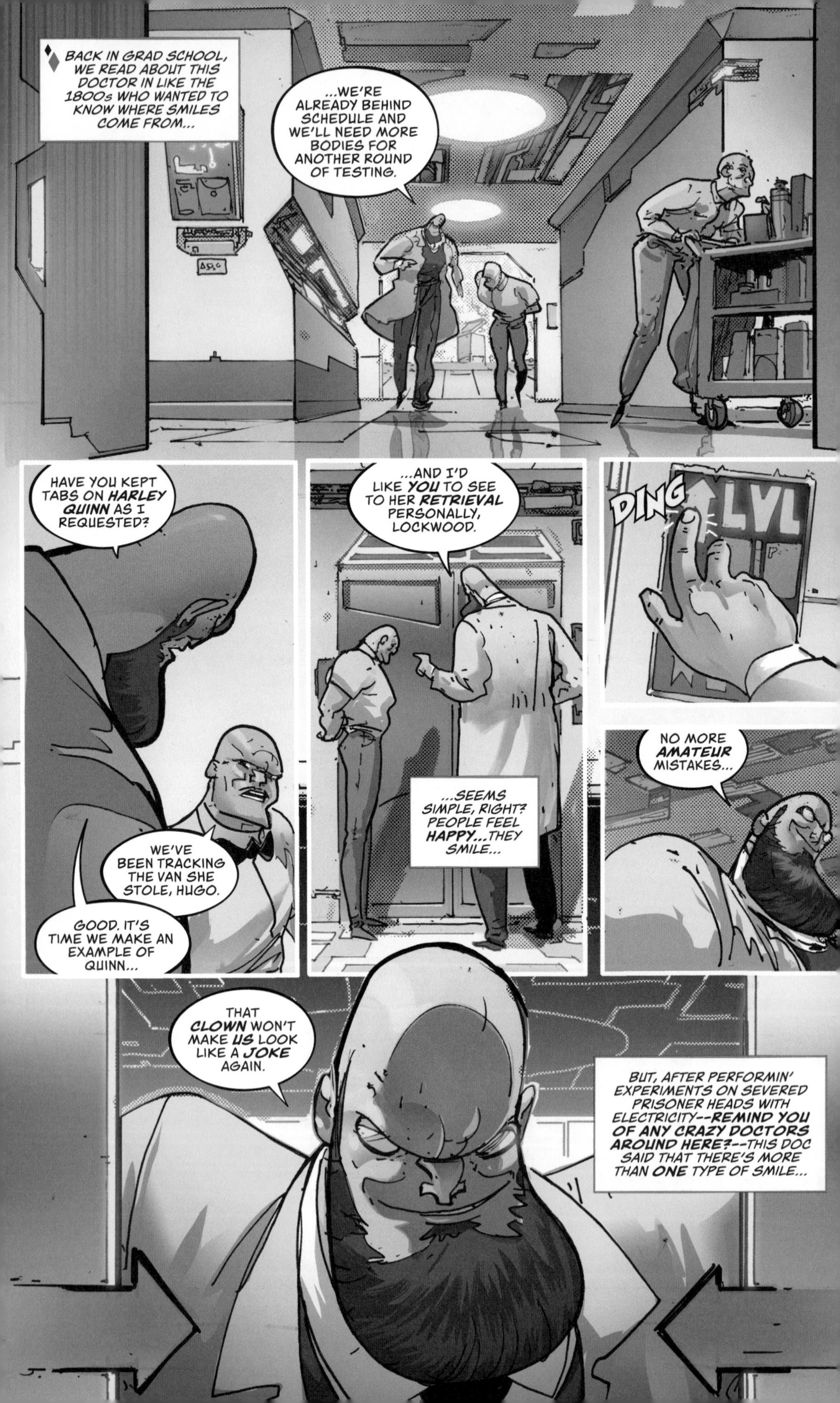
BACK IN GRAD SCHOOL, WE READ ABOUT THIS DOCTOR IN LIKE THE 1800s WHO WANTED TO KNOW WHERE SMILES COME FROM...
...WE'RE ALREADY BEHIND SCHEDULE AND WE'LL NEED MORE BODIES FOR ANOTHER ROUND OF TESTING.
HAVE YOU KEPT TABS ON HARLEY QUINN AS I REQUESTED?
WE'VE BEEN TRACKING THE VAN SHE STOLE, HUGO.
GOOD. IT'S TIME WE MAKE AN EXAMPLE OF QUINN...
...AND I'D LIKE YOU TO SEE TO HER RETRIEVAL PERSONALLY, LOCKWOOD.
...SEEMS SIMPLE, RIGHT? PEOPLE FEEL HAPPY...THEY SMILE...
DING
LVL
NO MORE AMATEUR MISTAKES...
THAT CLOWN WON'T MAKE US LOOK LIKE A JOKE AGAIN.
BUT, AFTER PERFORMIN' EXPERIMENTS ON SEVERED PRISONER HEADS WITH ELECTRICITY--REMIND YOU OF ANY CRAZY DOCTORS AROUND HERE?--THIS DOC SAID THAT THERE'S MORE THAN ONE TYPE OF SMILE...

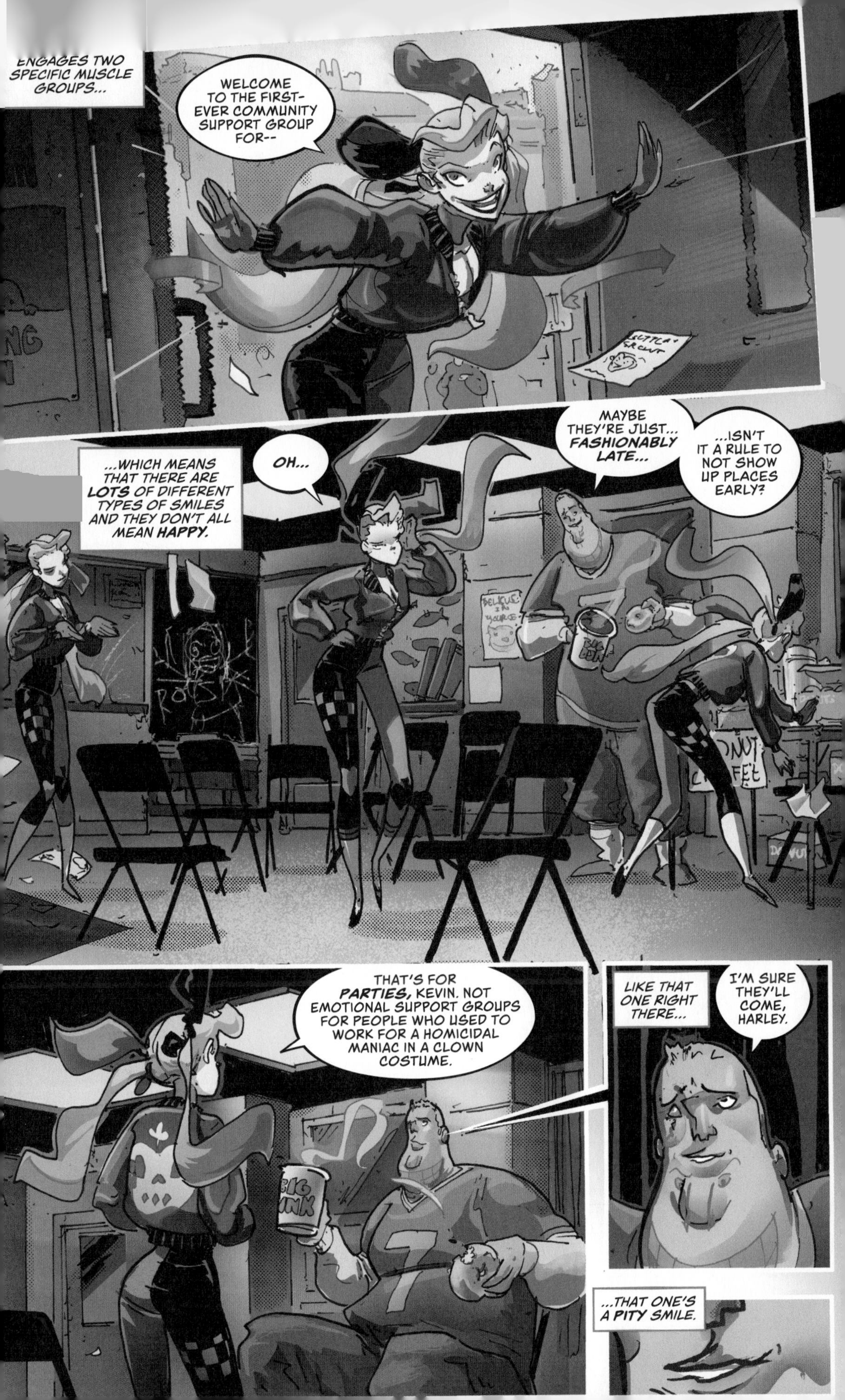
ENGAGES TWO SPECIFIC MUSCLE GROUPS...
WELCOME TO THE FIRST-EVER COMMUNITY SUPPORT GROUP FOR--
...WHICH MEANS THAT THERE ARE LOTS OF DIFFERENT TYPES OF SMILES AND THEY DON'T ALL MEAN HAPPY.
OH...
MAYBE THEY'RE JUST... FASHIONABLY LATE...
...ISN'T IT A RULE TO NOT SHOW UP PLACES EARLY?
THAT'S FOR PARTIES, KEVIN. NOT EMOTIONAL SUPPORT GROUPS FOR PEOPLE WHO USED TO WORK FOR A HOMICIDAL MANIAC IN A CLOWN COSTUME.
LIKE THAT ONE RIGHT THERE...
I'M SURE THEY'LL COME, HARLEY.
...THAT ONE'S A PITY SMILE.

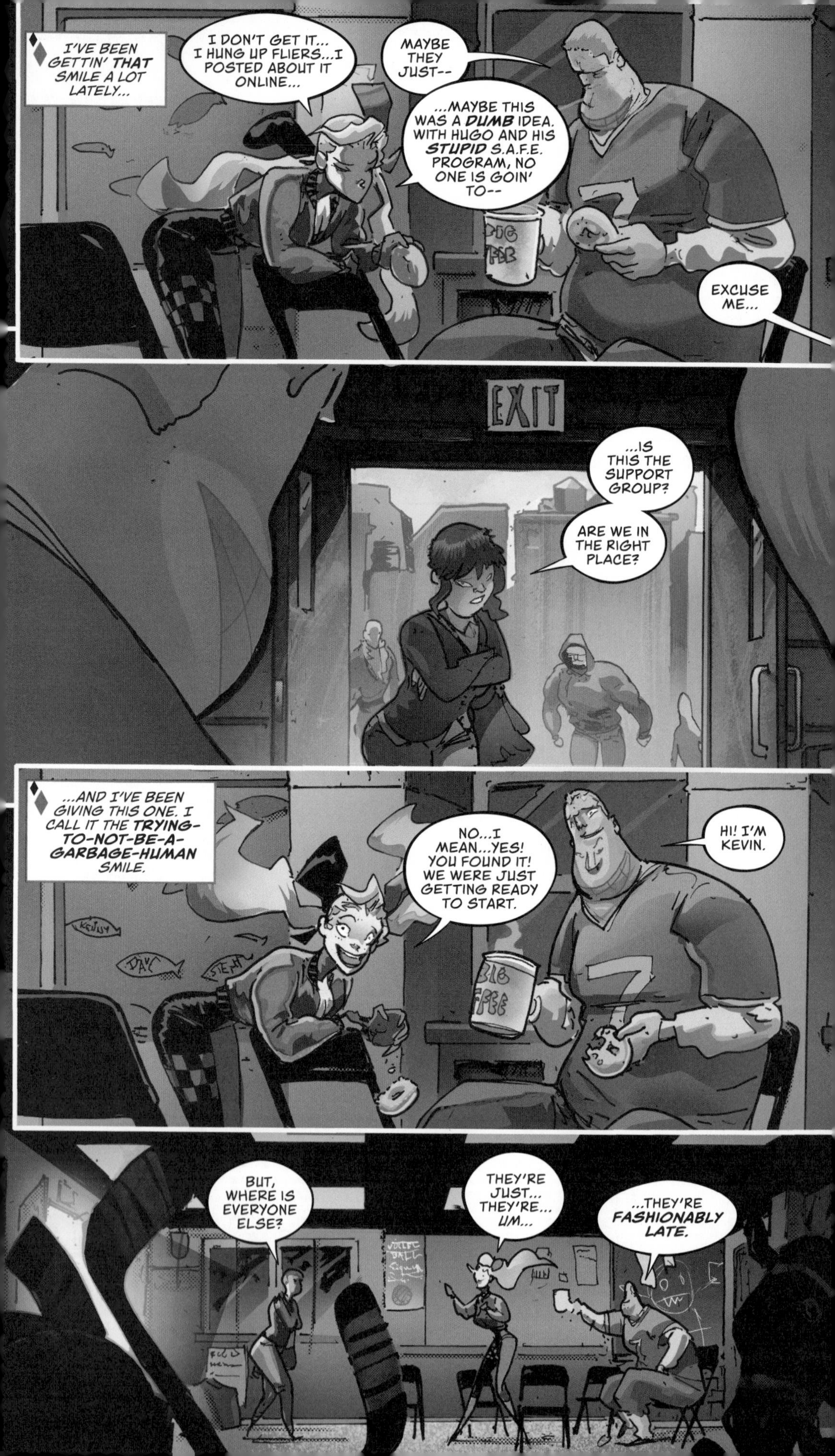

I'VE BEEN GETTIN' THAT SMILE A LOT LATELY...
I DON'T GET IT... I HUNG UP FLIERS...I POSTED ABOUT IT ONLINE...
MAYBE THEY JUST--
...MAYBE THIS WAS A DUMB IDEA. WITH HUGO AND HIS STUPID S.A.F.E. PROGRAM, NO ONE IS GOIN' TO--
EXCUSE ME...
EXIT
...IS THIS THE SUPPORT GROUP?
ARE WE IN THE RIGHT PLACE?
...AND I'VE BEEN GIVING THIS ONE. I CALL IT THE TRYING-TO-NOT-BE-A-GARBAGE-HUMAN SMILE.
NO...I MEAN...YES! YOU FOUND IT! WE WERE JUST GETTING READY TO START.
HI! I'M KEVIN.
BUT, WHERE IS EVERYONE ELSE?
THEY'RE JUST... THEY'RE... UM...
...THEY'RE FASHIONABLY LATE.

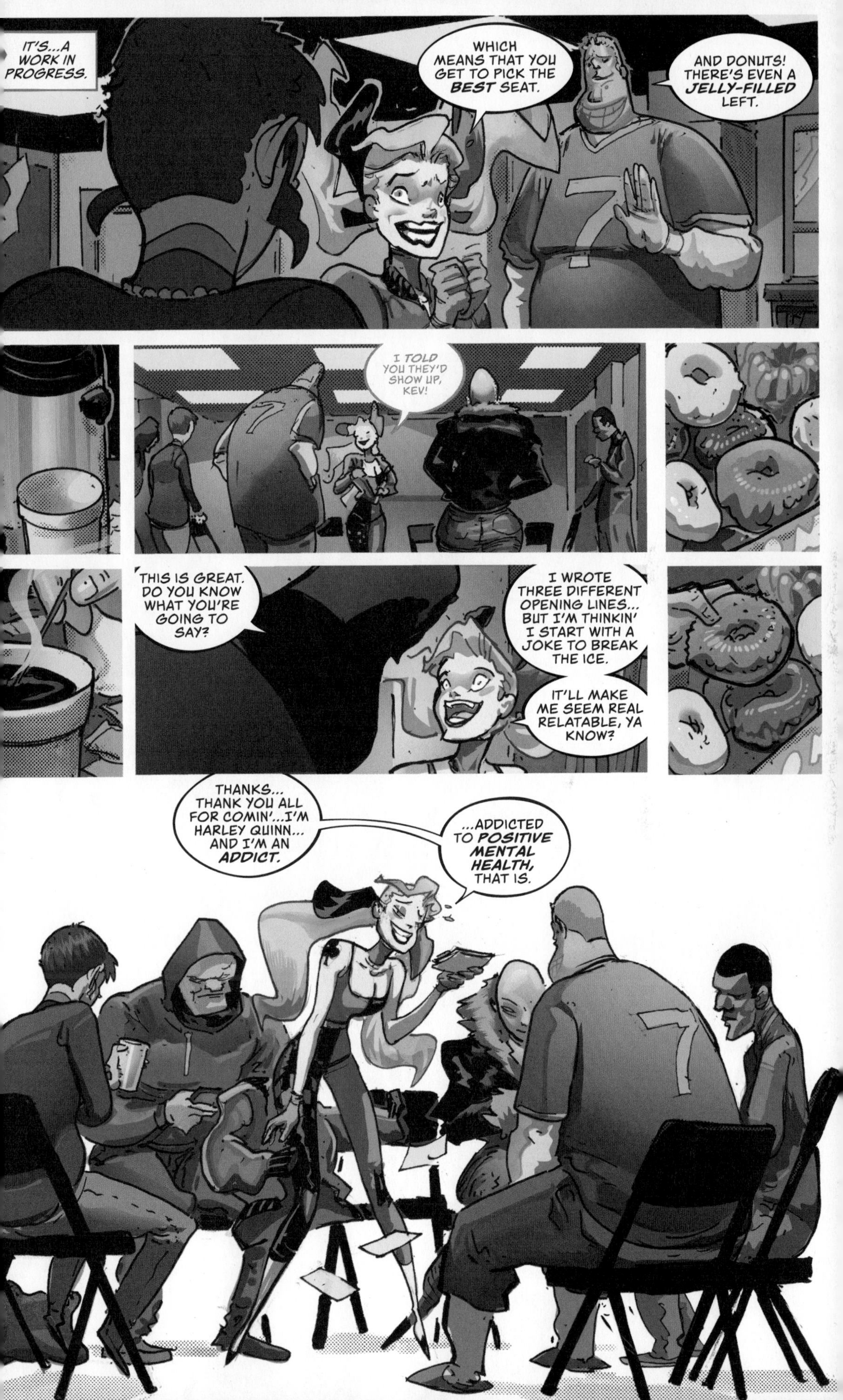
IT'S...A WORK IN PROGRESS.
WHICH MEANS THAT YOU GET TO PICK THE BEST SEAT.
AND DONUTS! THERE'S EVEN A JELLY-FILLED LEFT.
I TOLD YOU THEY'D SHOW UP, KEV!
THIS IS GREAT. DO YOU KNOW WHAT YOU'RE GOING TO SAY?
I WROTE THREE DIFFERENT OPENING LINES... BUT I'M THINKIN' I START WITH A JOKE TO BREAK THE ICE.
IT'LL MAKE ME SEEM REAL RELATABLE, YA KNOW?
THANKS... THANK YOU ALL FOR COMIN'...I'M HARLEY QUINN... AND I'M AN ADDICT.
...ADDICTED TO POSITIVE MENTAL HEALTH, THAT IS.

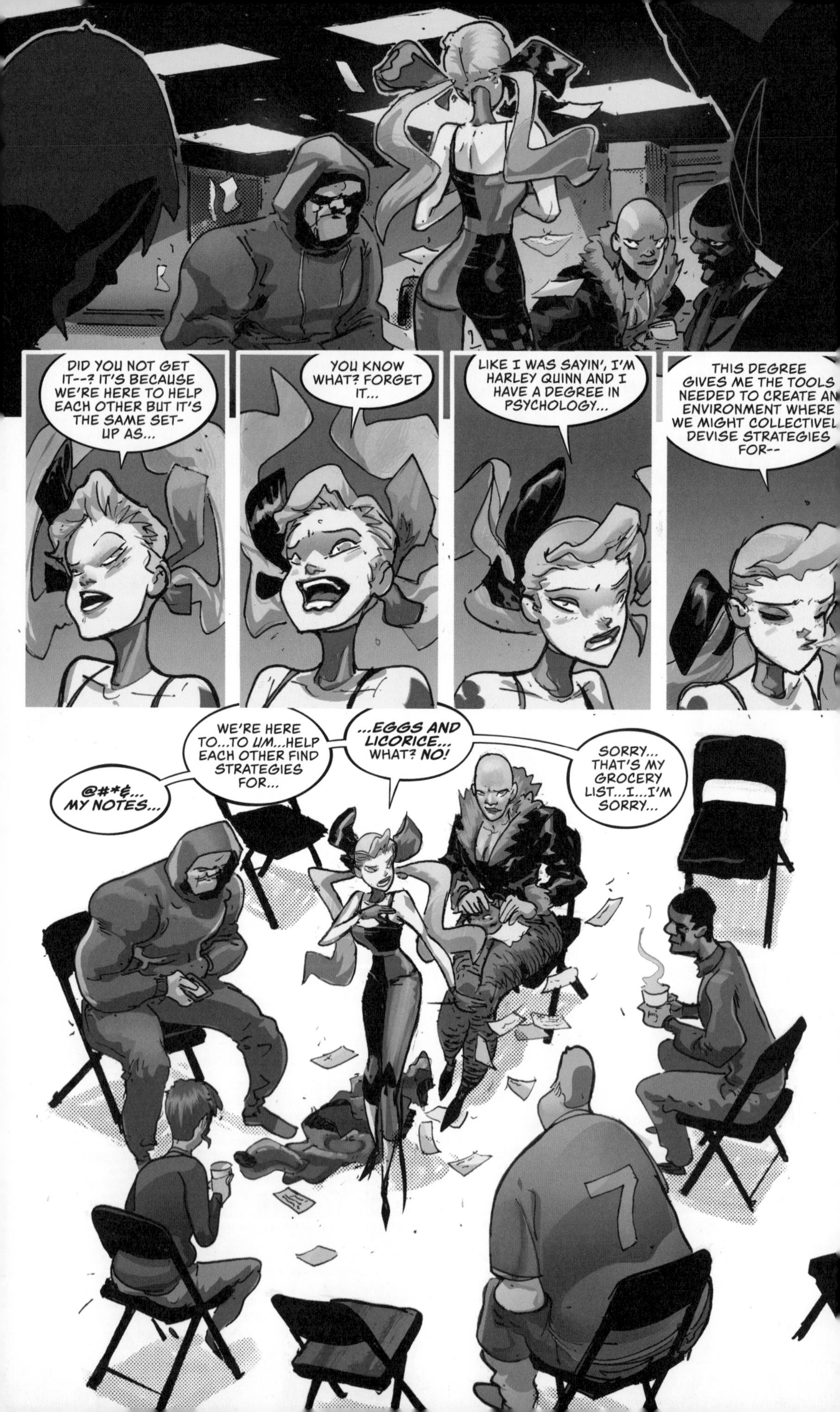
DID YOU NOT GET IT--? IT'S BECAUSE WE'RE HERE TO HELP EACH OTHER BUT IT'S THE SAME SET-UP AS...
YOU KNOW WHAT? FORGET IT...
LIKE I WAS SAYIN', I'M HARLEY QUINN AND I HAVE A DEGREE IN PSYCHOLOGY...
THIS DEGREE GIVES ME THE TOOLS NEEDED TO CREATE AN ENVIRONMENT WHERE WE MIGHT COLLECTIVEL DEVISE STRATEGIES FOR--
@#*&... MY NOTES...
WE'RE HERE TO...TO UM...HELP EACH OTHER FIND STRATEGIES FOR...
...EGGS AND LICORICE... WHAT? NO!
SORRY... THAT'S MY GROCERY LIST...I...I'M SORRY...
7

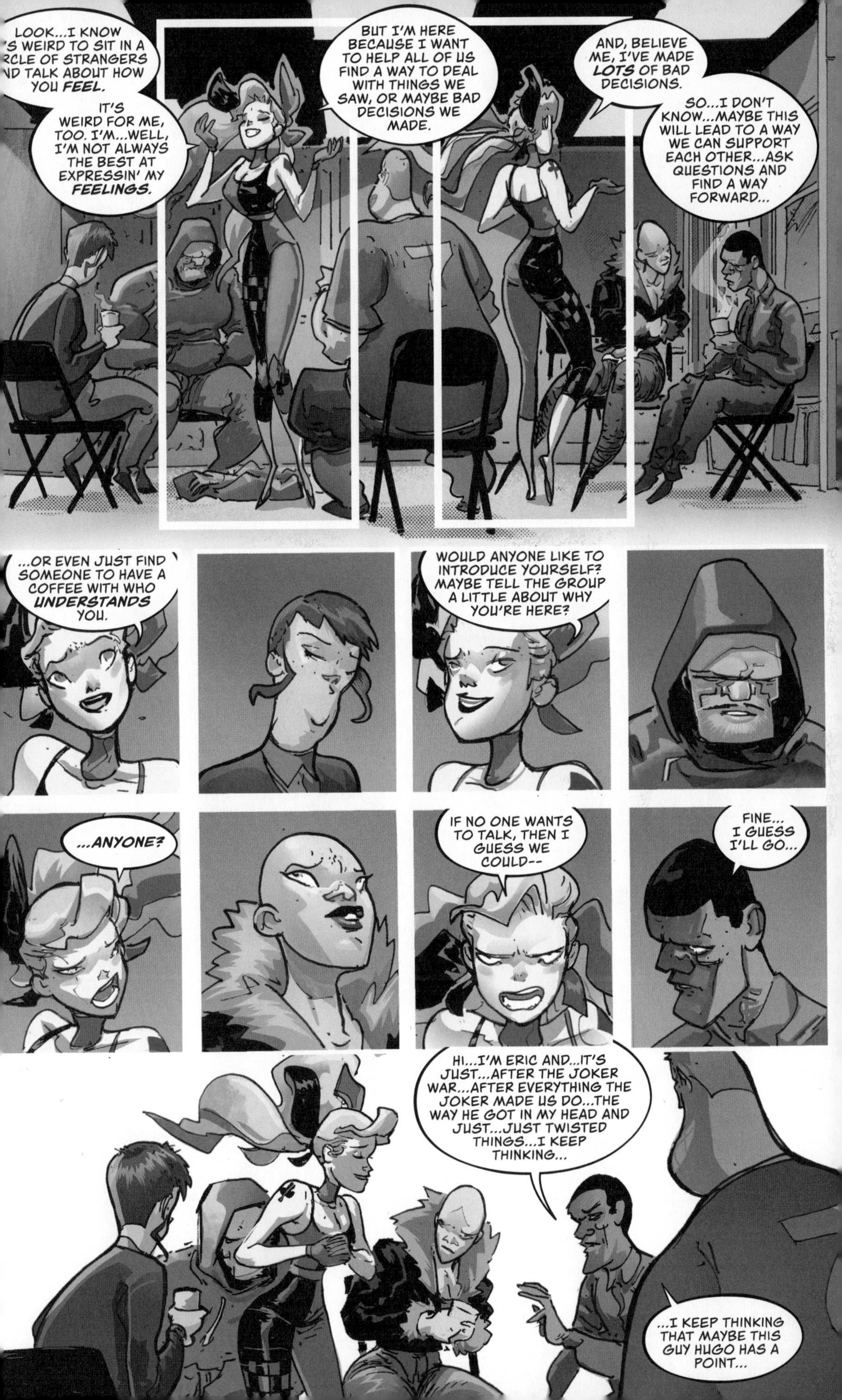
LOOK...I KNOW 'S WEIRD TO SIT IN A RCLE OF STRANGERS ND TALK ABOUT HOW YOU FEEL.
IT'S WEIRD FOR ME, TOO. I'M...WELL, I'M NOT ALWAYS THE BEST AT EXPRESSIN' MY FEELINGS.
BUT I'M HERE BECAUSE I WANT TO HELP ALL OF US FIND A WAY TO DEAL WITH THINGS WE SAW, OR MAYBE BAD DECISIONS WE MADE.
AND, BELIEVE ME, I'VE MADE LOTS OF BAD DECISIONS.
SO...I DON'T KNOW...MAYBE THIS WILL LEAD TO A WAY WE CAN SUPPORT EACH OTHER...ASK QUESTIONS AND FIND A WAY FORWARD...
...OR EVEN JUST FIND SOMEONE TO HAVE A COFFEE WITH WHO UNDERSTANDS YOU.
WOULD ANYONE LIKE TO INTRODUCE YOURSELF? MAYBE TELL THE GROUP A LITTLE ABOUT WHY YOU'RE HERE?
...ANYONE?
IF NO ONE WANTS TO TALK, THEN I GUESS WE COULD--
FINE... I GUESS I'LL GO...
HI...I'M ERIC AND...IT'S JUST...AFTER THE JOKER WAR...AFTER EVERYTHING THE JOKER MADE US DO...THE WAY HE GOT IN MY HEAD AND JUST...JUST TWISTED THINGS...I KEEP THINKING...
...I KEEP THINKING THAT MAYBE THIS GUY HUGO HAS A POINT...

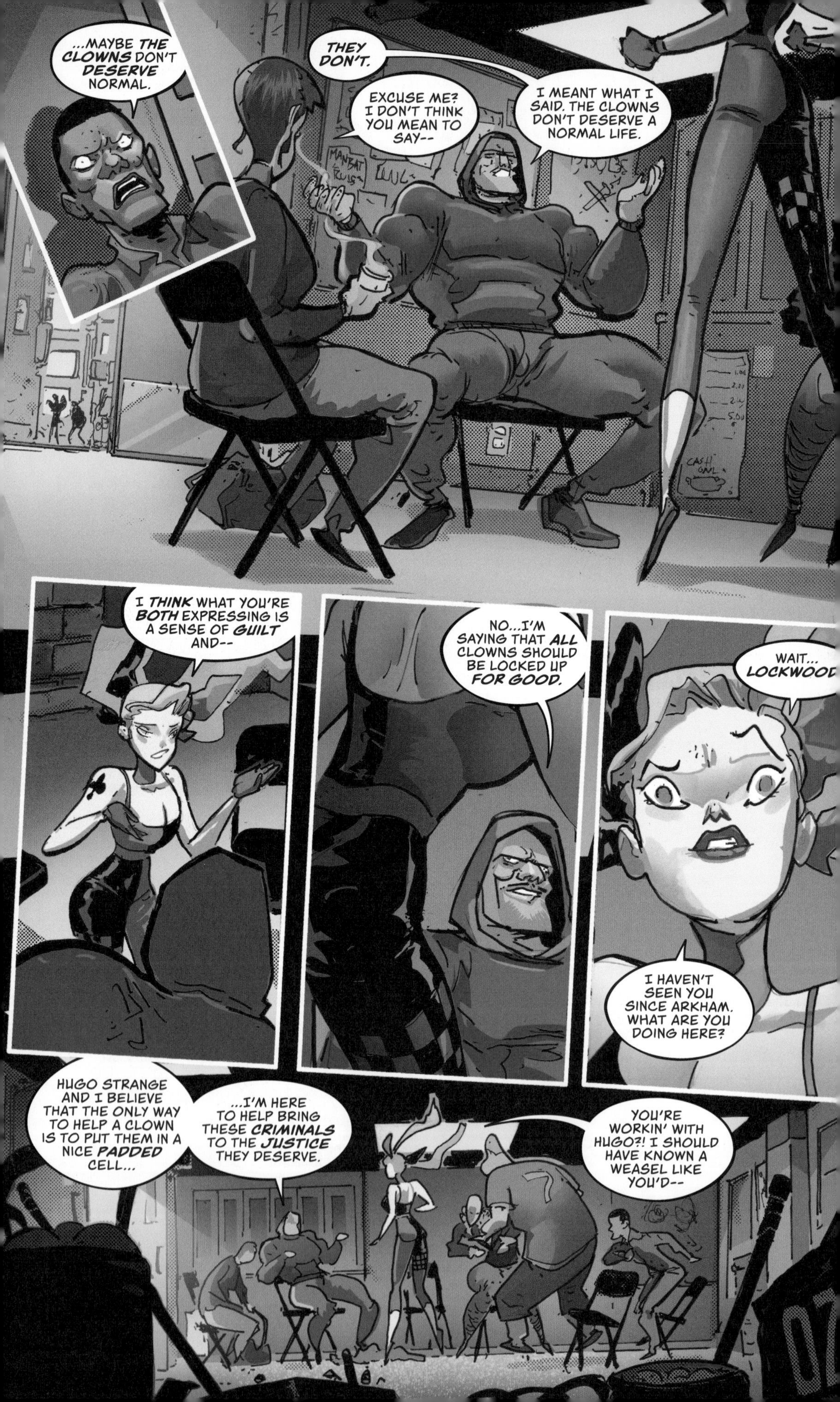
...MAYBE THE CLOWNS DON'T DESERVE NORMAL.
THEY DON'T.
EXCUSE ME? I DON'T THINK YOU MEAN TO SAY--
I MEANT WHAT I SAID. THE CLOWNS DON'T DESERVE A NORMAL LIFE.
I THINK WHAT YOU'RE BOTH EXPRESSING IS A SENSE OF GUILT AND--
NO...I'M SAYING THAT ALL CLOWNS SHOULD BE LOCKED UP FOR GOOD.
WAIT... LOCKWOOD
I HAVEN'T SEEN YOU SINCE ARKHAM. WHAT ARE YOU DOING HERE?
HUGO STRANGE AND I BELIEVE THAT THE ONLY WAY TO HELP A CLOWN IS TO PUT THEM IN A NICE PADDED CELL...
...I'M HERE TO HELP BRING THESE CRIMINALS TO THE JUSTICE THEY DESERVE.
YOU'RE WORKIN' WITH HUGO?! I SHOULD HAVE KNOWN A WEASEL LIKE YOU'D--

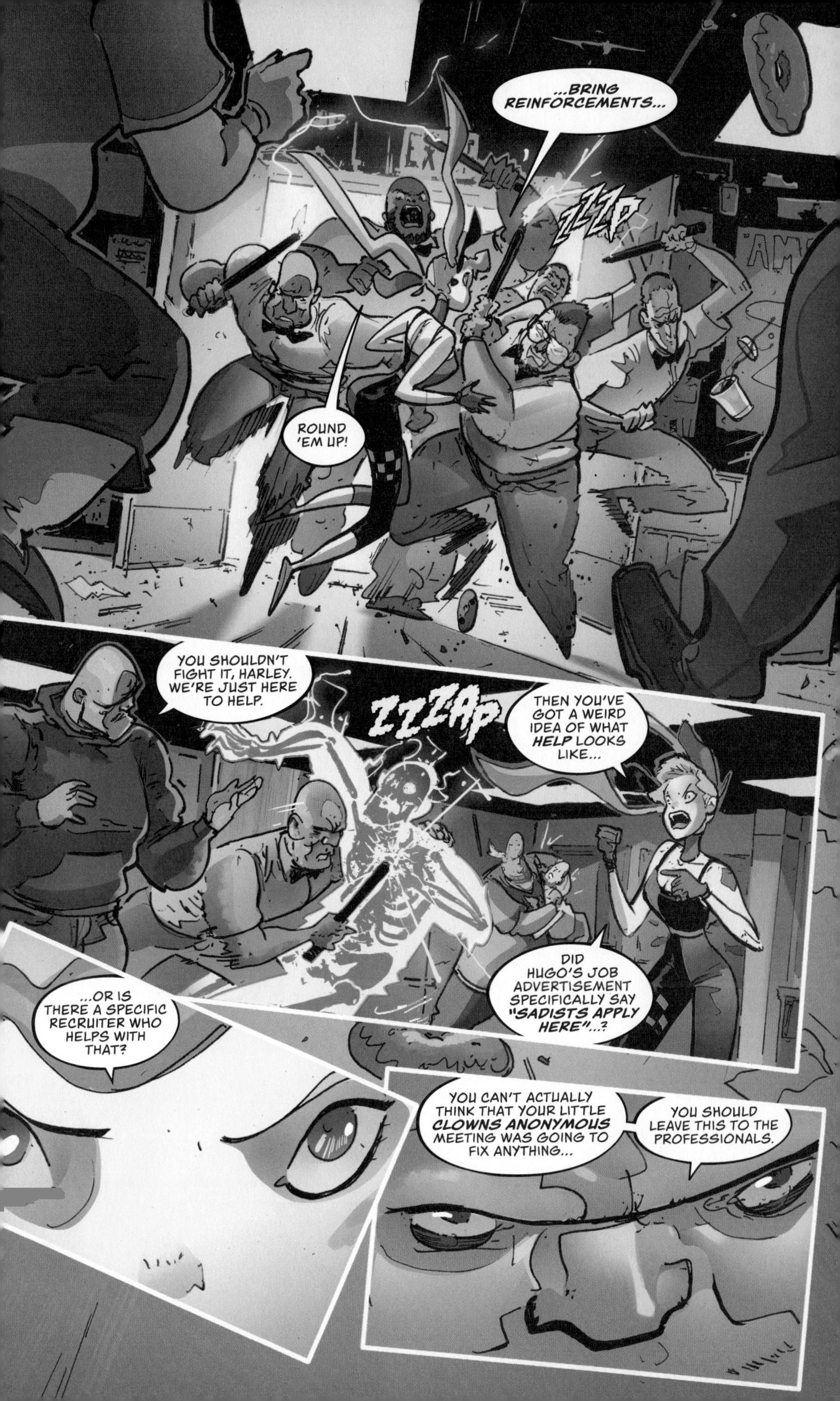
...BRING REINFORCEMENTS...
ZZZAP
ROUND 'EM UP!
YOU SHOULDN'T FIGHT IT, HARLEY. WE'RE JUST HERE TO HELP.
ZZZAP
THEN YOU'VE GOT A WEIRD IDEA OF WHAT HELP LOOKS LIKE...
DID HUGO'S JOB ADVERTISEMENT SPECIFICALLY SAY "SADISTS APPLY HERE"...?
...OR IS THERE A SPECIFIC RECRUITER WHO HELPS WITH THAT?
YOU CAN'T ACTUALLY THINK THAT YOUR LITTLE CLOWNS ANONYMOUS MEETING WAS GOING TO FIX ANYTHING...
YOU SHOULD LEAVE THIS TO THE PROFESSIONALS.

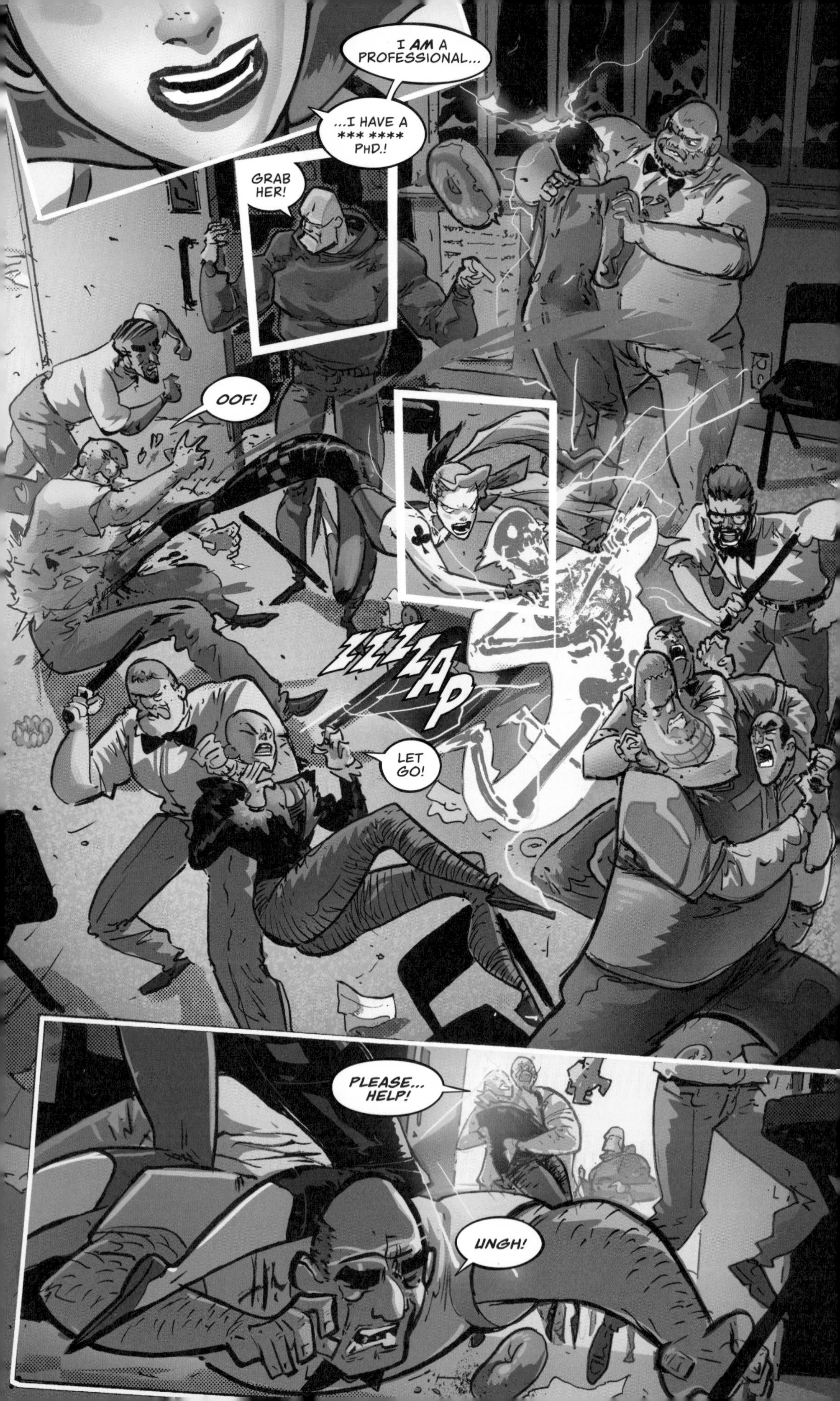
I AM A PROFESSIONAL...
...I HAVE A *** **** PHD.!
GRAB HER!
OOF!
ZZZZAP
LET GO!
PLEASE... HELP!
UNGH!

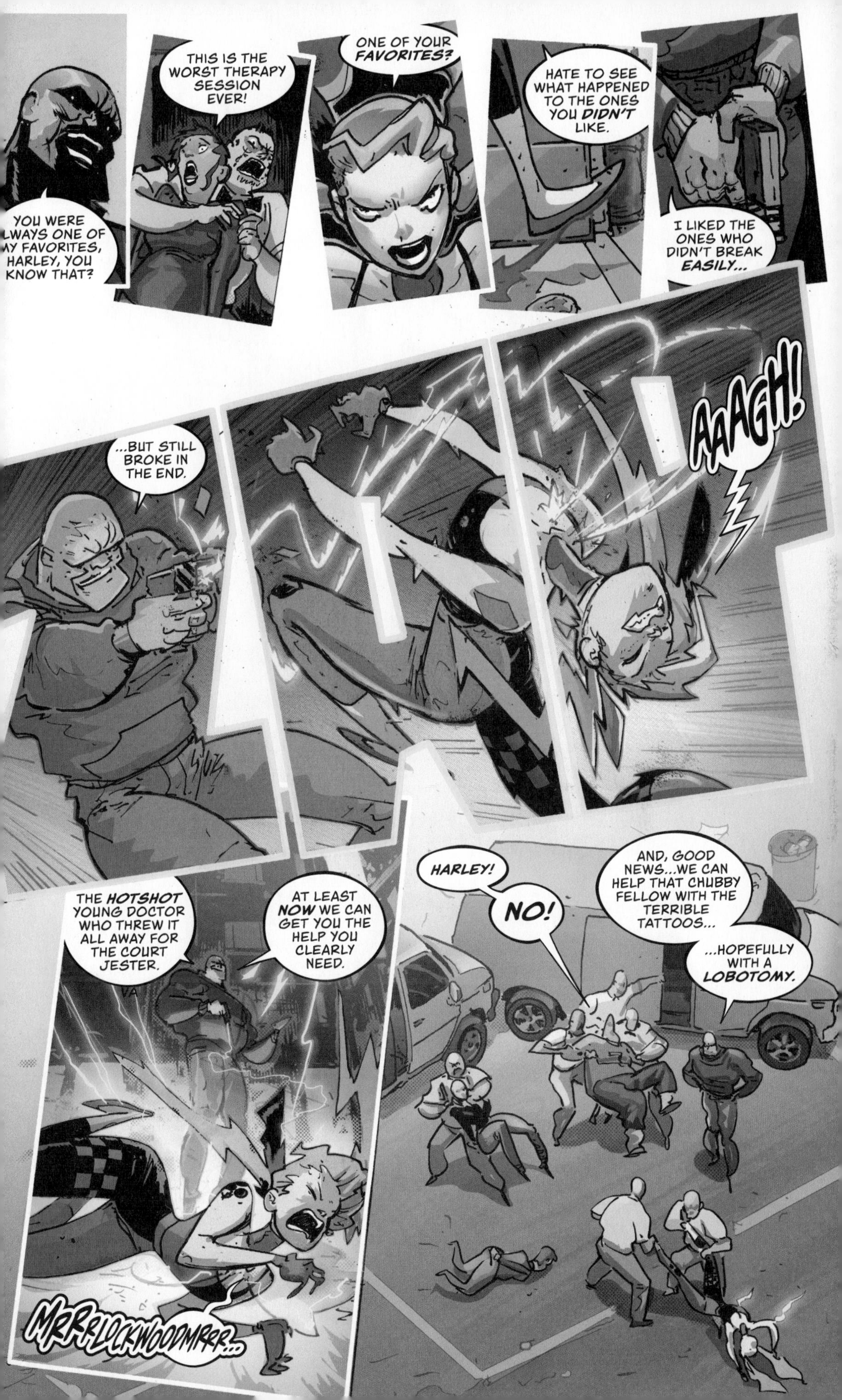

YOU WERE ALWAYS ONE OF MY FAVORITES, HARLEY, YOU KNOW THAT?
THIS IS THE WORST THERAPY SESSION EVER!
ONE OF YOUR FAVORITES?
HATE TO SEE WHAT HAPPENED TO THE ONES YOU DIDN'T LIKE.
I LIKED THE ONES WHO DIDN'T BREAK EASILY...
...BUT STILL BROKE IN THE END.
AAAGH!
THE HOTSHOT YOUNG DOCTOR WHO THREW IT ALL AWAY FOR THE COURT JESTER.
AT LEAST NOW WE CAN GET YOU THE HELP YOU CLEARLY NEED.
MRRRLOCKWOODMRRR...
HARLEY!
NO!
AND, GOOD NEWS...WE CAN HELP THAT CHUBBY FELLOW WITH THE TERRIBLE TATTOOS...
...HOPEFULLY WITH A LOBOTOMY.

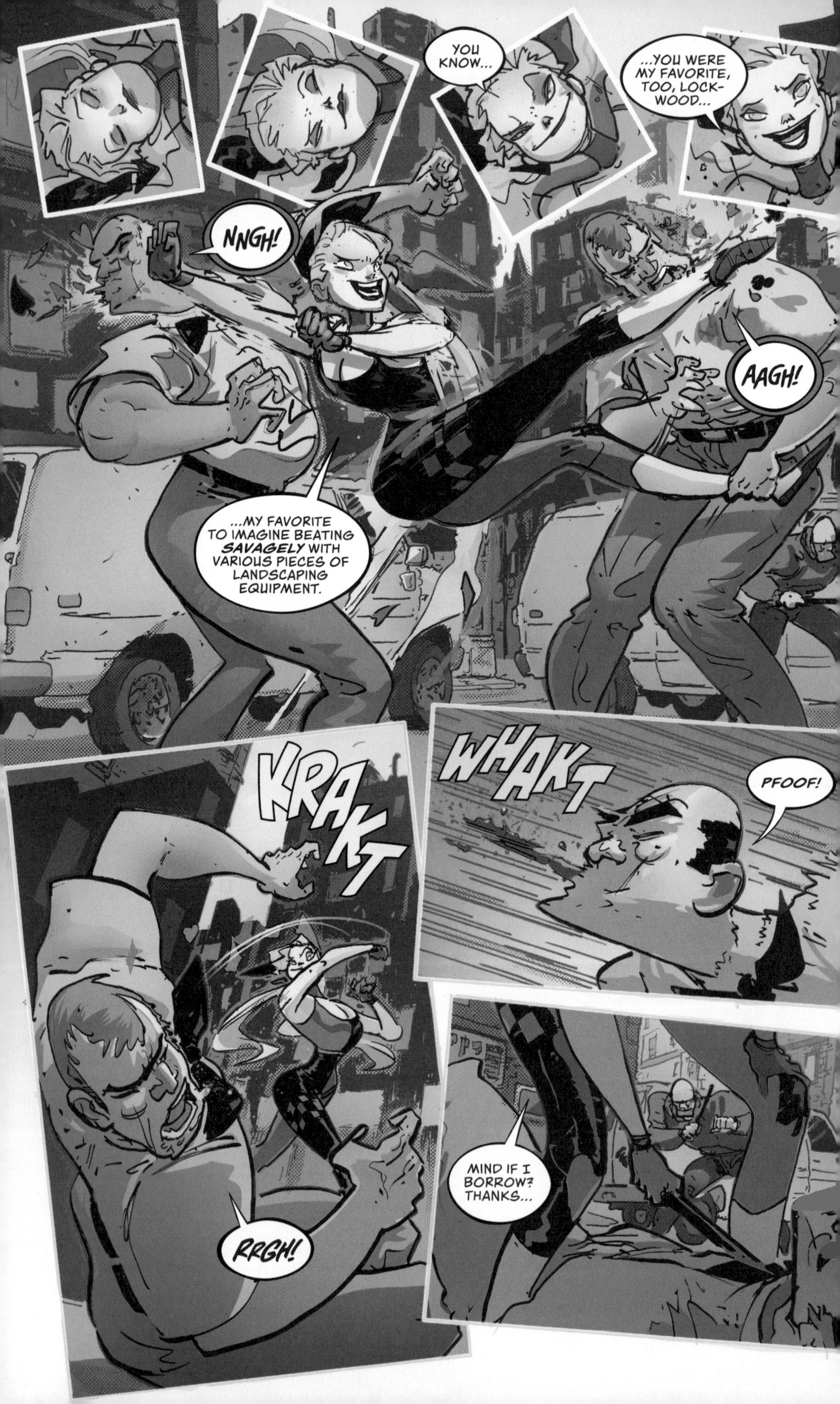
YOU KNOW...
...YOU WERE MY FAVORITE, TOO, LOCK-WOOD...
NNGH!
AAGH!
...MY FAVORITE TO IMAGINE BEATING SAVAGELY WITH VARIOUS PIECES OF LANDSCAPING EQUIPMENT.
KRAKT
RRGH!
WHAKT
PFOOF!
MIND IF I BORROW? THANKS...

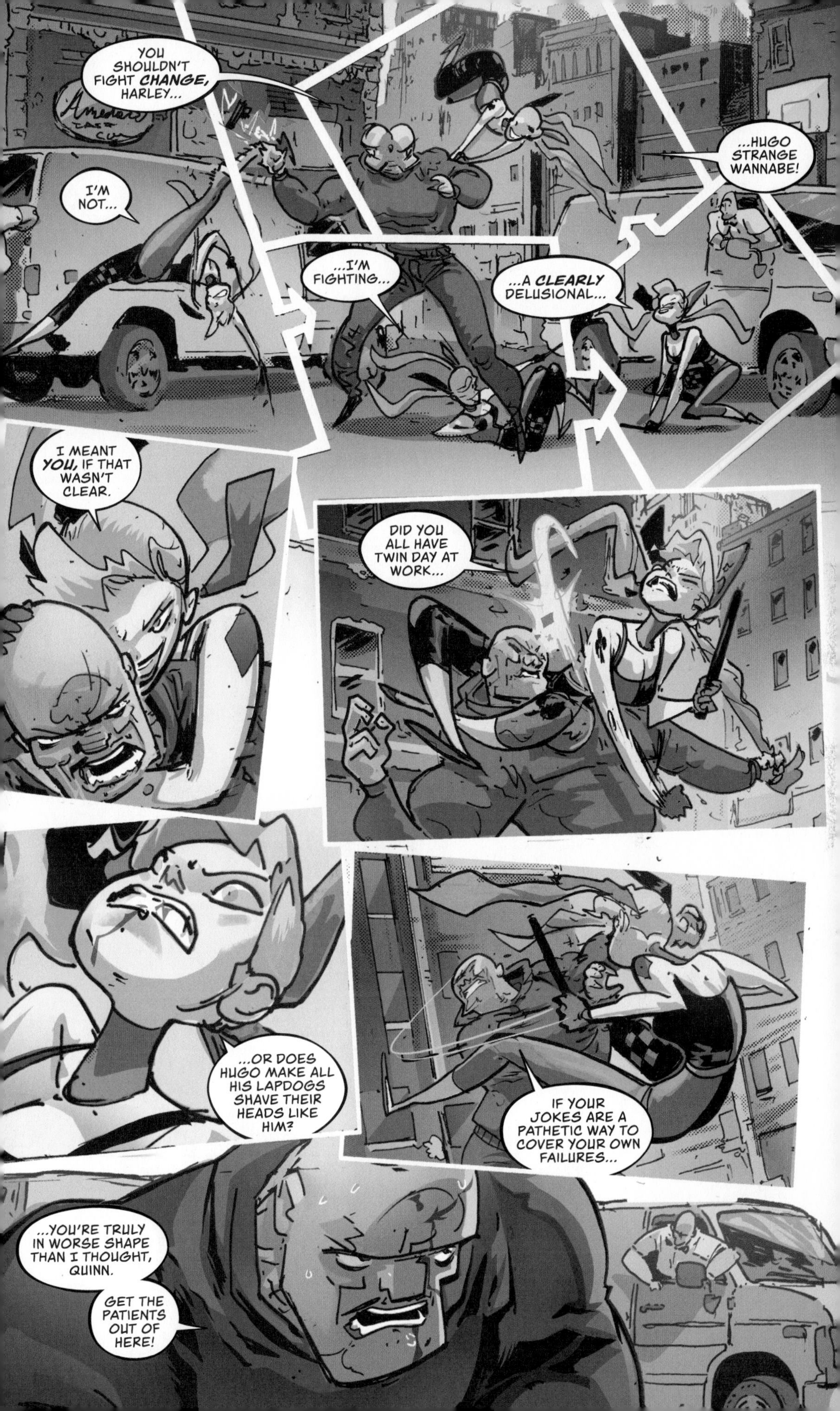
YOU SHOULDN'T FIGHT CHANGE, HARLEY...
I'M NOT...
...I'M FIGHTING...
...A CLEARLY DELUSIONAL...
...HUGO STRANGE WANNABE!
I MEANT YOU, IF THAT WASN'T CLEAR.
DID YOU ALL HAVE TWIN DAY AT WORK...
...OR DOES HUGO MAKE ALL HIS LAPDOGS SHAVE THEIR HEADS LIKE HIM?
IF YOUR JOKES ARE A PATHETIC WAY TO COVER YOUR OWN FAILURES...
...YOU'RE TRULY IN WORSE SHAPE THAN I THOUGHT, QUINN.
GET THE PATIENTS OUT OF HERE!

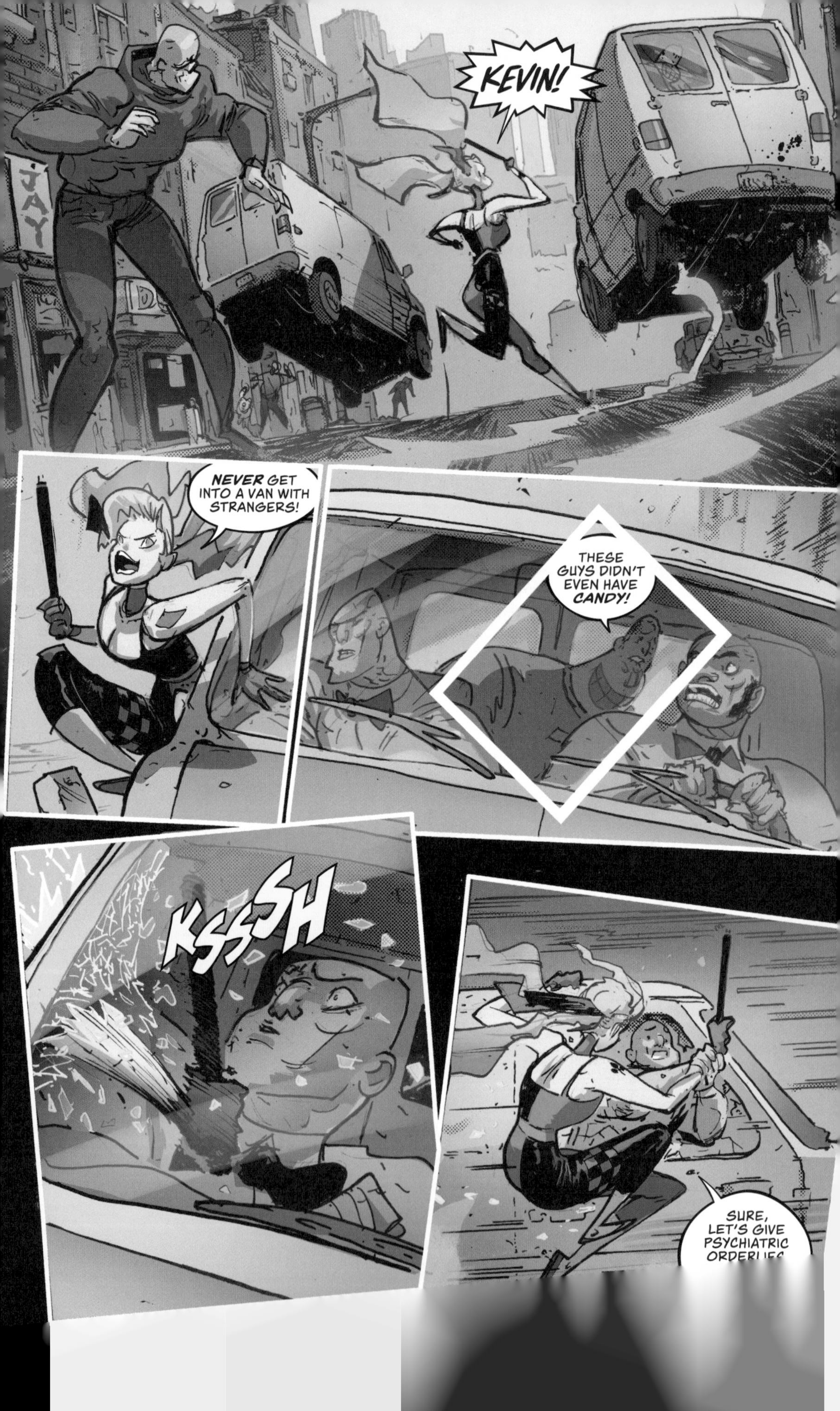
JAY
KEVIN!
NEVER GET INTO A VAN WITH STRANGERS!
THESE GUYS DIDN'T EVEN HAVE CANDY!
KSSSH
SURE, LET'S GIVE PSYCHIATRIC

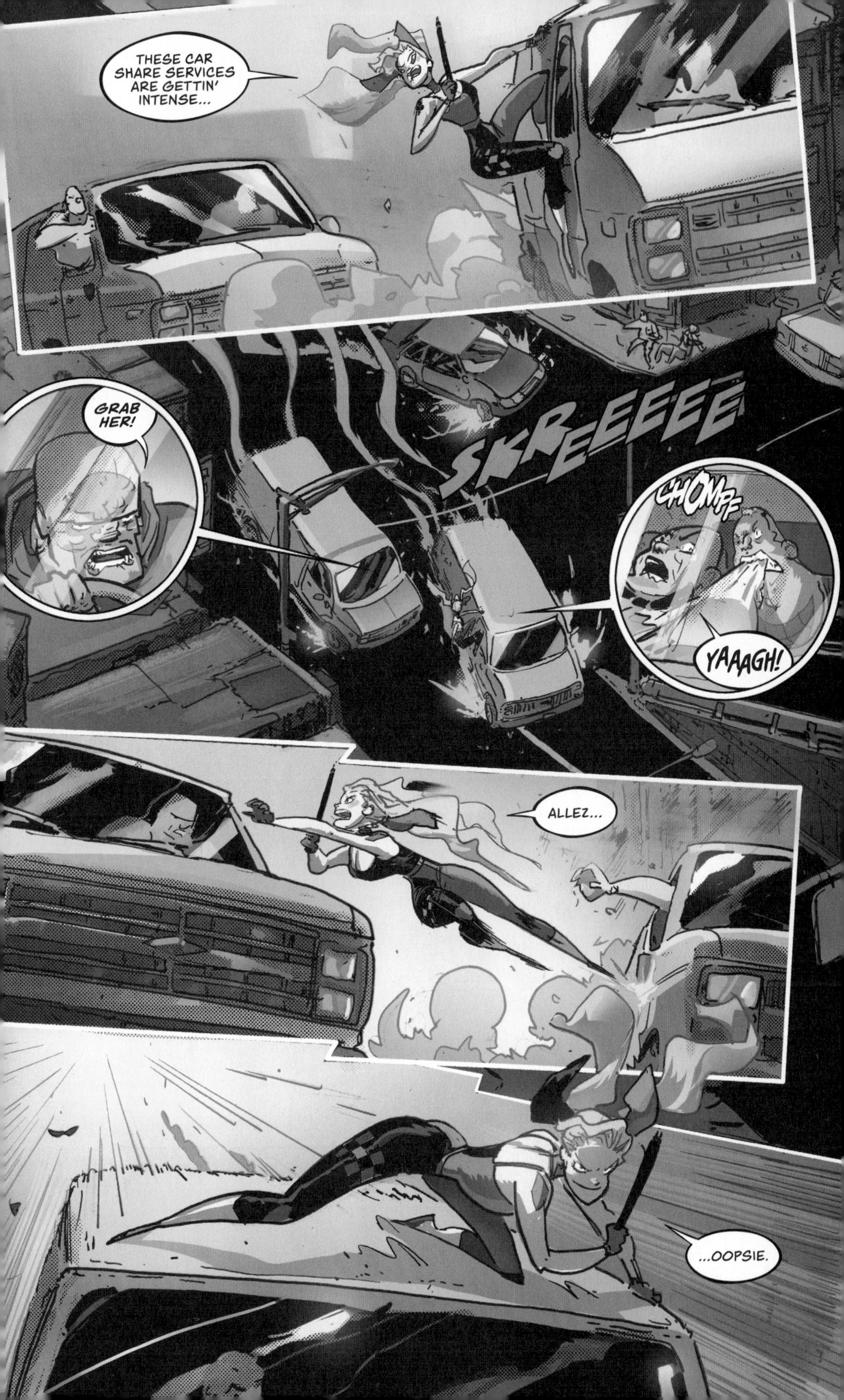
THESE CAR SHARE SERVICES ARE GETTIN' INTENSE...
GRAB HER!
SKREEEEEE
CHOMPF
YAAAGH!
ALLEZ...
...OOPSIE.

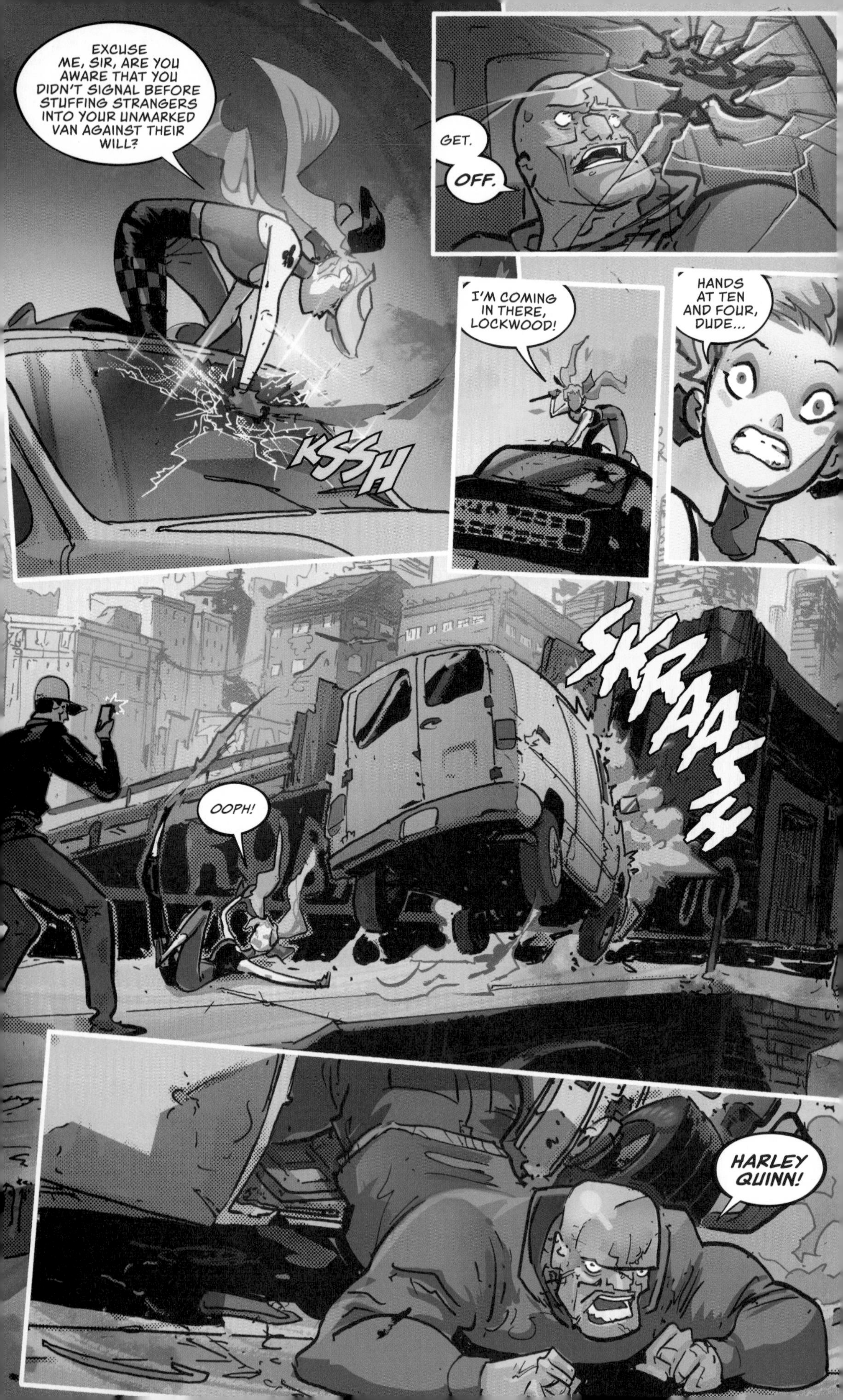
EXCUSE ME, SIR, ARE YOU AWARE THAT YOU DIDN'T SIGNAL BEFORE STUFFING STRANGERS INTO YOUR UNMARKED VAN AGAINST THEIR WILL?
KSSH
GET.
OFF.
I'M COMING IN THERE, LOCKWOOD!
HANDS AT TEN AND FOUR, DUDE...
SKRAASH
OOPH!
HARLEY QUINN!

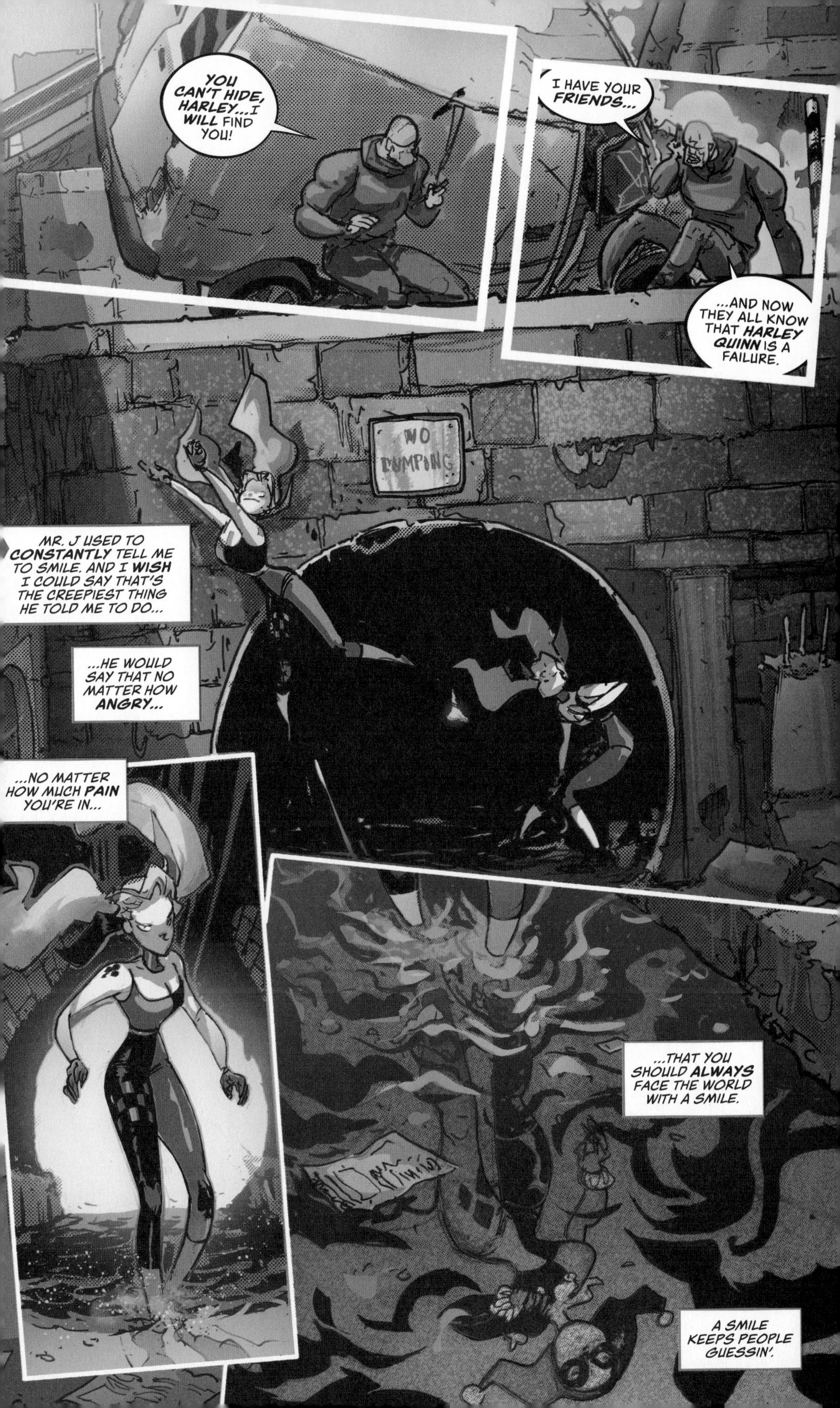

YOU CAN'T HIDE, HARLEY...I WILL FIND YOU!
I HAVE YOUR FRIENDS...
...AND NOW THEY ALL KNOW THAT HARLEY QUINN IS A FAILURE.
NO DUMPING
MR. J USED TO CONSTANTLY TELL ME TO SMILE. AND I WISH I COULD SAY THAT'S THE CREEPIEST THING HE TOLD ME TO DO...
...HE WOULD SAY THAT NO MATTER HOW ANGRY...
...NO MATTER HOW MUCH PAIN YOU'RE IN...
...THAT YOU SHOULD ALWAYS FACE THE WORLD WITH A SMILE.
A SMILE KEEPS PEOPLE GUESSIN'.

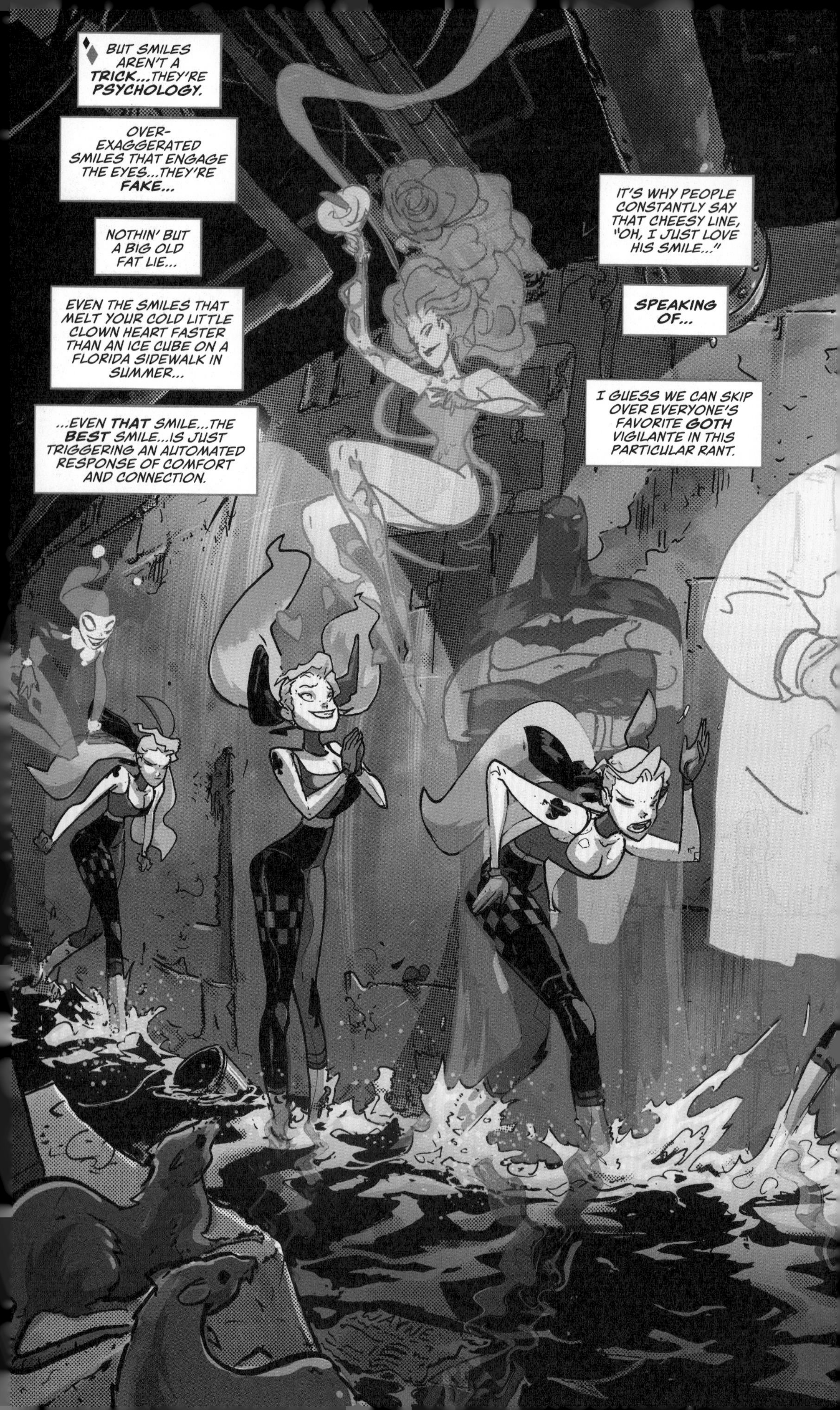
BUT SMILES AREN'T A TRICK...THEY'RE PSYCHOLOGY.
OVER-EXAGGERATED SMILES THAT ENGAGE THE EYES...THEY'RE FAKE...
NOTHIN' BUT A BIG OLD FAT LIE...
EVEN THE SMILES THAT MELT YOUR COLD LITTLE CLOWN HEART FASTER THAN AN ICE CUBE ON A FLORIDA SIDEWALK IN SUMMER...
...EVEN THAT SMILE...THE BEST SMILE...IS JUST TRIGGERING AN AUTOMATED RESPONSE OF COMFORT AND CONNECTION.
IT'S WHY PEOPLE CONSTANTLY SAY THAT CHEESY LINE, "OH, I JUST LOVE HIS SMILE..."
SPEAKING OF...
I GUESS WE CAN SKIP OVER EVERYONE'S FAVORITE GOTH VIGILANTE IN THIS PARTICULAR RANT.

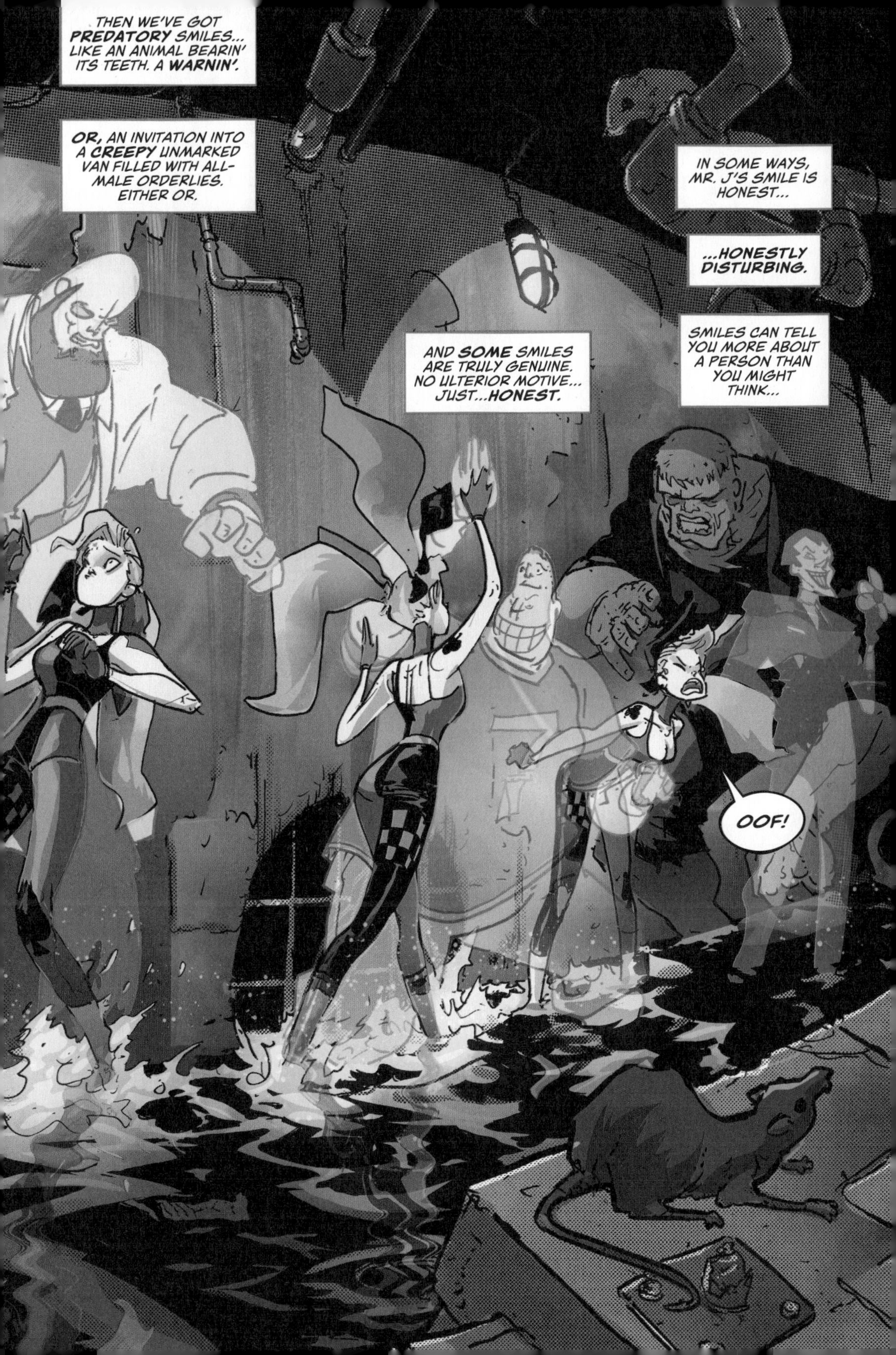
THEN WE'VE GOT PREDATORY SMILES... LIKE AN ANIMAL BEARIN' ITS TEETH. A WARNIN'.
OR, AN INVITATION INTO A CREEPY UNMARKED VAN FILLED WITH ALL-MALE ORDERLIES. EITHER OR.
IN SOME WAYS, MR. J'S SMILE IS HONEST...
...HONESTLY DISTURBING.
AND SOME SMILES ARE TRULY GENUINE. NO ULTERIOR MOTIVE... JUST...HONEST.
SMILES CAN TELL YOU MORE ABOUT A PERSON THAN YOU MIGHT THINK...
OOF!

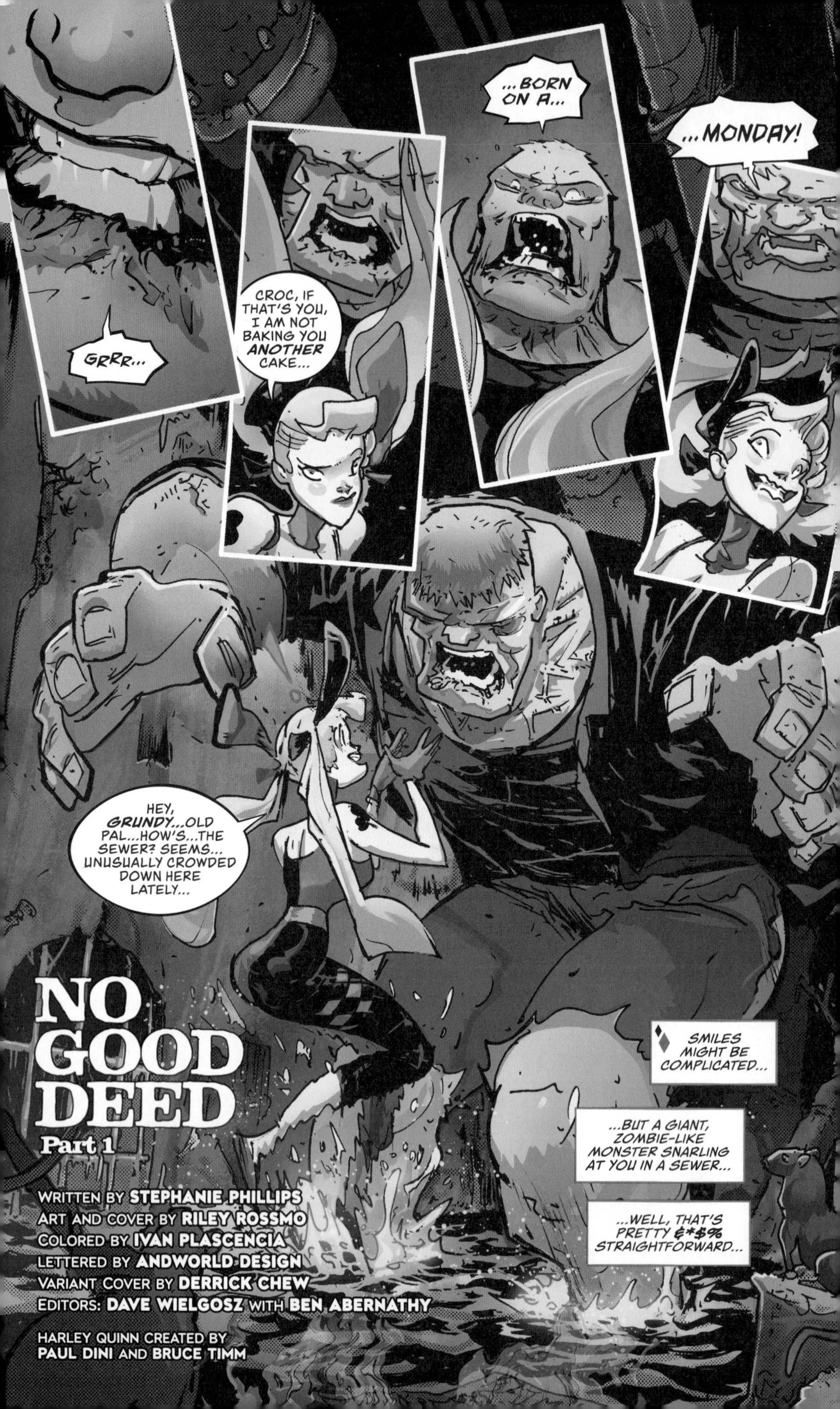
GRRR...
CROC, IF THAT'S YOU, I AM NOT BAKING YOU ANOTHER CAKE...
...BORN ON A...
...MONDAY!
HEY, GRUNDY...OLD PAL...HOW'S...THE SEWER? SEEMS... UNUSUALLY CROWDED DOWN HERE LATELY...
NO GOOD DEED
Part 1
SMILES MIGHT BE COMPLICATED...
...BUT A GIANT, ZOMBIE-LIKE MONSTER SNARLING AT YOU IN A SEWER...
...WELL, THAT'S PRETTY &*$% STRAIGHTFORWARD...
WRITTEN BY STEPHANIE PHILLIPS
ART AND COVER BY RILEY ROSSMO
COLORED BY IVAN PLASCENCIA
LETTERED BY ANDWORLD DESIGN
VARIANT COVER BY DERRICK CHEW
EDITORS: DAVE WIELGOSZ WITH BEN ABERNATHY
HARLEY QUINN CREATED BY PAUL DINI AND BRUCE TIMM

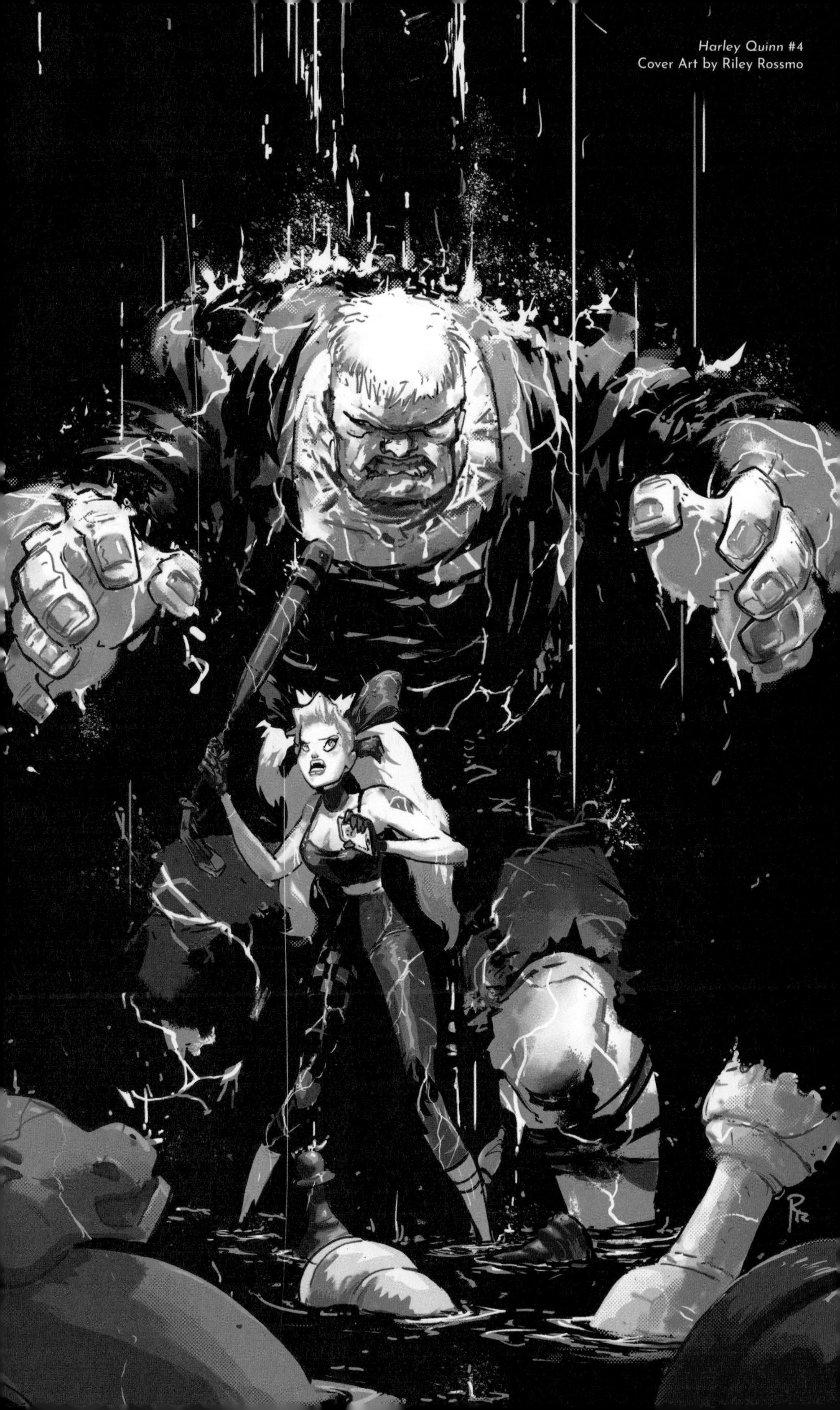

Harley Quinn #4
Cover Art by Riley Rossmo

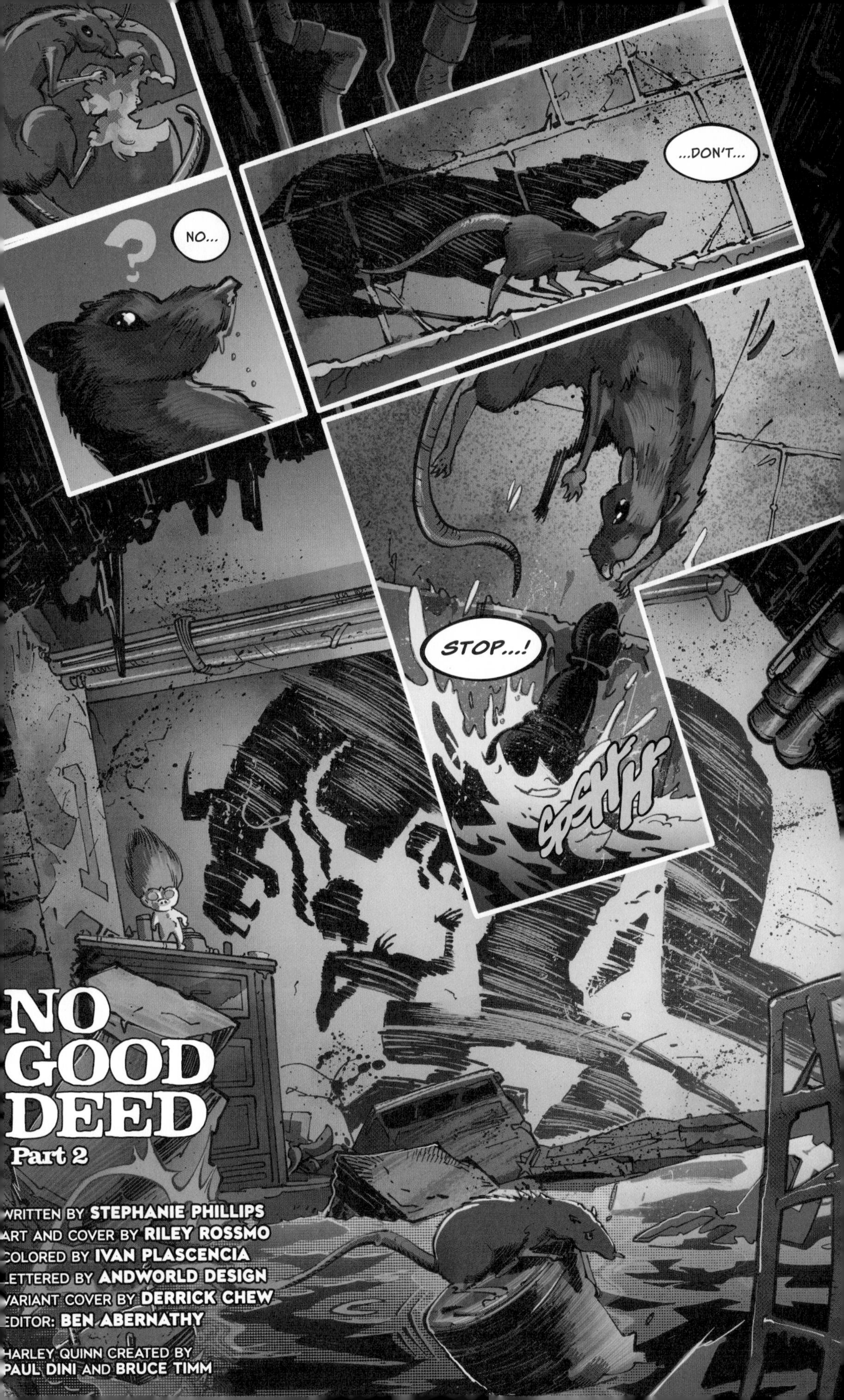
NO...
...DON'T...
STOP...!

NO GOOD DEED
Part 2

WRITTEN BY STEPHANIE PHILLIPS
ART AND COVER BY RILEY ROSSMO
COLORED BY IVAN PLASCENCIA
LETTERED BY ANDWORLD DESIGN
VARIANT COVER BY DERRICK CHEW
EDITOR: BEN ABERNATHY

HARLEY QUINN CREATED BY
PAUL DINI AND BRUCE TIMM

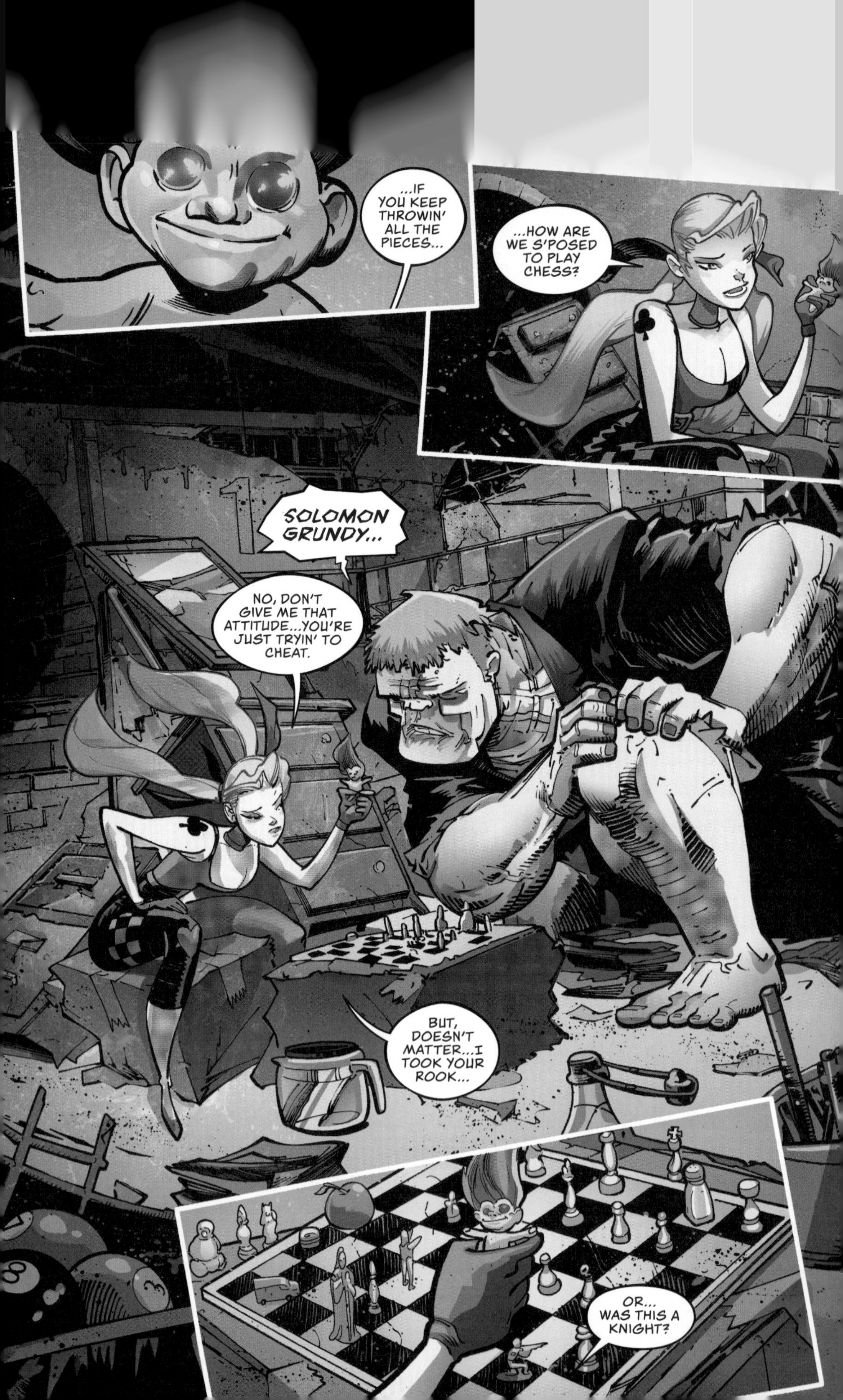
...IF YOU KEEP THROWIN' ALL THE PIECES...
...HOW ARE WE S'POSED TO PLAY CHESS?
SOLOMON GRUNDY...
NO, DON'T GIVE ME THAT ATTITUDE...YOU'RE JUST TRYIN' TO CHEAT.
BUT, DOESN'T MATTER...I TOOK YOUR ROOK...
OR... WAS THIS A KNIGHT?

...BORN ON A MONDAY!

OH PLEASE...

...I AM *NOT* HIDING WITH YOU IN THE SEWER AND PLAYING CHESS WITH LITERAL GARBAGE JUST TO AVOID MY *REAL* ISSUE, WHICH IS THE FACT THAT HUGO STRANGE CLOWN-NAPPED MY FRIEND KEVIN AND A BUNCHA FORMER JOKER CLOWNS...

I'M *DEFINITELY* NOT DOING *THAT.*

BUT...*UH*... SAY I *WAS* HAVIN' SOME ISSUES, S.G....

...SAY I *DID* MESS UP...

...I WOULDN'T EVEN KNOW *HOW* TO START FIXIN' THINGS, OR IF THINGS *CAN* BE FIXED.

I'M NO *BATMAN* OR NOTHIN'. HELL...I DON'T EVEN KNOW IF I'M ONE OF THE *GOOD GUYS* RIGHT NOW...

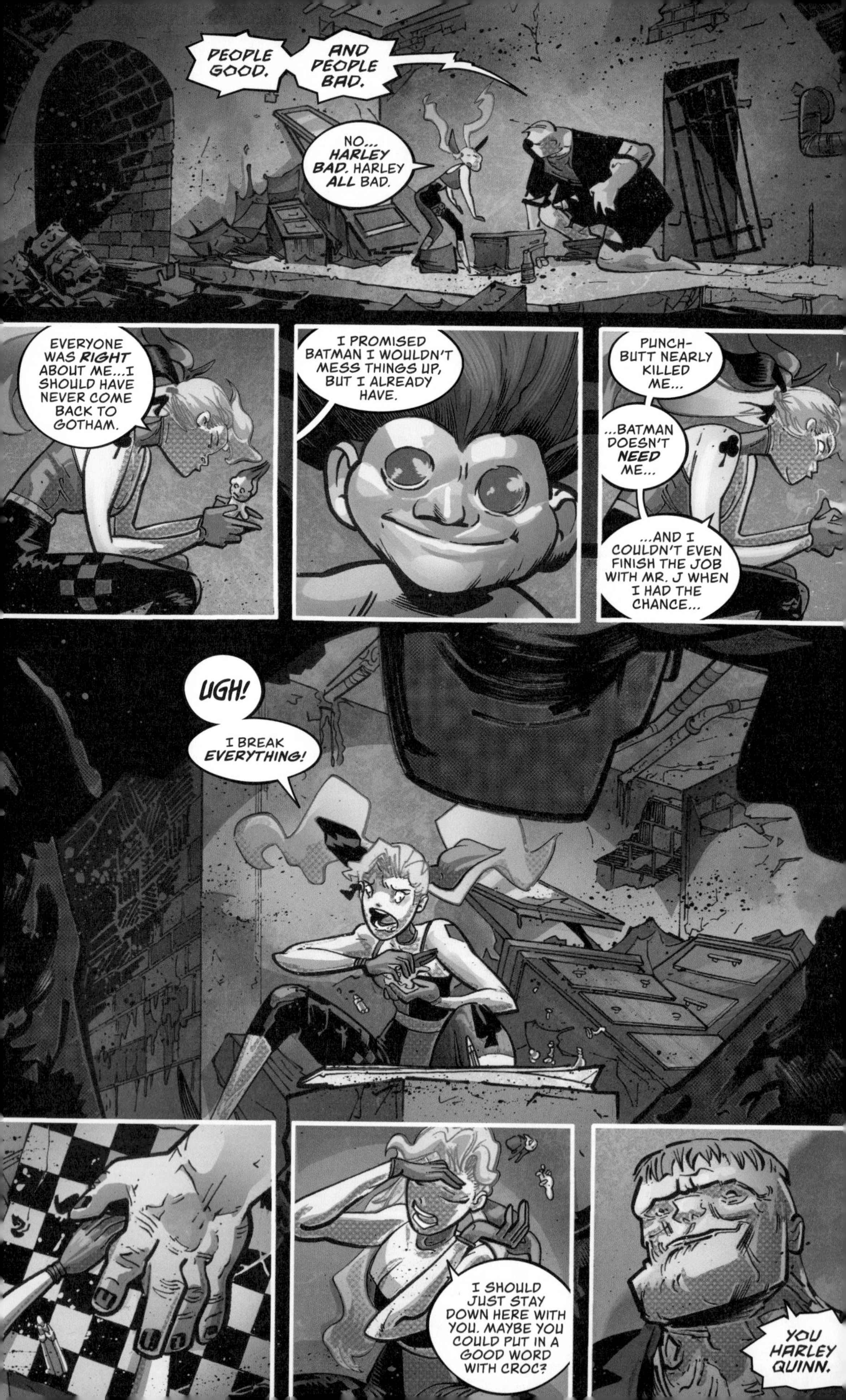
PEOPLE GOOD.
AND PEOPLE BAD.
NO... HARLEY BAD. HARLEY ALL BAD.
EVERYONE WAS RIGHT ABOUT ME...I SHOULD HAVE NEVER COME BACK TO GOTHAM.
I PROMISED BATMAN I WOULDN'T MESS THINGS UP, BUT I ALREADY HAVE.
PUNCH-BUTT NEARLY KILLED ME...
...BATMAN DOESN'T NEED ME...
...AND I COULDN'T EVEN FINISH THE JOB WITH MR. J WHEN I HAD THE CHANCE...
UGH!
I BREAK EVERYTHING!
I SHOULD JUST STAY DOWN HERE WITH YOU. MAYBE YOU COULD PUT IN A GOOD WORD WITH CROC?
YOU HARLEY QUINN.

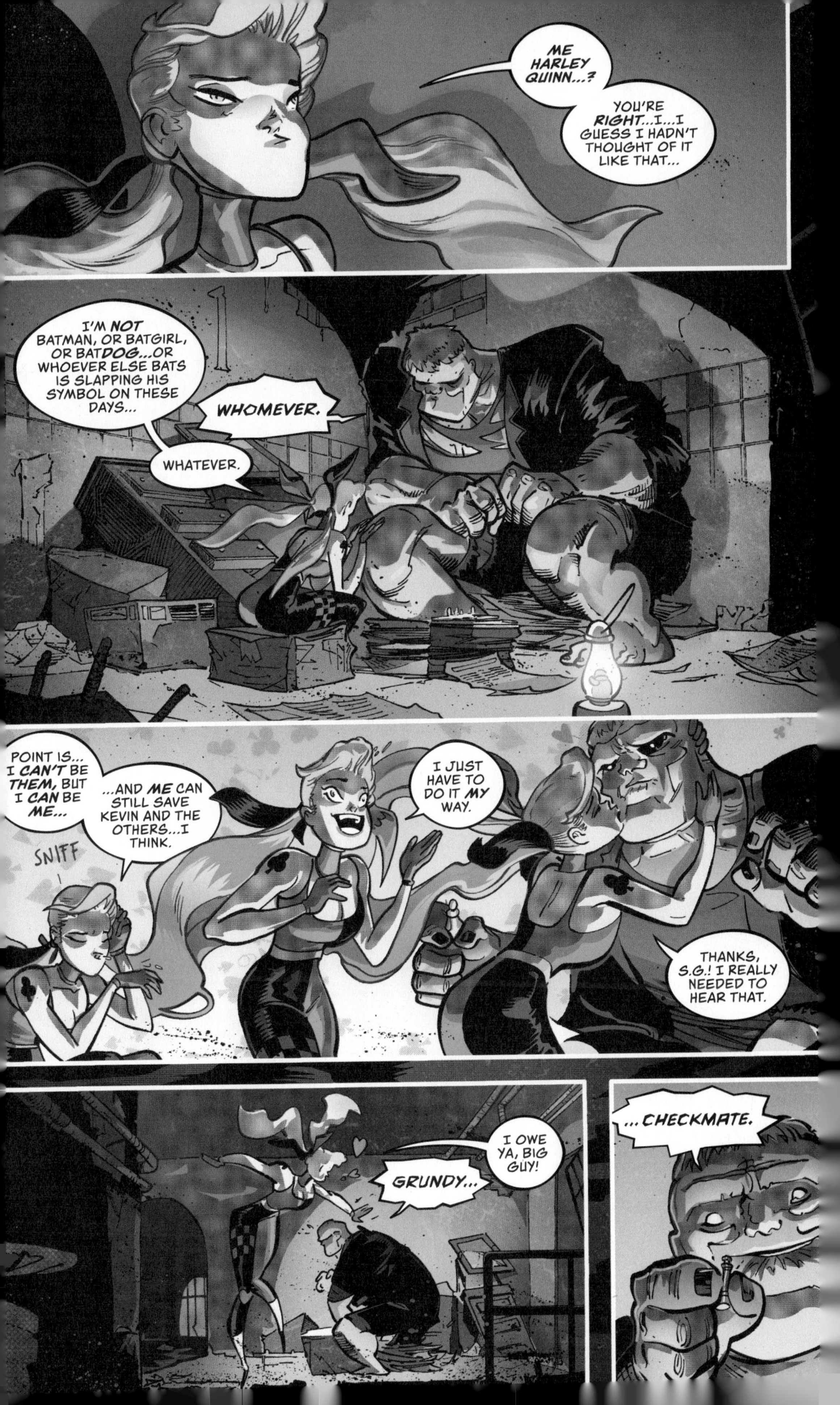

ME HARLEY QUINN...?
YOU'RE RIGHT...I...I GUESS I HADN'T THOUGHT OF IT LIKE THAT...
I'M NOT BATMAN, OR BATGIRL, OR BATDOG...OR WHOEVER ELSE BATS IS SLAPPING HIS SYMBOL ON THESE DAYS...
WHOMEVER.
WHATEVER.
POINT IS... I CAN'T BE THEM, BUT I CAN BE ME...
...AND ME CAN STILL SAVE KEVIN AND THE OTHERS...I THINK.
SNIFF
I JUST HAVE TO DO IT MY WAY.
THANKS, S.G.! I REALLY NEEDED TO HEAR THAT.
I OWE YA, BIG GUY!
GRUNDY...
...CHECKMATE.

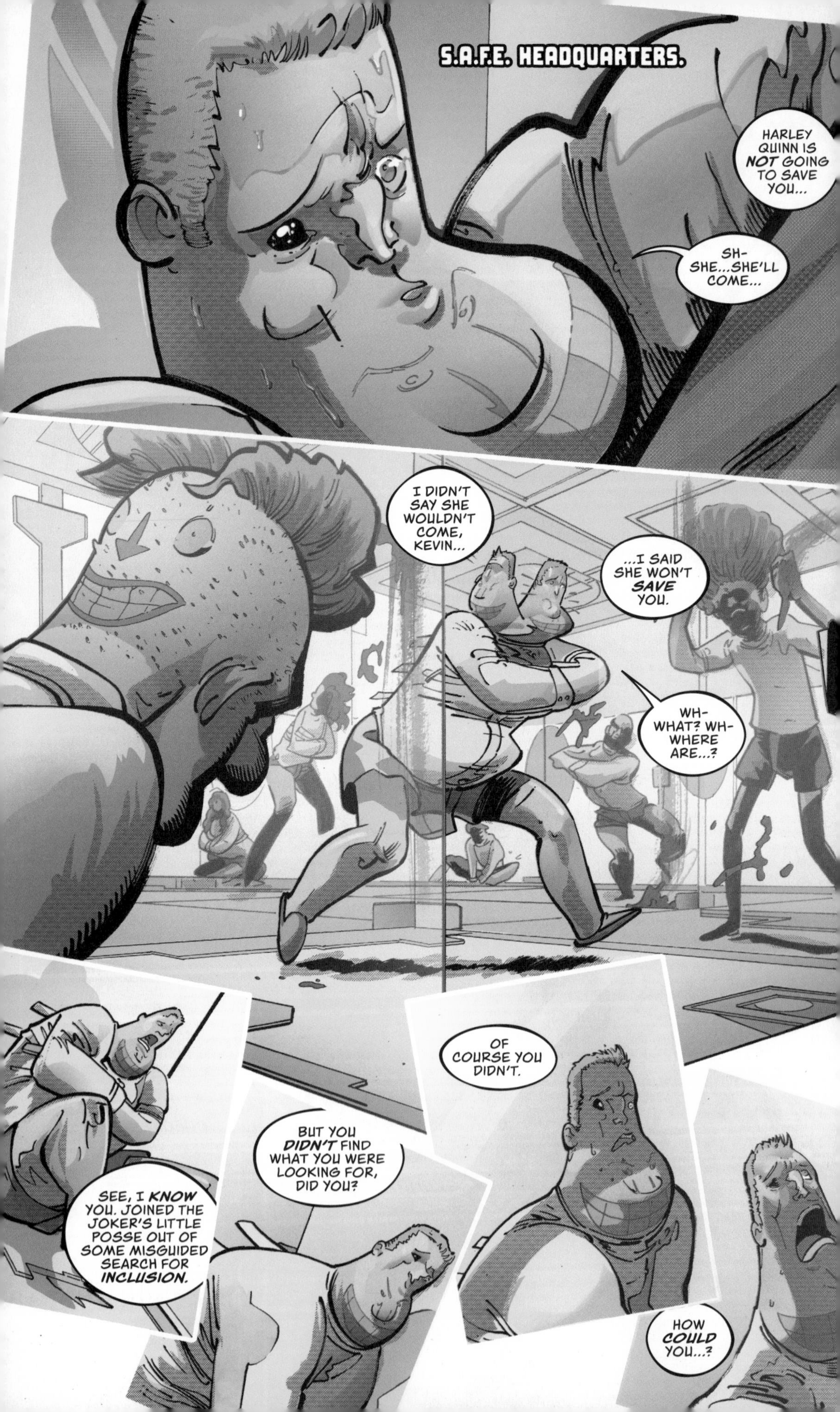
S.A.F.E. HEADQUARTERS.
HARLEY QUINN IS *NOT* GOING TO SAVE YOU...
SH- SHE...SHE'LL COME...
I DIDN'T SAY SHE WOULDN'T COME, KEVIN...
...I SAID SHE WON'T *SAVE* YOU.
WH- WHAT? WH- WHERE ARE...?
OF COURSE YOU DIDN'T.
SEE, I *KNOW* YOU. JOINED THE JOKER'S LITTLE POSSE OUT OF SOME MISGUIDED SEARCH FOR *INCLUSION.*
BUT YOU *DIDN'T* FIND WHAT YOU WERE LOOKING FOR, DID YOU?
HOW *COULD* YOU...?

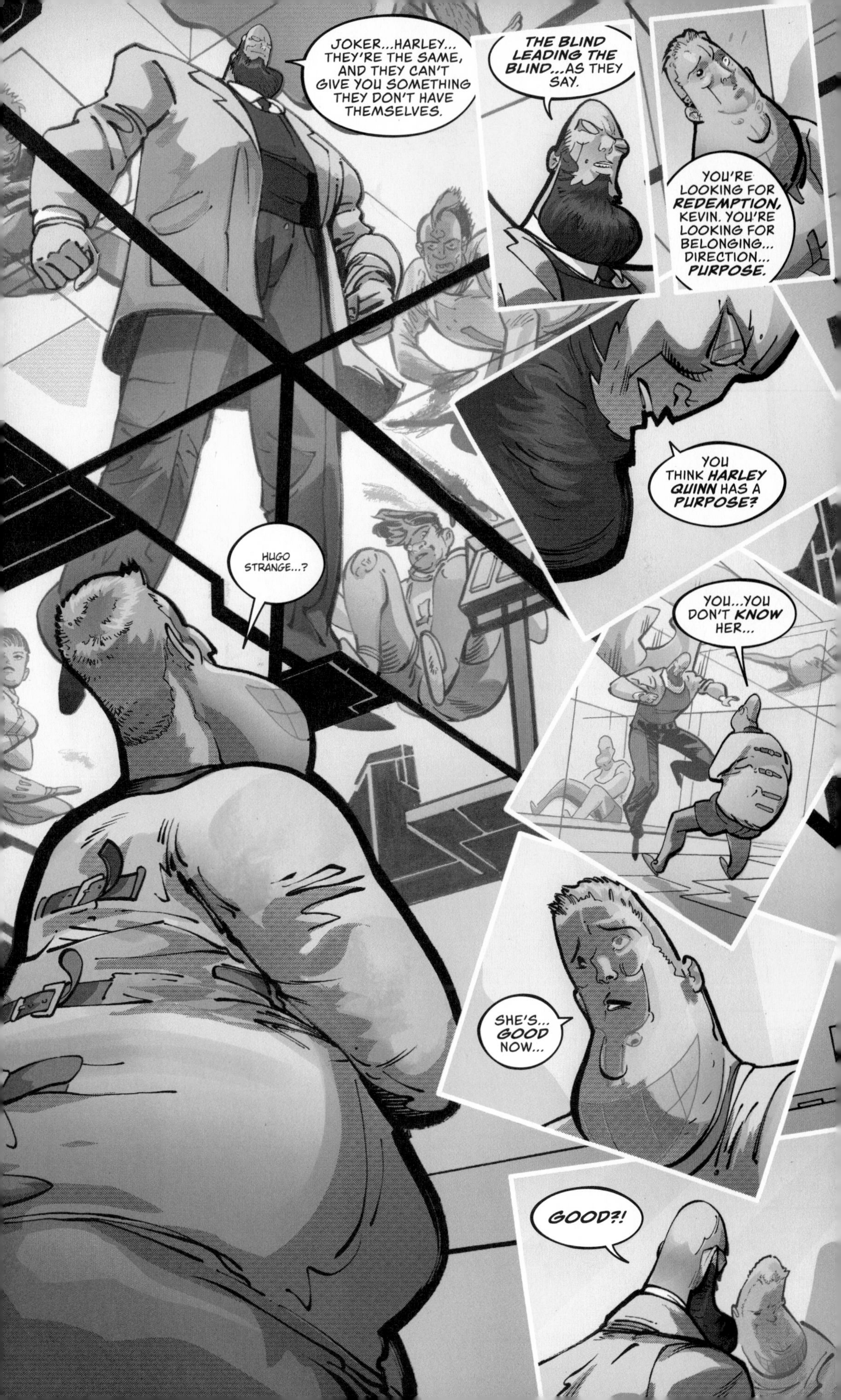

JOKER...HARLEY... THEY'RE THE SAME, AND THEY CAN'T GIVE YOU SOMETHING THEY DON'T HAVE THEMSELVES.
THE BLIND LEADING THE BLIND...AS THEY SAY.
YOU'RE LOOKING FOR REDEMPTION, KEVIN. YOU'RE LOOKING FOR BELONGING... DIRECTION... PURPOSE.
YOU THINK HARLEY QUINN HAS A PURPOSE?
HUGO STRANGE...?
YOU...YOU DON'T KNOW HER...
SHE'S... GOOD NOW...
GOOD?!

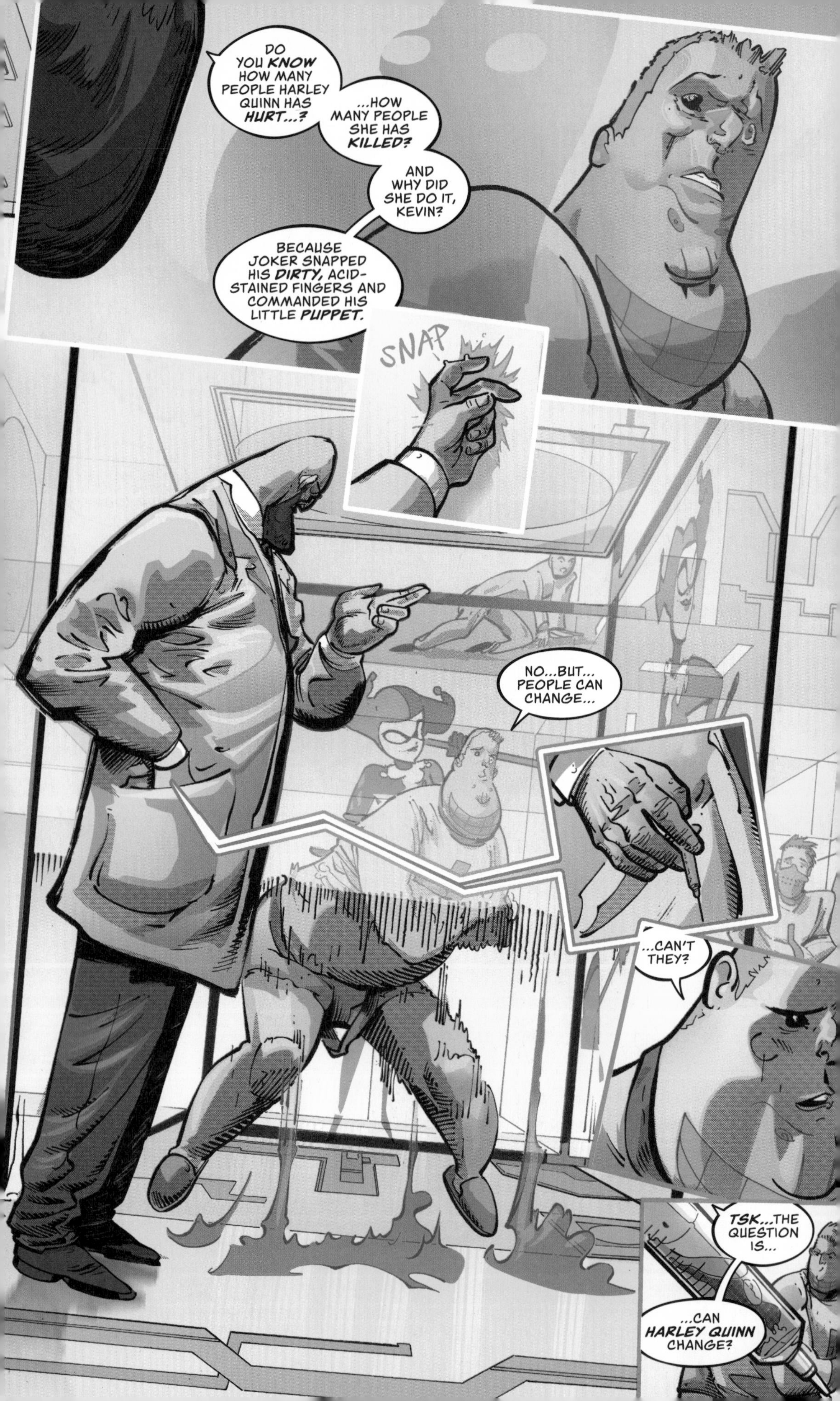
DO YOU **KNOW** HOW MANY PEOPLE HARLEY QUINN HAS **HURT...?**
...HOW MANY PEOPLE SHE HAS **KILLED?**
AND WHY DID SHE DO IT, KEVIN?
BECAUSE JOKER SNAPPED HIS **DIRTY,** ACID-STAINED FINGERS AND COMMANDED HIS LITTLE **PUPPET.**
SNAP
NO...BUT... PEOPLE CAN CHANGE...
...CAN'T THEY?
TSK...THE QUESTION IS...
...CAN **HARLEY QUINN** CHANGE?

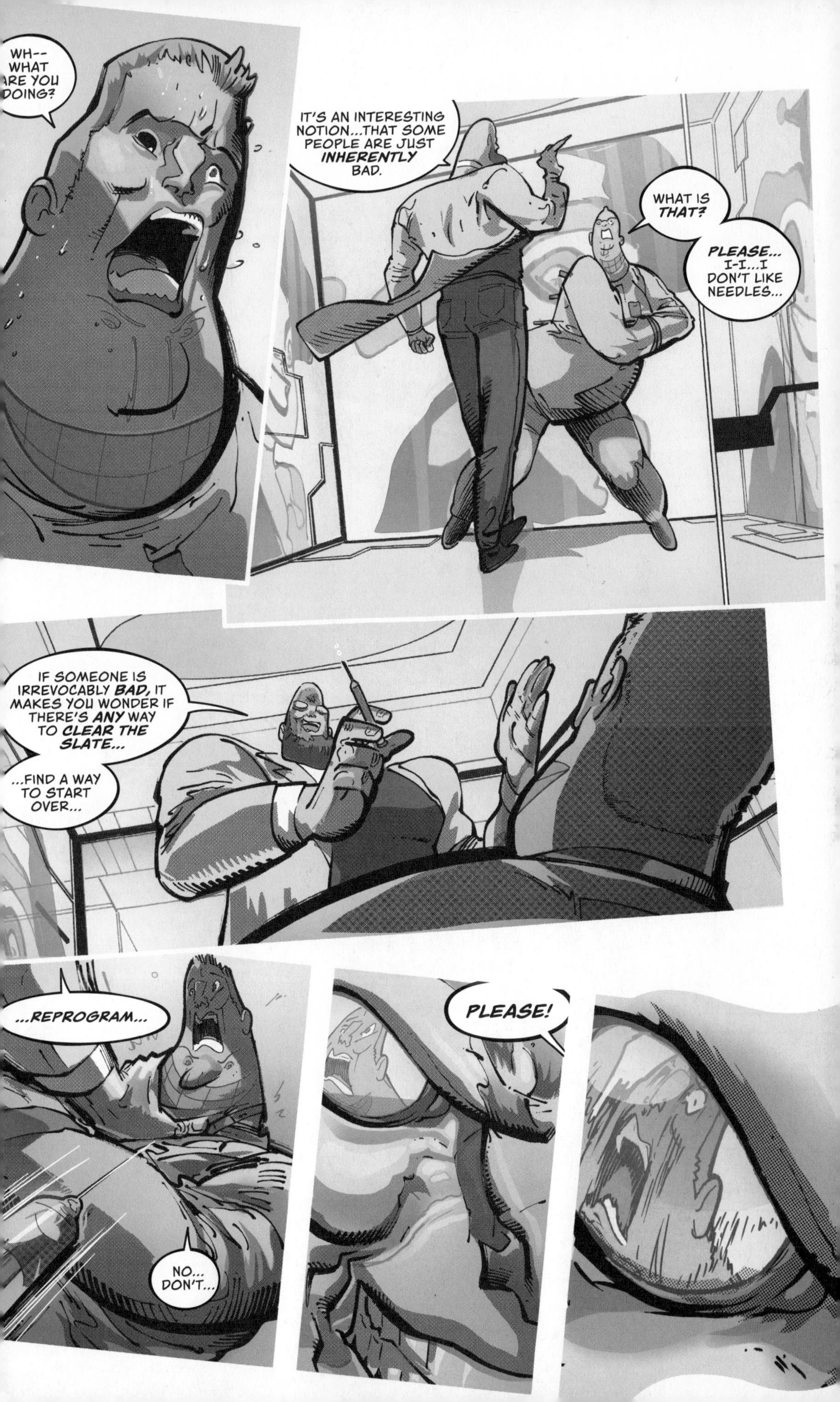

WH-- WHAT ARE YOU DOING?
IT'S AN INTERESTING NOTION...THAT SOME PEOPLE ARE JUST INHERENTLY BAD.
WHAT IS THAT?
PLEASE... I-I...I DON'T LIKE NEEDLES...
IF SOMEONE IS IRREVOCABLY BAD, IT MAKES YOU WONDER IF THERE'S ANY WAY TO CLEAR THE SLATE...
...FIND A WAY TO START OVER...
...REPROGRAM...
NO... DON'T...
PLEASE!

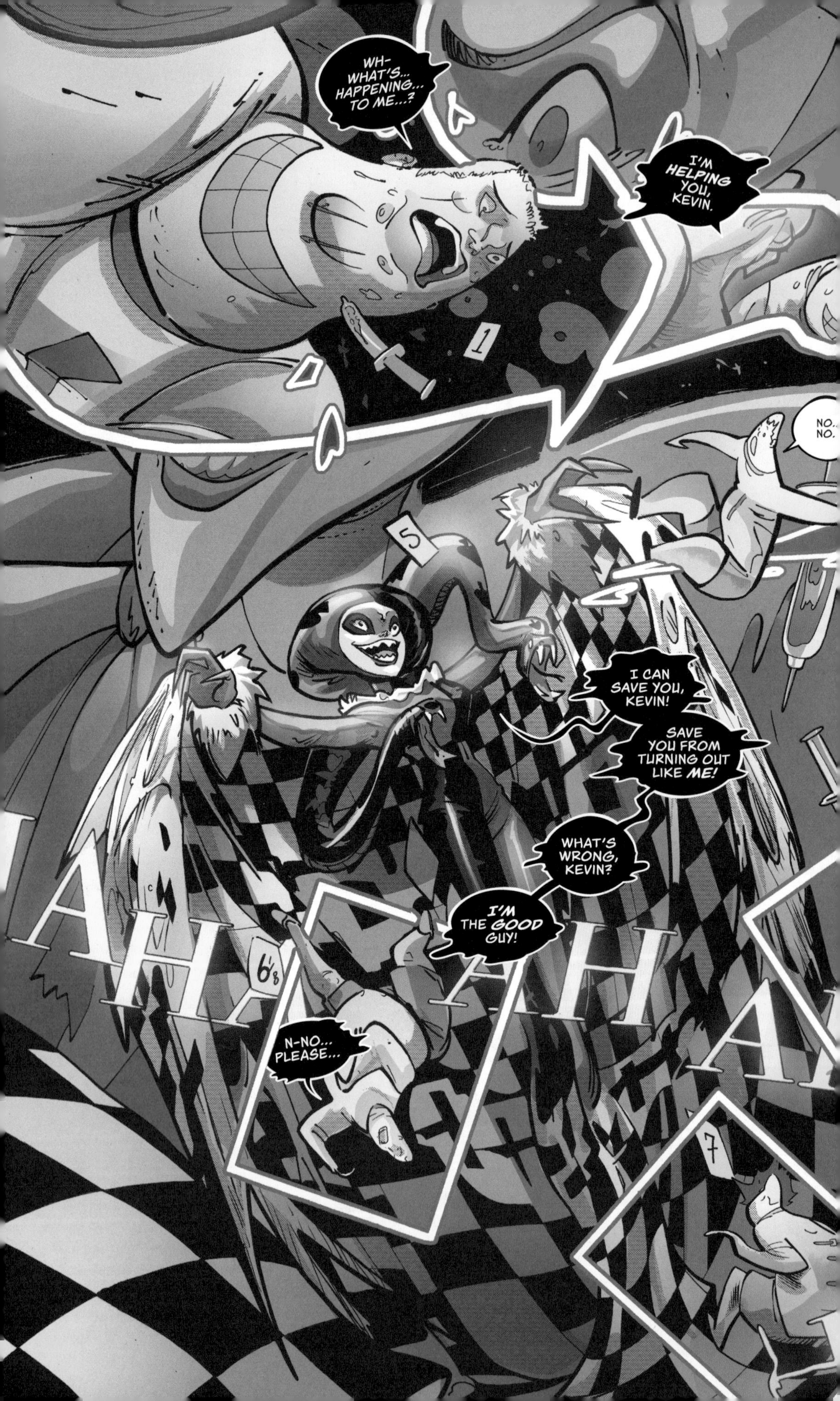

WH- WHAT'S... HAPPENING... TO ME...?
I'M HELPING YOU, KEVIN.
NO... NO.
I CAN SAVE YOU, KEVIN!
SAVE YOU FROM TURNING OUT LIKE ME!
WHAT'S WRONG, KEVIN?
I'M THE GOOD GUY!
N-NO... PLEASE...

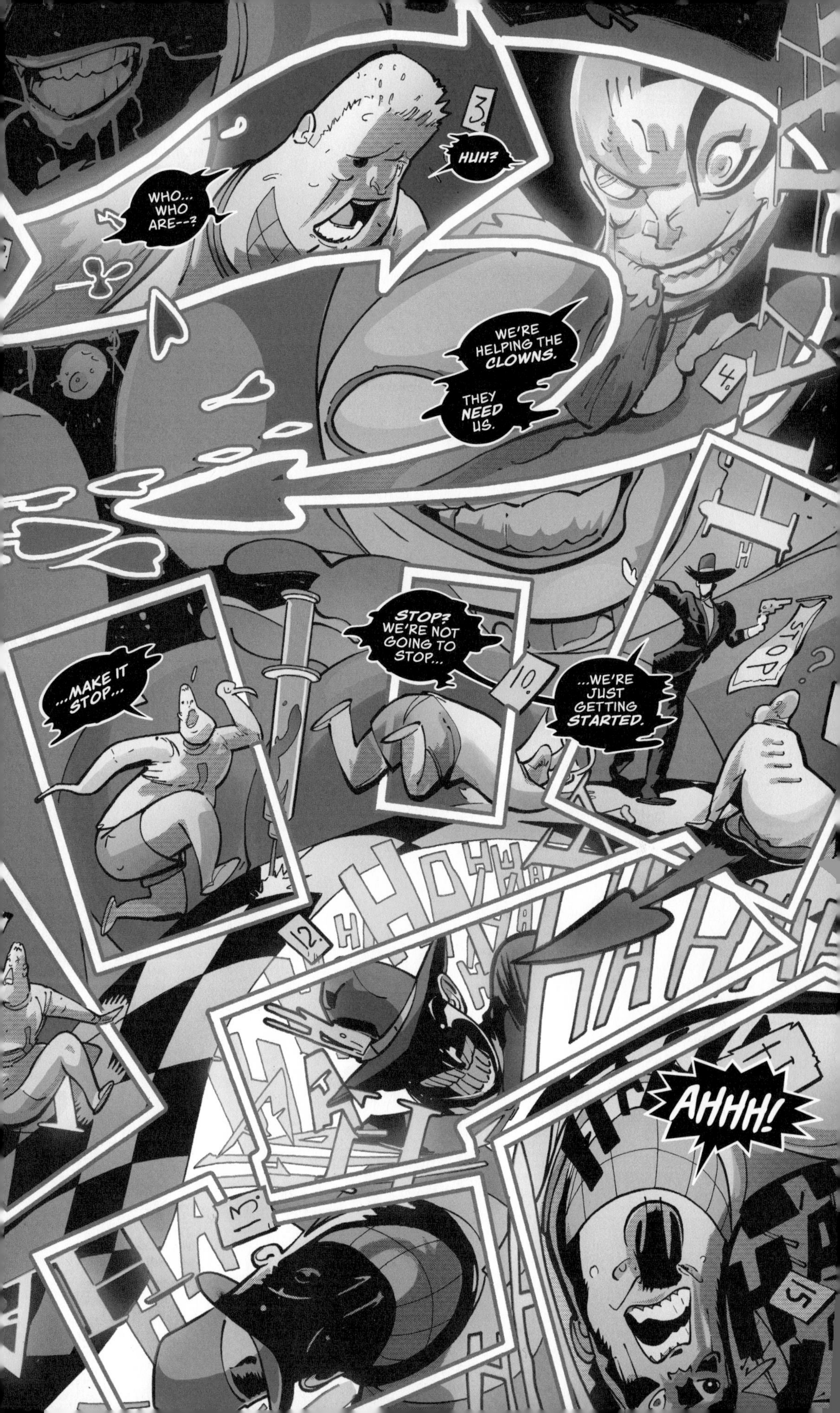
HUH?
WHO... WHO ARE--?
WE'RE HELPING THE CLOWNS.
THEY NEED US.
...MAKE IT STOP...
STOP? WE'RE NOT GOING TO STOP...
...WE'RE JUST GETTING STARTED.
AHHH!

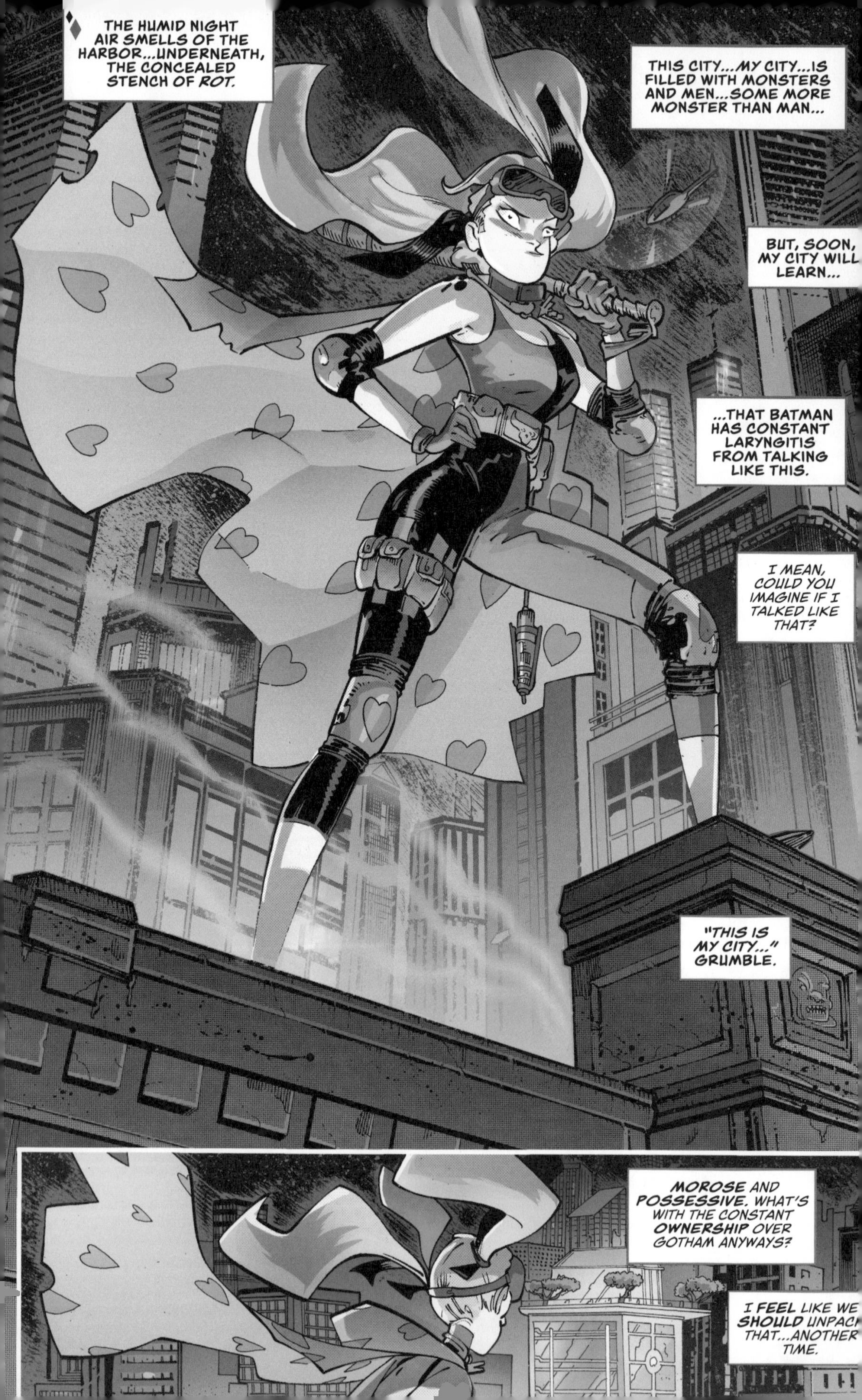
THE HUMID NIGHT AIR SMELLS OF THE HARBOR...UNDERNEATH, THE CONCEALED STENCH OF *ROT*.
THIS CITY...*MY CITY*...IS FILLED WITH MONSTERS AND MEN...SOME MORE MONSTER THAN MAN...
BUT, SOON, MY CITY WILL LEARN...
...THAT BATMAN HAS CONSTANT LARYNGITIS FROM TALKING LIKE THIS.
I MEAN, COULD YOU IMAGINE IF I TALKED LIKE THAT?
"THIS IS MY CITY..." GRUMBLE.
MOROSE AND POSSESSIVE. WHAT'S WITH THE CONSTANT OWNERSHIP OVER GOTHAM ANYWAYS?
I FEEL LIKE WE SHOULD UNPAC THAT...ANOTHER TIME.

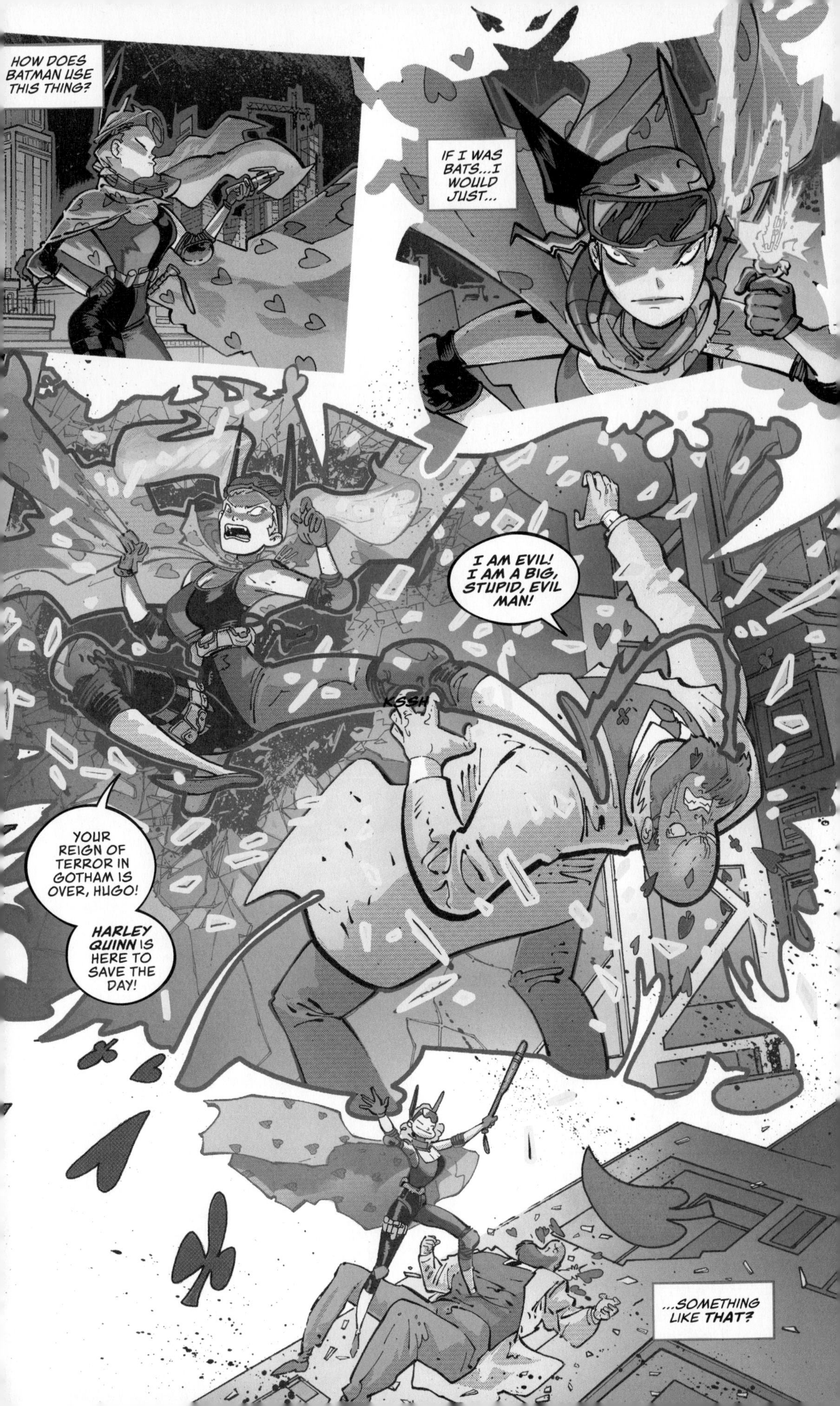
HOW DOES BATMAN USE THIS THING?
IF I WAS BATS...I WOULD JUST...
I AM EVIL! I AM A BIG, STUPID, EVIL MAN!
KSSH
YOUR REIGN OF TERROR IN GOTHAM IS OVER, HUGO!
HARLEY QUINN IS HERE TO SAVE THE DAY!
...SOMETHING LIKE THAT?

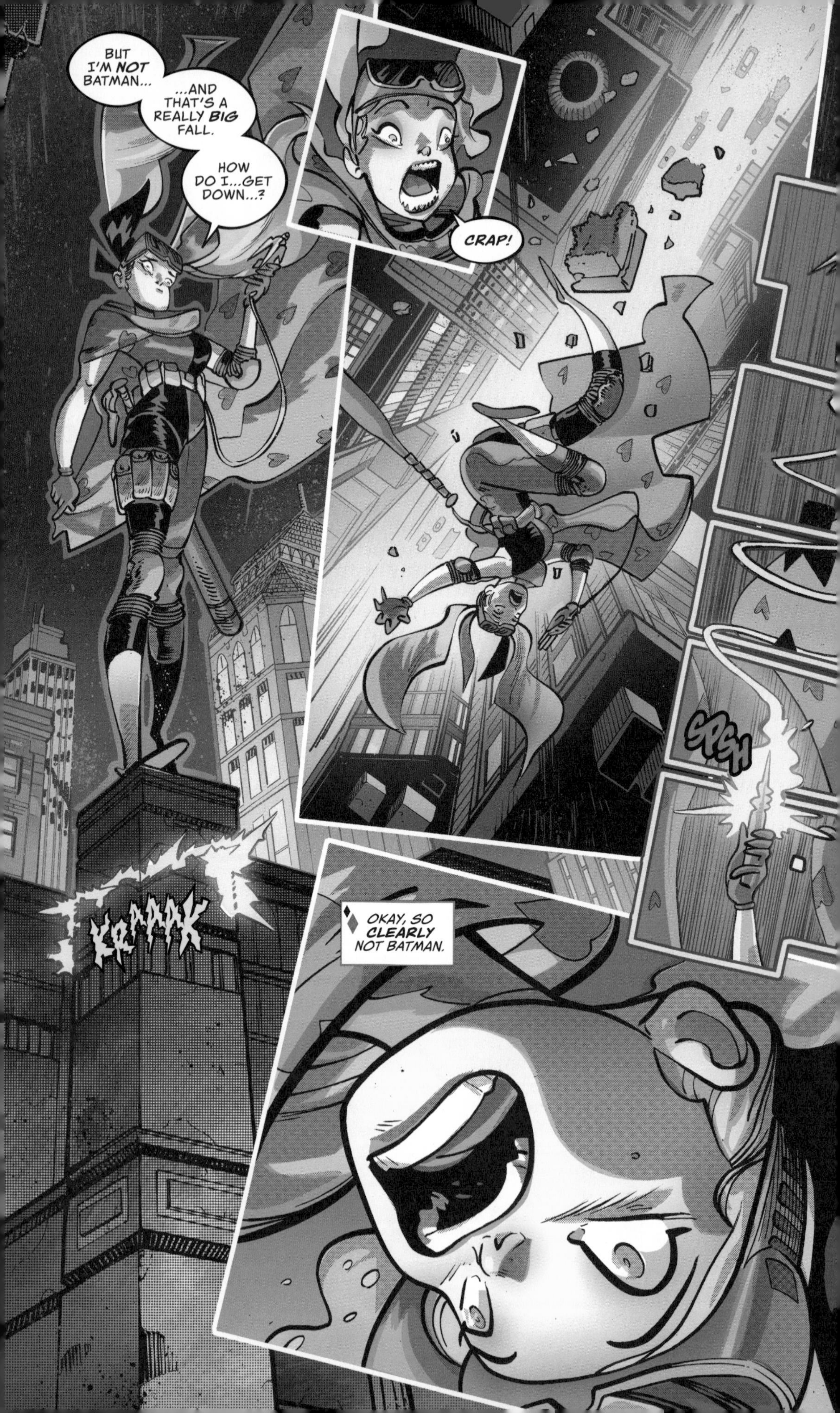
BUT I'M NOT BATMAN...
...AND THAT'S A REALLY BIG FALL.
HOW DO I...GET DOWN...?
CRAP!
KRAAAK
SPSH
OKAY, SO CLEARLY NOT BATMAN.

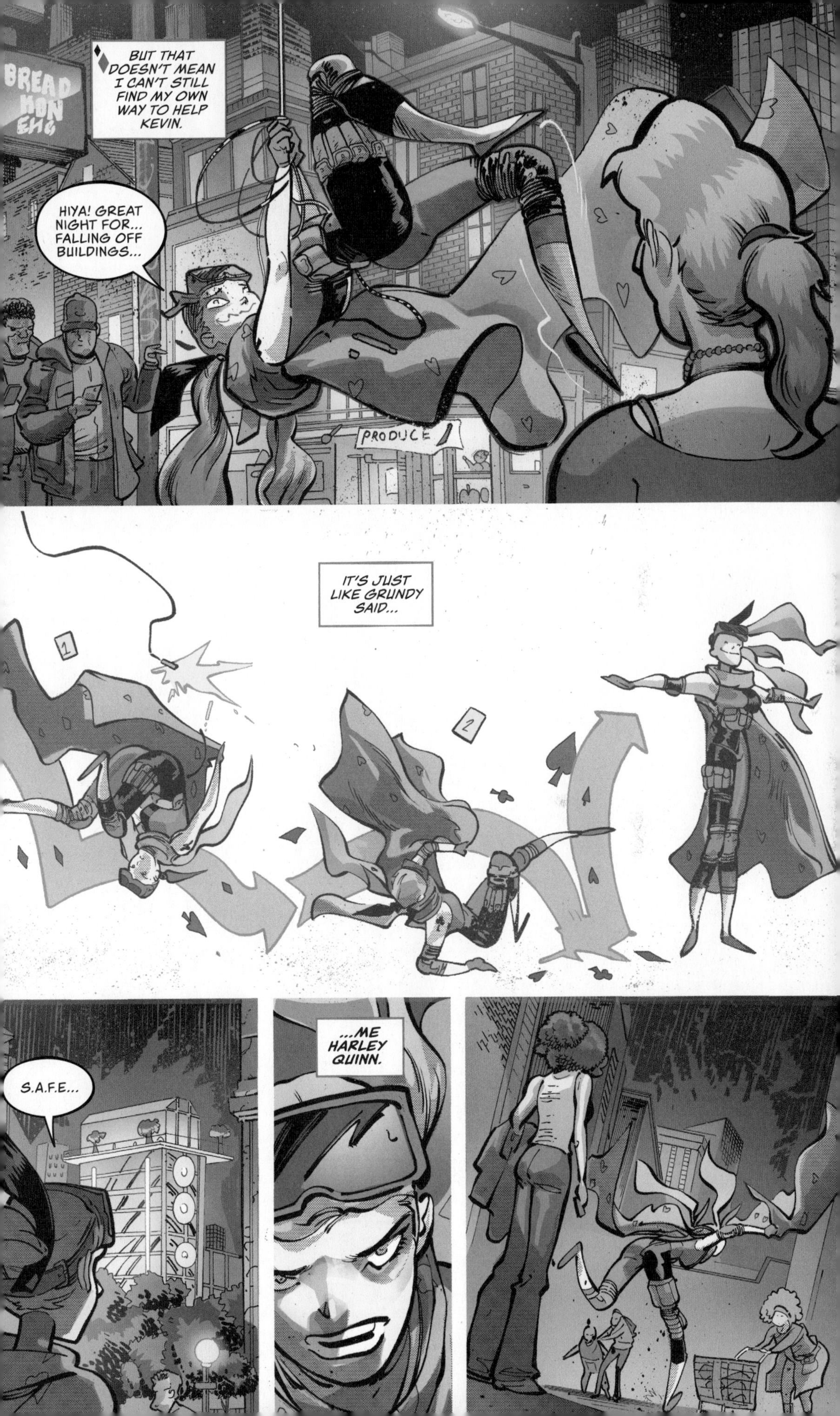
BREAD HON
BUT THAT DOESN'T MEAN I CAN'T STILL FIND MY OWN WAY TO HELP KEVIN.
HIYA! GREAT NIGHT FOR... FALLING OFF BUILDINGS...
PRODUCE
IT'S JUST LIKE GRUNDY SAID...
1
2
S.A.F.E...
...ME HARLEY QUINN.

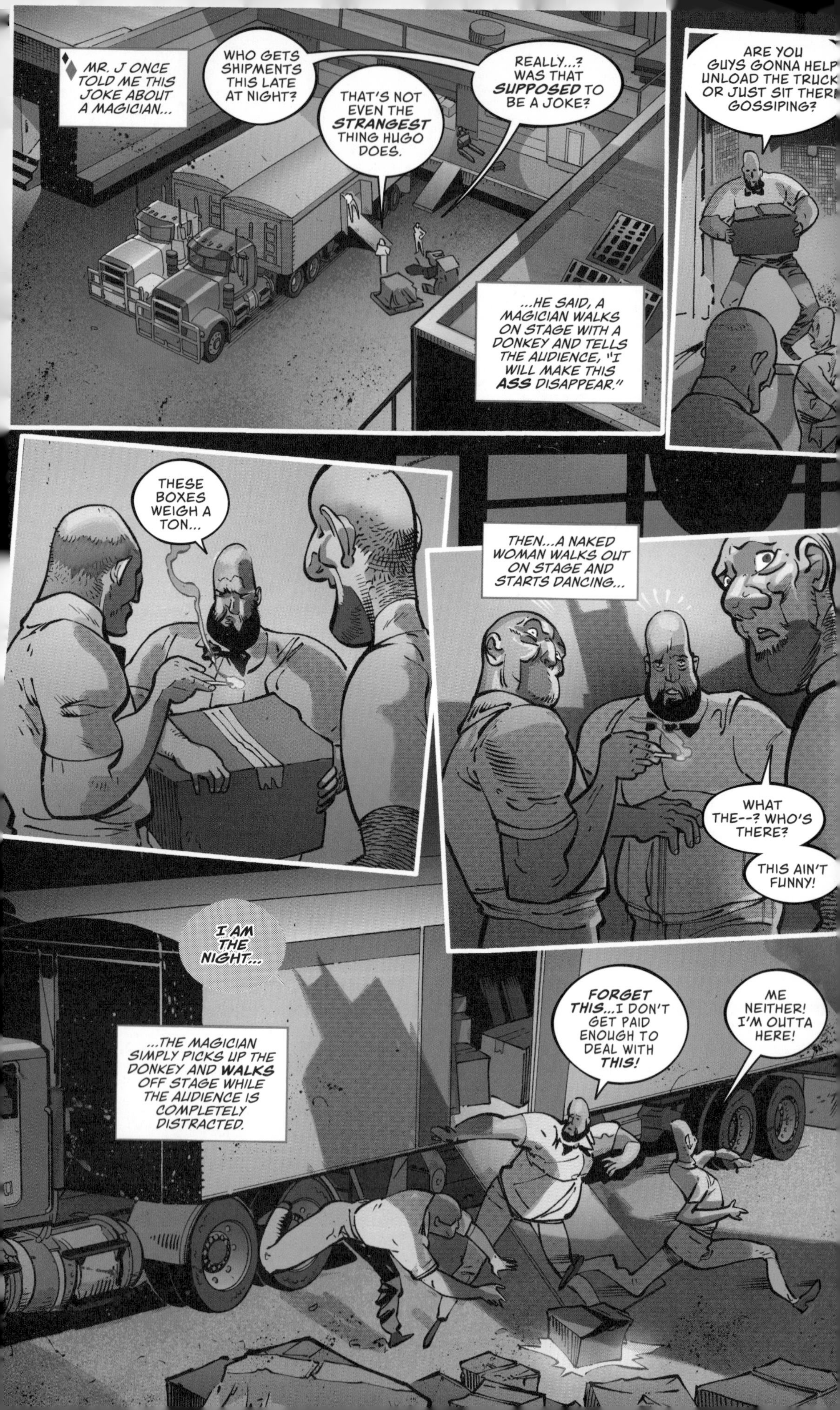

MR. J ONCE TOLD ME THIS JOKE ABOUT A MAGICIAN...
WHO GETS SHIPMENTS THIS LATE AT NIGHT?
THAT'S NOT EVEN THE STRANGEST THING HUGO DOES.
REALLY...? WAS THAT SUPPOSED TO BE A JOKE?
...HE SAID, A MAGICIAN WALKS ON STAGE WITH A DONKEY AND TELLS THE AUDIENCE, "I WILL MAKE THIS ASS DISAPPEAR."
ARE YOU GUYS GONNA HELP UNLOAD THE TRUCK OR JUST SIT THERE GOSSIPING?
THESE BOXES WEIGH A TON...
THEN...A NAKED WOMAN WALKS OUT ON STAGE AND STARTS DANCING...
WHAT THE--? WHO'S THERE?
THIS AIN'T FUNNY!
I AM THE NIGHT...
...THE MAGICIAN SIMPLY PICKS UP THE DONKEY AND WALKS OFF STAGE WHILE THE AUDIENCE IS COMPLETELY DISTRACTED.
FORGET THIS...I DON'T GET PAID ENOUGH TO DEAL WITH THIS!
ME NEITHER! I'M OUTTA HERE!

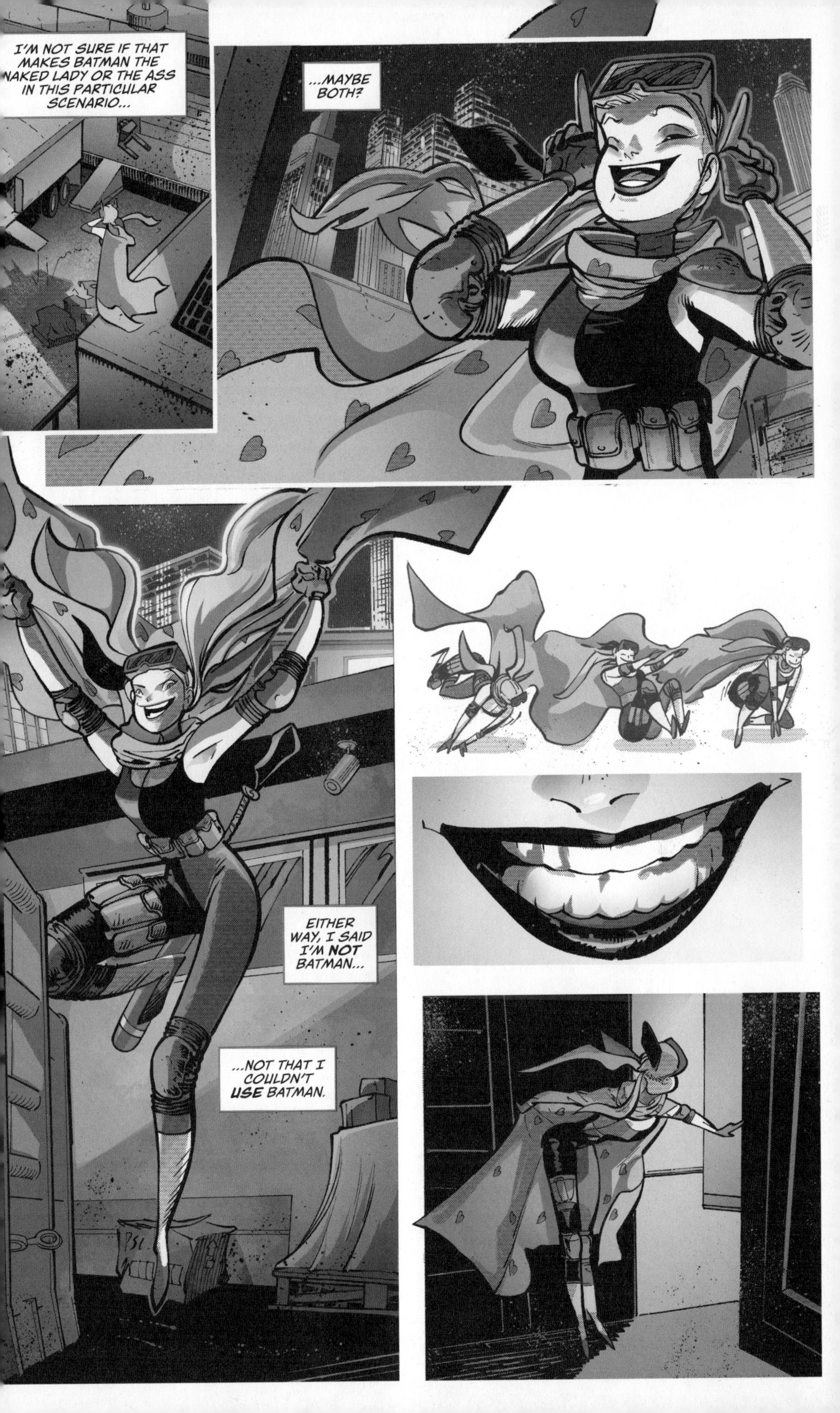
I'M NOT SURE IF THAT MAKES BATMAN THE NAKED LADY OR THE ASS IN THIS PARTICULAR SCENARIO...
...MAYBE BOTH?
EITHER WAY, I SAID I'M NOT BATMAN...
...NOT THAT I COULDN'T USE BATMAN.

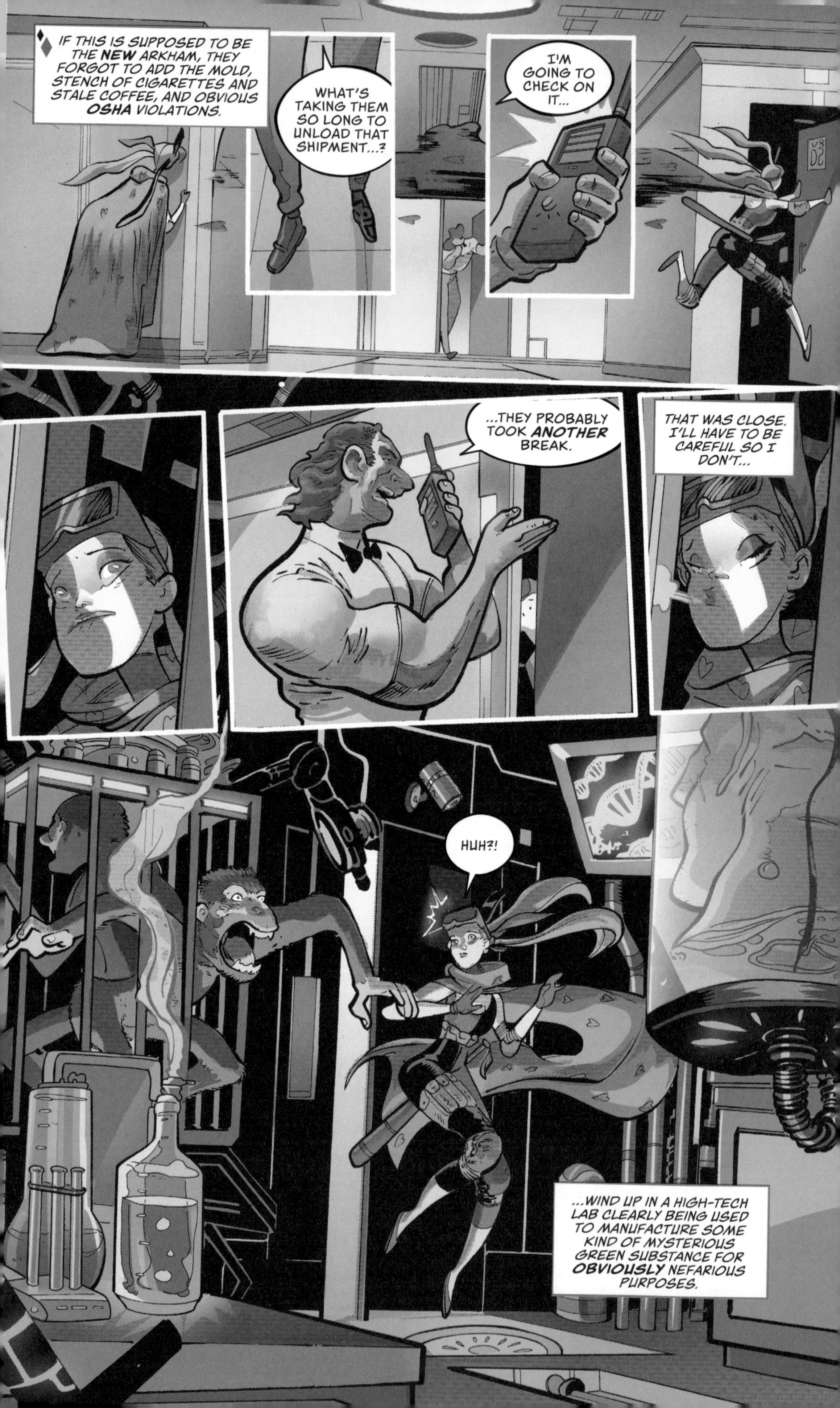
IF THIS IS SUPPOSED TO BE THE NEW ARKHAM, THEY FORGOT TO ADD THE MOLD, STENCH OF CIGARETTES AND STALE COFFEE, AND OBVIOUS OSHA VIOLATIONS.
WHAT'S TAKING THEM SO LONG TO UNLOAD THAT SHIPMENT...?
I'M GOING TO CHECK ON IT...
...THEY PROBABLY TOOK ANOTHER BREAK.
THAT WAS CLOSE. I'LL HAVE TO BE CAREFUL SO I DON'T...
HUH?!
...WIND UP IN A HIGH-TECH LAB CLEARLY BEING USED TO MANUFACTURE SOME KIND OF MYSTERIOUS GREEN SUBSTANCE FOR OBVIOUSLY NEFARIOUS PURPOSES.

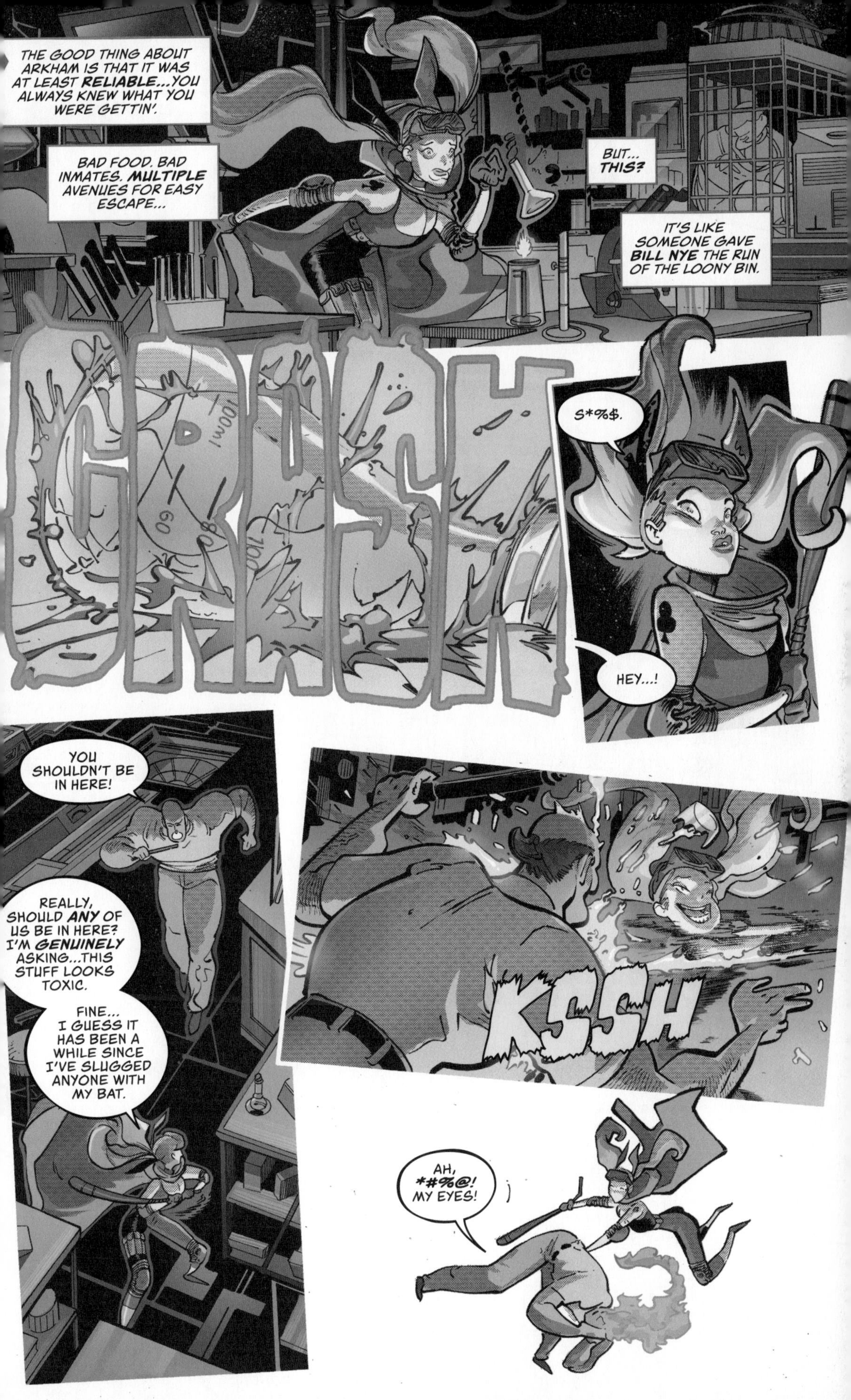
THE GOOD THING ABOUT ARKHAM IS THAT IT WAS AT LEAST RELIABLE...YOU ALWAYS KNEW WHAT YOU WERE GETTIN'.
BAD FOOD. BAD INMATES. MULTIPLE AVENUES FOR EASY ESCAPE...
BUT... THIS?
IT'S LIKE SOMEONE GAVE BILL NYE THE RUN OF THE LOONY BIN.
CRASH
100ml
S*%$.
HEY...!
YOU SHOULDN'T BE IN HERE!
REALLY, SHOULD ANY OF US BE IN HERE? I'M GENUINELY ASKING...THIS STUFF LOOKS TOXIC.
FINE... I GUESS IT HAS BEEN A WHILE SINCE I'VE SLUGGED ANYONE WITH MY BAT.
KSSH
AH, *#%@! MY EYES!

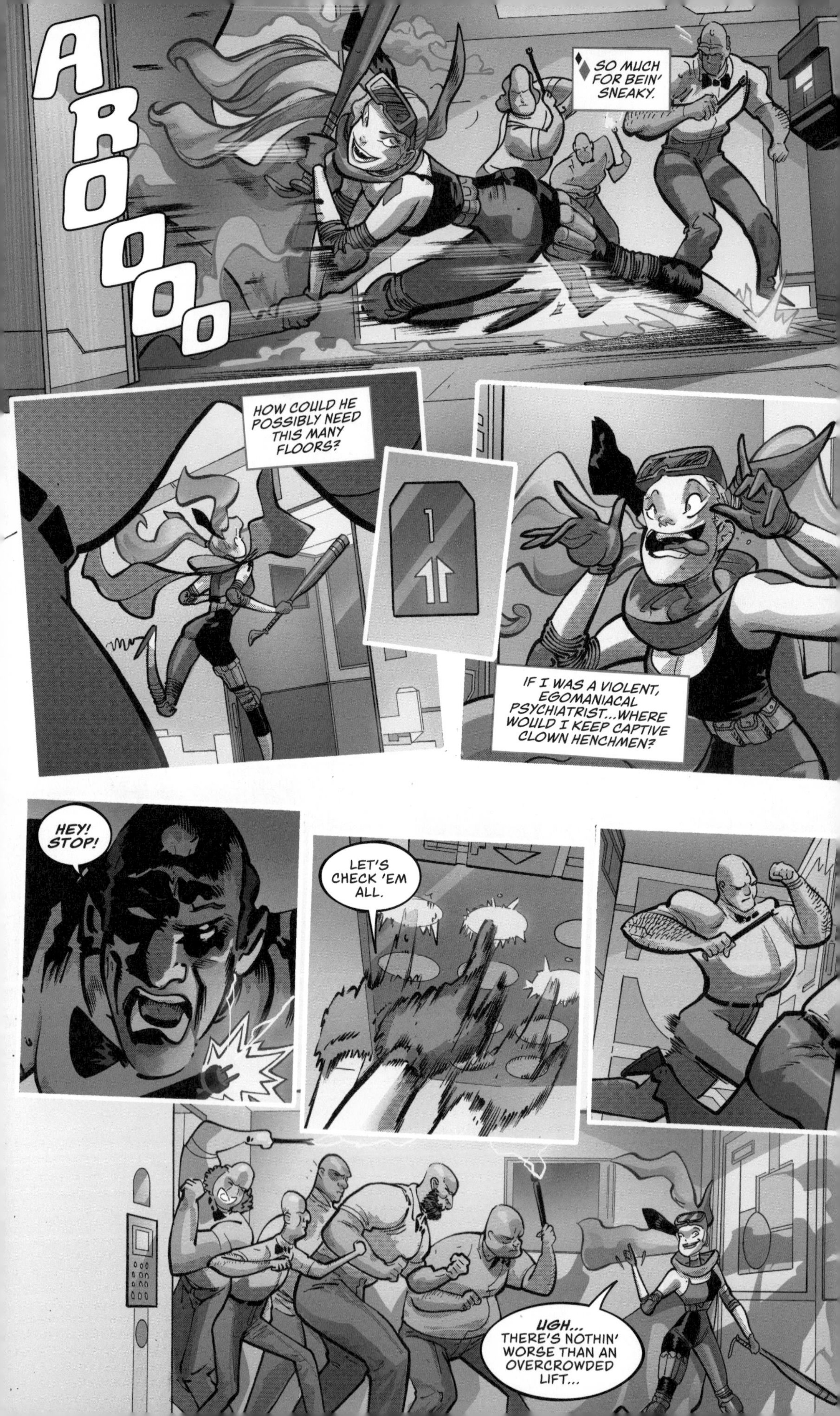
AROOOO
SO MUCH FOR BEIN' SNEAKY.
HOW COULD HE POSSIBLY NEED THIS MANY FLOORS?
1
IF I WAS A VIOLENT, EGOMANIACAL PSYCHIATRIST...WHERE WOULD I KEEP CAPTIVE CLOWN HENCHMEN?
HEY! STOP!
LET'S CHECK 'EM ALL.
UGH... THERE'S NOTHIN' WORSE THAN AN OVERCROWDED LIFT...

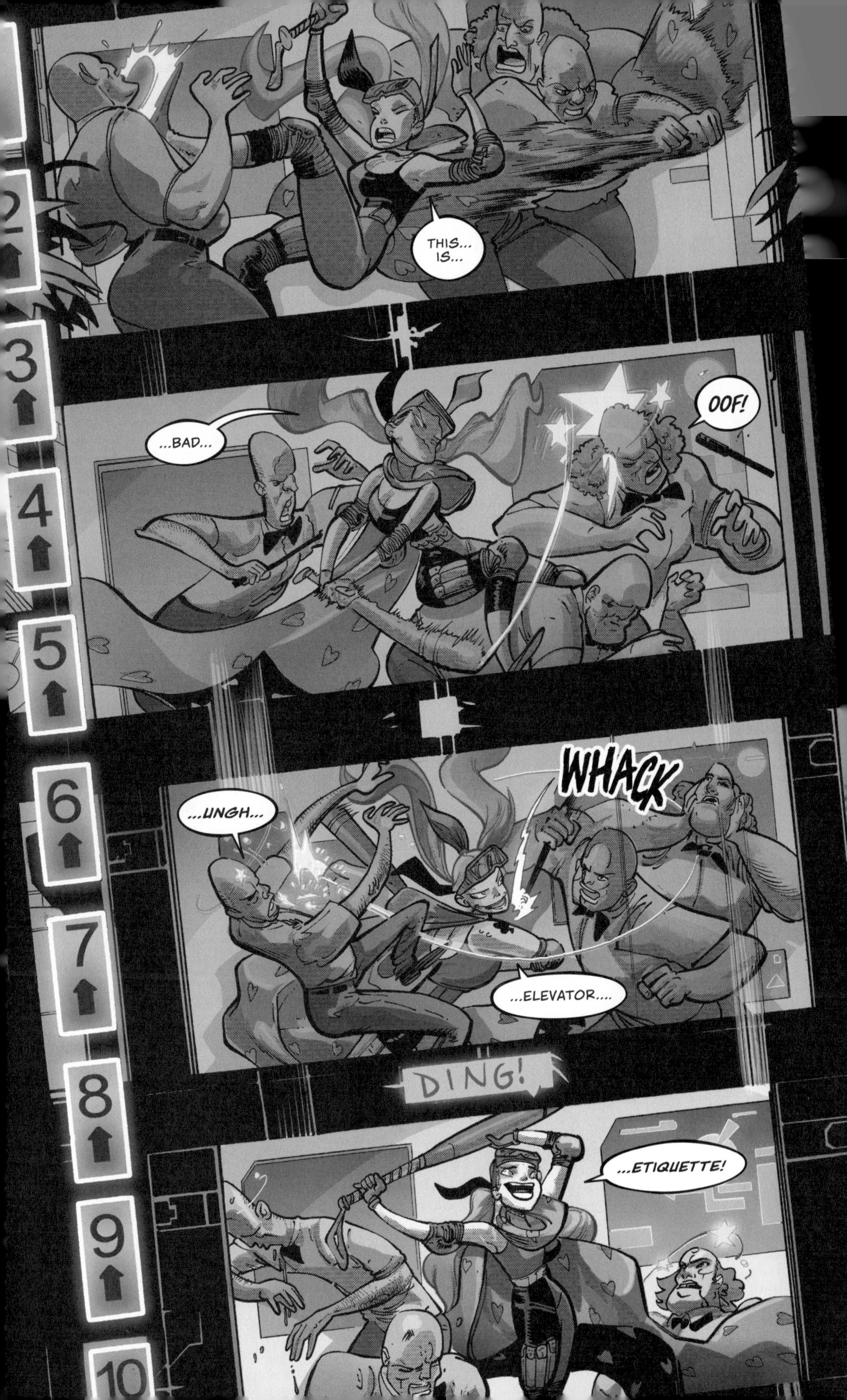

THIS... IS...
...BAD...
OOF!
...UNGH...
WHACK
...ELEVATOR....
DING!
...ETIQUETTE!

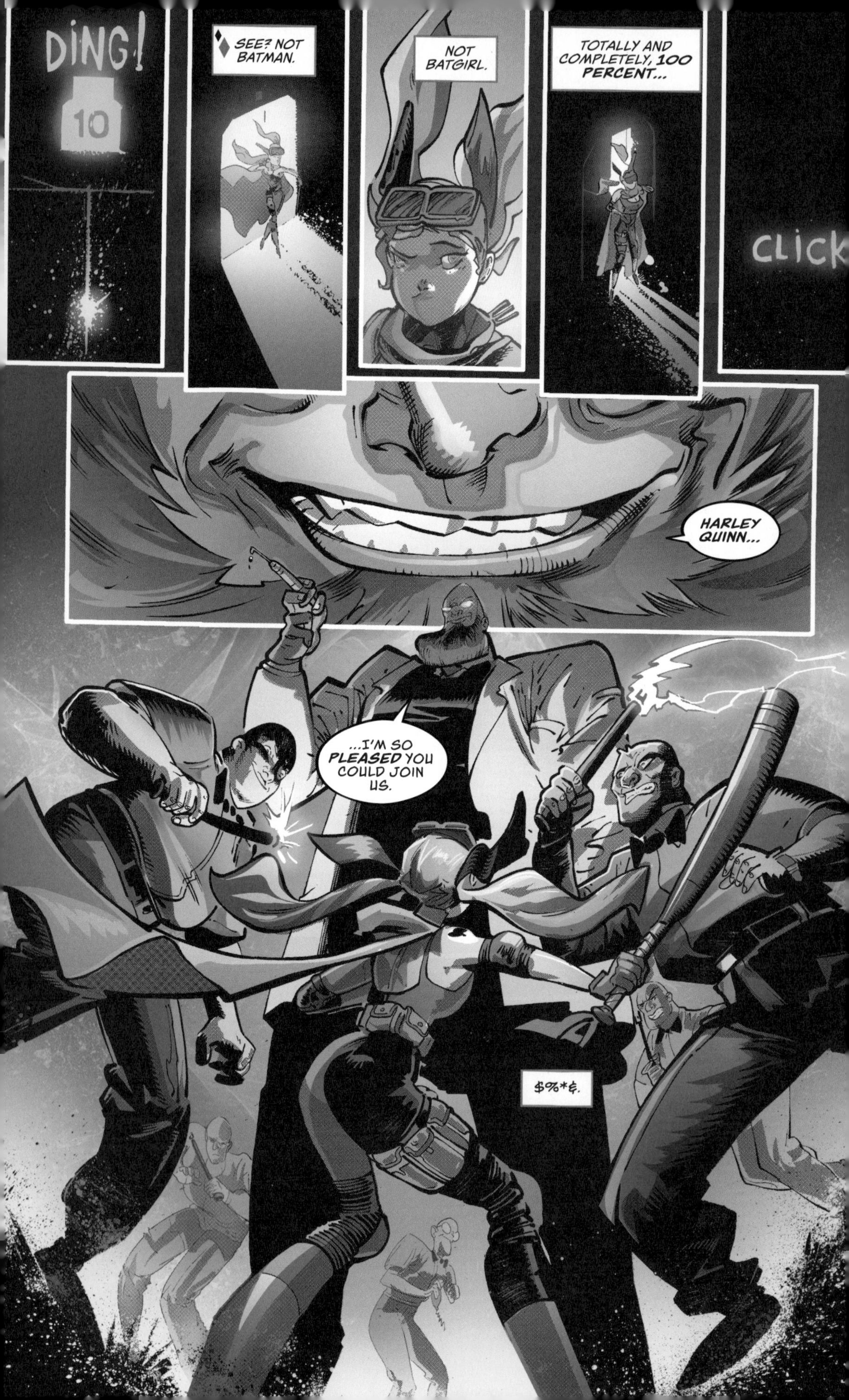
DING!
10
SEE? NOT BATMAN.
NOT BATGIRL.
TOTALLY AND COMPLETELY, 100 PERCENT...
CLICK
HARLEY QUINN...
...I'M SO PLEASED YOU COULD JOIN US.
$%*&.

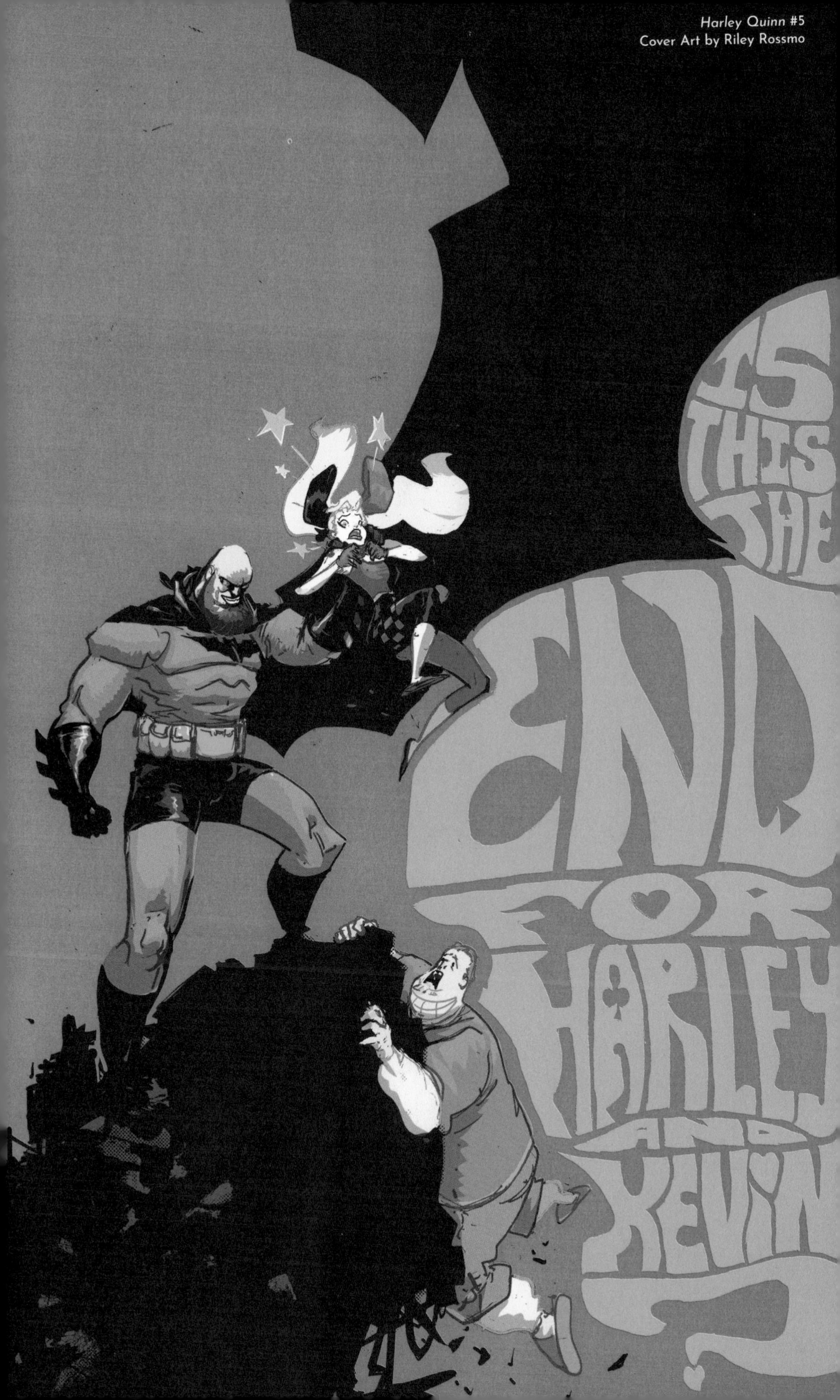
IS THIS THE END FOR HARLEY AND KEVIN?

Harley Quinn #5
Cover Art by Riley Rossmo

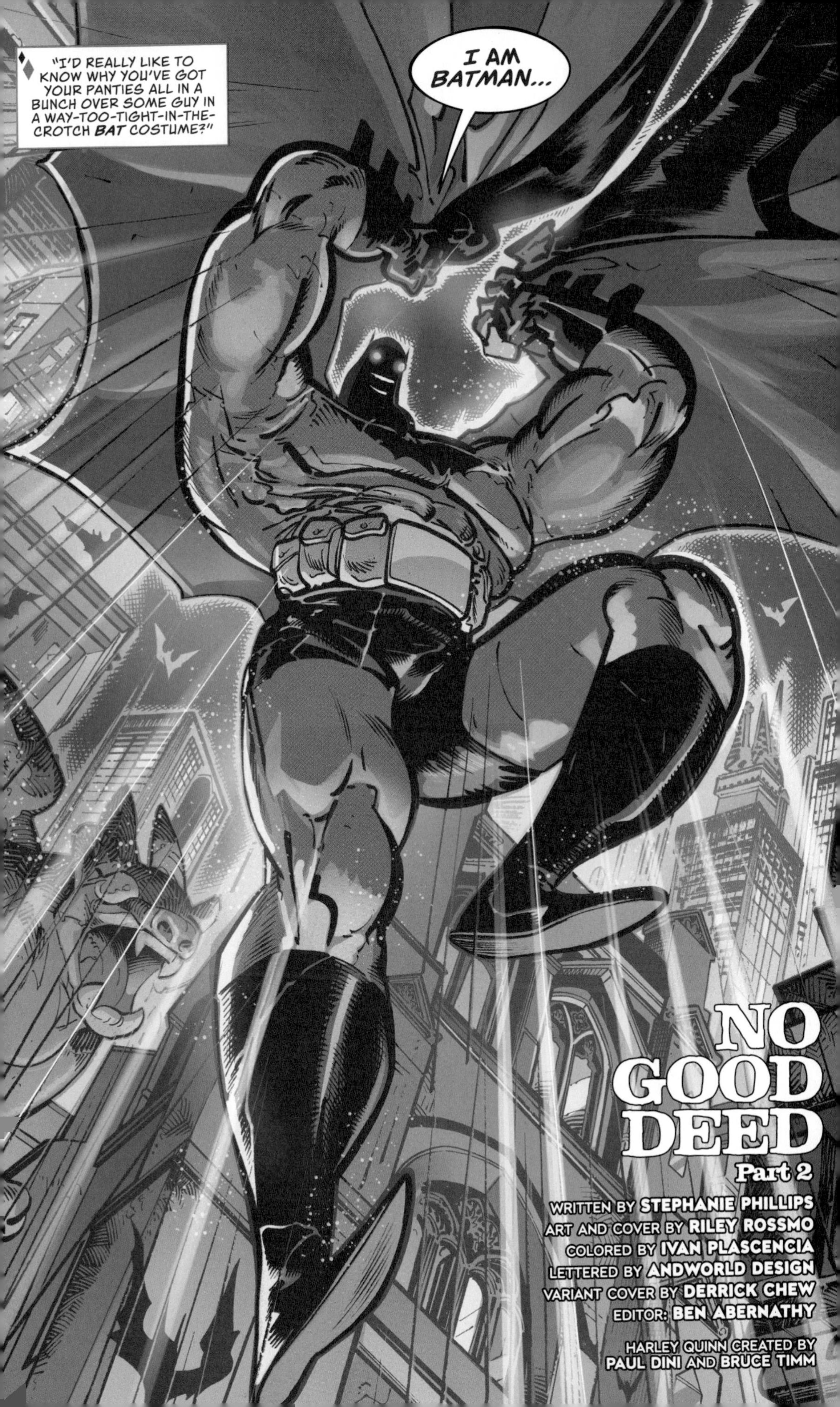

"I'D REALLY LIKE TO KNOW WHY YOU'VE GOT YOUR PANTIES ALL IN A BUNCH OVER SOME GUY IN A WAY-TOO-TIGHT-IN-THE-CROTCH BAT COSTUME?"
I AM BATMAN...
NO GOOD DEED
Part 2
WRITTEN BY STEPHANIE PHILLIPS
ART AND COVER BY RILEY ROSSMO
COLORED BY IVAN PLASCENCIA
LETTERED BY ANDWORLD DESIGN
VARIANT COVER BY DERRICK CHEW
EDITOR: BEN ABERNATHY
HARLEY QUINN CREATED BY PAUL DINI AND BRUCE TIMM

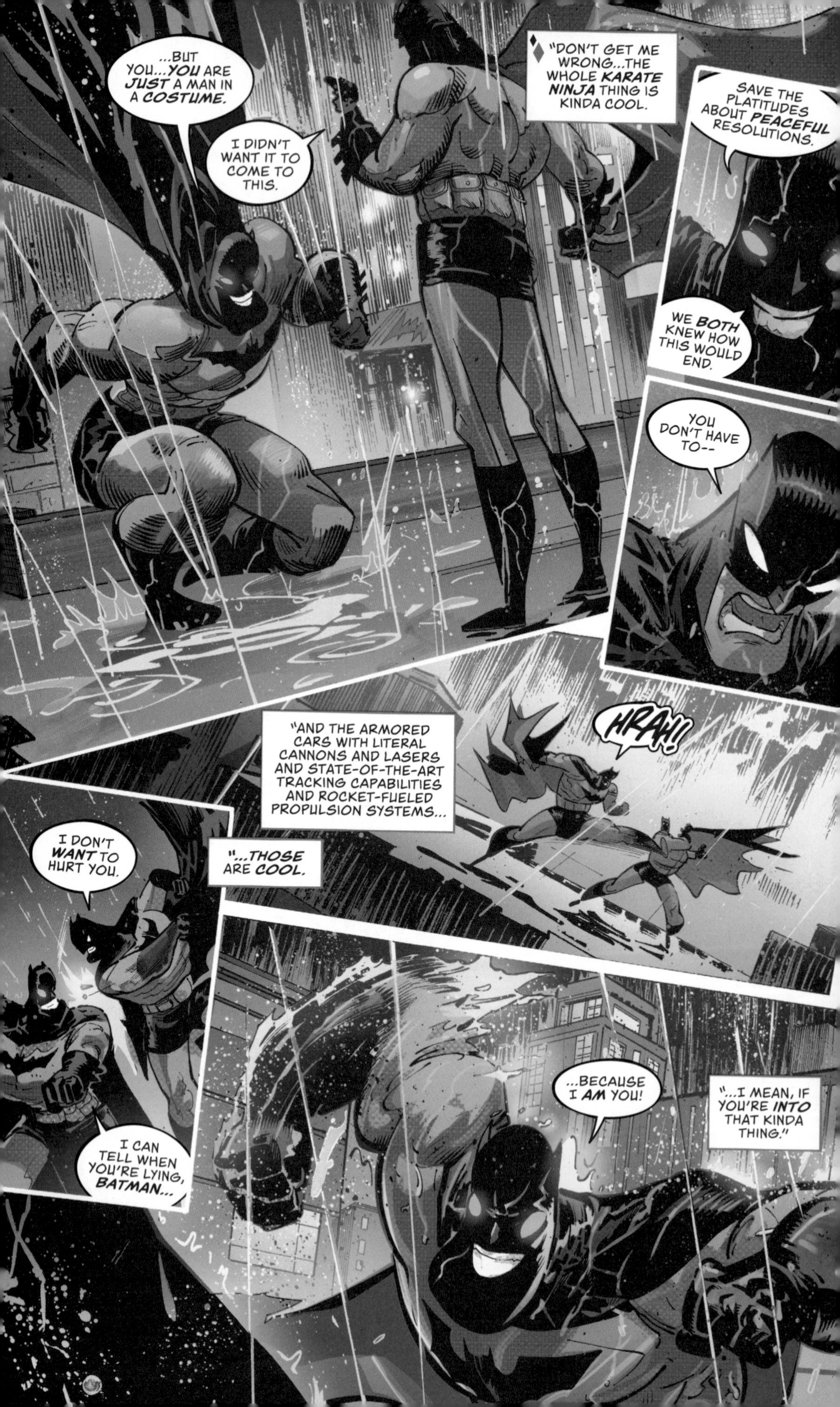

...BUT YOU...YOU ARE JUST A MAN IN A COSTUME.
I DIDN'T WANT IT TO COME TO THIS.
"DON'T GET ME WRONG...THE WHOLE KARATE NINJA THING IS KINDA COOL.
SAVE THE PLATITUDES ABOUT PEACEFUL RESOLUTIONS.
WE BOTH KNEW HOW THIS WOULD END.
YOU DON'T HAVE TO--
"AND THE ARMORED CARS WITH LITERAL CANNONS AND LASERS AND STATE-OF-THE-ART TRACKING CAPABILITIES AND ROCKET-FUELED PROPULSION SYSTEMS...
HRAH!!
I DON'T WANT TO HURT YOU.
"...THOSE ARE COOL.
I CAN TELL WHEN YOU'RE LYING, BATMAN...
...BECAUSE I AM YOU!
"...I MEAN, IF YOU'RE INTO THAT KINDA THING."

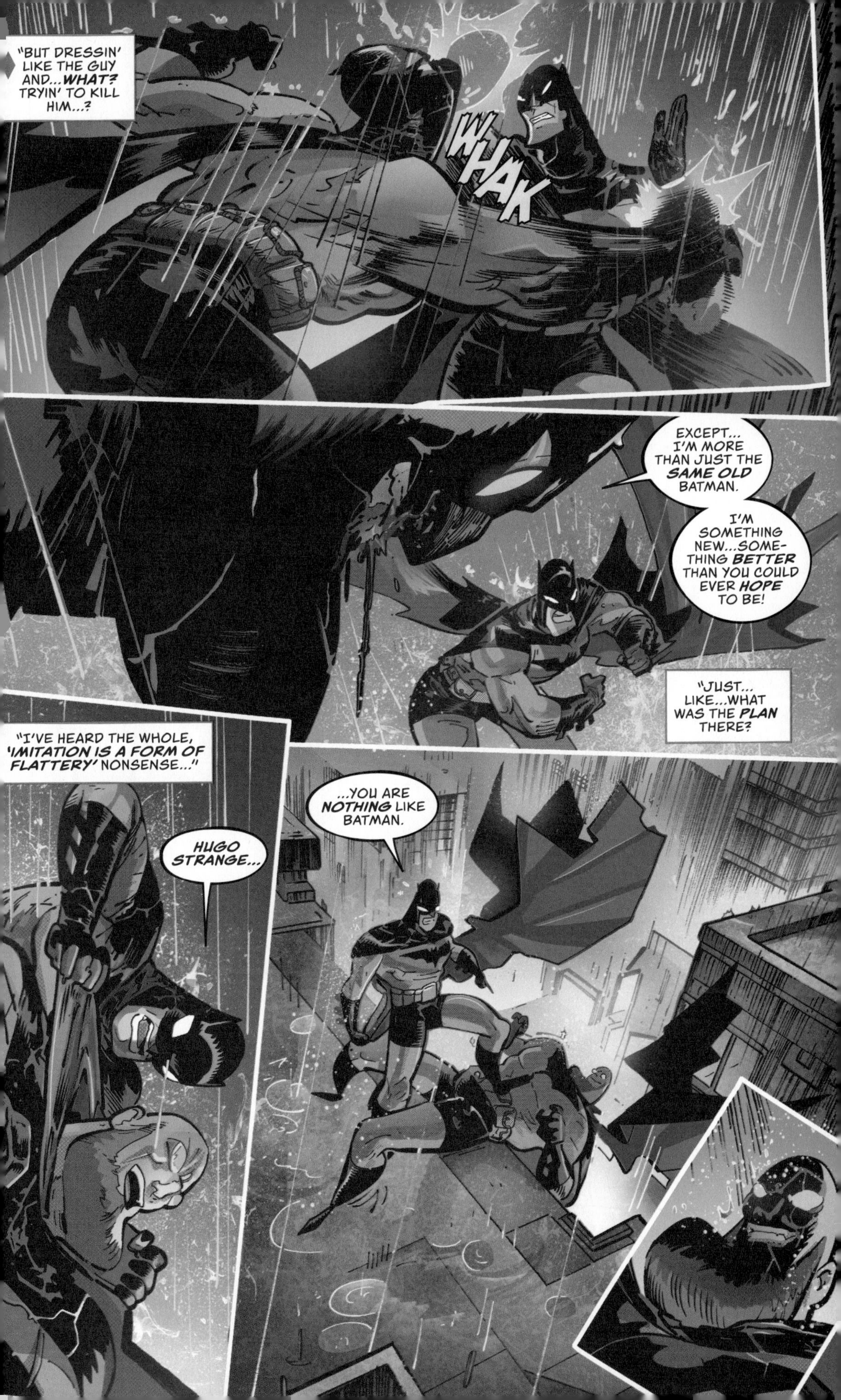
"BUT DRESSIN' LIKE THE GUY AND...WHAT? TRYIN' TO KILL HIM...?
WHAK
EXCEPT... I'M MORE THAN JUST THE SAME OLD BATMAN.
I'M SOMETHING NEW...SOMETHING BETTER THAN YOU COULD EVER HOPE TO BE!
"JUST... LIKE...WHAT WAS THE PLAN THERE?
"I'VE HEARD THE WHOLE, 'IMITATION IS A FORM OF FLATTERY' NONSENSE..."
HUGO STRANGE...
...YOU ARE NOTHING LIKE BATMAN.

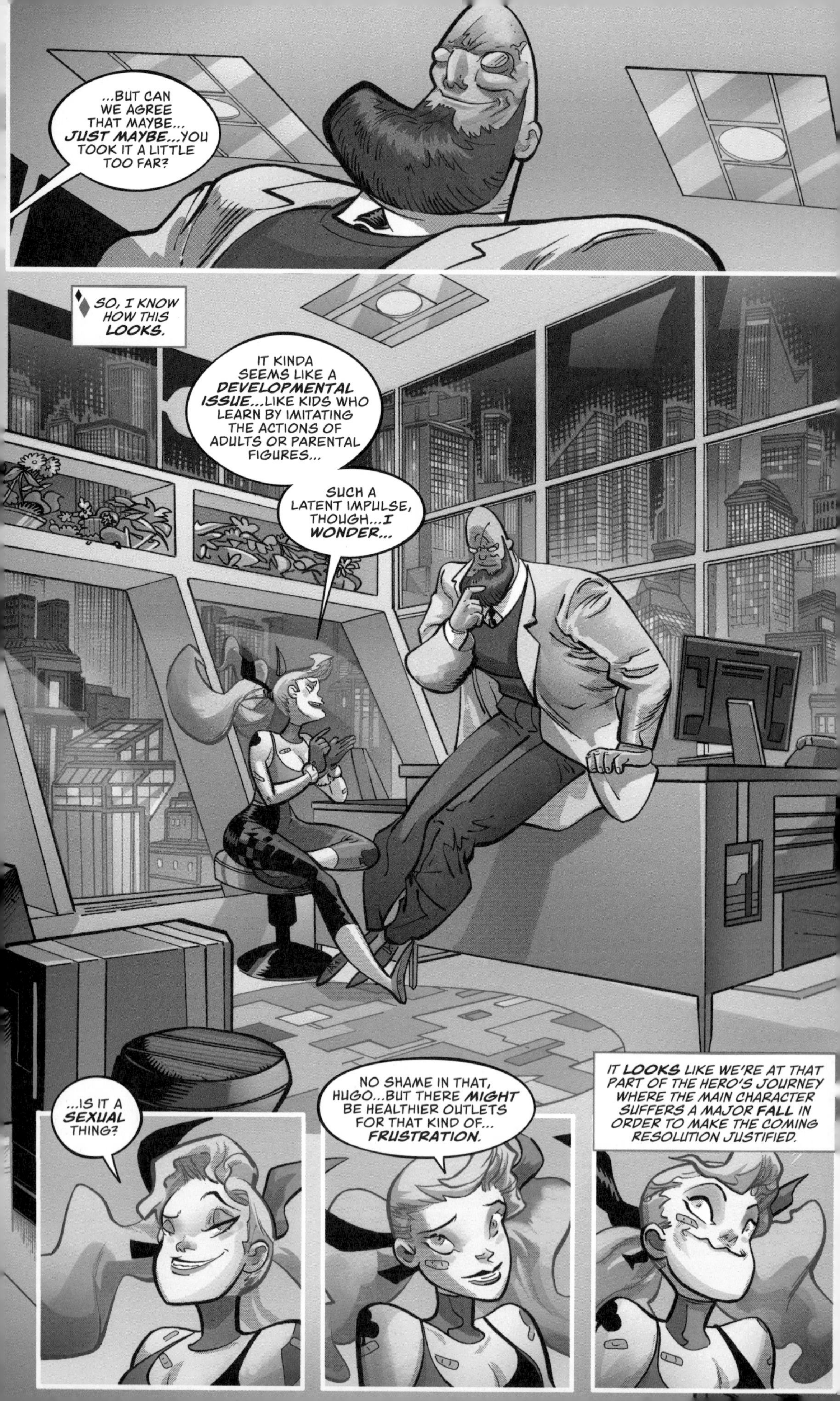

...BUT CAN WE AGREE THAT MAYBE... JUST MAYBE... YOU TOOK IT A LITTLE TOO FAR?
SO, I KNOW HOW THIS LOOKS.
IT KINDA SEEMS LIKE A DEVELOPMENTAL ISSUE... LIKE KIDS WHO LEARN BY IMITATING THE ACTIONS OF ADULTS OR PARENTAL FIGURES...
SUCH A LATENT IMPULSE, THOUGH... I WONDER...
...IS IT A SEXUAL THING?
NO SHAME IN THAT, HUGO... BUT THERE MIGHT BE HEALTHIER OUTLETS FOR THAT KIND OF... FRUSTRATION.
IT LOOKS LIKE WE'RE AT THAT PART OF THE HERO'S JOURNEY WHERE THE MAIN CHARACTER SUFFERS A MAJOR FALL IN ORDER TO MAKE THE COMING RESOLUTION JUSTIFIED.

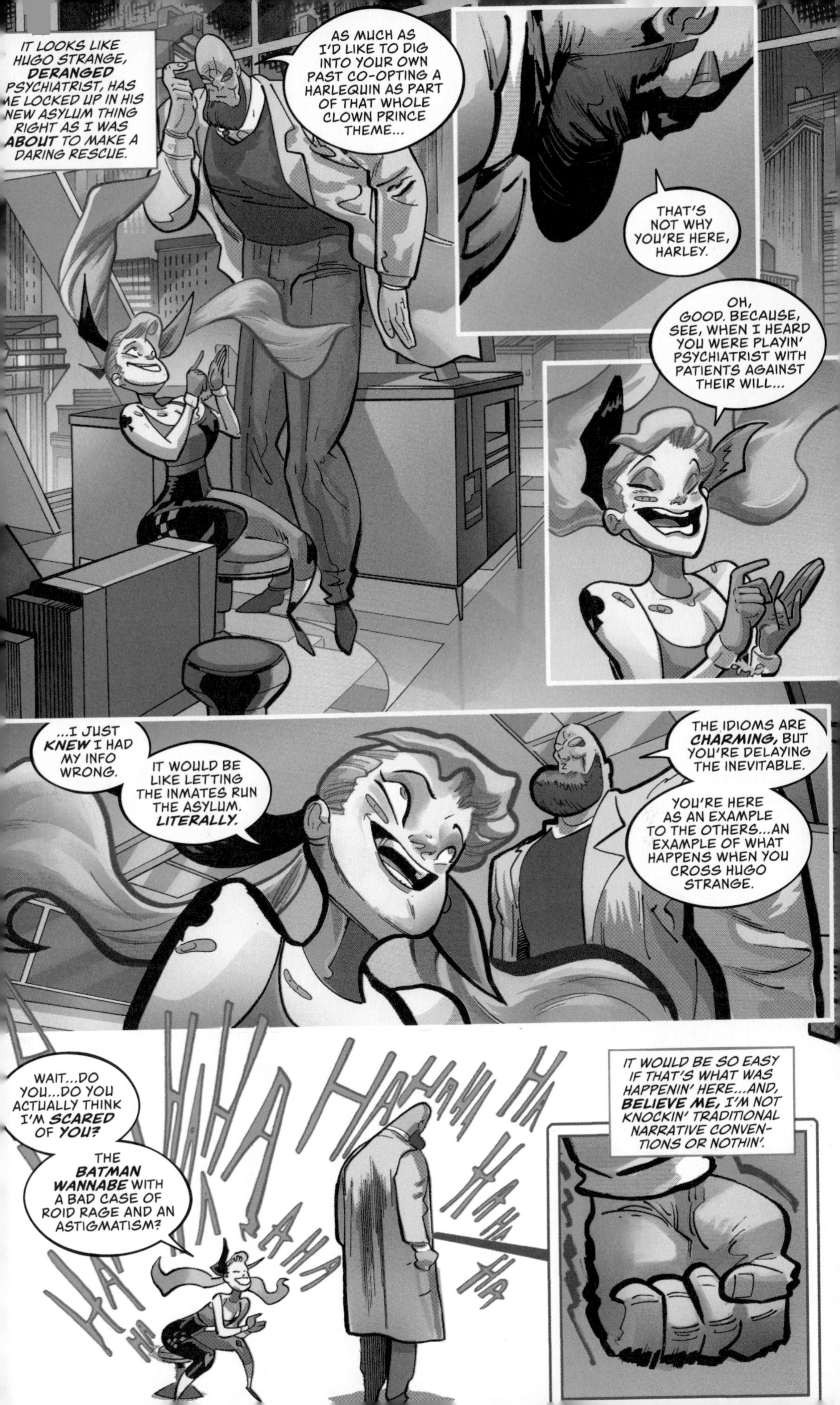
IT LOOKS LIKE HUGO STRANGE, **DERANGED** PSYCHIATRIST, HAS ME LOCKED UP IN HIS NEW ASYLUM THING RIGHT AS I WAS **ABOUT** TO MAKE A DARING RESCUE.
AS MUCH AS I'D LIKE TO DIG INTO YOUR OWN PAST CO-OPTING A HARLEQUIN AS PART OF THAT WHOLE CLOWN PRINCE THEME...
THAT'S NOT WHY YOU'RE HERE, HARLEY.
OH, GOOD. BECAUSE, SEE, WHEN I HEARD YOU WERE PLAYIN' PSYCHIATRIST WITH PATIENTS AGAINST THEIR WILL...
...I JUST **KNEW** I HAD MY INFO WRONG.
IT WOULD BE LIKE LETTING THE INMATES RUN THE ASYLUM. ***LITERALLY.***
THE IDIOMS ARE ***CHARMING,*** BUT YOU'RE DELAYING THE INEVITABLE.
YOU'RE HERE AS AN EXAMPLE TO THE OTHERS...AN EXAMPLE OF WHAT HAPPENS WHEN YOU CROSS HUGO STRANGE.
WAIT...DO YOU...DO YOU ACTUALLY THINK I'M ***SCARED*** OF ***YOU?***
THE ***BATMAN WANNABE*** WITH A BAD CASE OF ROID RAGE AND AN ASTIGMATISM?
HAHAHAHAHAHA HAHAHAHA
IT WOULD BE SO EASY IF THAT'S WHAT WAS HAPPENIN' HERE...AND, **BELIEVE ME,** I'M NOT KNOCKIN' TRADITIONAL NARRATIVE CONVENTIONS OR NOTHIN'.

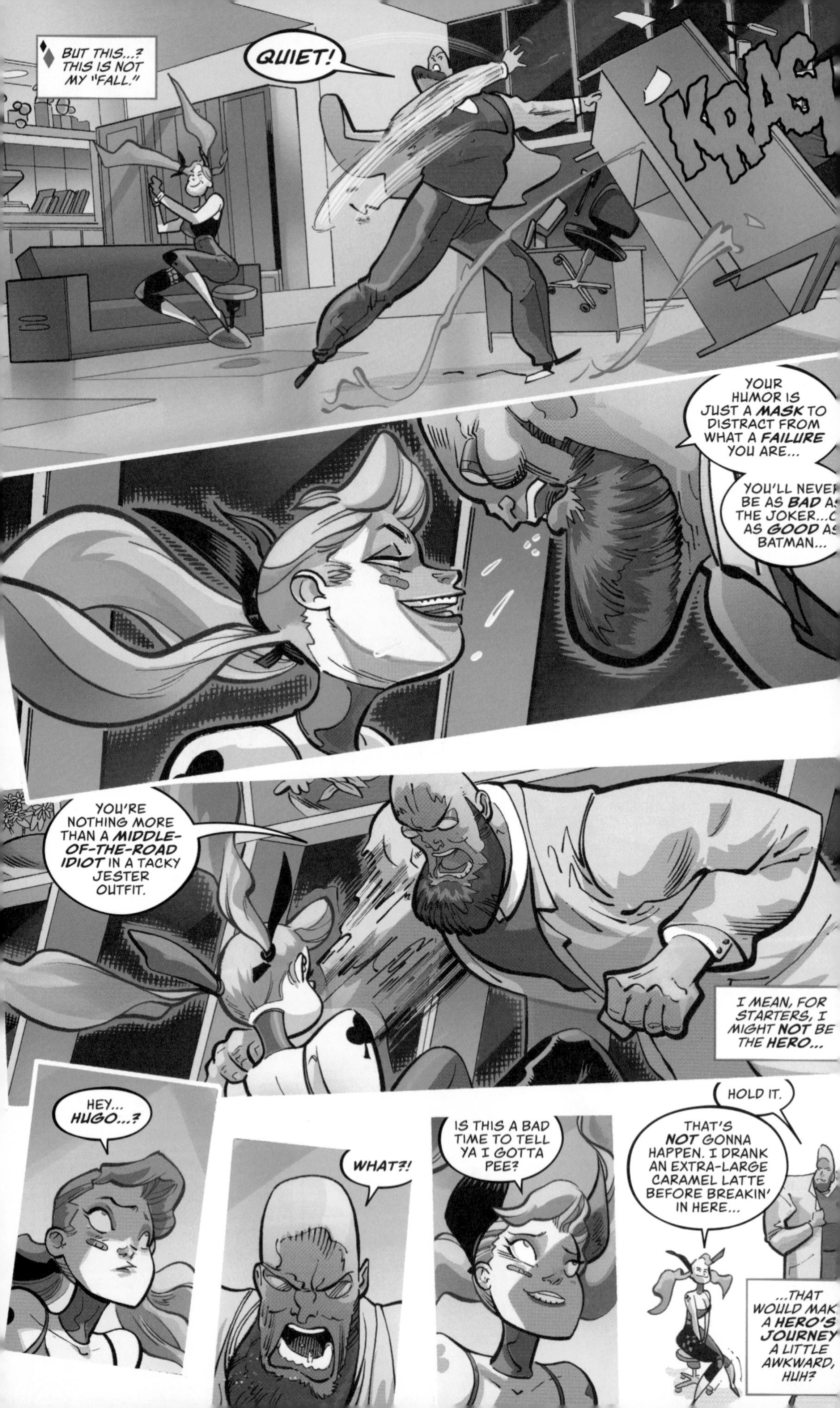

BUT THIS...? THIS IS NOT MY "FALL."
QUIET!
KRASH
YOUR HUMOR IS JUST A MASK TO DISTRACT FROM WHAT A FAILURE YOU ARE...
YOU'LL NEVER BE AS BAD AS THE JOKER...OR AS GOOD AS BATMAN...
YOU'RE NOTHING MORE THAN A MIDDLE-OF-THE-ROAD IDIOT IN A TACKY JESTER OUTFIT.
I MEAN, FOR STARTERS, I MIGHT NOT BE THE HERO...
HEY... HUGO...?
WHAT?!
IS THIS A BAD TIME TO TELL YA I GOTTA PEE?
HOLD IT.
THAT'S NOT GONNA HAPPEN. I DRANK AN EXTRA-LARGE CARAMEL LATTE BEFORE BREAKIN' IN HERE...
...THAT WOULD MAKE A HERO'S JOURNEY A LITTLE AWKWARD, HUH?

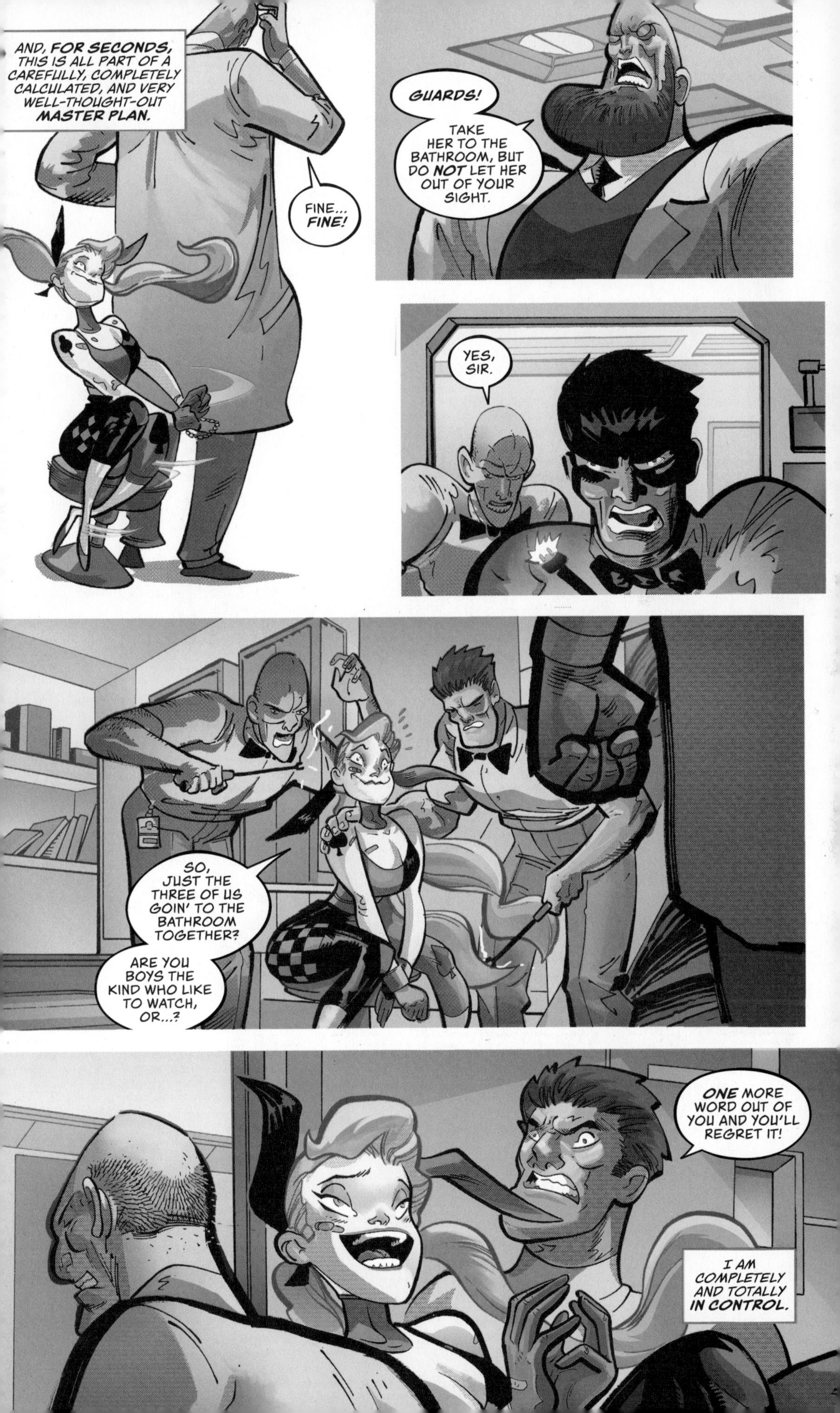
AND, FOR SECONDS, THIS IS ALL PART OF A CAREFULLY, COMPLETELY CALCULATED, AND VERY WELL-THOUGHT-OUT MASTER PLAN.
FINE... FINE!
GUARDS!
TAKE HER TO THE BATHROOM, BUT DO NOT LET HER OUT OF YOUR SIGHT.
YES, SIR.
SO, JUST THE THREE OF US GOIN' TO THE BATHROOM TOGETHER?
ARE YOU BOYS THE KIND WHO LIKE TO WATCH, OR...?
ONE MORE WORD OUT OF YOU AND YOU'LL REGRET IT!
I AM COMPLETELY AND TOTALLY IN CONTROL.

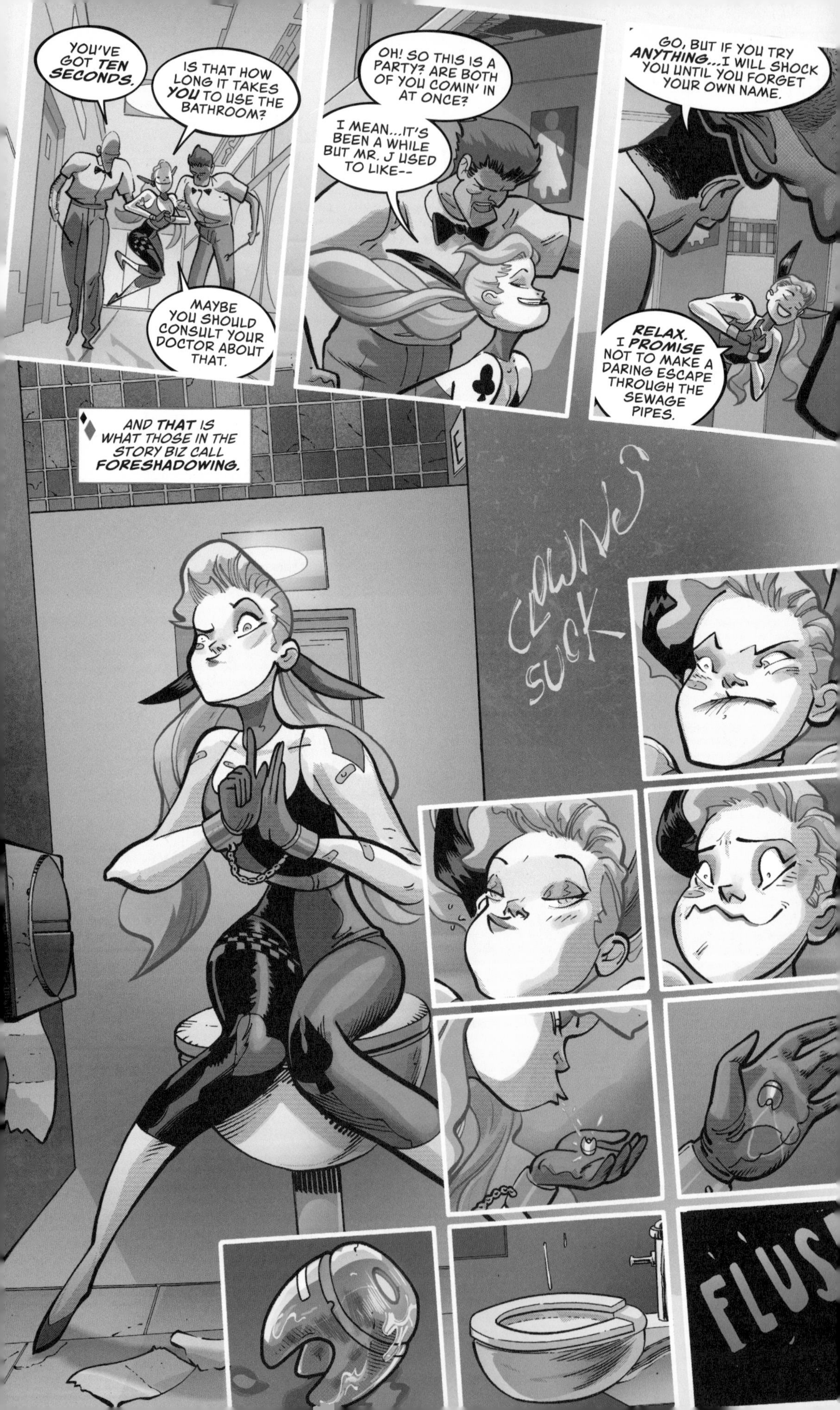
YOU'VE GOT TEN SECONDS.
IS THAT HOW LONG IT TAKES YOU TO USE THE BATHROOM?
MAYBE YOU SHOULD CONSULT YOUR DOCTOR ABOUT THAT.
OH! SO THIS IS A PARTY? ARE BOTH OF YOU COMIN' IN AT ONCE?
I MEAN...IT'S BEEN A WHILE BUT MR. J USED TO LIKE--
GO, BUT IF YOU TRY ANYTHING...I WILL SHOCK YOU UNTIL YOU FORGET YOUR OWN NAME.
RELAX. I PROMISE NOT TO MAKE A DARING ESCAPE THROUGH THE SEWAGE PIPES.
AND THAT IS WHAT THOSE IN THE STORY BIZ CALL FORESHADOWING.
CLOWNS SUCK

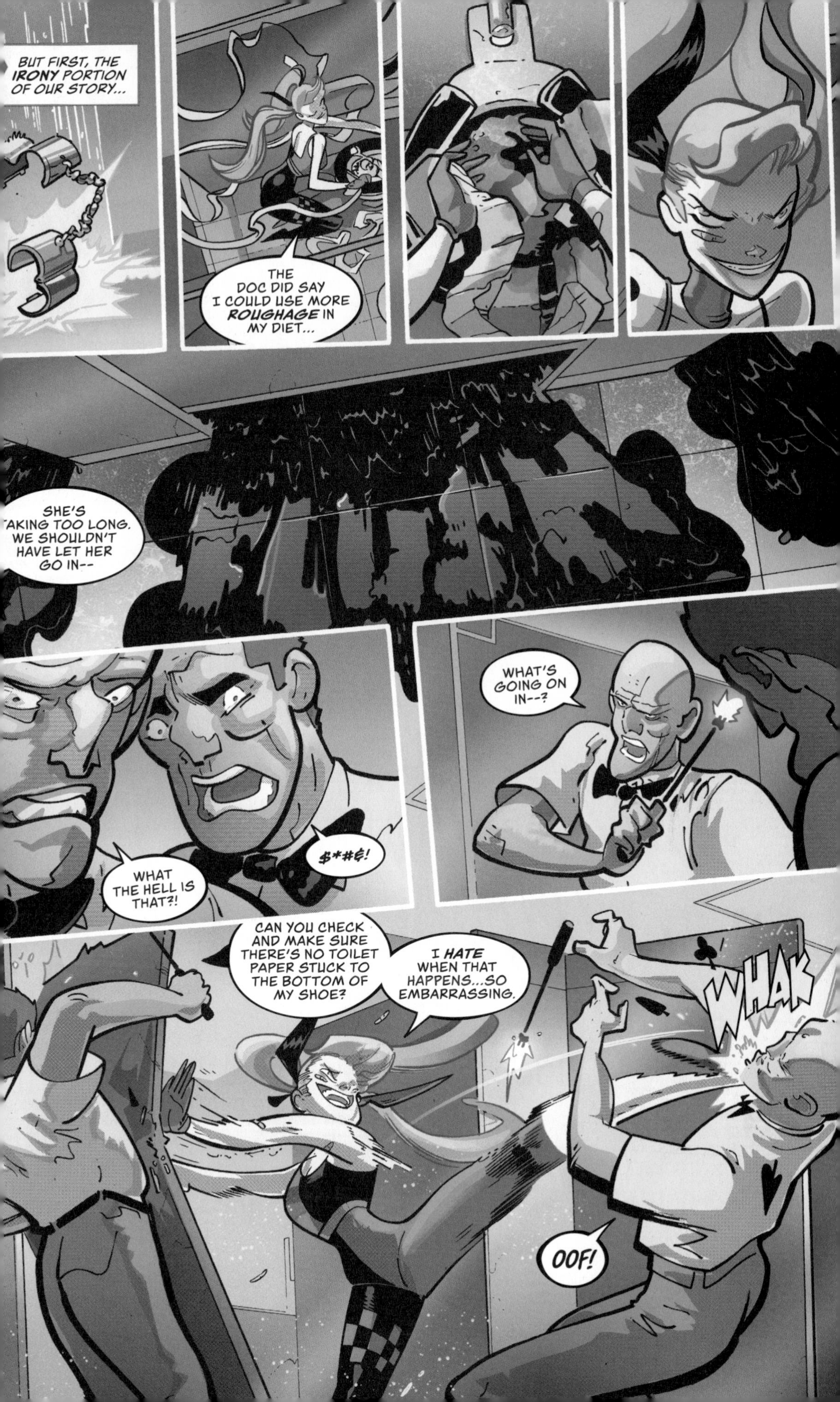

BUT FIRST, THE IRONY PORTION OF OUR STORY...
THE DOC DID SAY I COULD USE MORE ROUGHAGE IN MY DIET...
SHE'S TAKING TOO LONG. WE SHOULDN'T HAVE LET HER GO IN--
WHAT THE HELL IS THAT?!
$*#€!
WHAT'S GOING ON IN--?
CAN YOU CHECK AND MAKE SURE THERE'S NO TOILET PAPER STUCK TO THE BOTTOM OF MY SHOE?
I HATE WHEN THAT HAPPENS...SO EMBARRASSING.
WHAK
OOF!

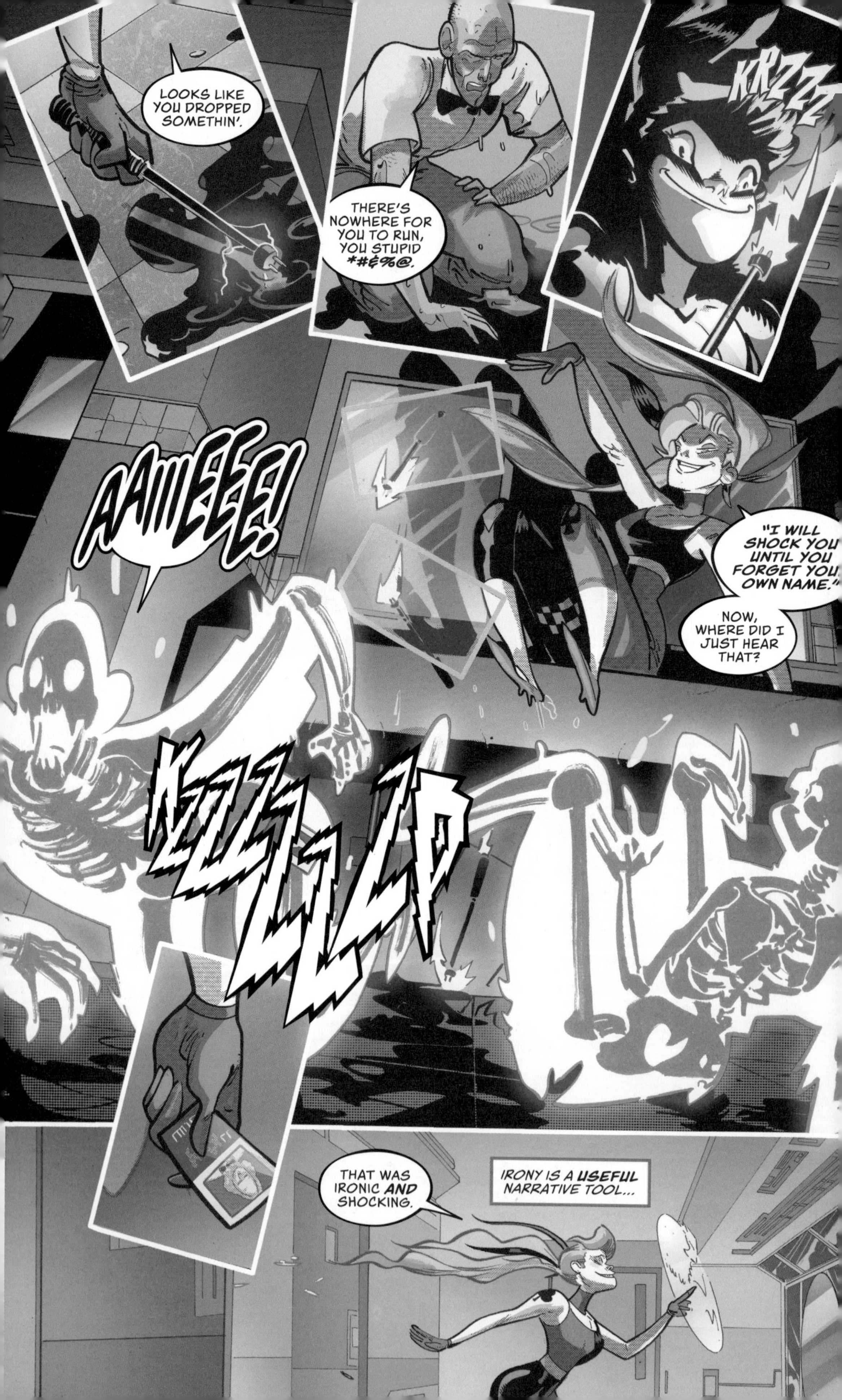
LOOKS LIKE YOU DROPPED SOMETHIN'.
THERE'S NOWHERE FOR YOU TO RUN, YOU STUPID *#&%@.
KRZZZT
AAIIIEEEE!
"I WILL SHOCK YOU UNTIL YOU FORGET YOUR OWN NAME."
NOW, WHERE DID I JUST HEAR THAT?
KZZZZZZZP
THAT WAS IRONIC AND SHOCKING.
IRONY IS A USEFUL NARRATIVE TOOL...

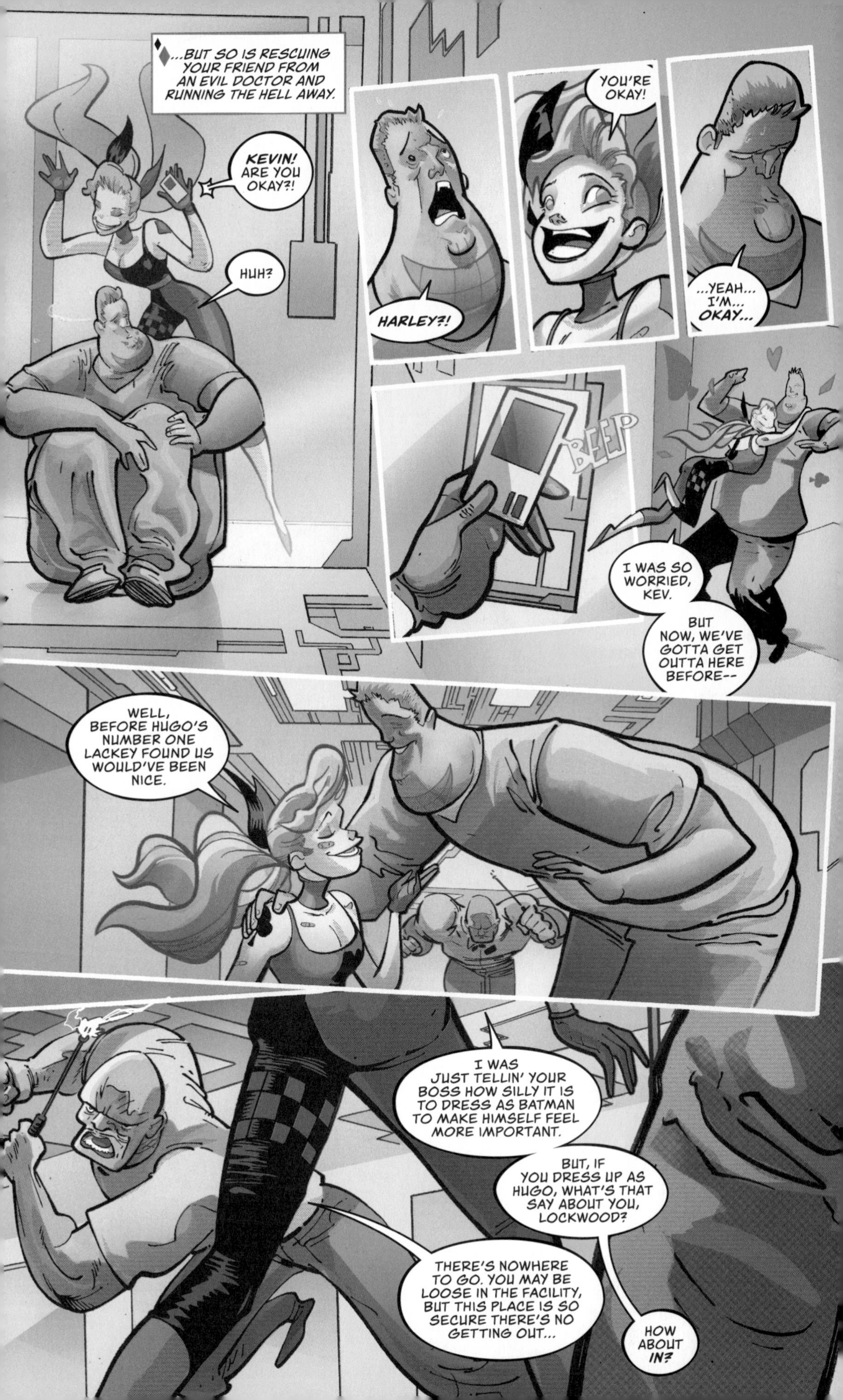
...BUT SO IS RESCUING YOUR FRIEND FROM AN EVIL DOCTOR AND RUNNING THE HELL AWAY.
KEVIN! ARE YOU OKAY?!
HUH?
HARLEY?!
YOU'RE OKAY!
...YEAH... I'M... OKAY...
BEEP
I WAS SO WORRIED, KEV.
BUT NOW, WE'VE GOTTA GET OUTTA HERE BEFORE--
WELL, BEFORE HUGO'S NUMBER ONE LACKEY FOUND US WOULD'VE BEEN NICE.
I WAS JUST TELLIN' YOUR BOSS HOW SILLY IT IS TO DRESS AS BATMAN TO MAKE HIMSELF FEEL MORE IMPORTANT.
BUT, IF YOU DRESS UP AS HUGO, WHAT'S THAT SAY ABOUT YOU, LOCKWOOD?
THERE'S NOWHERE TO GO. YOU MAY BE LOOSE IN THE FACILITY, BUT THIS PLACE IS SO SECURE THERE'S NO GETTING OUT...
HOW ABOUT IN?

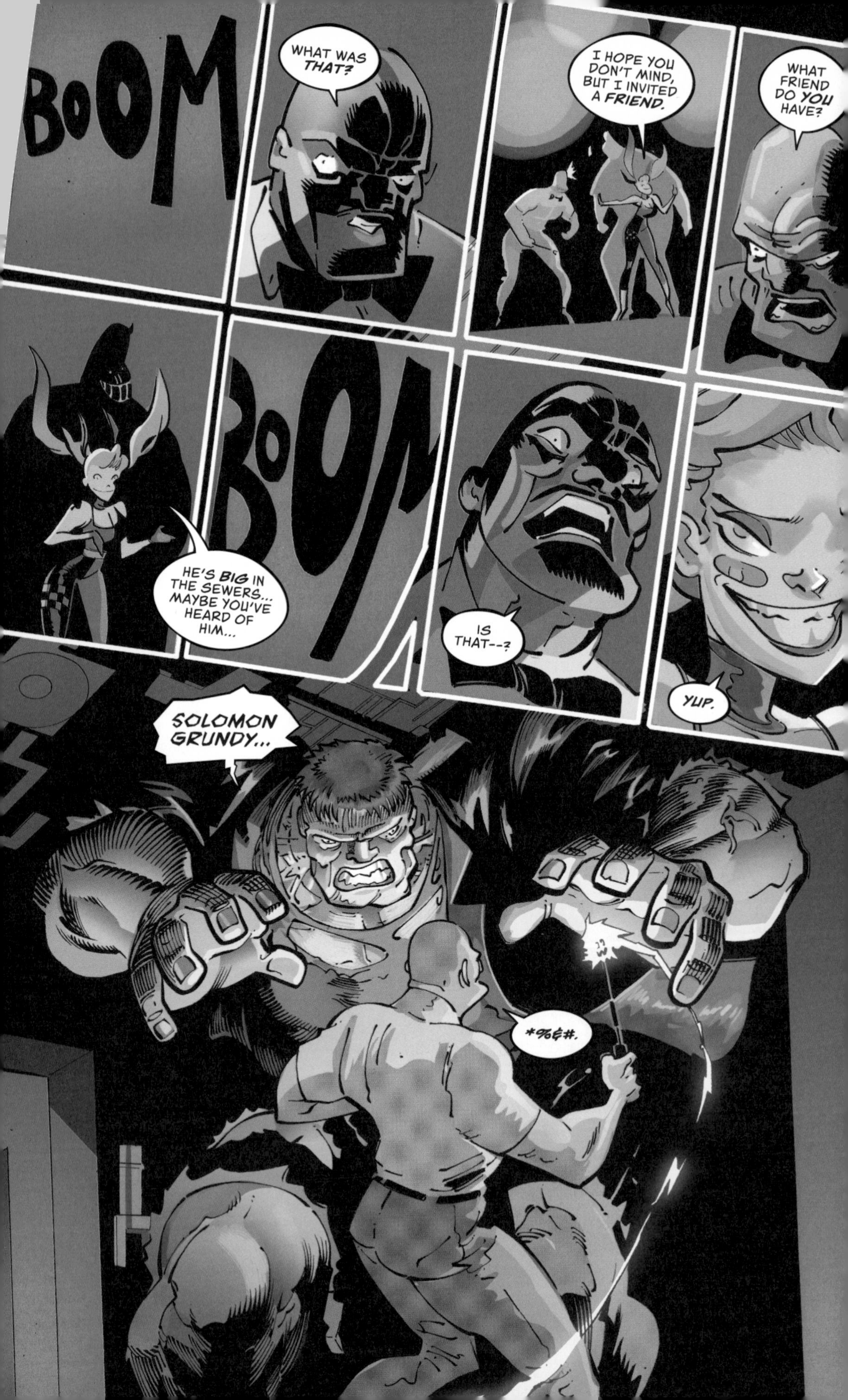
BOOM
WHAT WAS THAT?
I HOPE YOU DON'T MIND, BUT I INVITED A FRIEND.
WHAT FRIEND DO YOU HAVE?
HE'S BIG IN THE SEWERS... MAYBE YOU'VE HEARD OF HIM...
BOOM
IS THAT--?
YUP.
SOLOMON GRUNDY...
*%¢#.

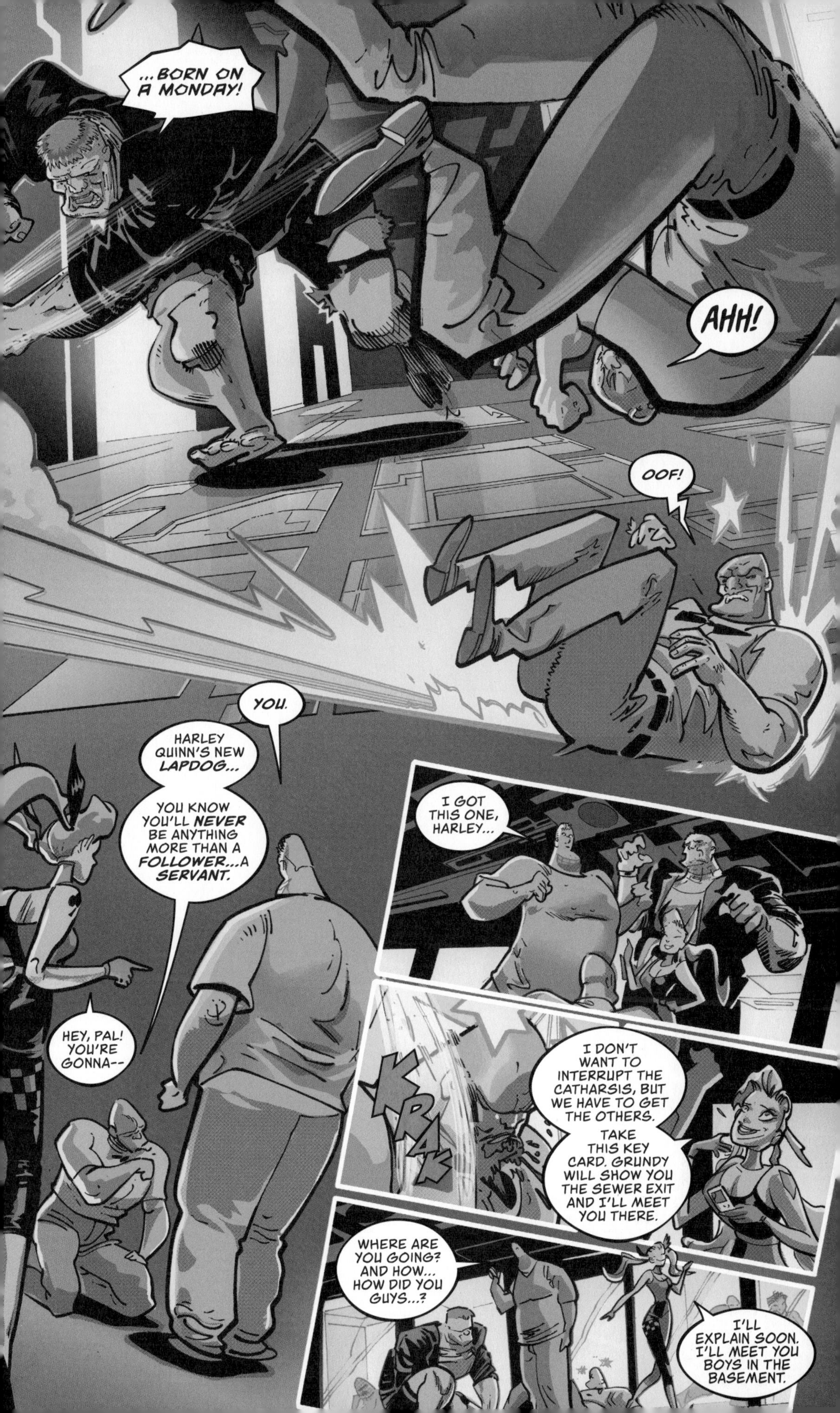
...BORN ON A MONDAY!
AHH!
OOF!
YOU.
HARLEY QUINN'S NEW LAPDOG...
YOU KNOW YOU'LL NEVER BE ANYTHING MORE THAN A FOLLOWER...A SERVANT.
HEY, PAL! YOU'RE GONNA--
I GOT THIS ONE, HARLEY...
KRAK
I DON'T WANT TO INTERRUPT THE CATHARSIS, BUT WE HAVE TO GET THE OTHERS.
TAKE THIS KEY CARD. GRUNDY WILL SHOW YOU THE SEWER EXIT AND I'LL MEET YOU THERE.
WHERE ARE YOU GOING? AND HOW... HOW DID YOU GUYS...?
I'LL EXPLAIN SOON. I'LL MEET YOU BOYS IN THE BASEMENT.

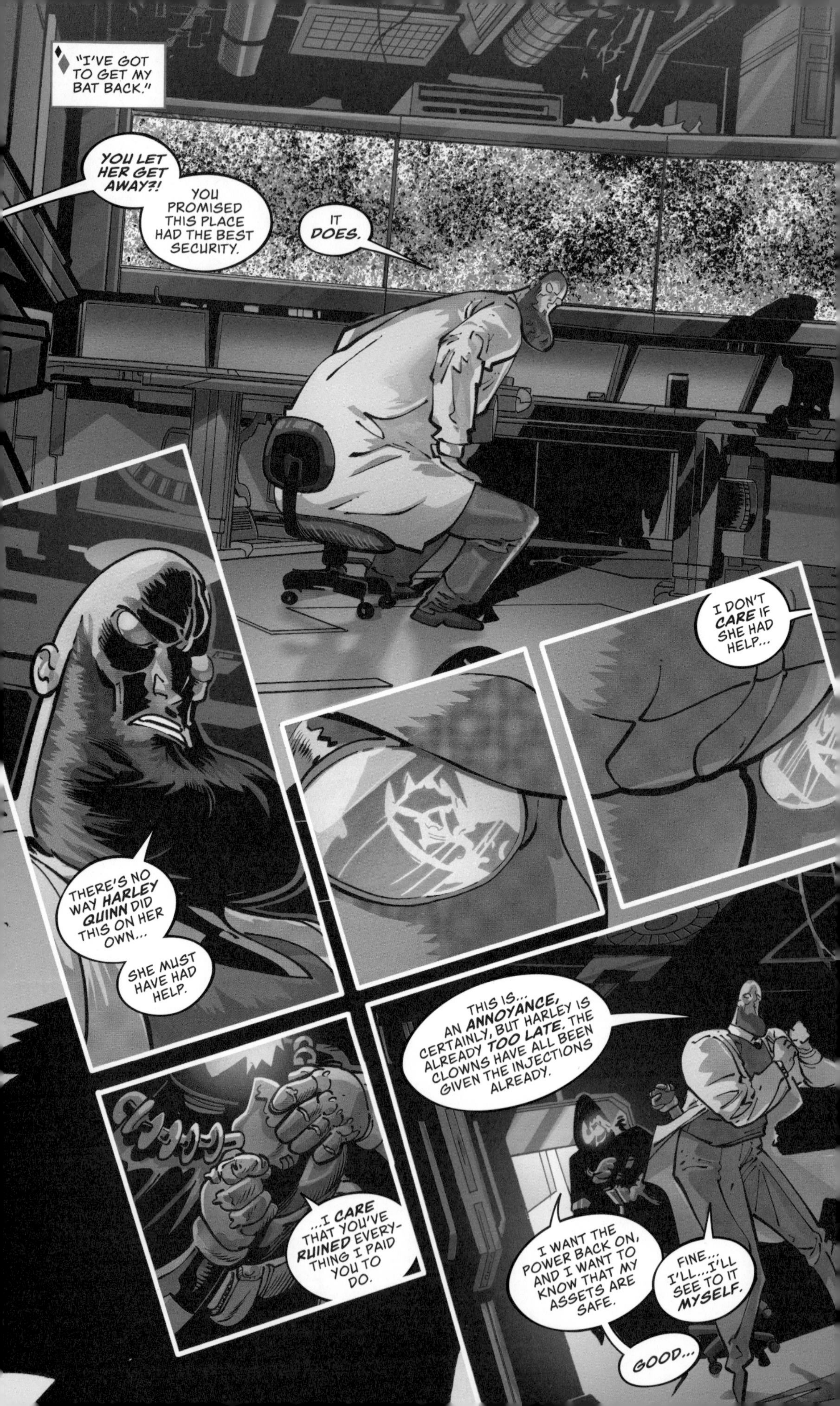
"I'VE GOT TO GET MY BAT BACK."
YOU LET HER GET AWAY?!
YOU PROMISED THIS PLACE HAD THE BEST SECURITY.
IT DOES.
THERE'S NO WAY HARLEY QUINN DID THIS ON HER OWN...
SHE MUST HAVE HAD HELP.
I DON'T CARE IF SHE HAD HELP...
...I CARE THAT YOU'VE RUINED EVERY-THING I PAID YOU TO DO.
THIS IS... AN ANNOYANCE, CERTAINLY, BUT HARLEY IS ALREADY TOO LATE. THE CLOWNS HAVE ALL BEEN GIVEN THE INJECTIONS ALREADY.
I WANT THE POWER BACK ON, AND I WANT TO KNOW THAT MY ASSETS ARE SAFE.
FINE... I'LL... I'LL SEE TO IT MYSELF.
GOOD...

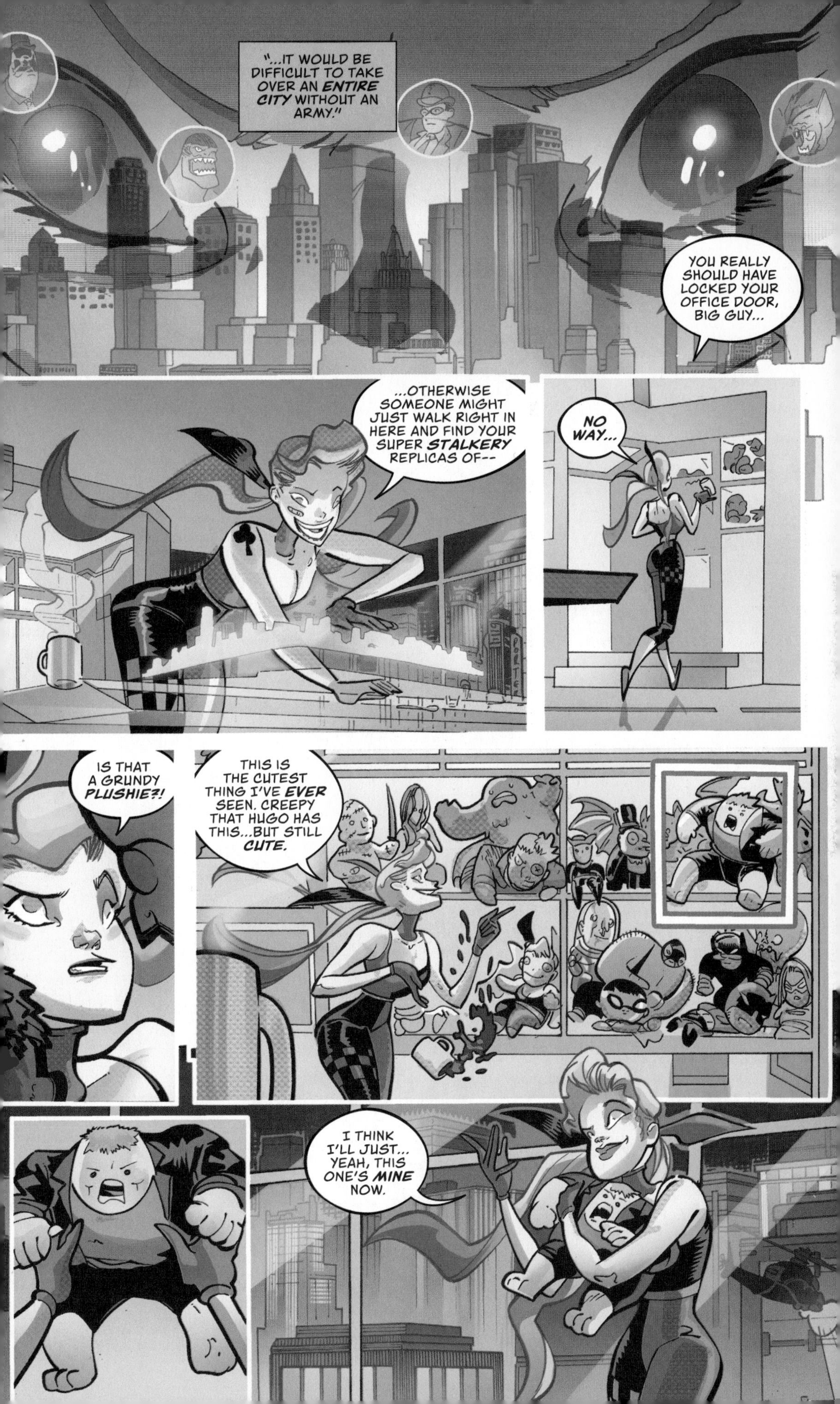
"...IT WOULD BE DIFFICULT TO TAKE OVER AN ENTIRE CITY WITHOUT AN ARMY."
YOU REALLY SHOULD HAVE LOCKED YOUR OFFICE DOOR, BIG GUY...
...OTHERWISE SOMEONE MIGHT JUST WALK RIGHT IN HERE AND FIND YOUR SUPER STALKERY REPLICAS OF--
NO WAY...
IS THAT A GRUNDY PLUSHIE?!
THIS IS THE CUTEST THING I'VE EVER SEEN. CREEPY THAT HUGO HAS THIS...BUT STILL CUTE.
I THINK I'LL JUST... YEAH, THIS ONE'S MINE NOW.

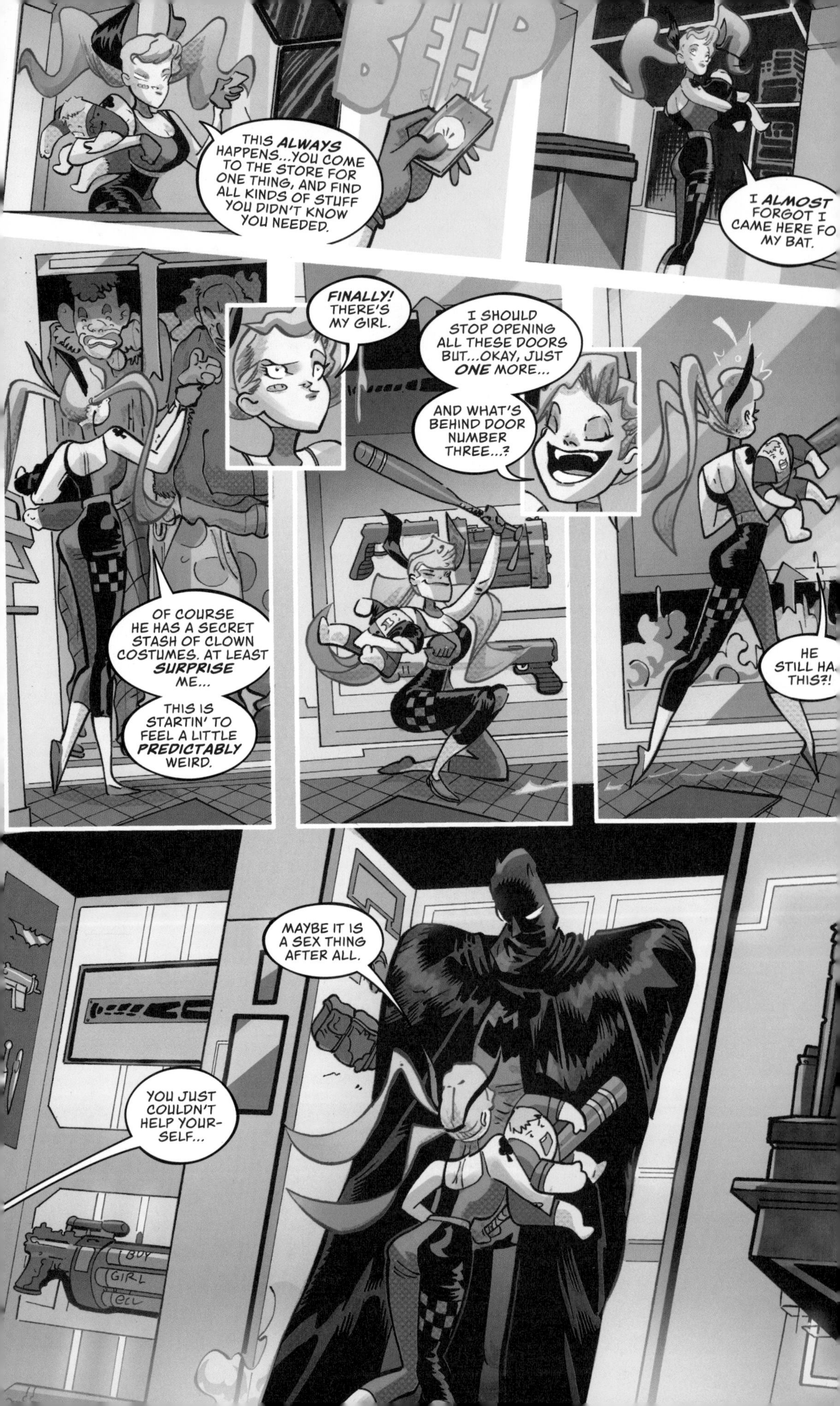
BEEP
THIS ALWAYS HAPPENS...YOU COME TO THE STORE FOR ONE THING, AND FIND ALL KINDS OF STUFF YOU DIDN'T KNOW YOU NEEDED.
I ALMOST FORGOT I CAME HERE FO MY BAT.
OF COURSE HE HAS A SECRET STASH OF CLOWN COSTUMES. AT LEAST SURPRISE ME...
THIS IS STARTIN' TO FEEL A LITTLE PREDICTABLY WEIRD.
FINALLY! THERE'S MY GIRL.
I SHOULD STOP OPENING ALL THESE DOORS BUT...OKAY, JUST ONE MORE...
AND WHAT'S BEHIND DOOR NUMBER THREE...?
HE STILL HA THIS?!
MAYBE IT IS A SEX THING AFTER ALL.
YOU JUST COULDN'T HELP YOUR-SELF...
BOY
GIRL

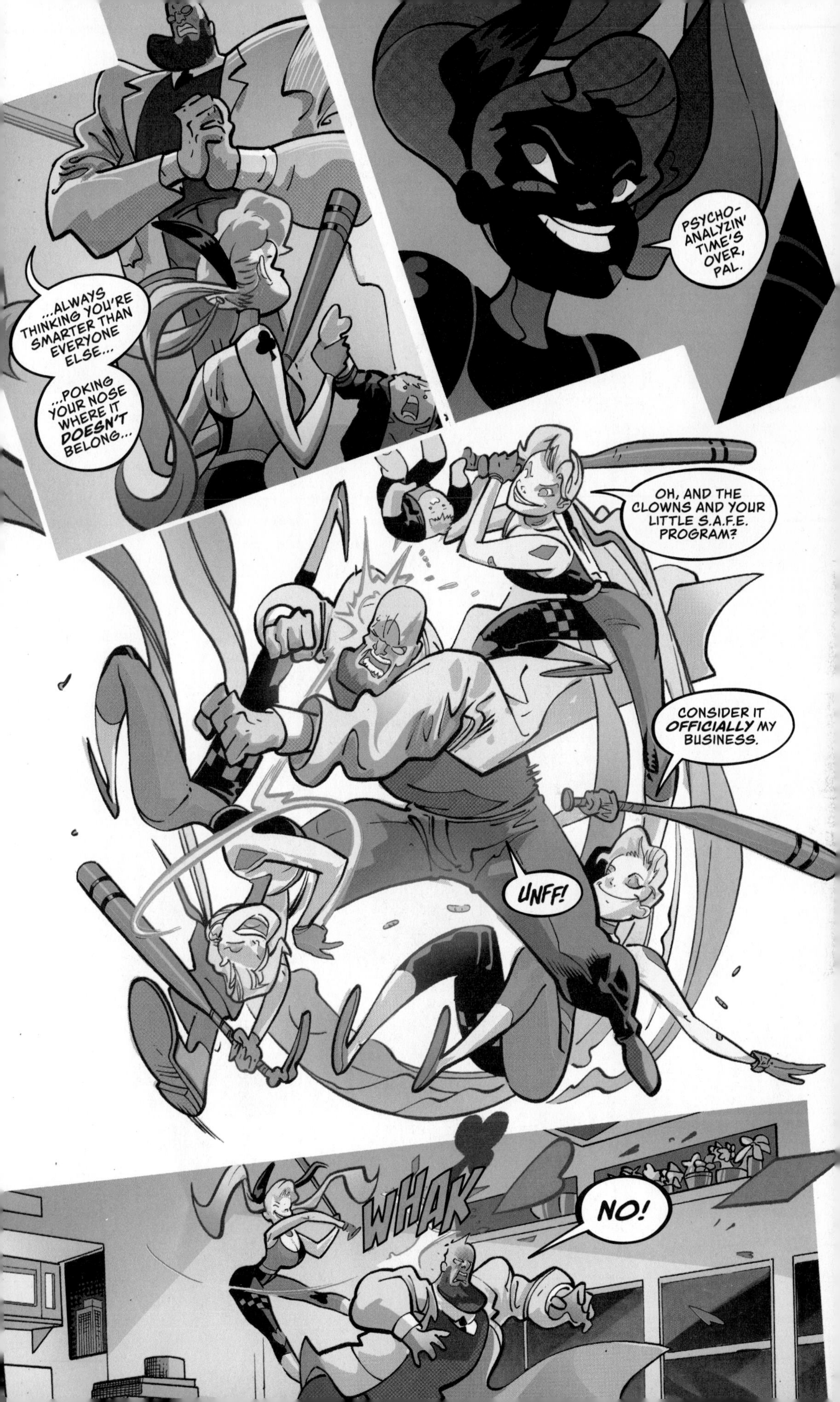
...ALWAYS THINKING YOU'RE SMARTER THAN EVERYONE ELSE...
...POKING YOUR NOSE WHERE IT DOESN'T BELONG...
PSYCHO-ANALYZIN' TIME'S OVER, PAL.
OH, AND THE CLOWNS AND YOUR LITTLE S.A.F.E. PROGRAM?
CONSIDER IT OFFICIALLY MY BUSINESS.
UNFF!
WHAK
NO!

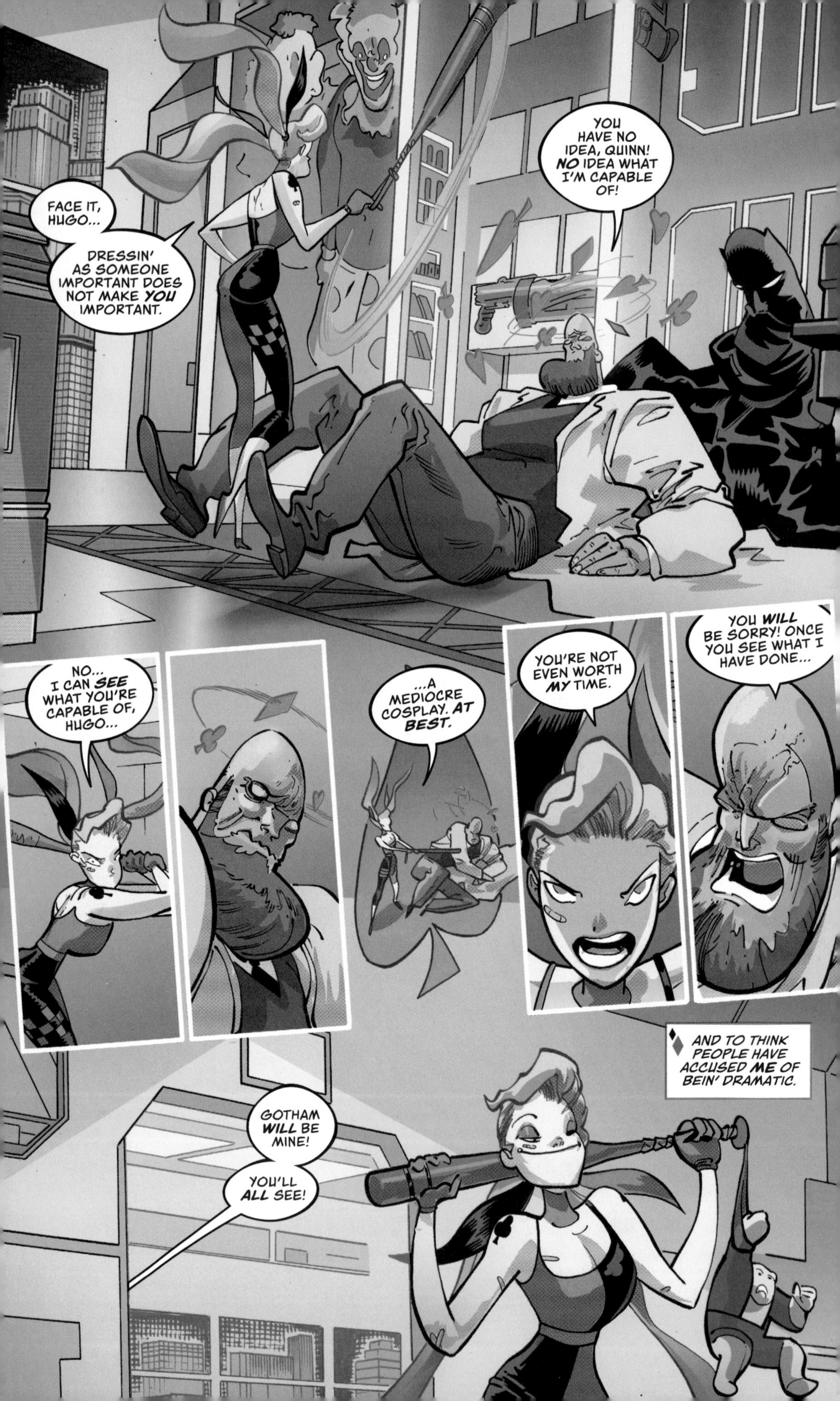
FACE IT, HUGO...
DRESSIN' AS SOMEONE IMPORTANT DOES NOT MAKE YOU IMPORTANT.
YOU HAVE NO IDEA, QUINN! NO IDEA WHAT I'M CAPABLE OF!
NO... I CAN SEE WHAT YOU'RE CAPABLE OF, HUGO...
...A MEDIOCRE COSPLAY. AT BEST.
YOU'RE NOT EVEN WORTH MY TIME.
YOU WILL BE SORRY! ONCE YOU SEE WHAT I HAVE DONE...
AND TO THINK PEOPLE HAVE ACCUSED ME OF BEIN' DRAMATIC.
GOTHAM WILL BE MINE!
YOU'LL ALL SEE!

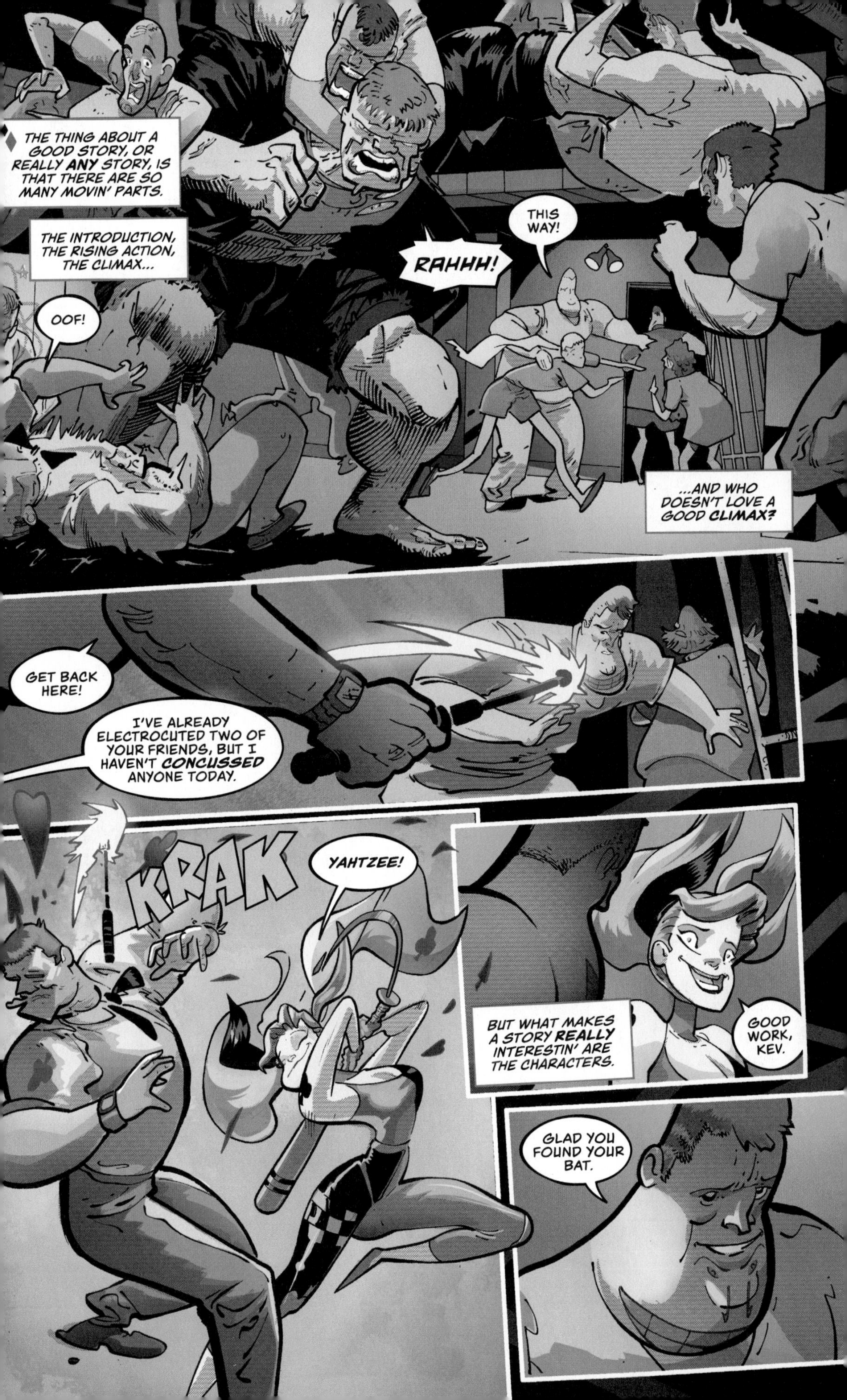
THE THING ABOUT A GOOD STORY, OR REALLY **ANY** STORY, IS THAT THERE ARE SO MANY MOVIN' PARTS.
THE INTRODUCTION, THE RISING ACTION, THE CLIMAX...
OOF!
RAHHH!
THIS WAY!
...AND WHO DOESN'T LOVE A GOOD **CLIMAX**?
GET BACK HERE!
I'VE ALREADY ELECTROCUTED TWO OF YOUR FRIENDS, BUT I HAVEN'T **CONCUSSED** ANYONE TODAY.
KRAK
YAHTZEE!
BUT WHAT MAKES A STORY **REALLY** INTERESTIN' ARE THE CHARACTERS.
GOOD WORK, KEV.
GLAD YOU FOUND YOUR BAT.

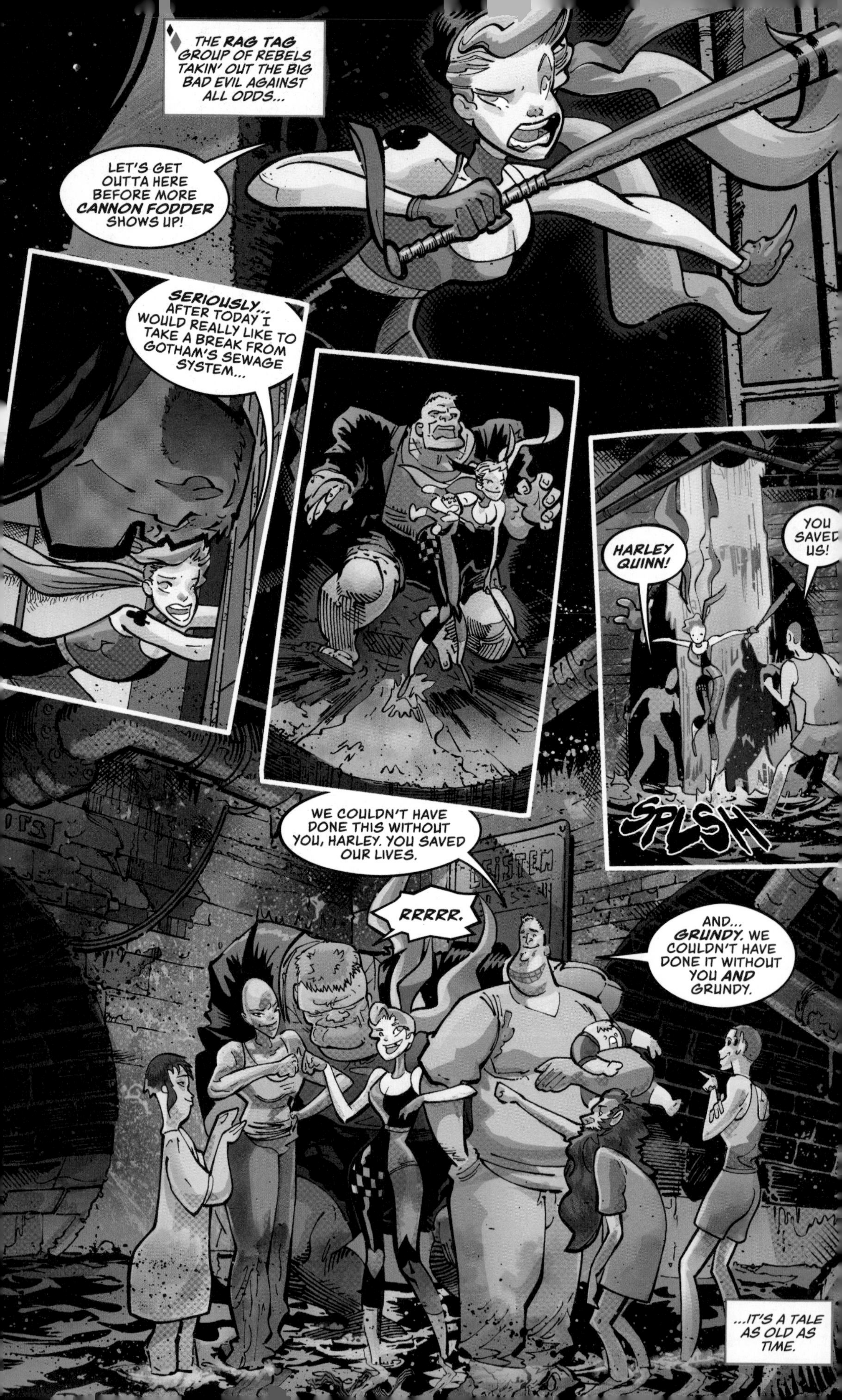
THE RAG TAG GROUP OF REBELS TAKIN' OUT THE BIG BAD EVIL AGAINST ALL ODDS...
LET'S GET OUTTA HERE BEFORE MORE CANNON FODDER SHOWS UP!
SERIOUSLY... AFTER TODAY I WOULD REALLY LIKE TO TAKE A BREAK FROM GOTHAM'S SEWAGE SYSTEM...
HARLEY QUINN!
YOU SAVED US!
SPLSH
WE COULDN'T HAVE DONE THIS WITHOUT YOU, HARLEY. YOU SAVED OUR LIVES.
RRRRR.
AND... GRUNDY. WE COULDN'T HAVE DONE IT WITHOUT YOU AND GRUNDY.
...IT'S A TALE AS OLD AS TIME.

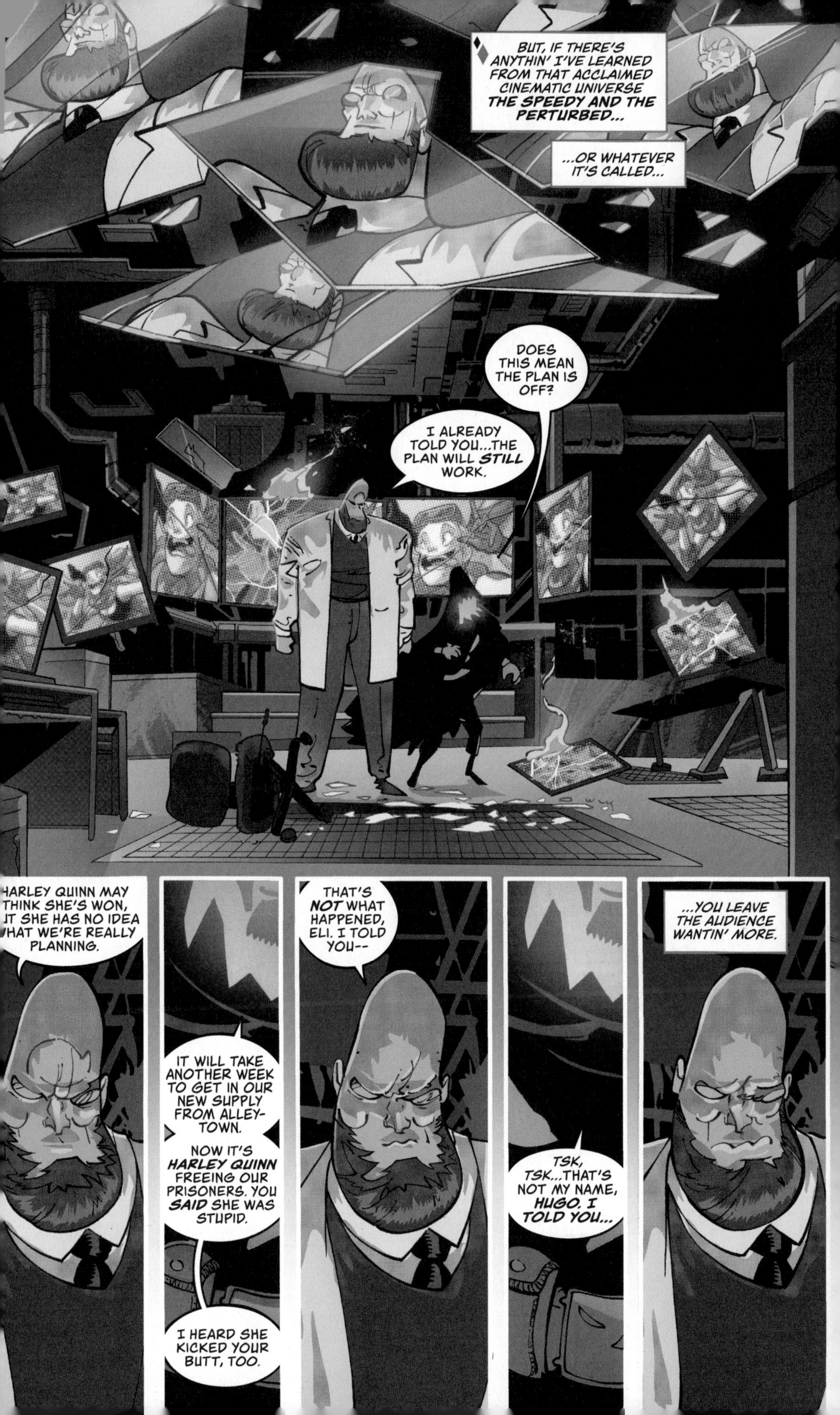
BUT, IF THERE'S ANYTHIN' I'VE LEARNED FROM THAT ACCLAIMED CINEMATIC UNIVERSE ***THE SPEEDY AND THE PERTURBED...***
...OR WHATEVER IT'S CALLED...
DOES THIS MEAN THE PLAN IS OFF?
I ALREADY TOLD YOU...THE PLAN WILL ***STILL*** WORK.
HARLEY QUINN MAY THINK SHE'S WON, IT SHE HAS NO IDEA WHAT WE'RE REALLY PLANNING.
IT WILL TAKE ANOTHER WEEK TO GET IN OUR NEW SUPPLY FROM ALLEY-TOWN.
NOW IT'S ***HARLEY QUINN*** FREEING OUR PRISONERS. YOU ***SAID*** SHE WAS STUPID.
I HEARD SHE KICKED YOUR BUTT, TOO.
THAT'S ***NOT*** WHAT HAPPENED, ELI. I TOLD YOU--
TSK, TSK...THAT'S NOT MY NAME, ***HUGO. I TOLD YOU...***
...YOU LEAVE THE AUDIENCE WANTIN' MORE.

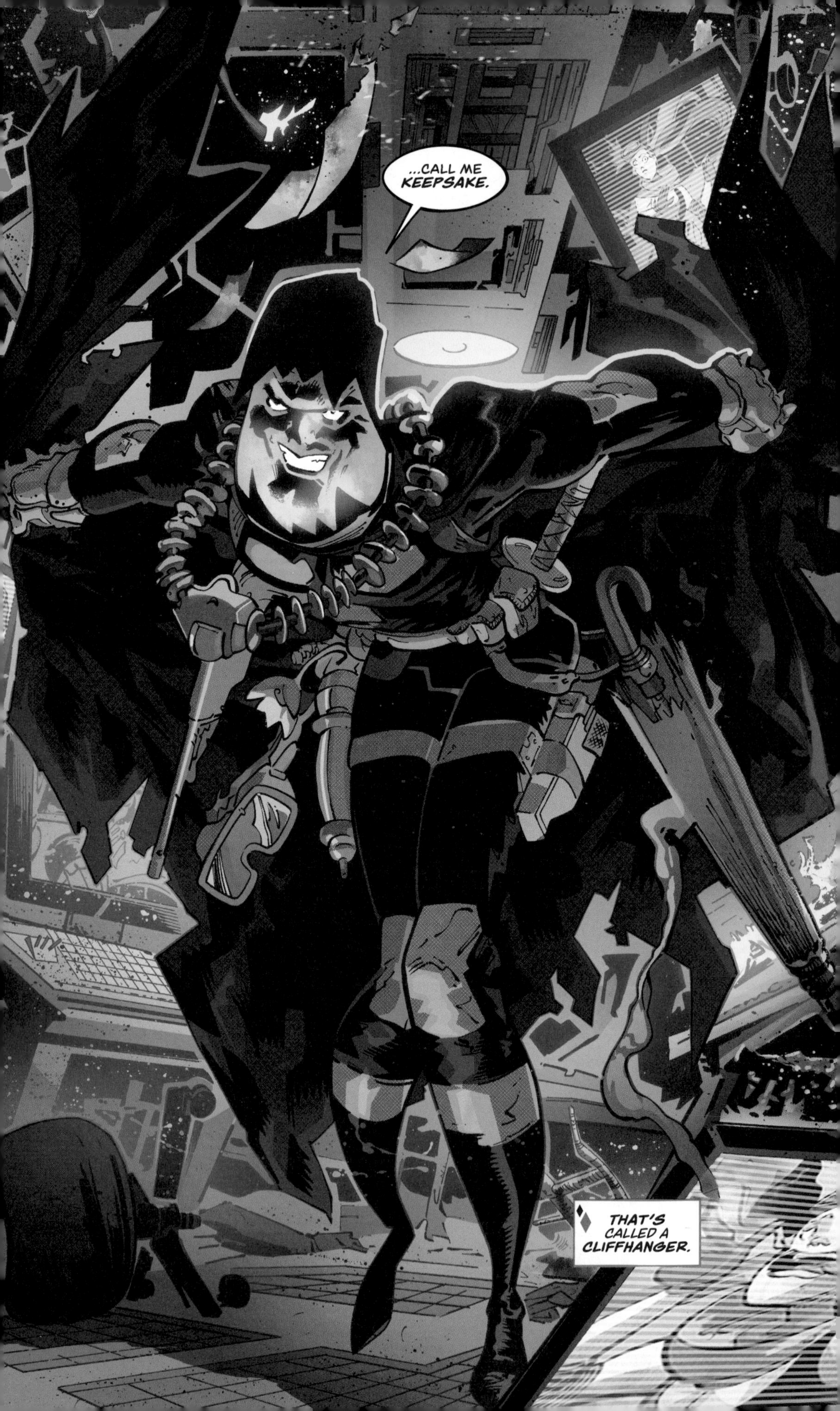
...CALL ME KEEPSAKE.
THAT'S CALLED A CLIFFHANGER.

Harley Quinn #6
Cover Art by Riley Rossmo

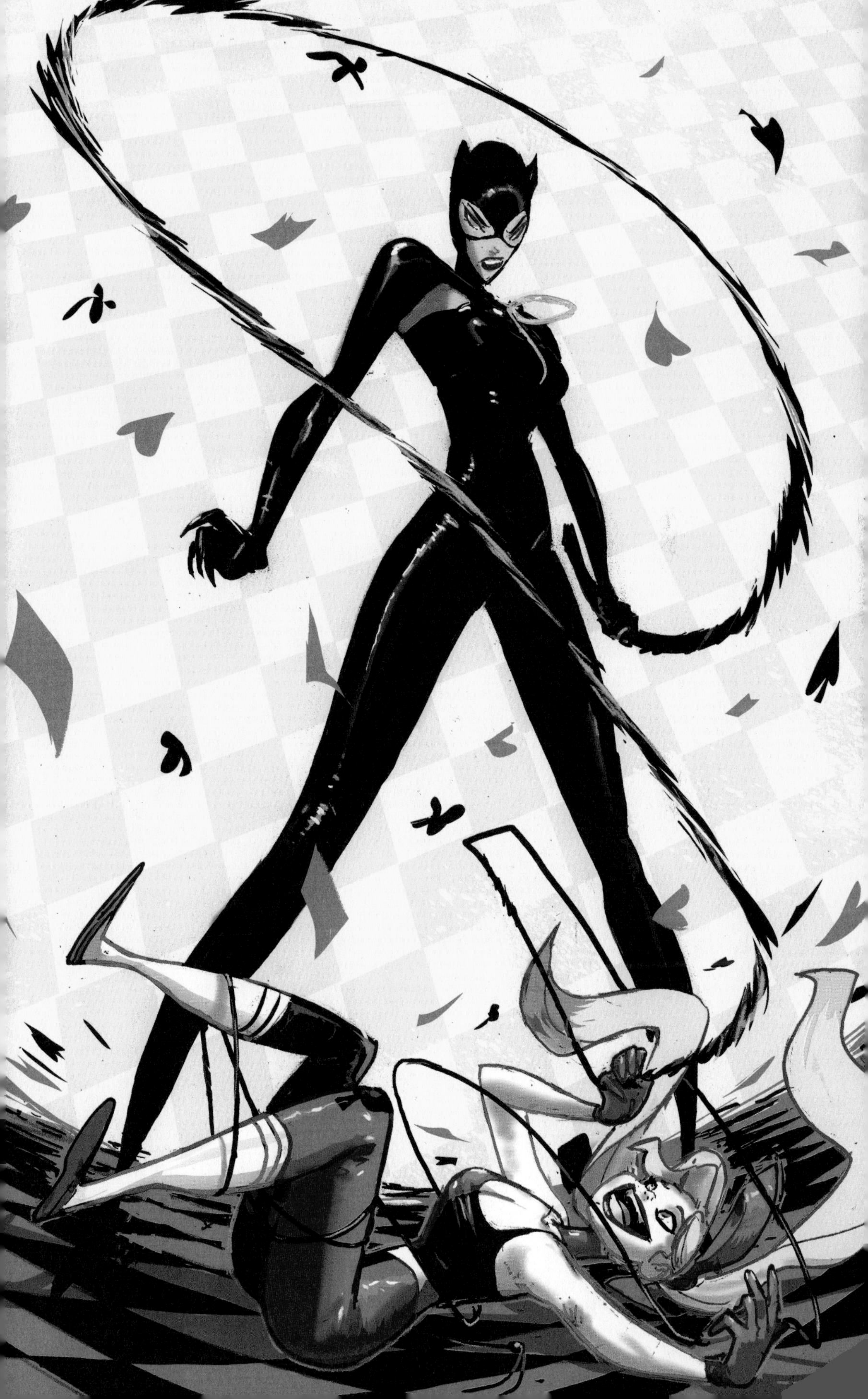

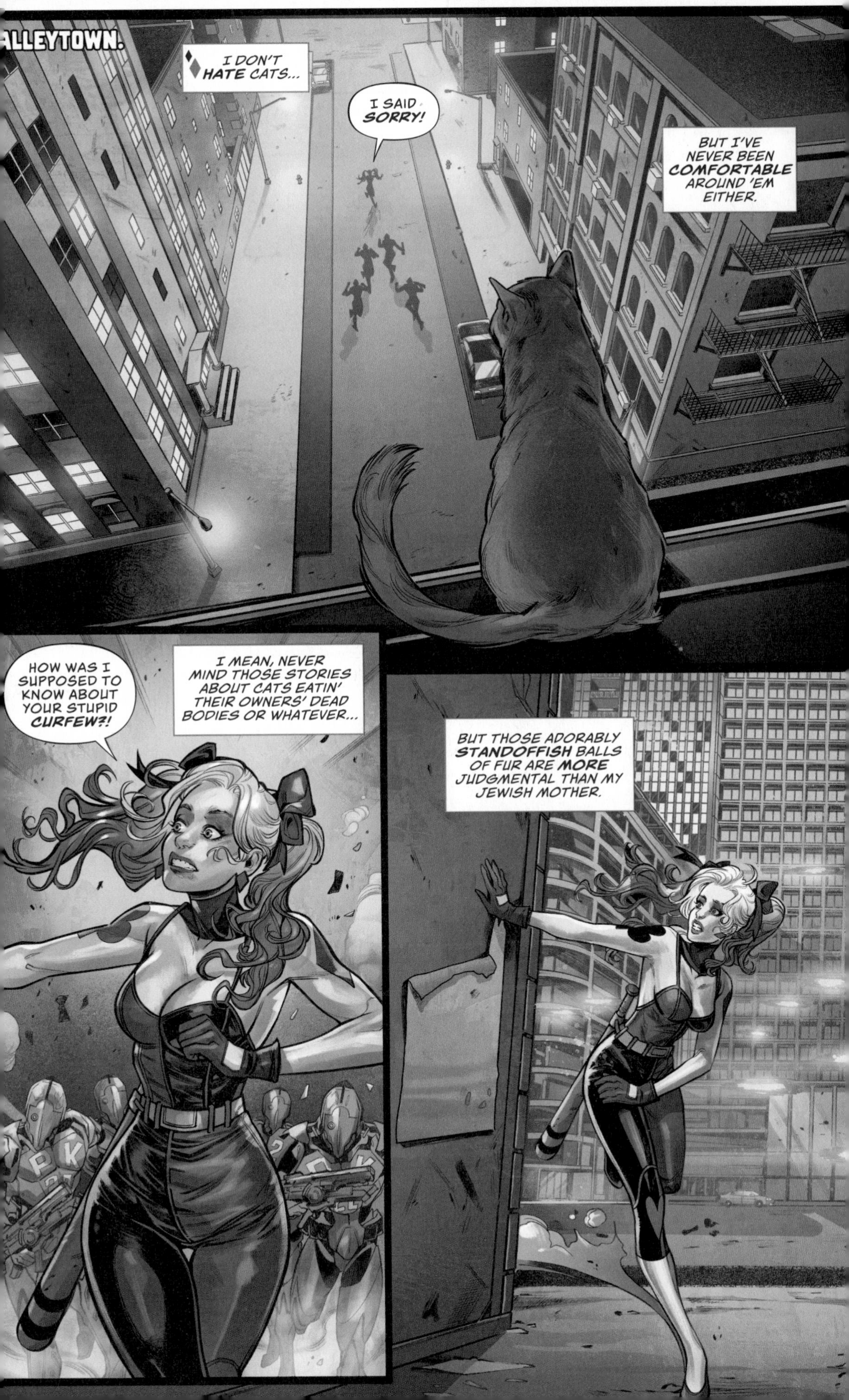
ALLEYTOWN.
I DON'T HATE CATS...
I SAID SORRY!
BUT I'VE NEVER BEEN COMFORTABLE AROUND 'EM EITHER.
HOW WAS I SUPPOSED TO KNOW ABOUT YOUR STUPID CURFEW?!
I MEAN, NEVER MIND THOSE STORIES ABOUT CATS EATIN' THEIR OWNERS' DEAD BODIES OR WHATEVER...
BUT THOSE ADORABLY STANDOFFISH BALLS OF FUR ARE MORE JUDGMENTAL THAN MY JEWISH MOTHER.

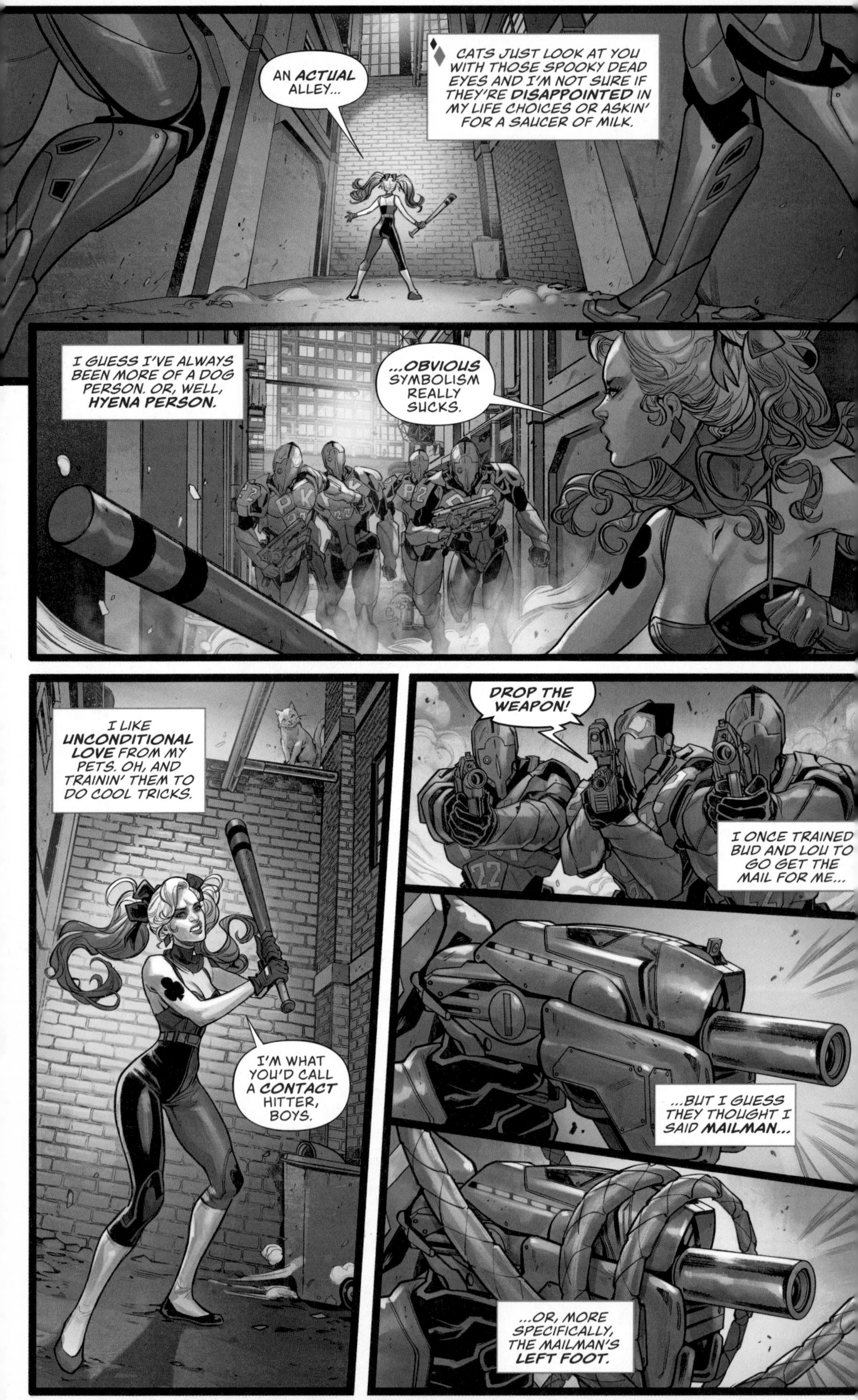
AN ACTUAL ALLEY...
CATS JUST LOOK AT YOU WITH THOSE SPOOKY DEAD EYES AND I'M NOT SURE IF THEY'RE DISAPPOINTED IN MY LIFE CHOICES OR ASKIN' FOR A SAUCER OF MILK.
I GUESS I'VE ALWAYS BEEN MORE OF A DOG PERSON. OR, WELL, HYENA PERSON.
...OBVIOUS SYMBOLISM REALLY SUCKS.
I LIKE UNCONDITIONAL LOVE FROM MY PETS. OH, AND TRAININ' THEM TO DO COOL TRICKS.
I'M WHAT YOU'D CALL A CONTACT HITTER, BOYS.
DROP THE WEAPON!
I ONCE TRAINED BUD AND LOU TO GO GET THE MAIL FOR ME...
...BUT I GUESS THEY THOUGHT I SAID MAILMAN...
...OR, MORE SPECIFICALLY, THE MAILMAN'S LEFT FOOT.

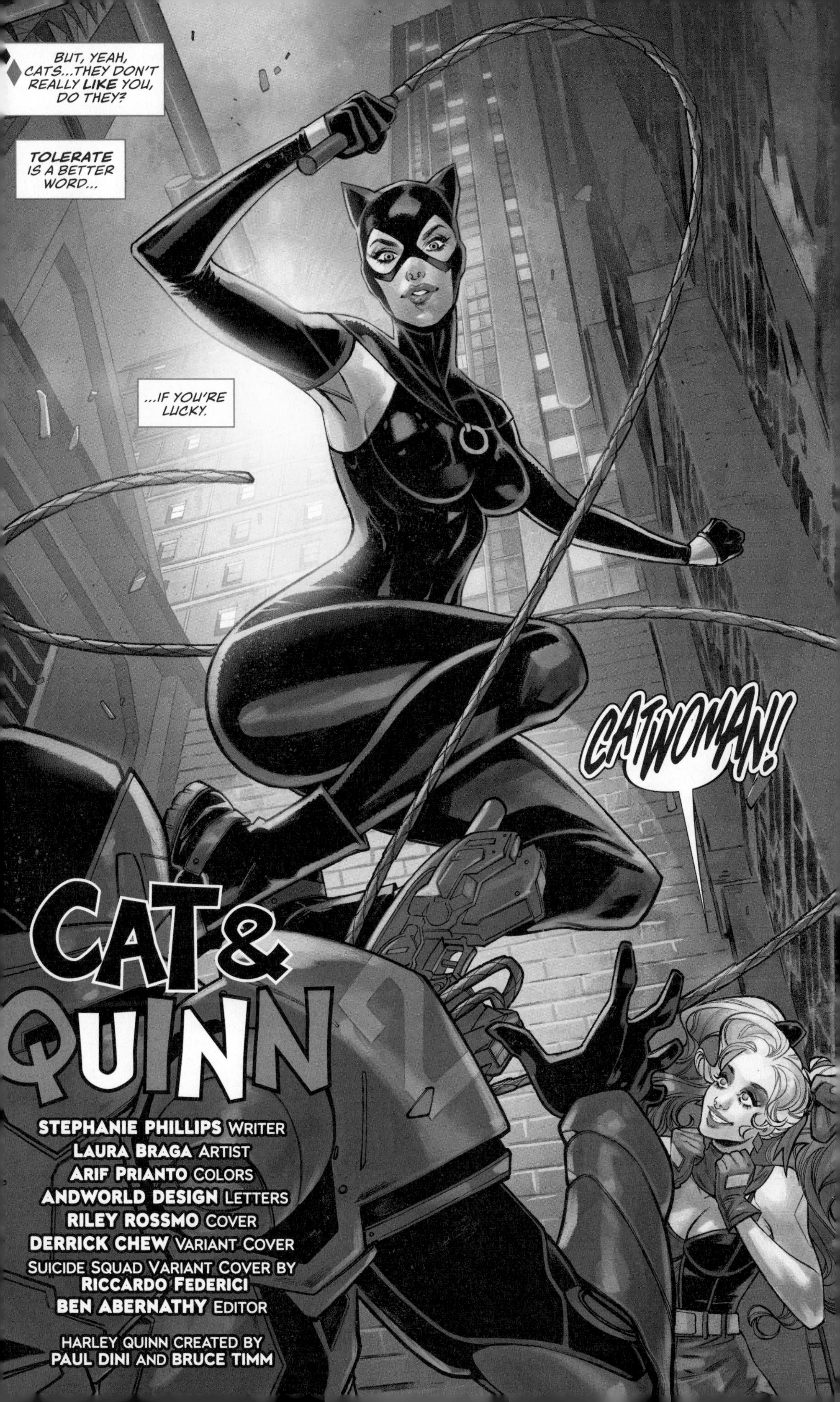
BUT, YEAH, CATS...THEY DON'T REALLY LIKE YOU, DO THEY?
TOLERATE IS A BETTER WORD...
...IF YOU'RE LUCKY.
CATWOMAN!
CAT& QUINN
STEPHANIE PHILLIPS WRITER
LAURA BRAGA ARTIST
ARIF PRIANTO COLORS
ANDWORLD DESIGN LETTERS
RILEY ROSSMO COVER
DERRICK CHEW VARIANT COVER
SUICIDE SQUAD VARIANT COVER BY RICCARDO FEDERICI
BEN ABERNATHY EDITOR
HARLEY QUINN CREATED BY PAUL DINI AND BRUCE TIMM

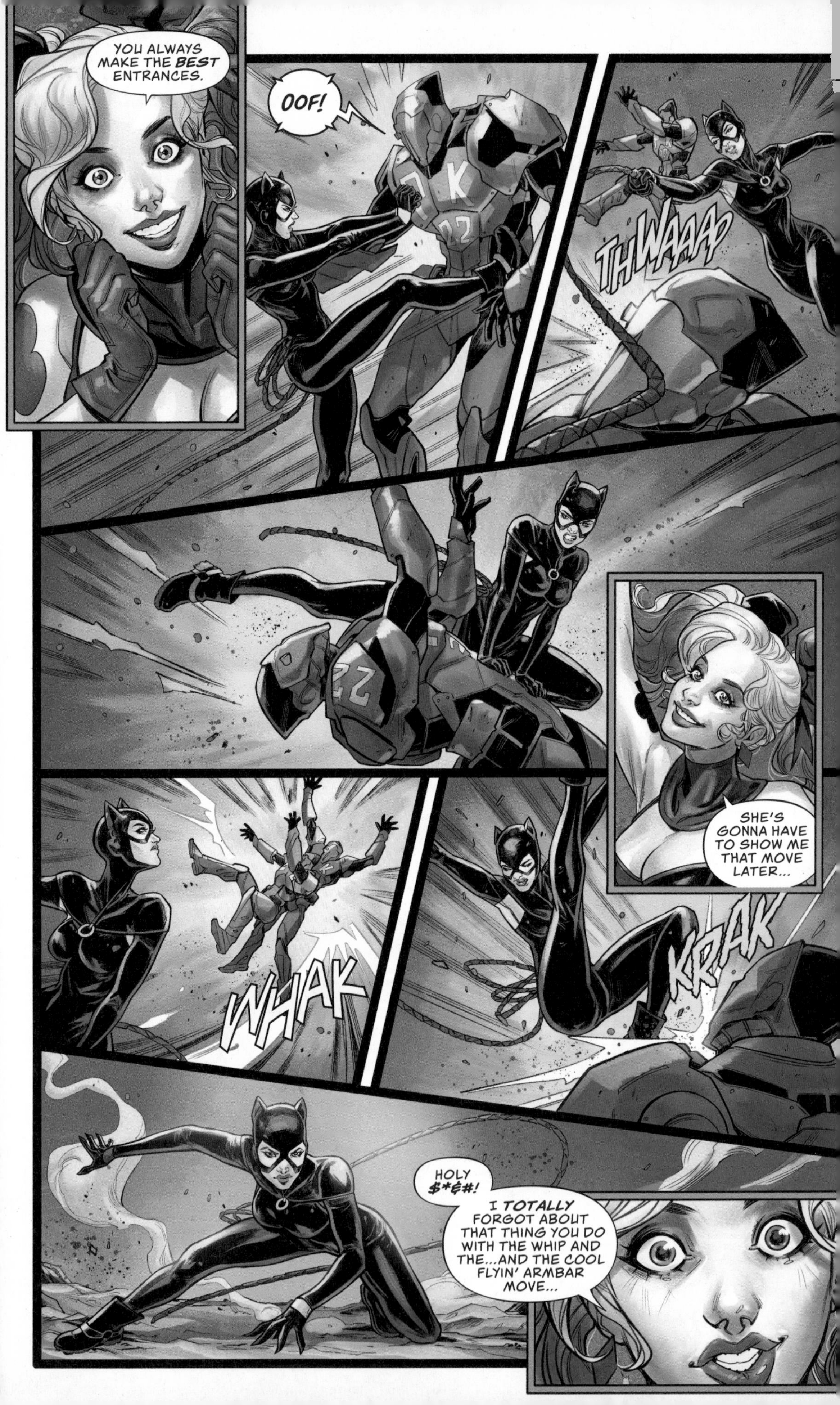

YOU ALWAYS MAKE THE BEST ENTRANCES.
OOF!
THWAAAP
SHE'S GONNA HAVE TO SHOW ME THAT MOVE LATER...
WHAK
KRAK
HOLY $*&#!
I TOTALLY FORGOT ABOUT THAT THING YOU DO WITH THE WHIP AND THE...AND THE COOL FLYIN' ARMBAR MOVE...

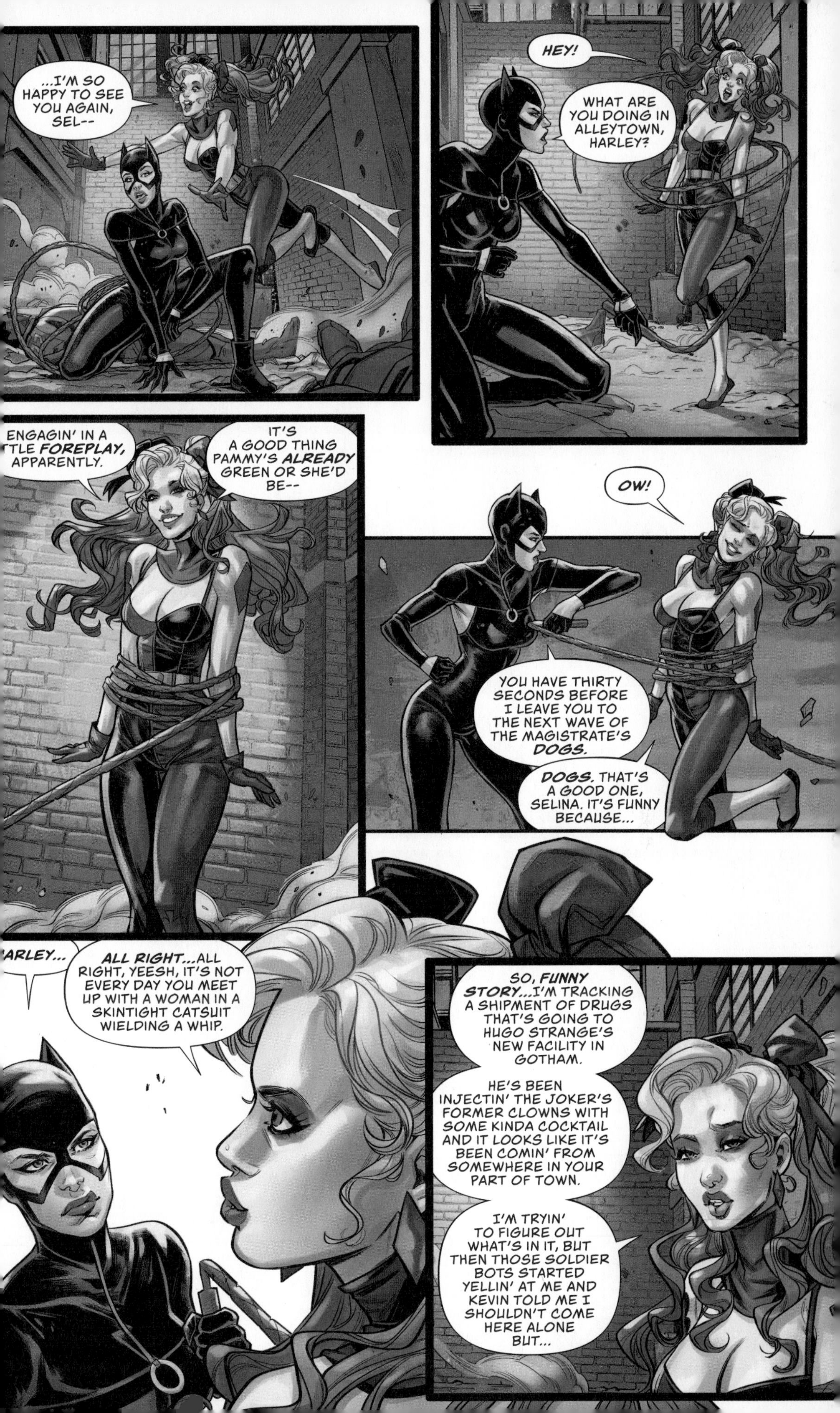
...I'M SO HAPPY TO SEE YOU AGAIN, SEL--
HEY!
WHAT ARE YOU DOING IN ALLEYTOWN, HARLEY?
ENGAGIN' IN A TTLE FOREPLAY, APPARENTLY.
IT'S A GOOD THING PAMMY'S ALREADY GREEN OR SHE'D BE--
OW!
YOU HAVE THIRTY SECONDS BEFORE I LEAVE YOU TO THE NEXT WAVE OF THE MAGISTRATE'S DOGS.
DOGS. THAT'S A GOOD ONE, SELINA. IT'S FUNNY BECAUSE...
ARLEY...
ALL RIGHT...ALL RIGHT, YEESH, IT'S NOT EVERY DAY YOU MEET UP WITH A WOMAN IN A SKINTIGHT CATSUIT WIELDING A WHIP.
SO, FUNNY STORY...I'M TRACKING A SHIPMENT OF DRUGS THAT'S GOING TO HUGO STRANGE'S NEW FACILITY IN GOTHAM.
HE'S BEEN INJECTIN' THE JOKER'S FORMER CLOWNS WITH SOME KINDA COCKTAIL AND IT LOOKS LIKE IT'S BEEN COMIN' FROM SOMEWHERE IN YOUR PART OF TOWN.
I'M TRYIN' TO FIGURE OUT WHAT'S IN IT, BUT THEN THOSE SOLDIER BOTS STARTED YELLIN' AT ME AND KEVIN TOLD ME I SHOULDN'T COME HERE ALONE BUT...

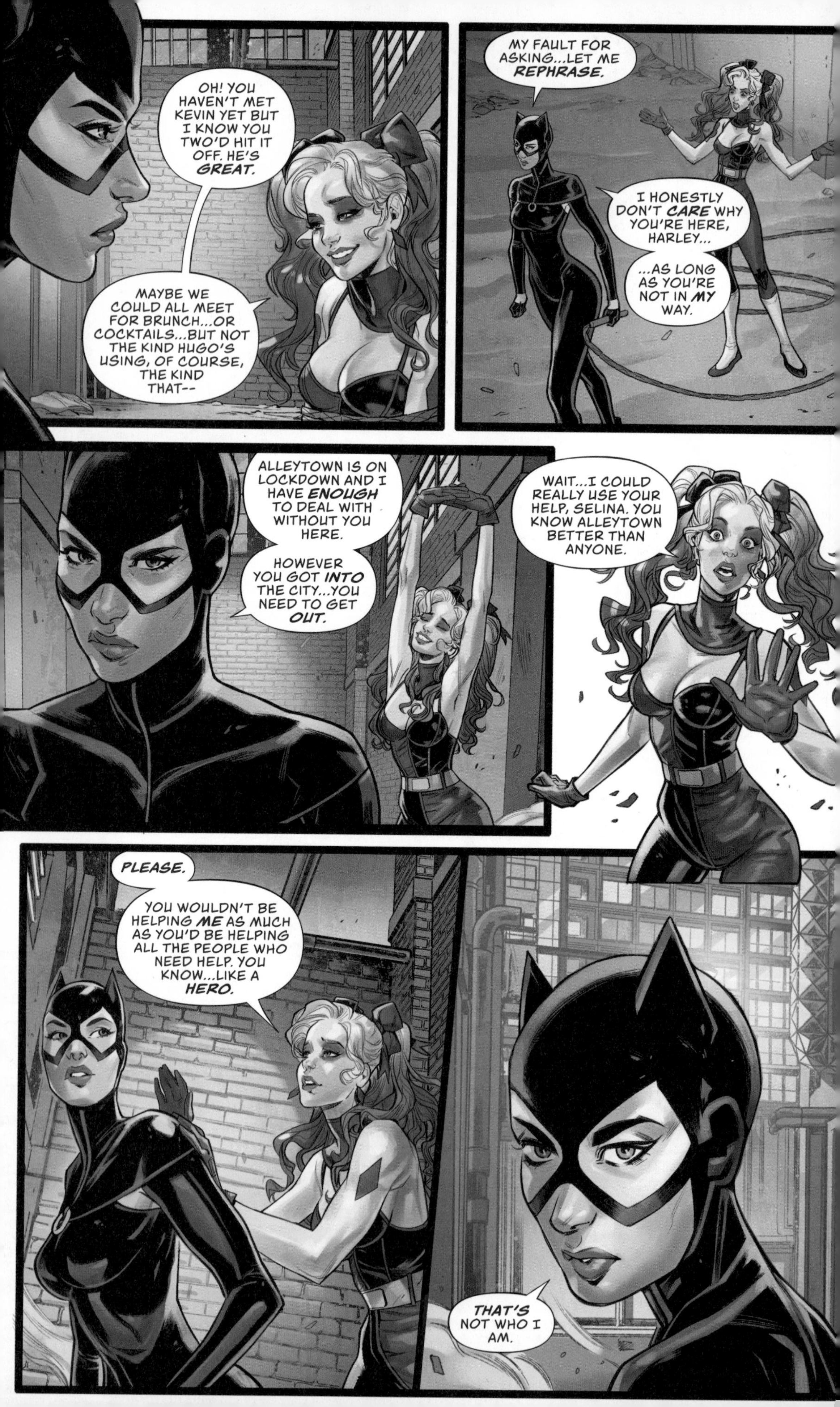
OH! YOU HAVEN'T MET KEVIN YET BUT I KNOW YOU TWO'D HIT IT OFF. HE'S GREAT.
MAYBE WE COULD ALL MEET FOR BRUNCH...OR COCKTAILS...BUT NOT THE KIND HUGO'S USING, OF COURSE, THE KIND THAT--
MY FAULT FOR ASKING...LET ME REPHRASE.
I HONESTLY DON'T CARE WHY YOU'RE HERE, HARLEY...
...AS LONG AS YOU'RE NOT IN MY WAY.
ALLEYTOWN IS ON LOCKDOWN AND I HAVE ENOUGH TO DEAL WITH WITHOUT YOU HERE.
HOWEVER YOU GOT INTO THE CITY...YOU NEED TO GET OUT.
WAIT...I COULD REALLY USE YOUR HELP, SELINA. YOU KNOW ALLEYTOWN BETTER THAN ANYONE.
PLEASE.
YOU WOULDN'T BE HELPING ME AS MUCH AS YOU'D BE HELPING ALL THE PEOPLE WHO NEED HELP. YOU KNOW...LIKE A HERO.
THAT'S NOT WHO I AM.

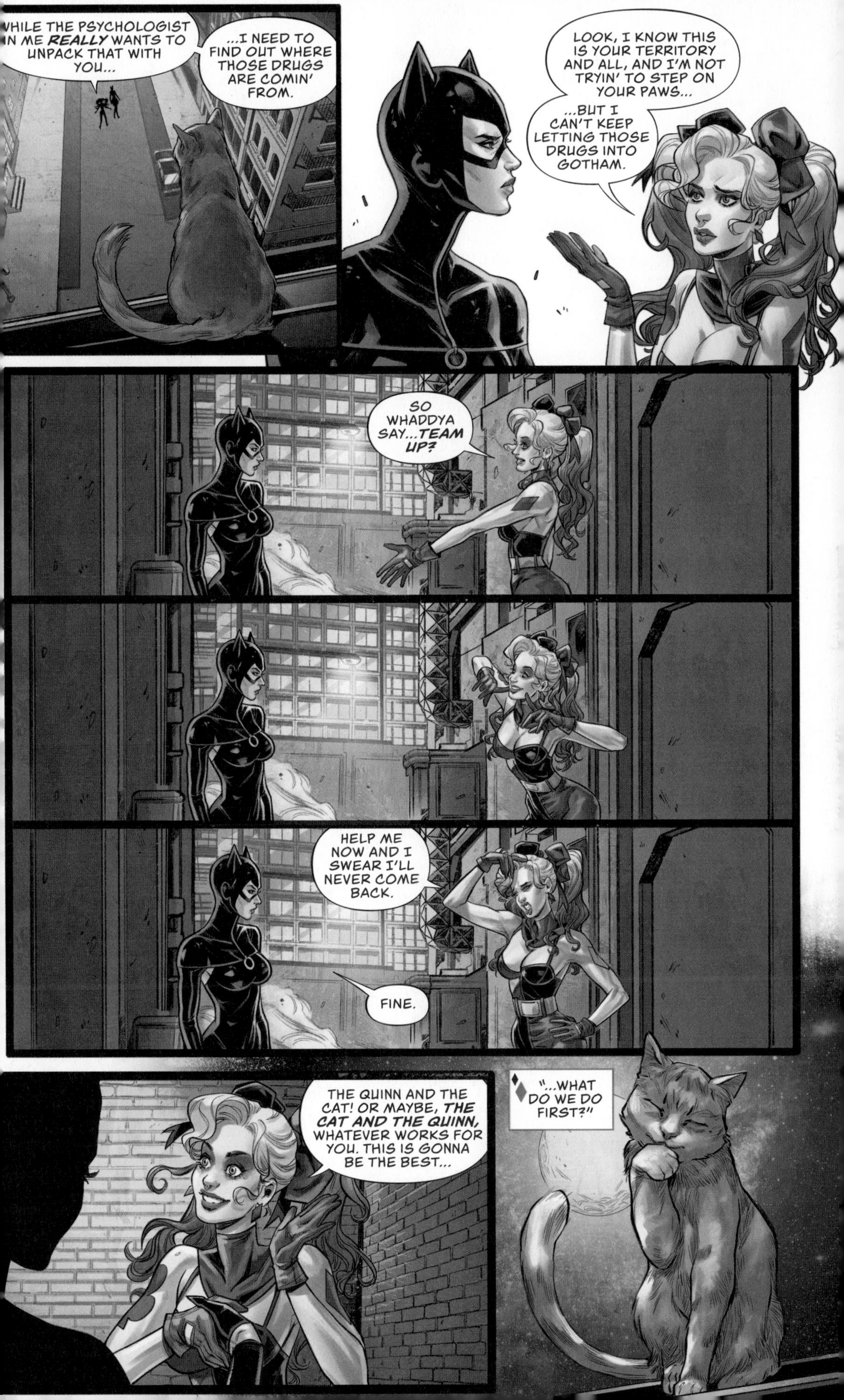
WHILE THE PSYCHOLOGIST IN ME *REALLY* WANTS TO UNPACK THAT WITH YOU...
...I NEED TO FIND OUT WHERE THOSE DRUGS ARE COMIN' FROM.
LOOK, I KNOW THIS IS YOUR TERRITORY AND ALL, AND I'M NOT TRYIN' TO STEP ON YOUR PAWS...
...BUT I CAN'T KEEP LETTING THOSE DRUGS INTO GOTHAM.
SO WHADDYA SAY...*TEAM UP?*
HELP ME NOW AND I SWEAR I'LL NEVER COME BACK.
FINE.
THE QUINN AND THE CAT! OR MAYBE, *THE CAT AND THE QUINN,* WHATEVER WORKS FOR YOU. THIS IS GONNA BE THE BEST...
"...WHAT DO WE DO FIRST?"

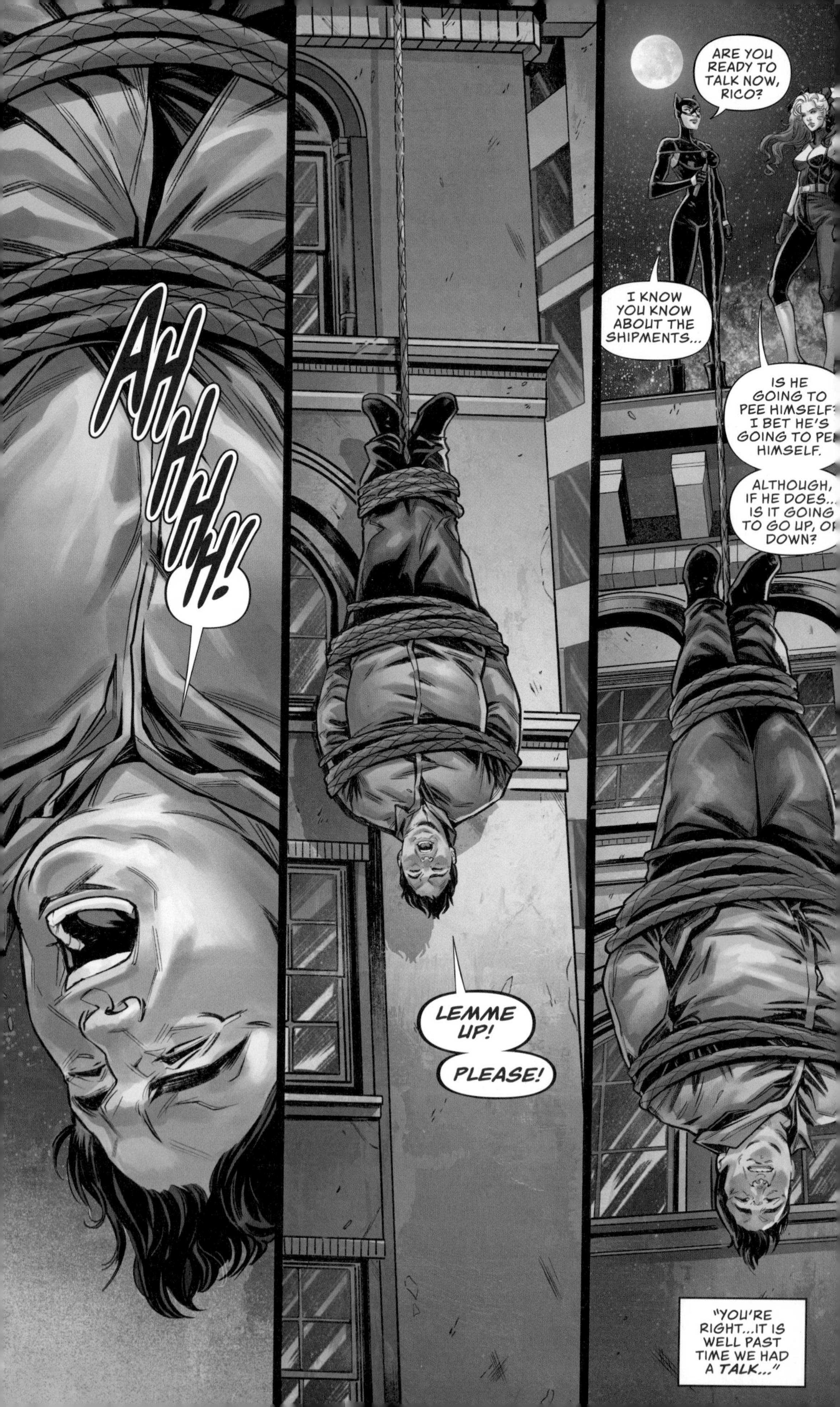
AHHHHH!
LEMME UP!
PLEASE!
ARE YOU READY TO TALK NOW, RICO?
I KNOW YOU KNOW ABOUT THE SHIPMENTS...
IS HE GOING TO PEE HIMSELF? I BET HE'S GOING TO PEE HIMSELF.
ALTHOUGH, IF HE DOES... IS IT GOING TO GO UP, OR DOWN?
"YOU'RE RIGHT...IT IS WELL PAST TIME WE HAD A *TALK*..."

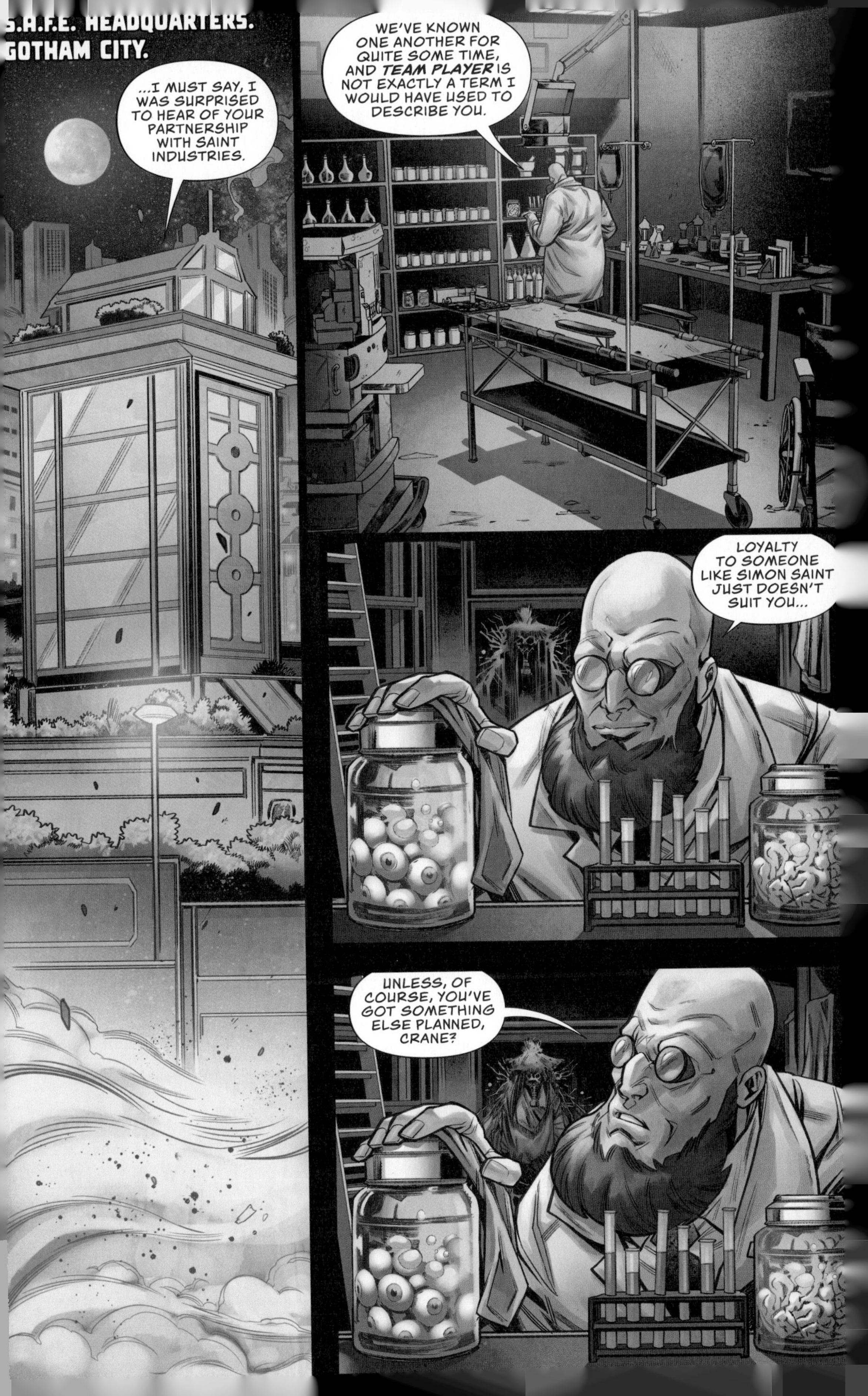
S.A.F.E. HEADQUARTERS. GOTHAM CITY.
...I MUST SAY, I WAS SURPRISED TO HEAR OF YOUR PARTNERSHIP WITH SAINT INDUSTRIES.
WE'VE KNOWN ONE ANOTHER FOR QUITE SOME TIME, AND TEAM PLAYER IS NOT EXACTLY A TERM I WOULD HAVE USED TO DESCRIBE YOU.
LOYALTY TO SOMEONE LIKE SIMON SAINT JUST DOESN'T SUIT YOU...
UNLESS, OF COURSE, YOU'VE GOT SOMETHING ELSE PLANNED, CRANE?

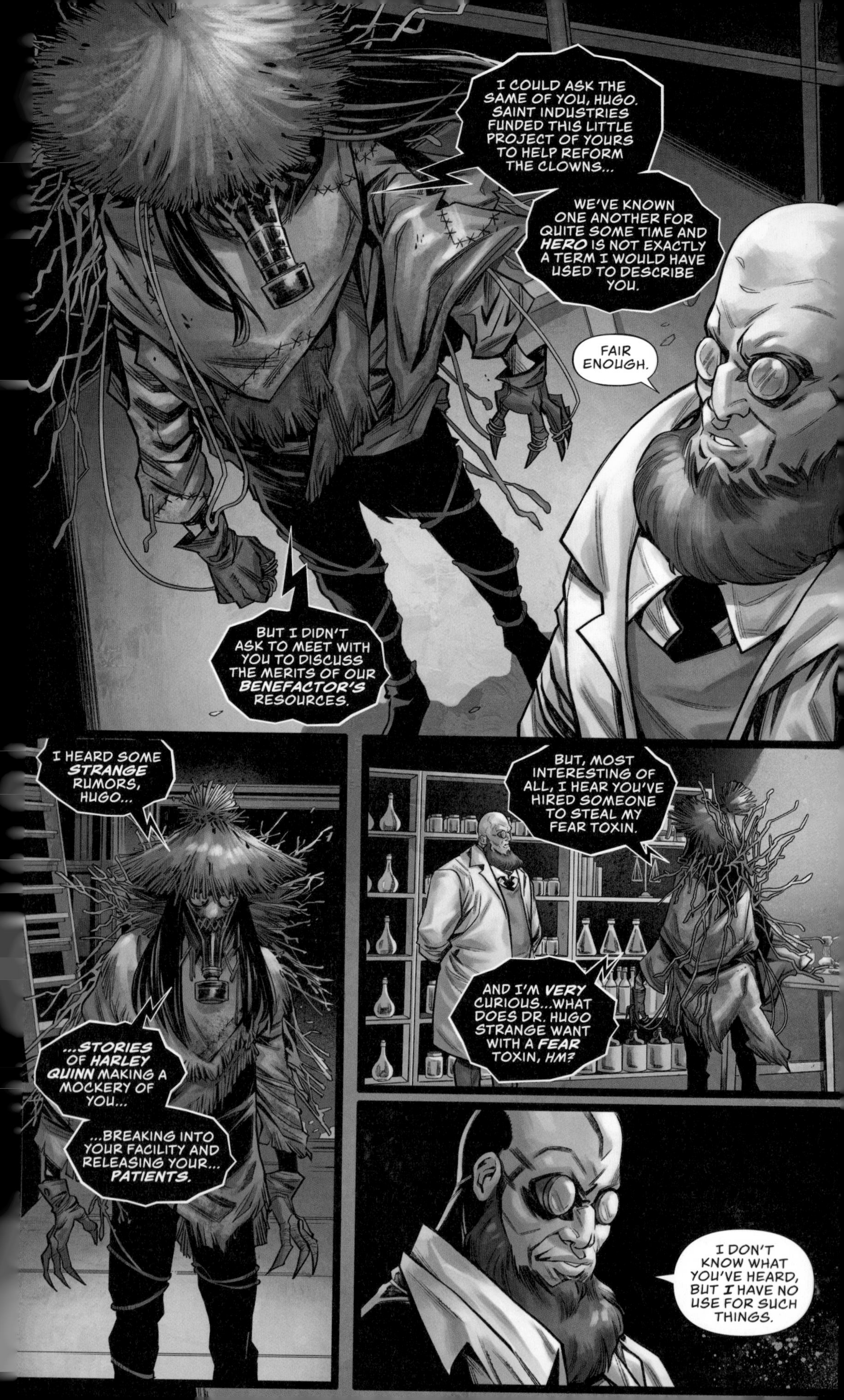

I COULD ASK THE SAME OF YOU, HUGO. SAINT INDUSTRIES FUNDED THIS LITTLE PROJECT OF YOURS TO HELP REFORM THE CLOWNS...
WE'VE KNOWN ONE ANOTHER FOR QUITE SOME TIME AND HERO IS NOT EXACTLY A TERM I WOULD HAVE USED TO DESCRIBE YOU.
FAIR ENOUGH.
BUT I DIDN'T ASK TO MEET WITH YOU TO DISCUSS THE MERITS OF OUR BENEFACTOR'S RESOURCES.
I HEARD SOME STRANGE RUMORS, HUGO...
...STORIES OF HARLEY QUINN MAKING A MOCKERY OF YOU...
...BREAKING INTO YOUR FACILITY AND RELEASING YOUR... PATIENTS.
BUT, MOST INTERESTING OF ALL, I HEAR YOU'VE HIRED SOMEONE TO STEAL MY FEAR TOXIN.
AND I'M VERY CURIOUS...WHAT DOES DR. HUGO STRANGE WANT WITH A FEAR TOXIN, HM?
I DON'T KNOW WHAT YOU'VE HEARD, BUT I HAVE NO USE FOR SUCH THINGS.

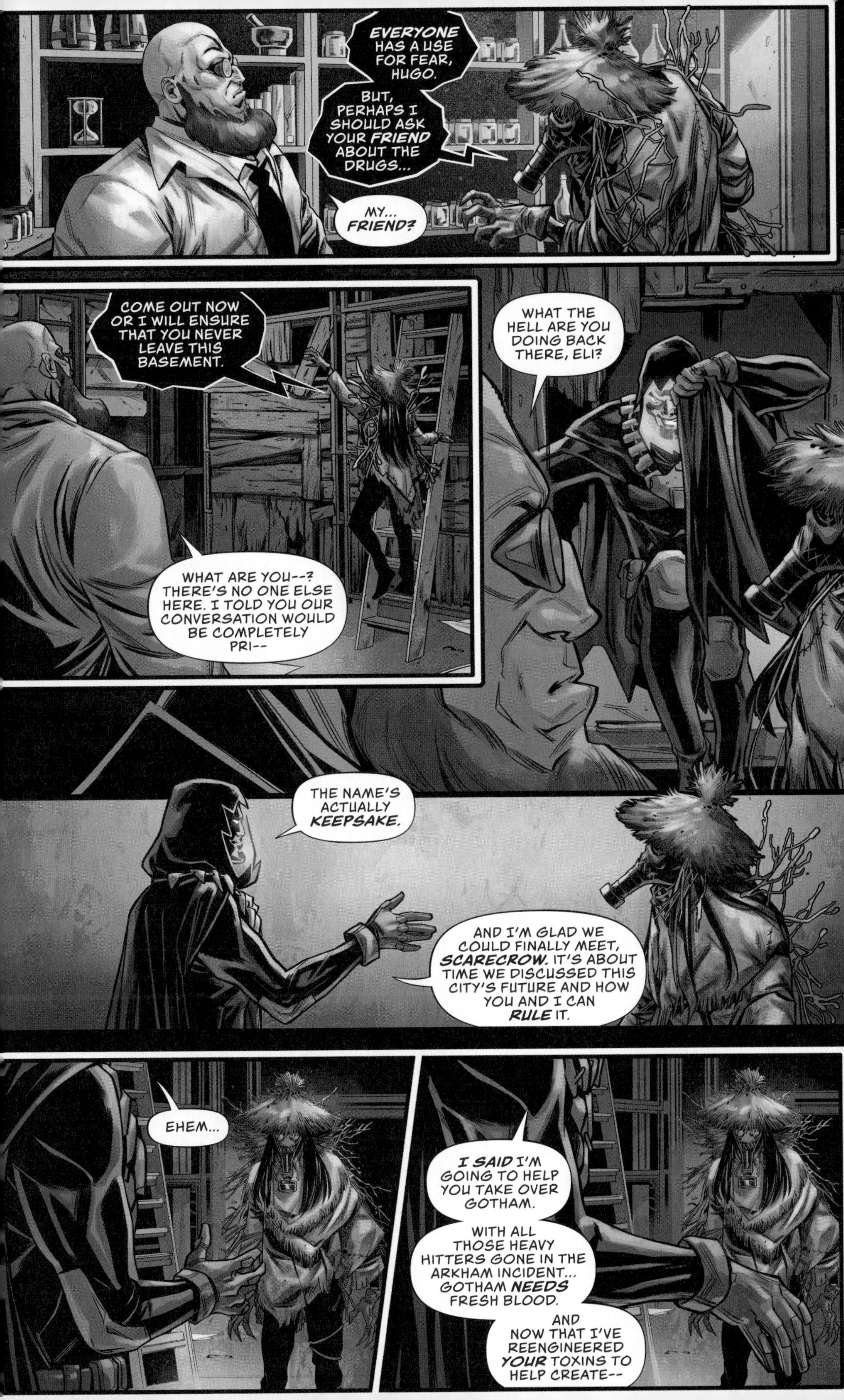
EVERYONE HAS A USE FOR FEAR, HUGO.
BUT, PERHAPS I SHOULD ASK YOUR FRIEND ABOUT THE DRUGS...
MY... FRIEND?
COME OUT NOW OR I WILL ENSURE THAT YOU NEVER LEAVE THIS BASEMENT.
WHAT ARE YOU--? THERE'S NO ONE ELSE HERE. I TOLD YOU OUR CONVERSATION WOULD BE COMPLETELY PRI--
WHAT THE HELL ARE YOU DOING BACK THERE, ELI?
THE NAME'S ACTUALLY KEEPSAKE.
AND I'M GLAD WE COULD FINALLY MEET, SCARECROW. IT'S ABOUT TIME WE DISCUSSED THIS CITY'S FUTURE AND HOW YOU AND I CAN RULE IT.
EHEM...
I SAID I'M GOING TO HELP YOU TAKE OVER GOTHAM.
WITH ALL THOSE HEAVY HITTERS GONE IN THE ARKHAM INCIDENT... GOTHAM NEEDS FRESH BLOOD.
AND NOW THAT I'VE REENGINEERED YOUR TOXINS TO HELP CREATE--

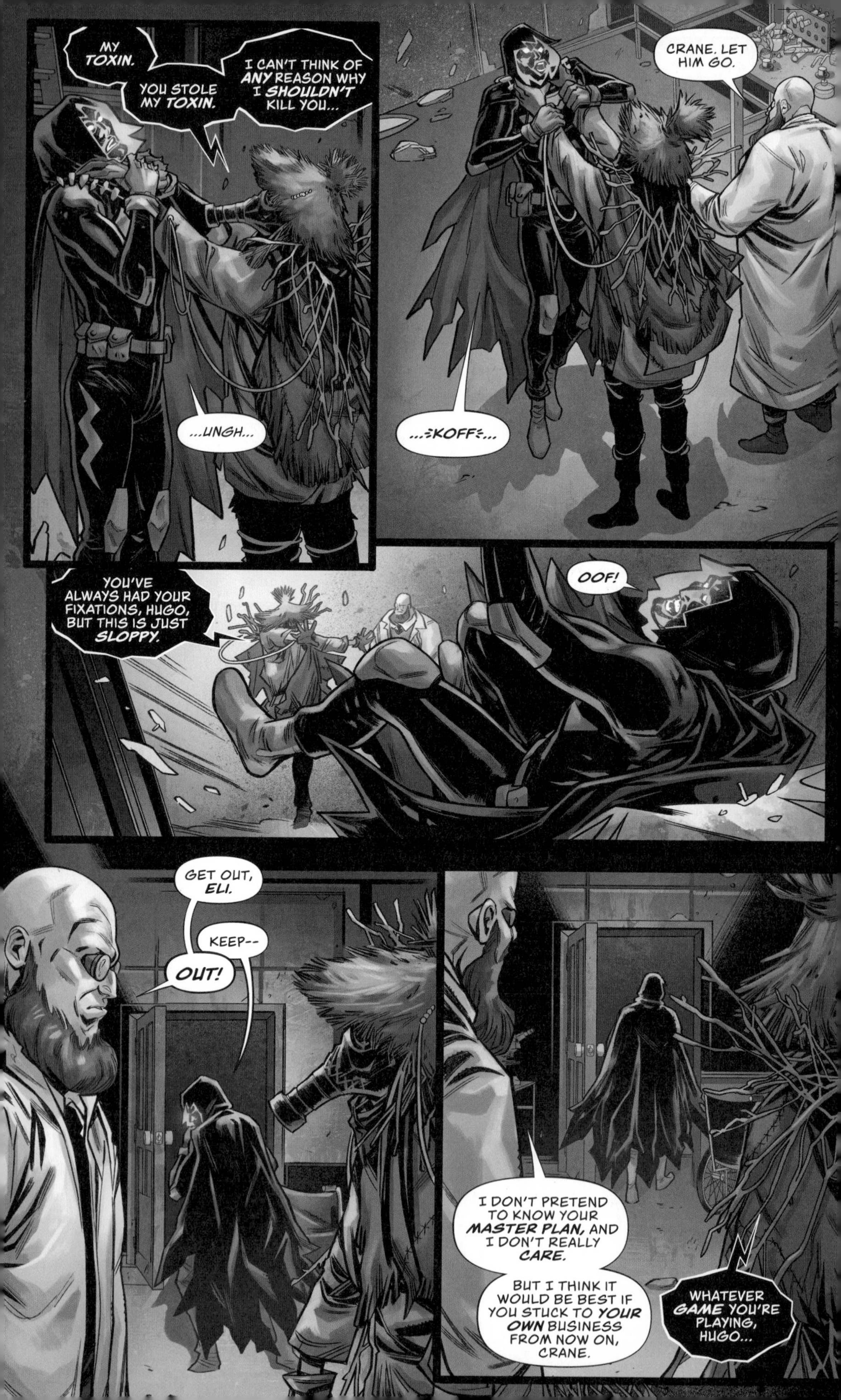

MY TOXIN.
YOU STOLE MY TOXIN.
I CAN'T THINK OF ANY REASON WHY I SHOULDN'T KILL YOU...
...UNGH...
CRANE. LET HIM GO.
...KOFF...
YOU'VE ALWAYS HAD YOUR FIXATIONS, HUGO, BUT THIS IS JUST SLOPPY.
OOF!
GET OUT, ELI.
KEEP--
OUT!
I DON'T PRETEND TO KNOW YOUR MASTER PLAN, AND I DON'T REALLY CARE.
BUT I THINK IT WOULD BE BEST IF YOU STUCK TO YOUR OWN BUSINESS FROM NOW ON, CRANE.
WHATEVER GAME YOU'RE PLAYING, HUGO...

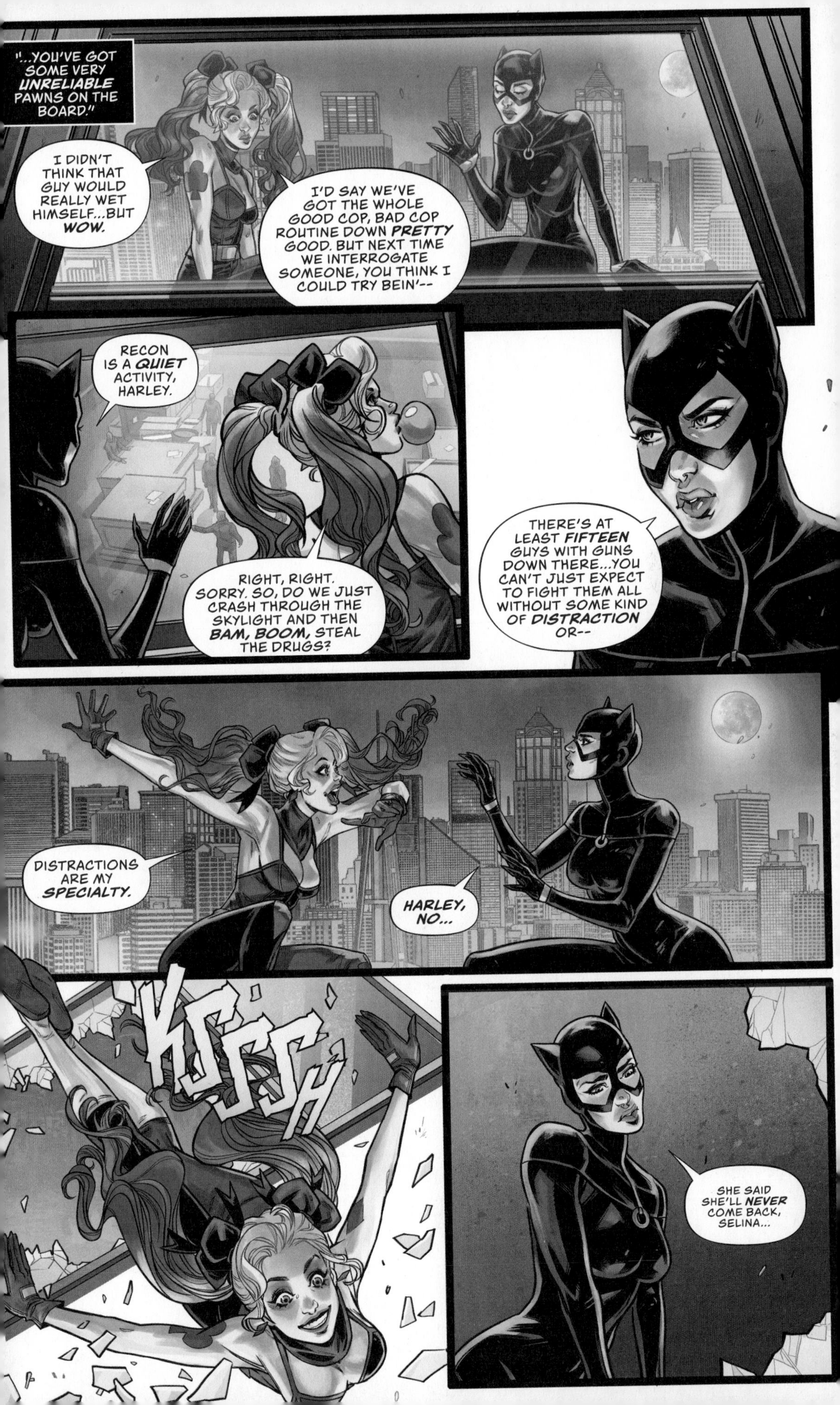
"...YOU'VE GOT SOME VERY UNRELIABLE PAWNS ON THE BOARD."
I DIDN'T THINK THAT GUY WOULD REALLY WET HIMSELF...BUT WOW.
I'D SAY WE'VE GOT THE WHOLE GOOD COP, BAD COP ROUTINE DOWN PRETTY GOOD. BUT NEXT TIME WE INTERROGATE SOMEONE, YOU THINK I COULD TRY BEIN'--
RECON IS A QUIET ACTIVITY, HARLEY.
RIGHT, RIGHT. SORRY. SO, DO WE JUST CRASH THROUGH THE SKYLIGHT AND THEN BAM, BOOM, STEAL THE DRUGS?
THERE'S AT LEAST FIFTEEN GUYS WITH GUNS DOWN THERE...YOU CAN'T JUST EXPECT TO FIGHT THEM ALL WITHOUT SOME KIND OF DISTRACTION OR--
DISTRACTIONS ARE MY SPECIALTY.
HARLEY, NO...
KSSSH
SHE SAID SHE'LL NEVER COME BACK, SELINA...

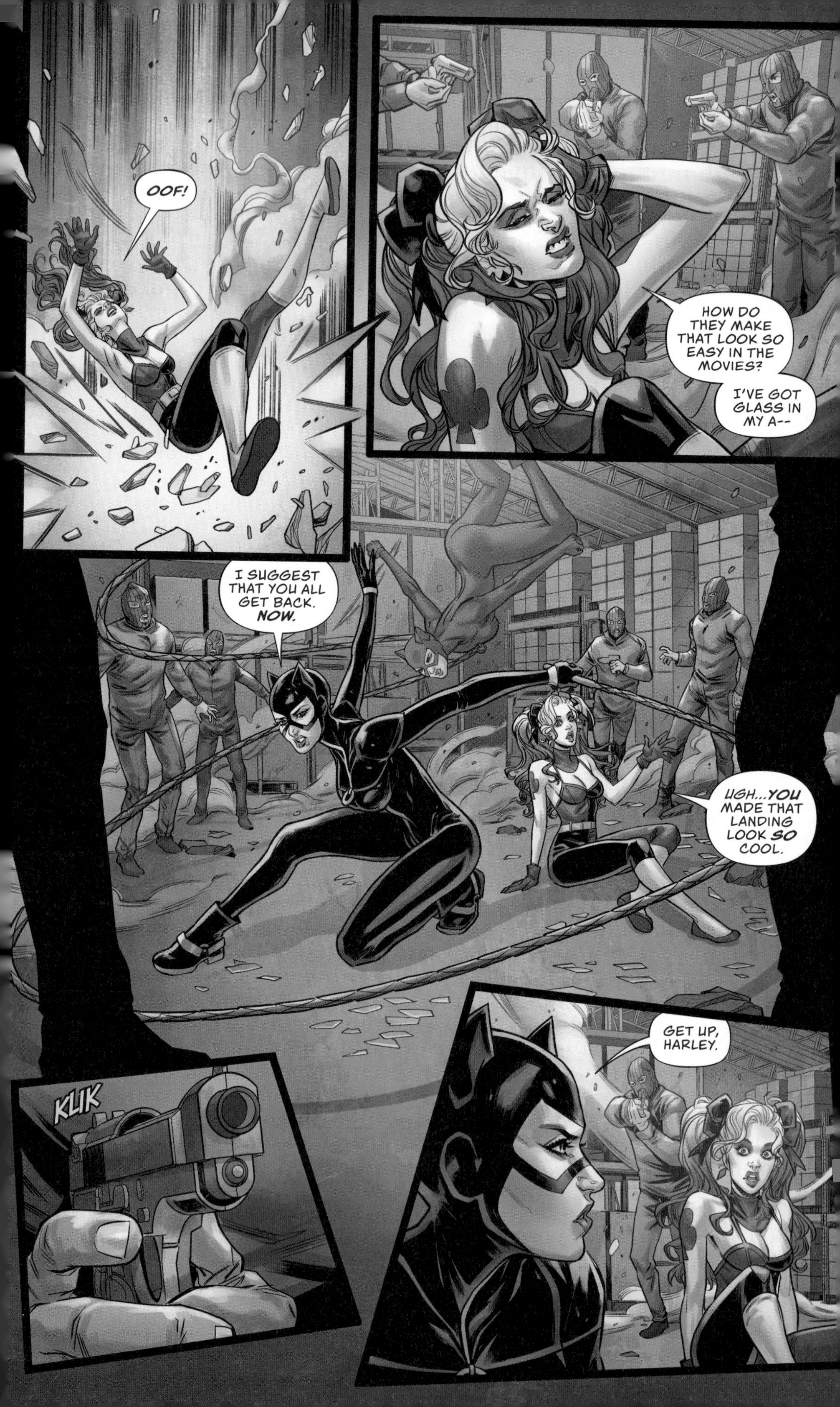
OOF!
HOW DO THEY MAKE THAT LOOK SO EASY IN THE MOVIES?
I'VE GOT GLASS IN MY A--
I SUGGEST THAT YOU ALL GET BACK. NOW.
UGH...YOU MADE THAT LANDING LOOK SO COOL.
KLIK
GET UP, HARLEY.

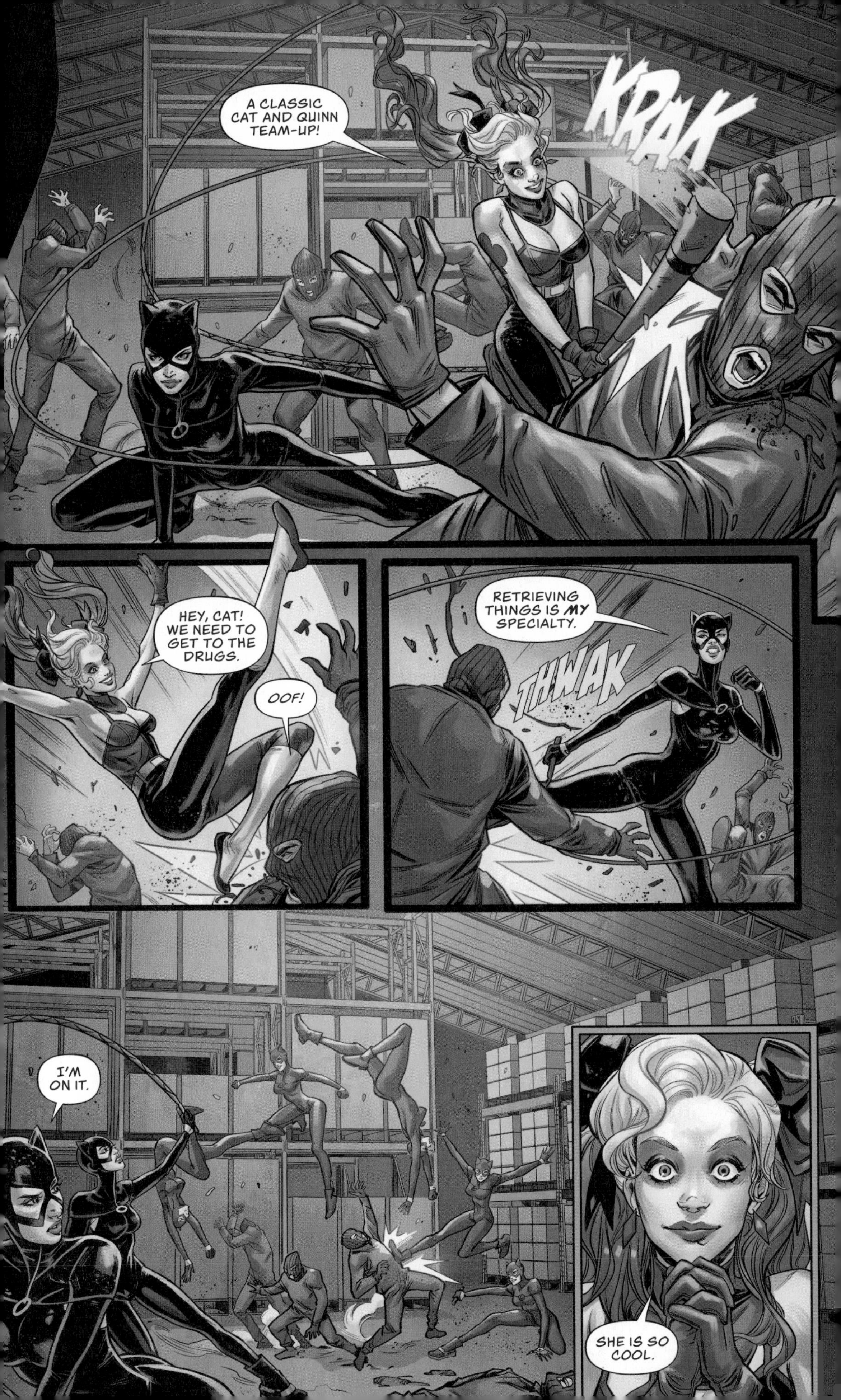

A CLASSIC CAT AND QUINN TEAM-UP!
KRAK
HEY, CAT! WE NEED TO GET TO THE DRUGS.
OOF!
RETRIEVING THINGS IS *MY* SPECIALTY.
THWAK
I'M ON IT.
SHE IS SO COOL.

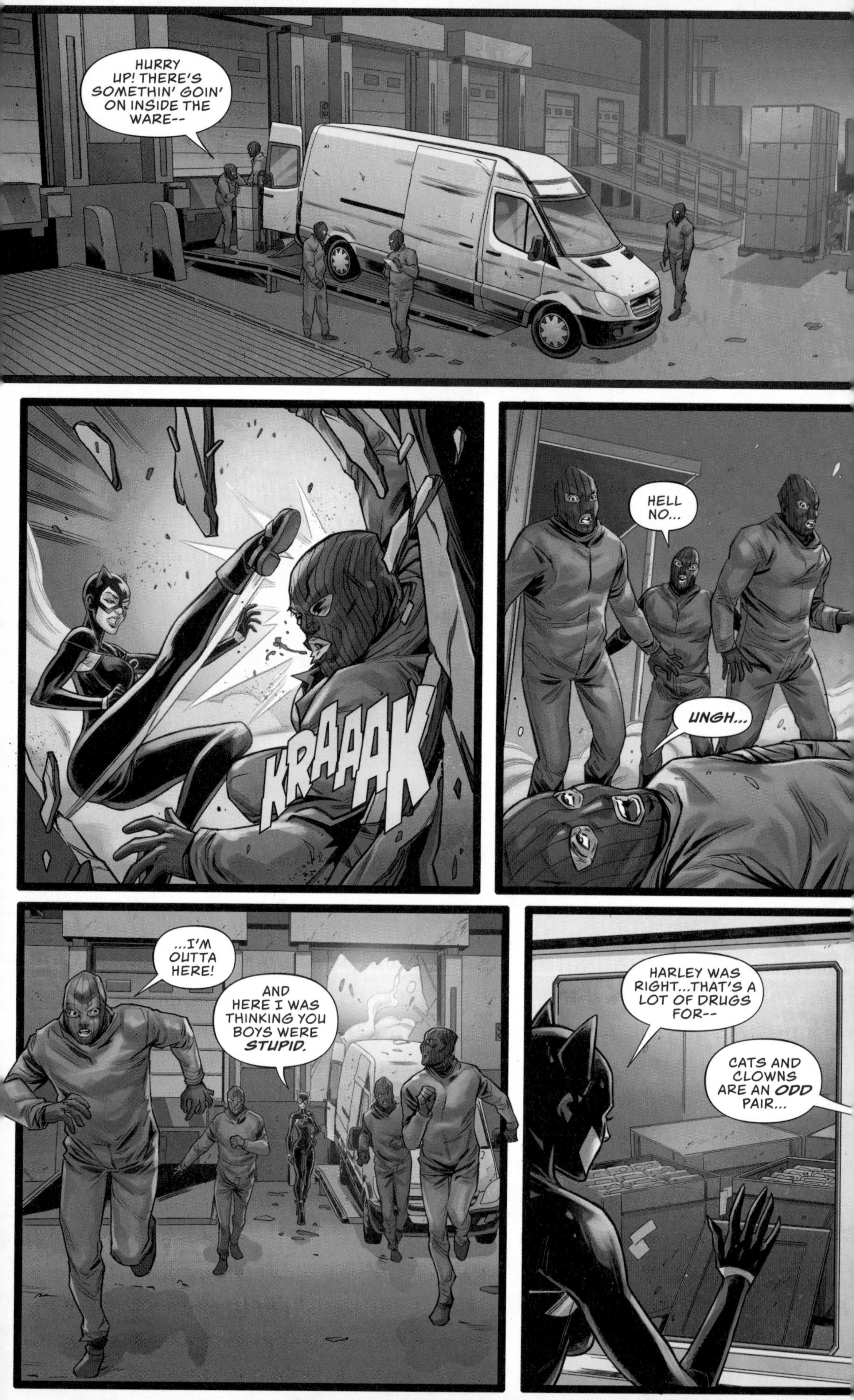

HURRY UP! THERE'S SOMETHIN' GOIN' ON INSIDE THE WARE--
KRAAAK
HELL NO...
UNGH...
...I'M OUTTA HERE!
AND HERE I WAS THINKING YOU BOYS WERE STUPID.
HARLEY WAS RIGHT...THAT'S A LOT OF DRUGS FOR--
CATS AND CLOWNS ARE AN ODD PAIR...

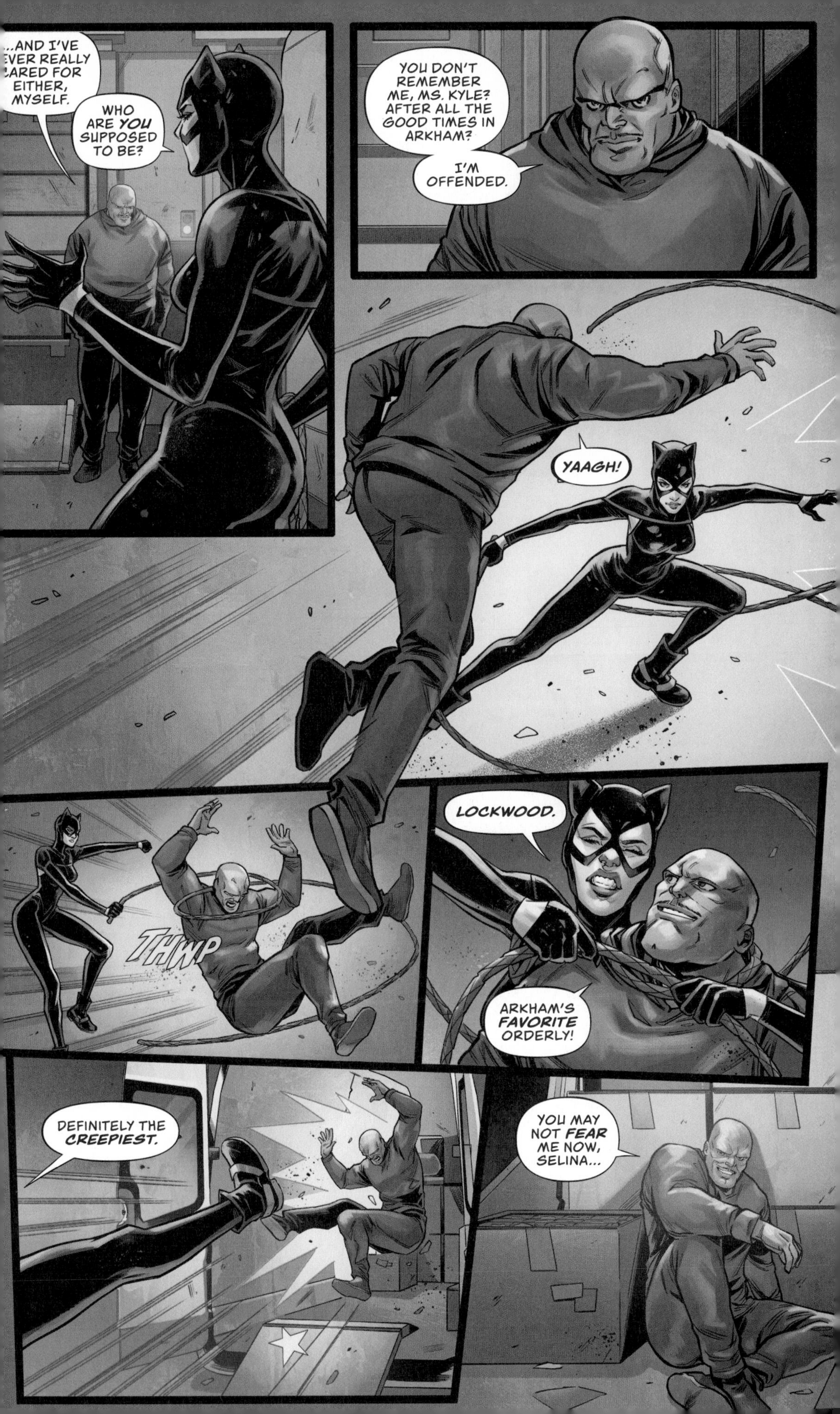
...AND I'VE
EVER REALLY
CARED FOR
EITHER,
MYSELF.
WHO ARE YOU SUPPOSED TO BE?
YOU DON'T REMEMBER ME, MS. KYLE? AFTER ALL THE GOOD TIMES IN ARKHAM?
I'M OFFENDED.
YAAGH!
THWP
LOCKWOOD.
ARKHAM'S FAVORITE ORDERLY!
DEFINITELY THE CREEPIEST.
YOU MAY NOT FEAR ME NOW, SELINA...

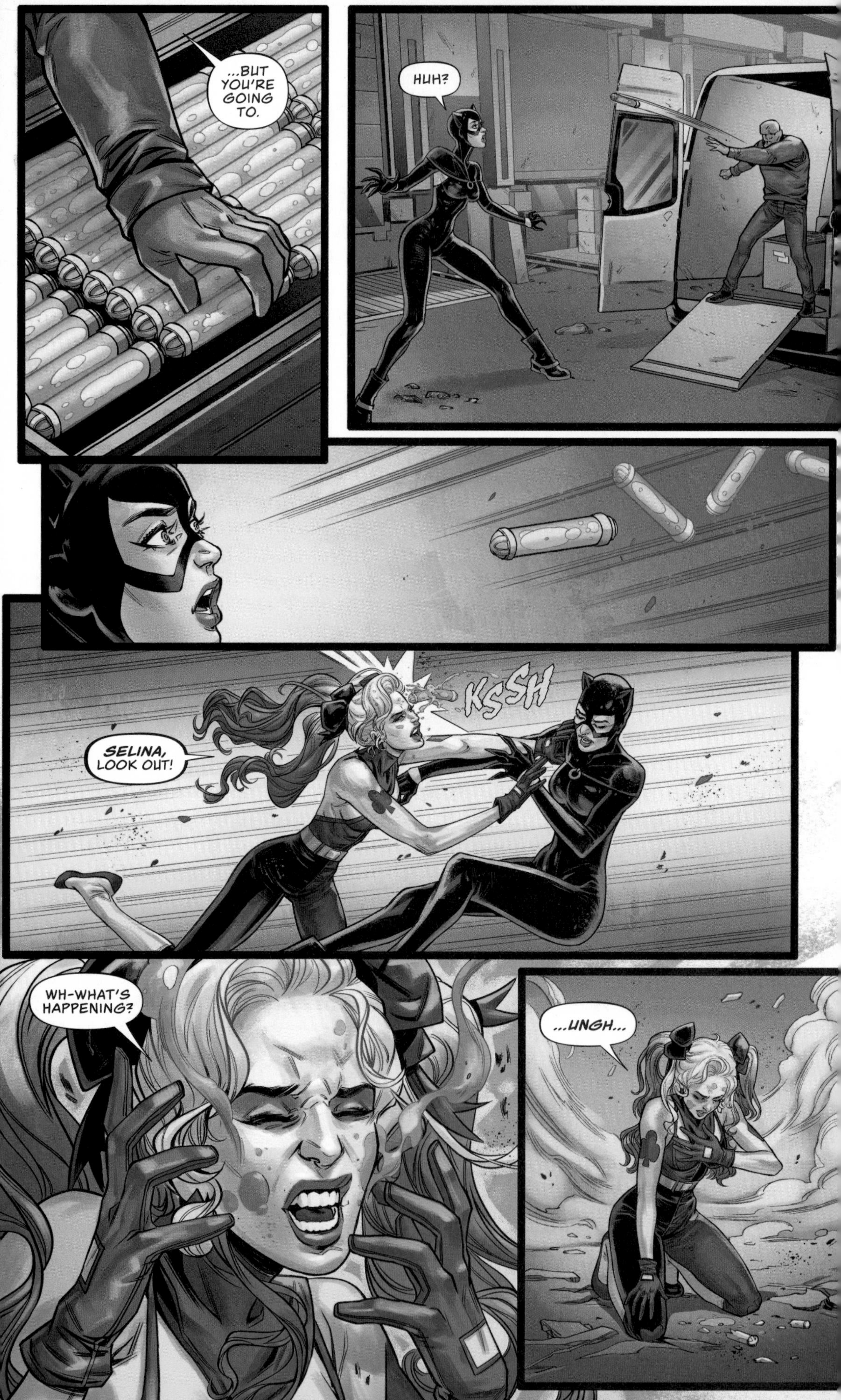
...BUT YOU'RE GOING TO.
HUH?
KSSH
SELINA, LOOK OUT!
WH-WHAT'S HAPPENING?
...UNGH...

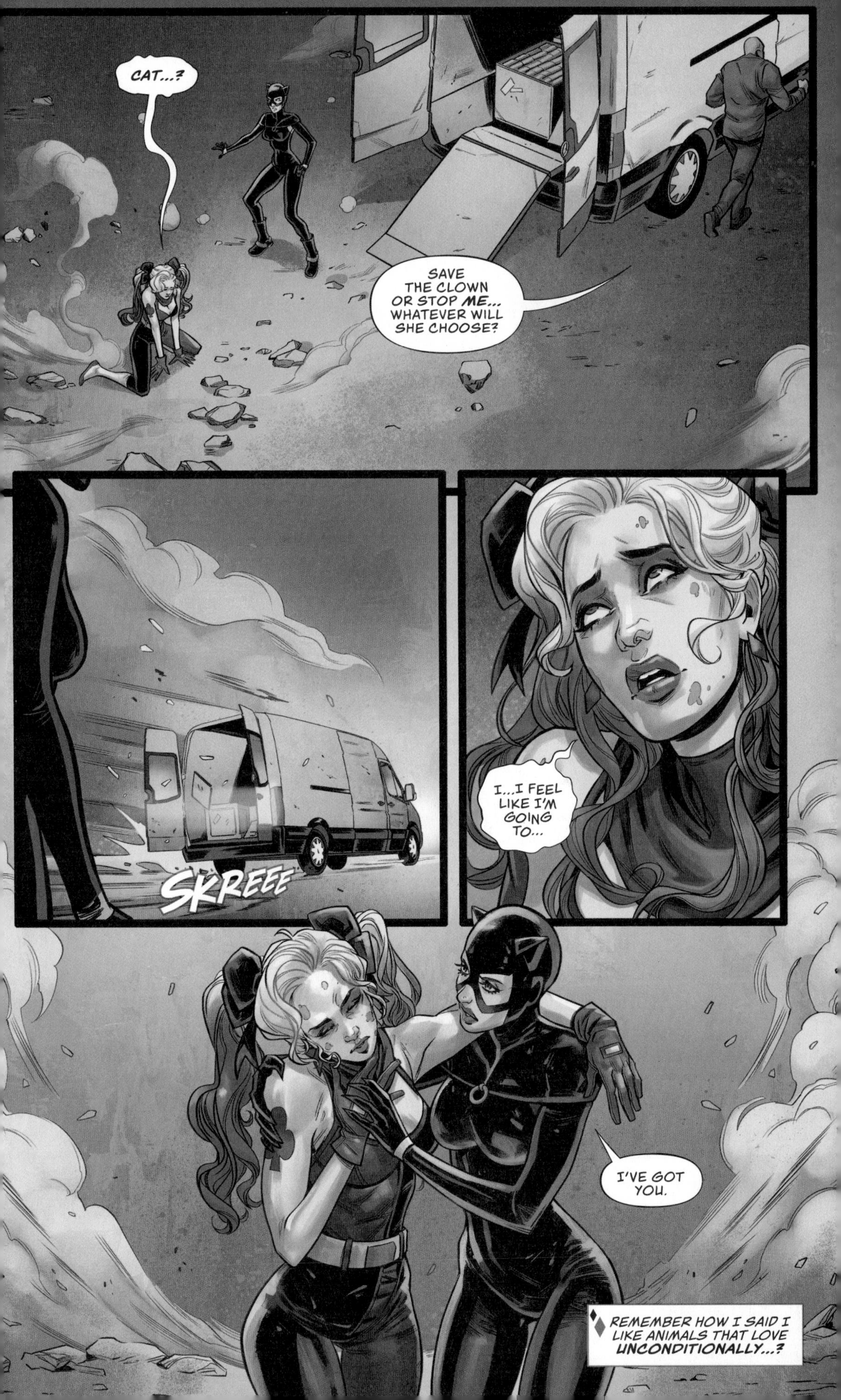

CAT...?
SAVE THE CLOWN OR STOP *ME*... WHATEVER WILL SHE CHOOSE?
SKREEE
I...I FEEL LIKE I'M GOING TO...
I'VE GOT YOU.
REMEMBER HOW I SAID I LIKE ANIMALS THAT LOVE **UNCONDITIONALLY**...?

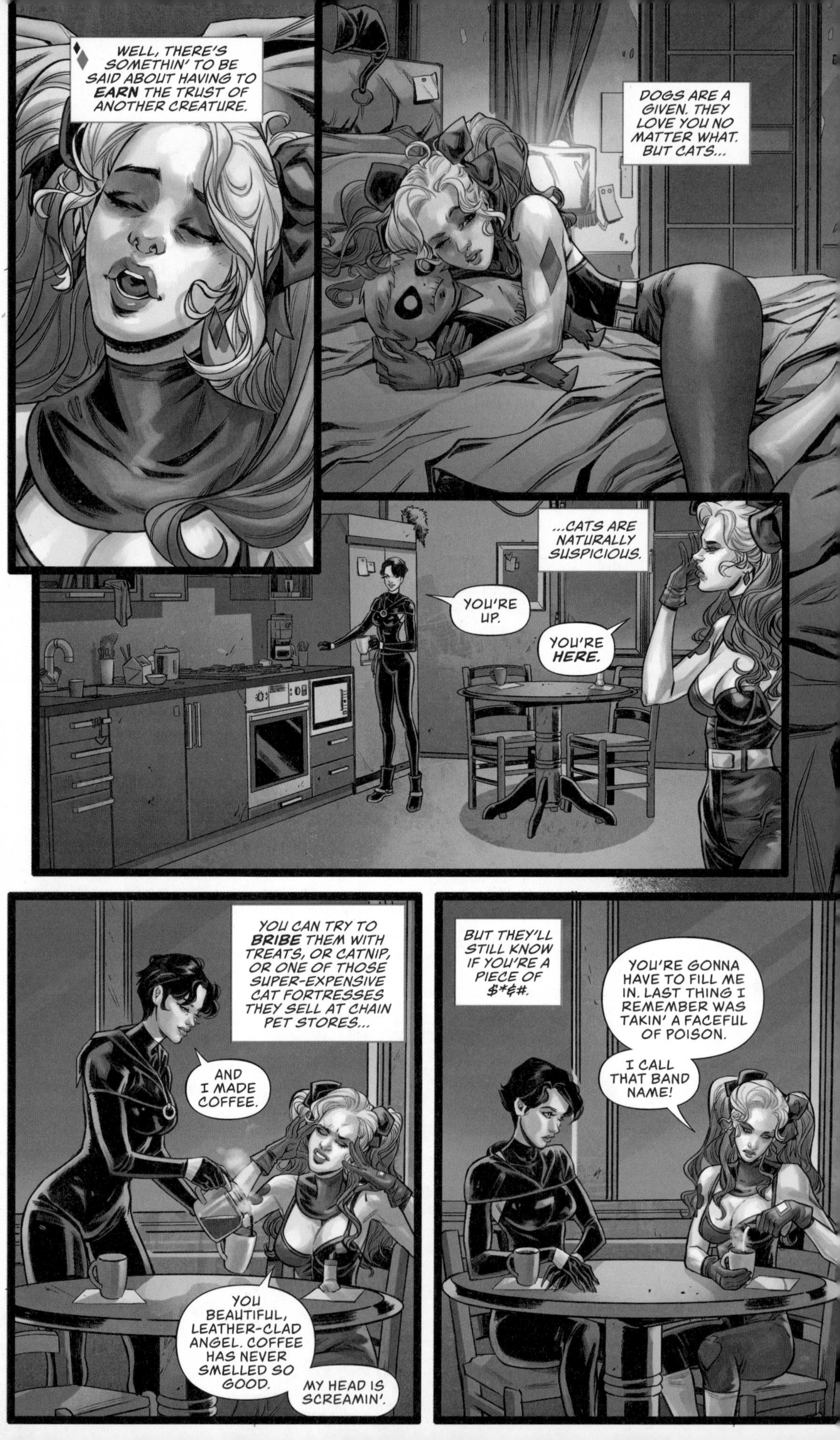
WELL, THERE'S SOMETHIN' TO BE SAID ABOUT HAVING TO EARN THE TRUST OF ANOTHER CREATURE.
DOGS ARE A GIVEN. THEY LOVE YOU NO MATTER WHAT. BUT CATS...
...CATS ARE NATURALLY SUSPICIOUS.
YOU'RE UP.
YOU'RE HERE.
YOU CAN TRY TO BRIBE THEM WITH TREATS, OR CATNIP, OR ONE OF THOSE SUPER-EXPENSIVE CAT FORTRESSES THEY SELL AT CHAIN PET STORES...
AND I MADE COFFEE.
YOU BEAUTIFUL, LEATHER-CLAD ANGEL. COFFEE HAS NEVER SMELLED SO GOOD.
MY HEAD IS SCREAMIN'.
BUT THEY'LL STILL KNOW IF YOU'RE A PIECE OF $*¢#.
YOU'RE GONNA HAVE TO FILL ME IN. LAST THING I REMEMBER WAS TAKIN' A FACEFUL OF POISON.
I CALL THAT BAND NAME!

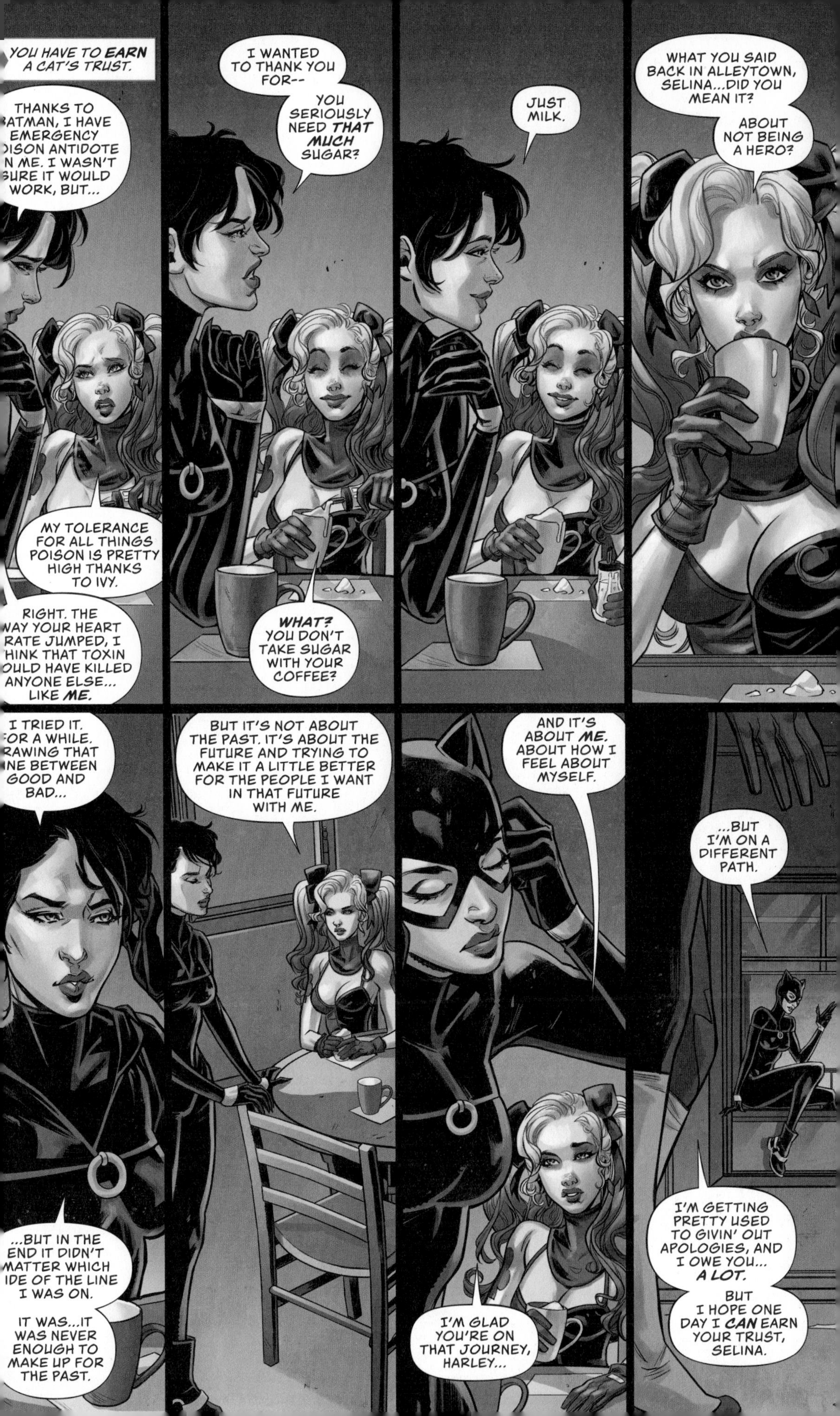
YOU HAVE TO EARN A CAT'S TRUST.
THANKS TO ATMAN, I HAVE EMERGENCY OISON ANTIDOTE N ME. I WASN'T SURE IT WOULD WORK, BUT...
MY TOLERANCE FOR ALL THINGS POISON IS PRETTY HIGH THANKS TO IVY.
RIGHT. THE WAY YOUR HEART RATE JUMPED, I HINK THAT TOXIN OULD HAVE KILLED ANYONE ELSE... LIKE ME.
I WANTED TO THANK YOU FOR--
YOU SERIOUSLY NEED THAT MUCH SUGAR?
WHAT? YOU DON'T TAKE SUGAR WITH YOUR COFFEE?
JUST MILK.
WHAT YOU SAID BACK IN ALLEYTOWN, SELINA...DID YOU MEAN IT?
ABOUT NOT BEING A HERO?
I TRIED IT. FOR A WHILE. RAWING THAT NE BETWEEN GOOD AND BAD...
...BUT IN THE END IT DIDN'T MATTER WHICH IDE OF THE LINE I WAS ON.
IT WAS...IT WAS NEVER ENOUGH TO MAKE UP FOR THE PAST.
BUT IT'S NOT ABOUT THE PAST. IT'S ABOUT THE FUTURE AND TRYING TO MAKE IT A LITTLE BETTER FOR THE PEOPLE I WANT IN THAT FUTURE WITH ME.
AND IT'S ABOUT ME. ABOUT HOW I FEEL ABOUT MYSELF.
I'M GLAD YOU'RE ON THAT JOURNEY, HARLEY...
...BUT I'M ON A DIFFERENT PATH.
I'M GETTING PRETTY USED TO GIVIN' OUT APOLOGIES, AND I OWE YOU... A LOT.
BUT I HOPE ONE DAY I CAN EARN YOUR TRUST, SELINA.

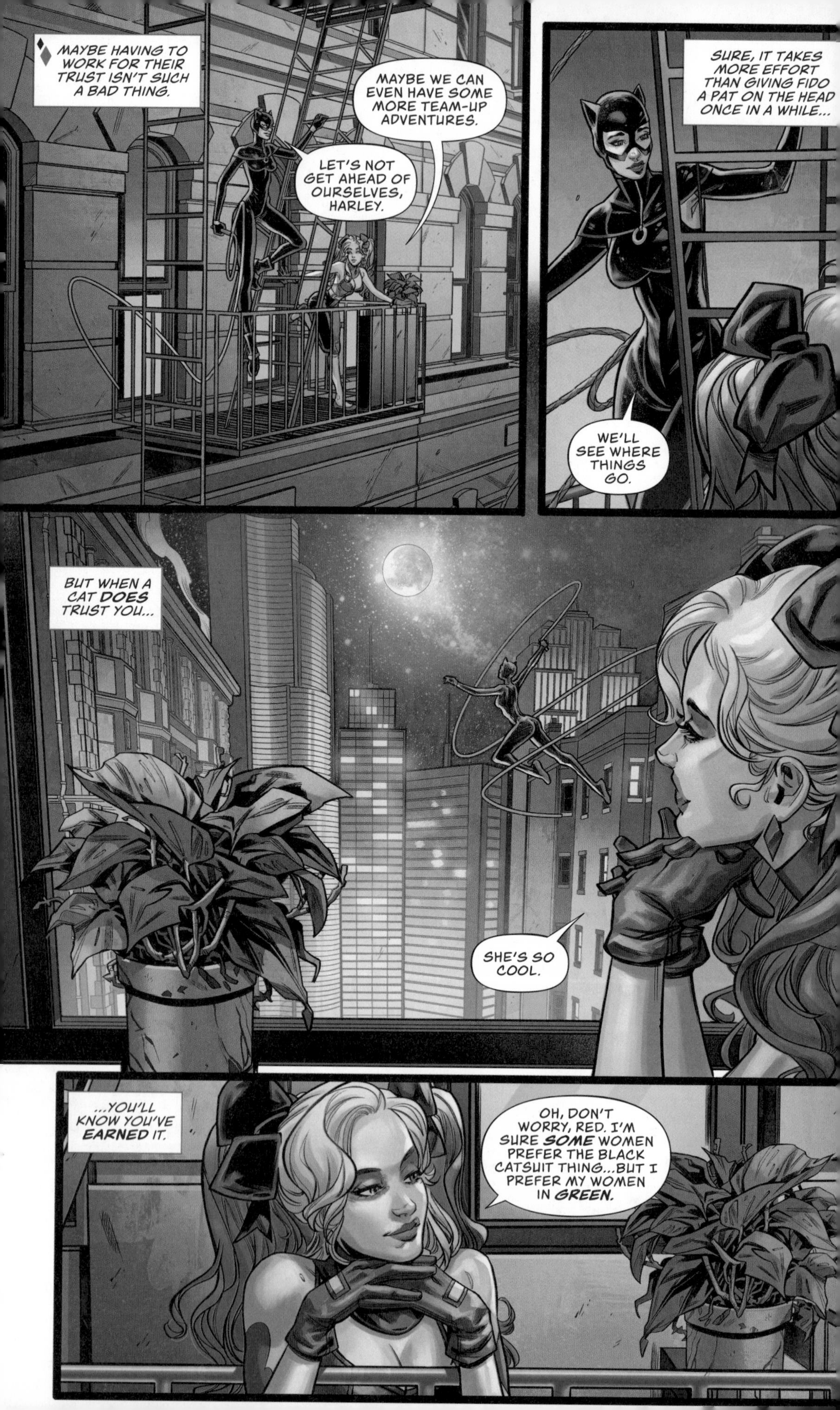

MAYBE HAVING TO WORK FOR THEIR TRUST ISN'T SUCH A BAD THING.
MAYBE WE CAN EVEN HAVE SOME MORE TEAM-UP ADVENTURES.
LET'S NOT GET AHEAD OF OURSELVES, HARLEY.
SURE, IT TAKES MORE EFFORT THAN GIVING FIDO A PAT ON THE HEAD ONCE IN A WHILE...
WE'LL SEE WHERE THINGS GO.
BUT WHEN A CAT DOES TRUST YOU...
SHE'S SO COOL.
...YOU'LL KNOW YOU'VE EARNED IT.
OH, DON'T WORRY, RED. I'M SURE SOME WOMEN PREFER THE BLACK CATSUIT THING...BUT I PREFER MY WOMEN IN GREEN.

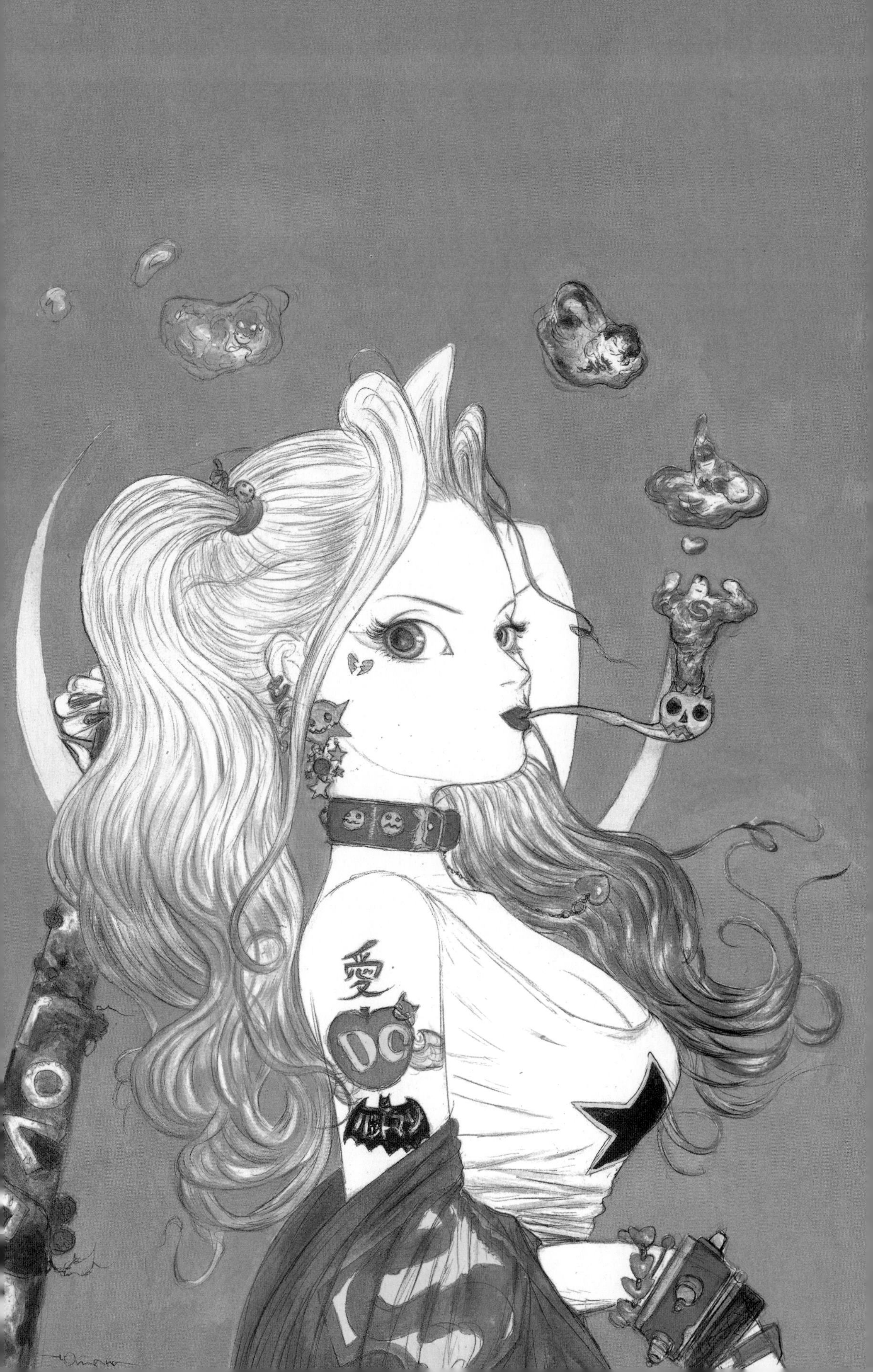
愛
DC

Harley Quinn #1
Variant Cover Art by Yoshitaka Amano

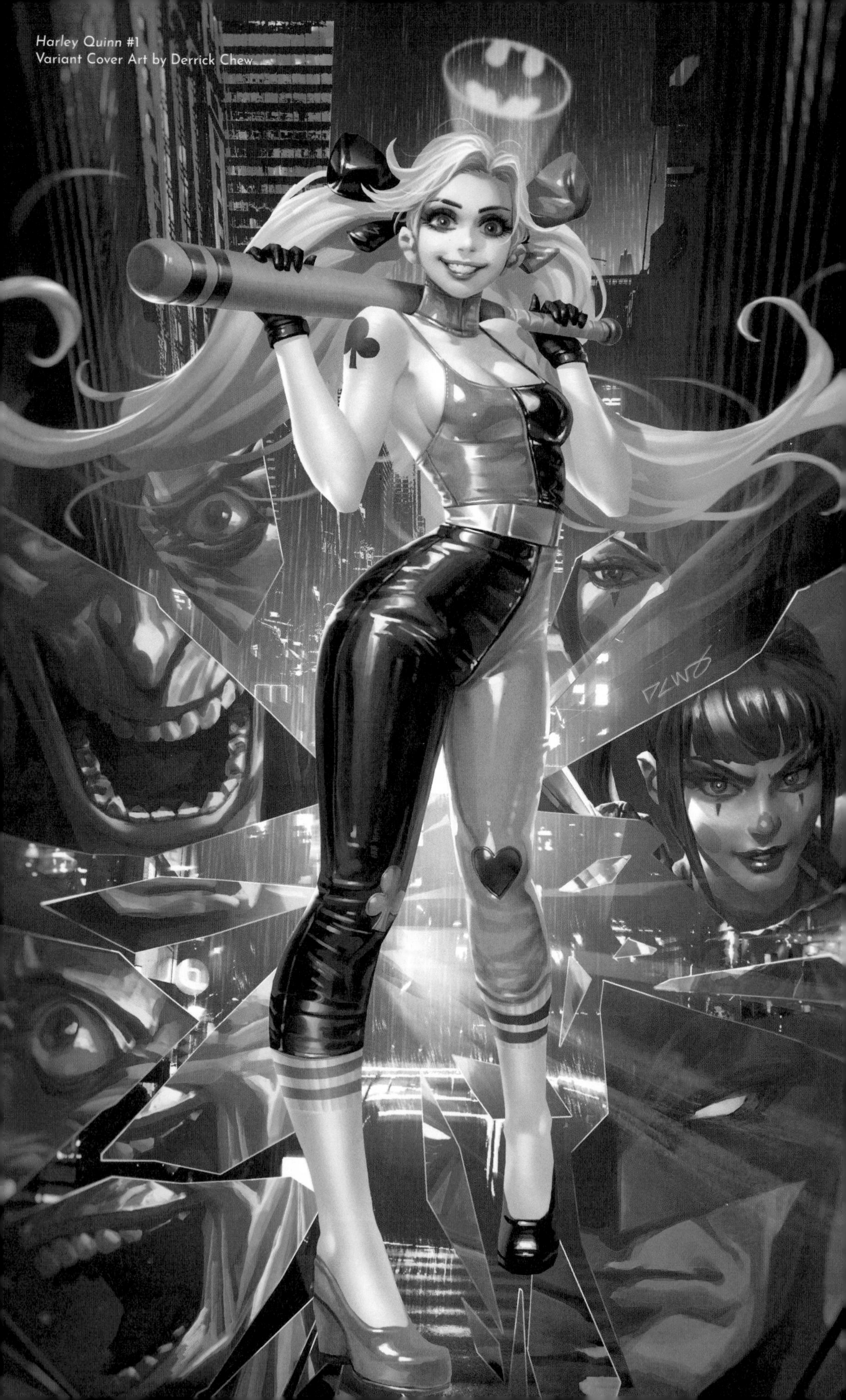

Harley Quinn #1
Variant Cover Art by Derrick Chew

Harley Quinn #2
Variant Cover Art by Derrick Chew

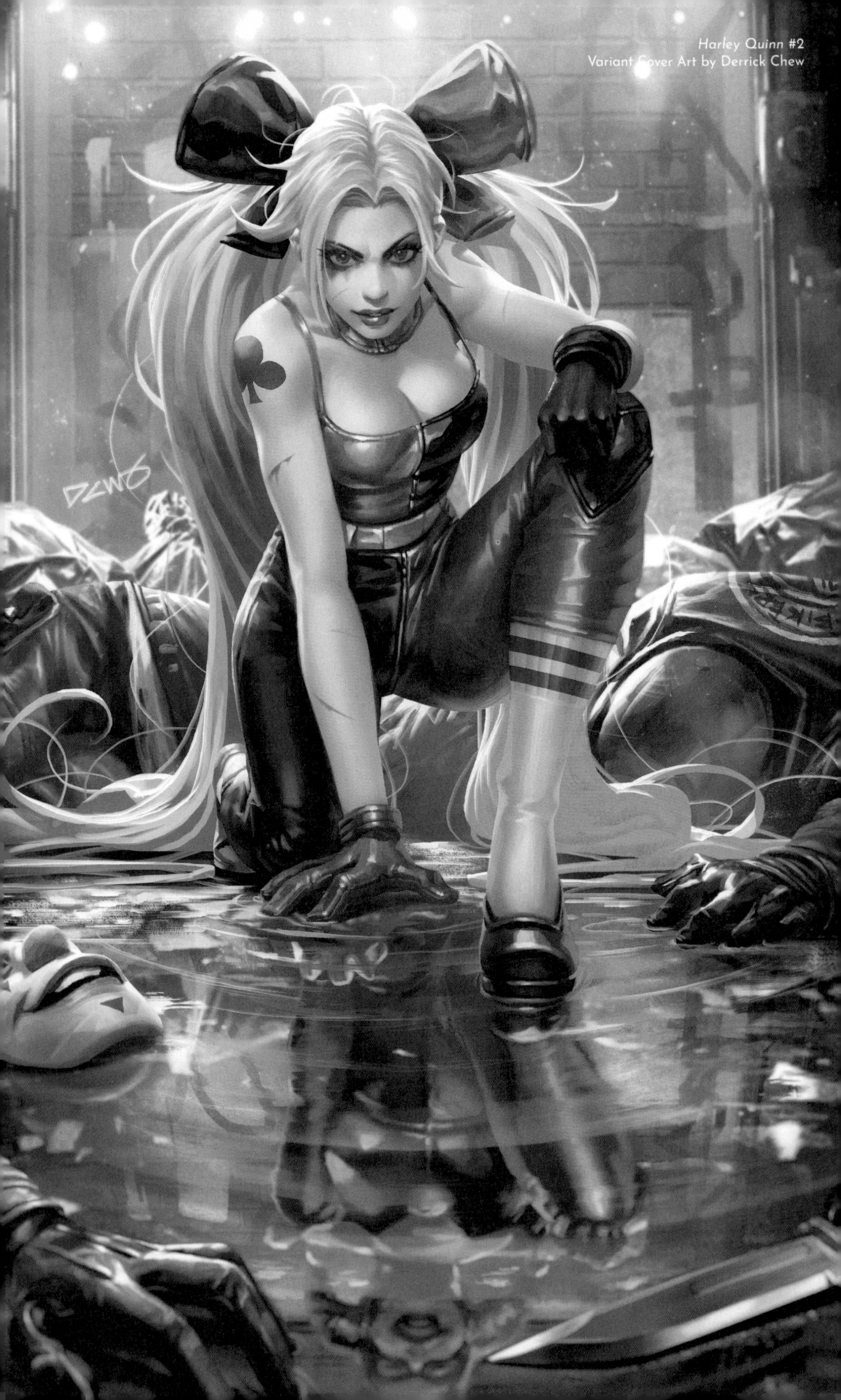
DCW

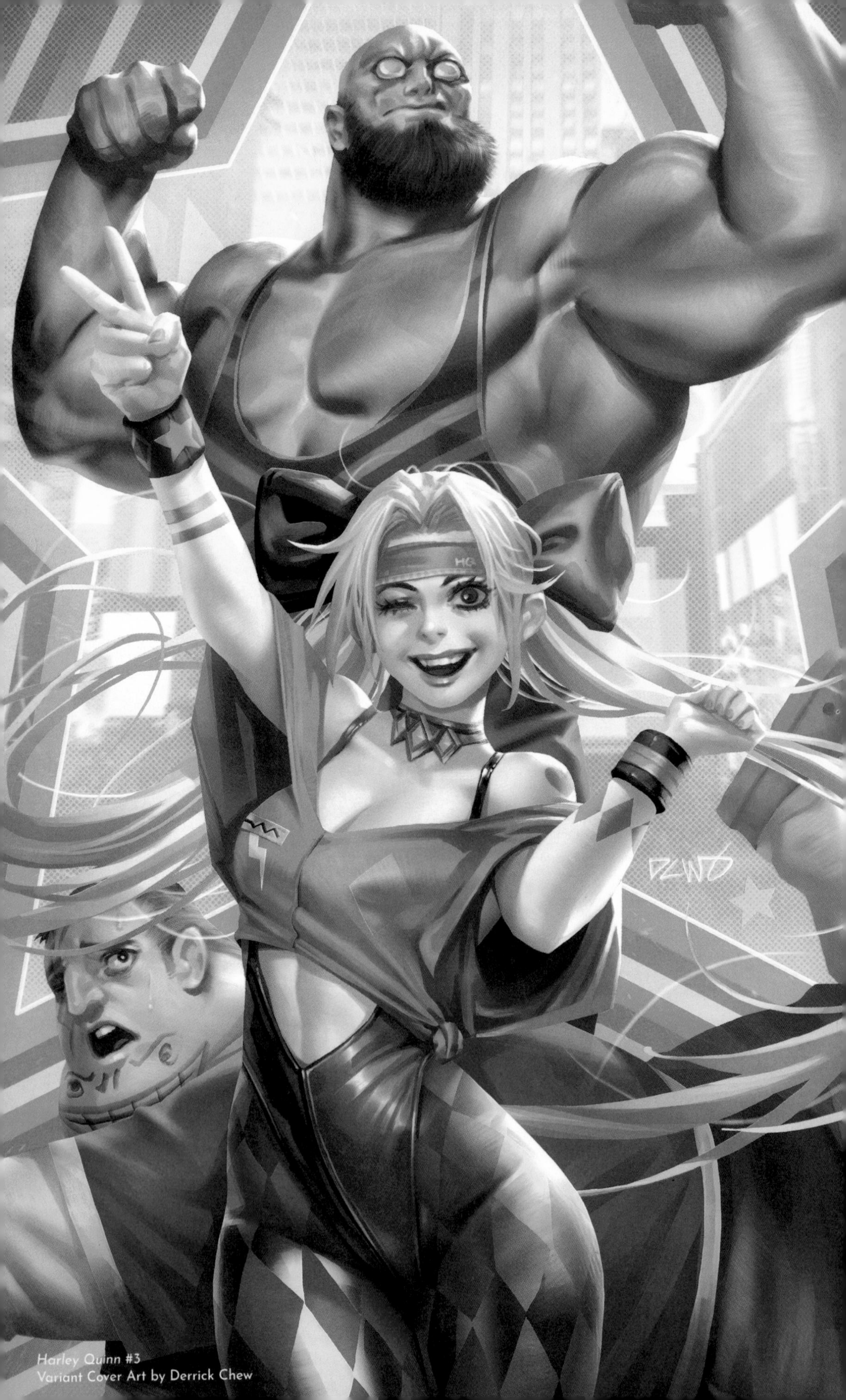
HQ

Harley Quinn #3
Variant Cover Art by Derrick Chew

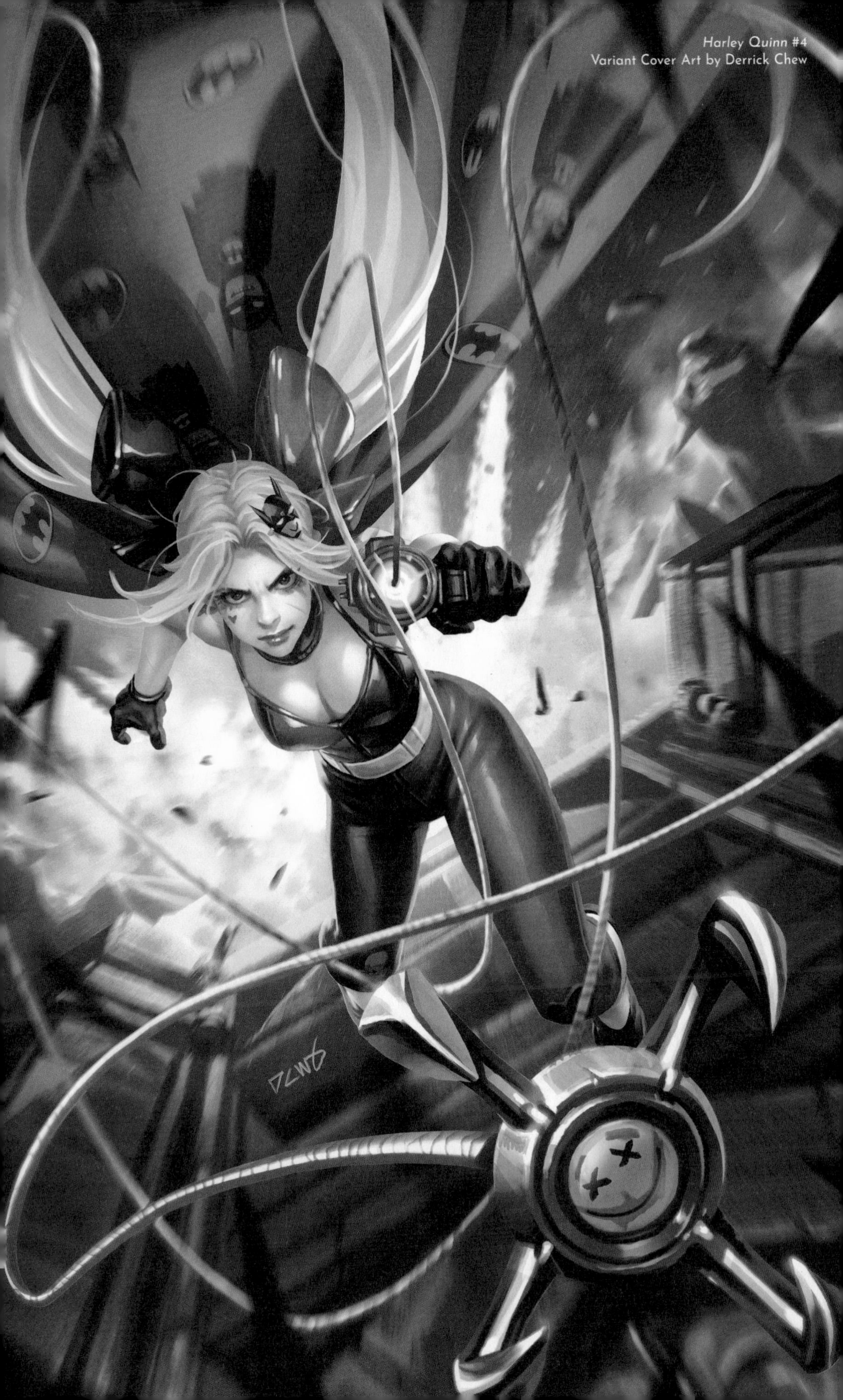

Harley Quinn #4
Variant Cover Art by Derrick Chew

Harley Quinn #5
Variant Cover Art by Derrick Chew

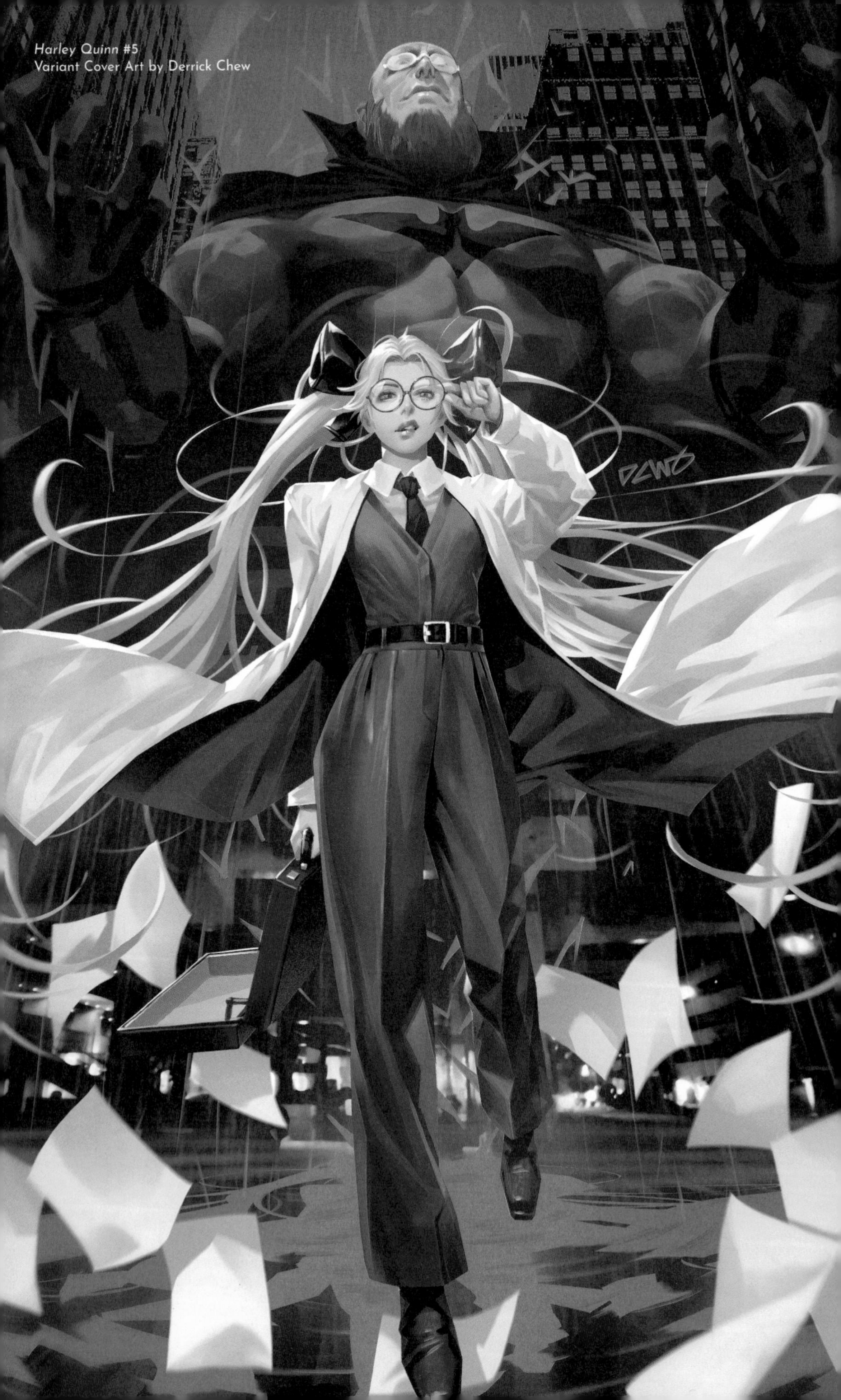

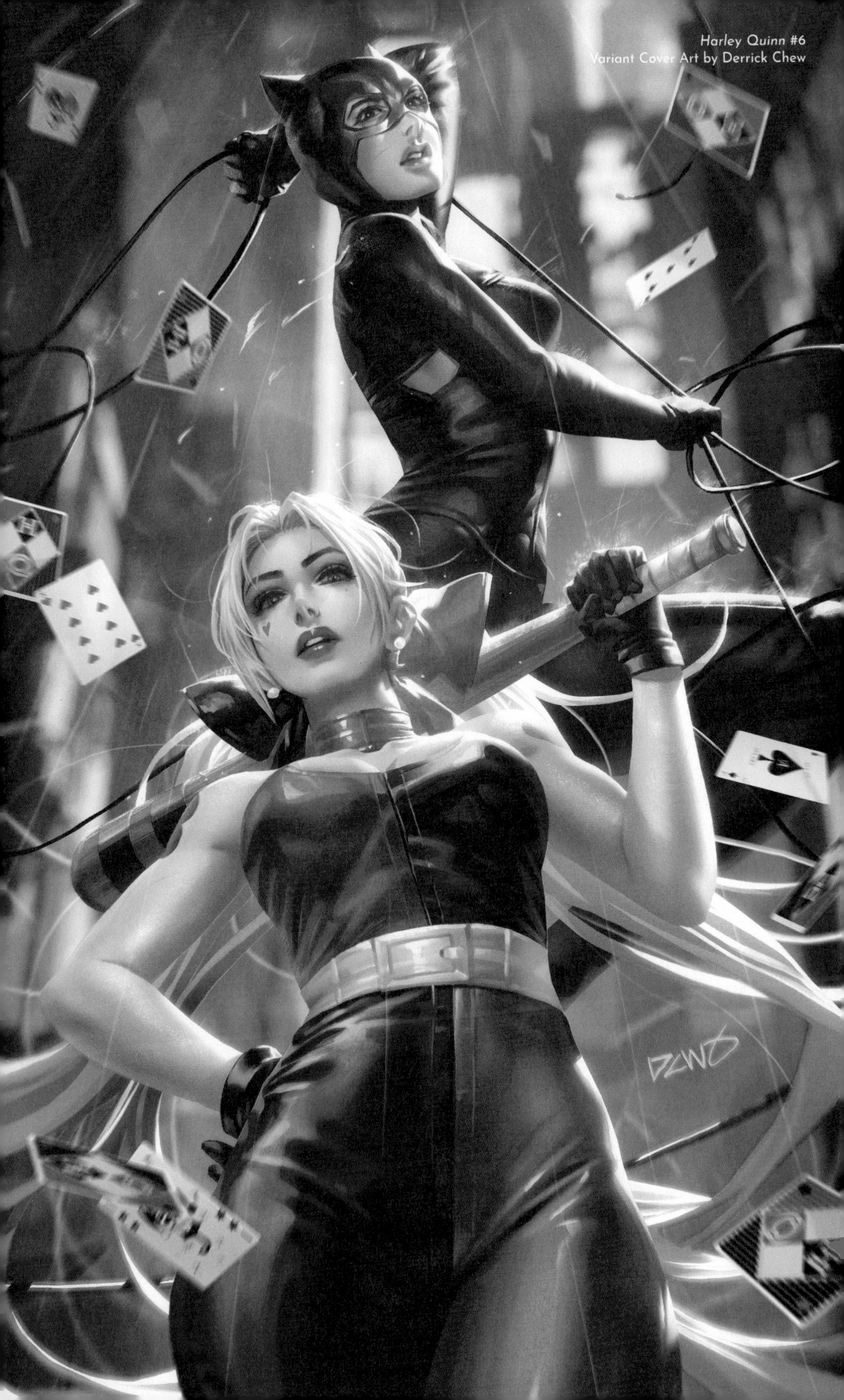

Harley Quinn #6
Variant Cover Art by Derrick Chew

Harley Quinn #6
The Suicide Squad Variant Cover Art
by Riccardo Federici

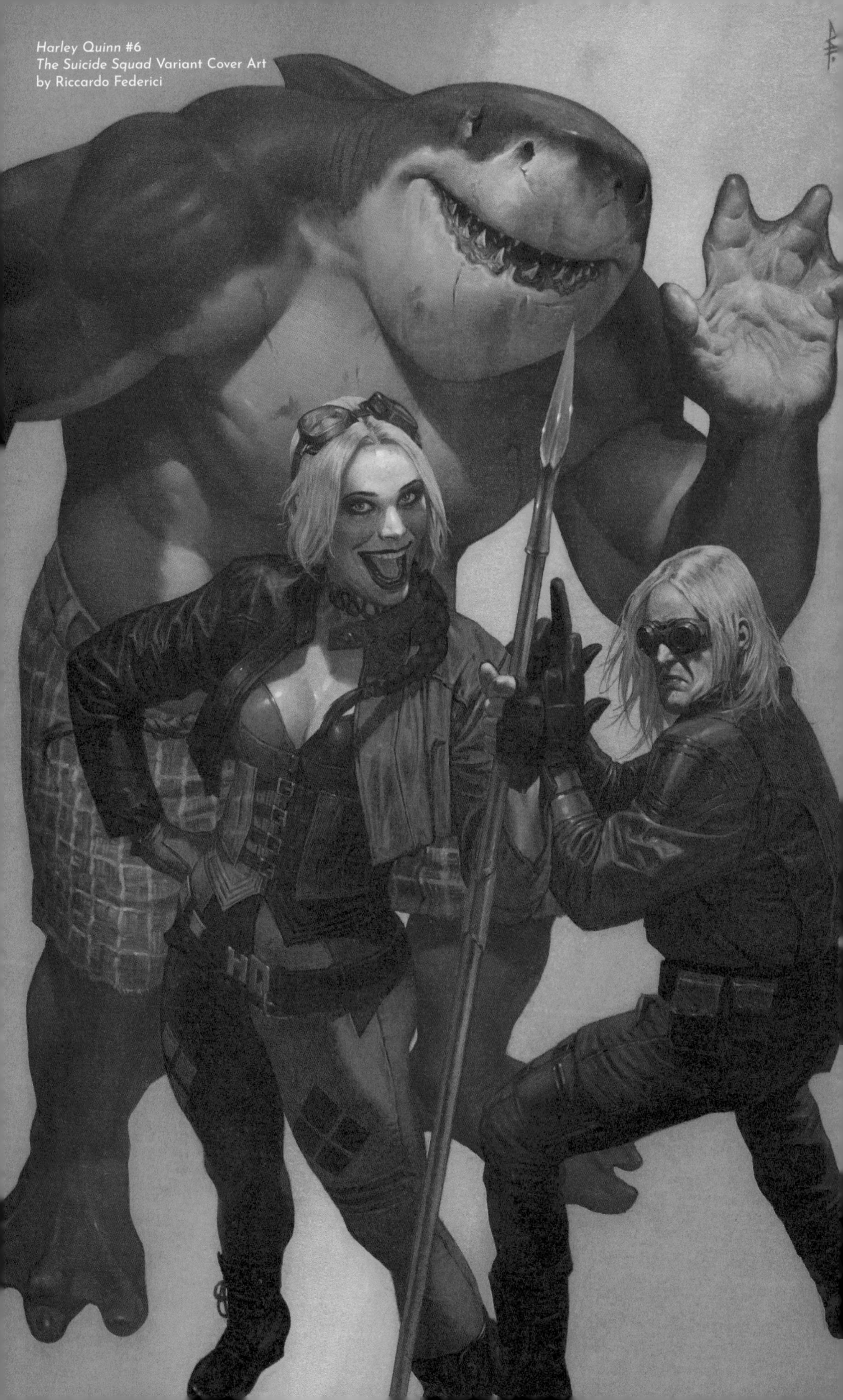

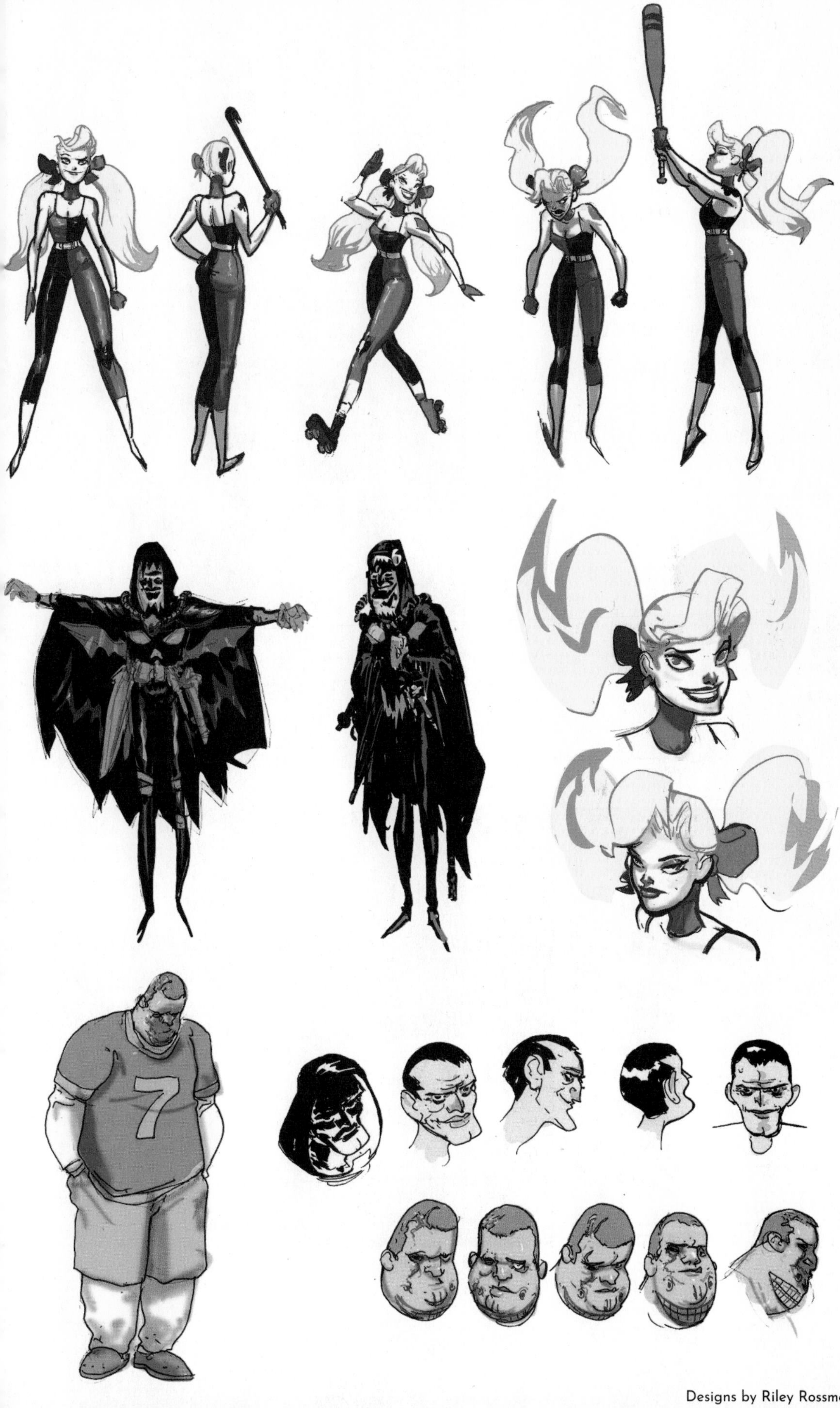
7

Designs by Riley Rossmo

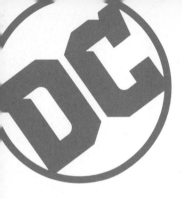

"A smart concept, snappy one-liners and a great twist to match a tag-team of talented artists."
–NEWSARAMA

"Every bit as chaotic and unabashedly fun as one would expect."
–IGN

HARLEY QUINN

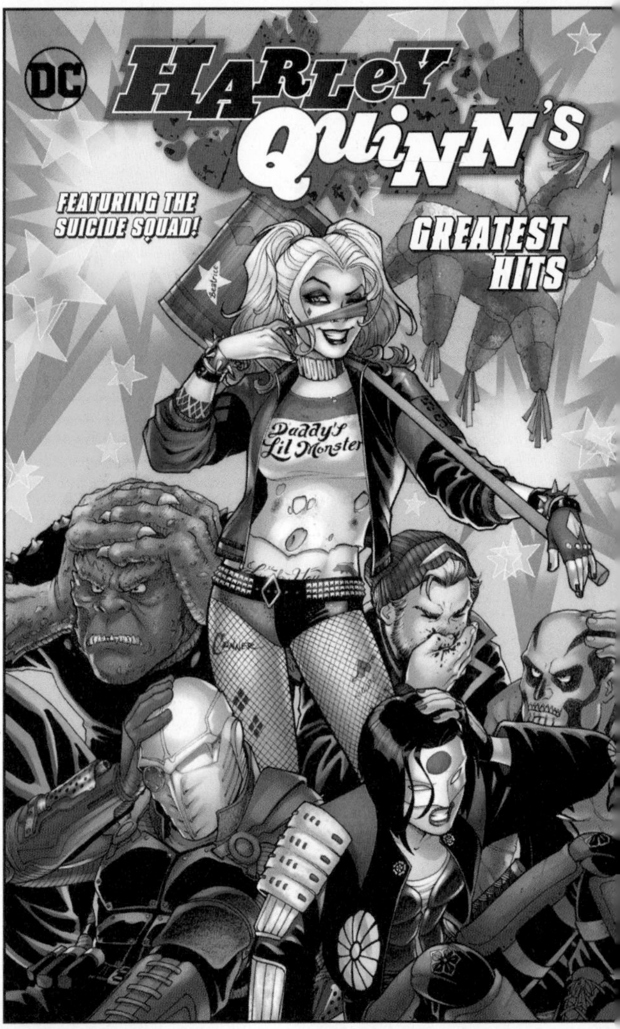
DC
HARLEY QUINN'S
FEATURING THE SUICIDE SQUAD!
GREATEST HITS
Daddy's Lil Monster

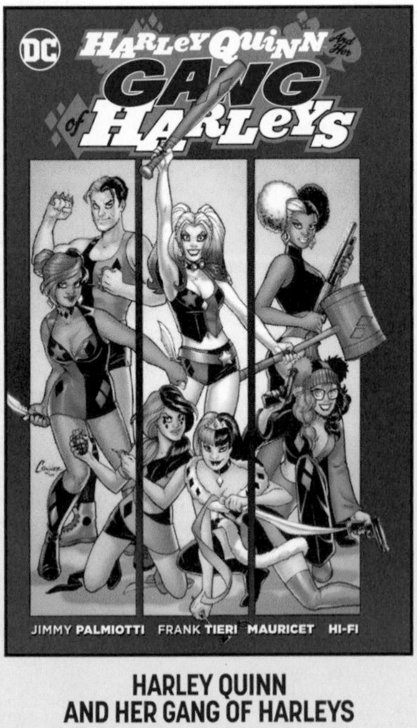
DC
HARLEY QUINN And Her GANG of HARLEYS
JIMMY PALMIOTTI FRANK TIERI MAURICET HI-FI

HARLEY QUINN
AND HER GANG OF HARLEYS

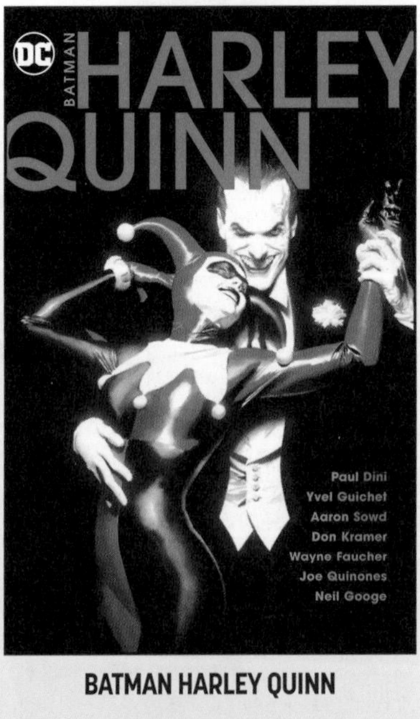
DC
BATMAN
HARLEY QUINN
Paul Dini
Yvel Guichet
Aaron Sowd
Don Kramer
Wayne Faucher
Joe Quinones
Neil Googe

BATMAN HARLEY QUINN

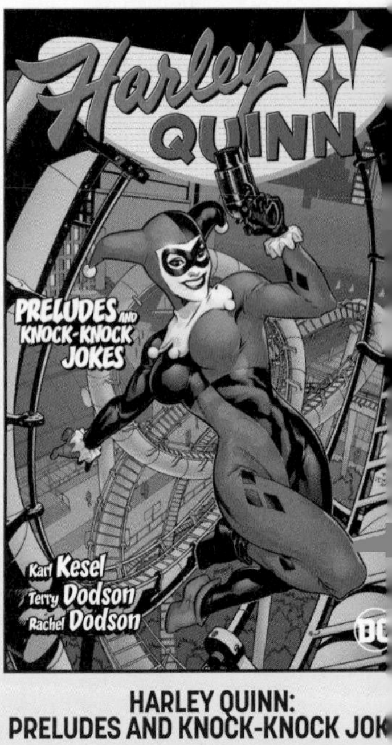
Harley QUINN
PRELUDES AND KNOCK-KNOCK JOKES
Karl Kesel
Terry Dodson
Rachel Dodson

HARLEY QUINN:
PRELUDES AND KNOCK-KNOCK JOK

Get more DC graphic novels wherever comics and books are sold!